07-GHOST 8

Yukino Ichihara
Yuki Amemiya

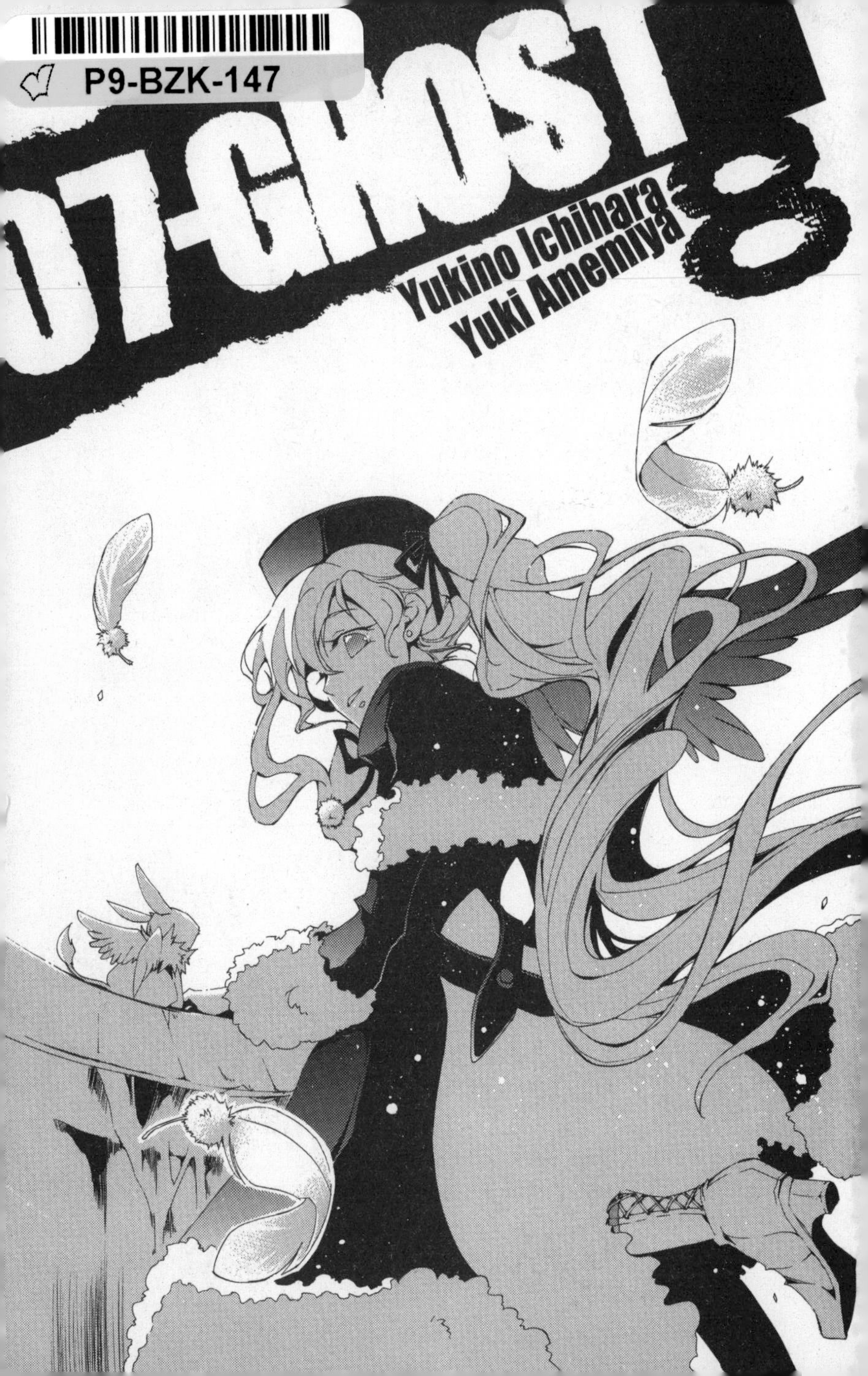

07-GHOST

Characters

One thousand years ago, two equally powerful nations coexisted. One was the Barsburg Empire, protected by the Eye of Rafael. The other was the Raggs Kingdom, protected by the Eye of Mikael. Now that the Raggs Kingdom has been destroyed, things have changed...

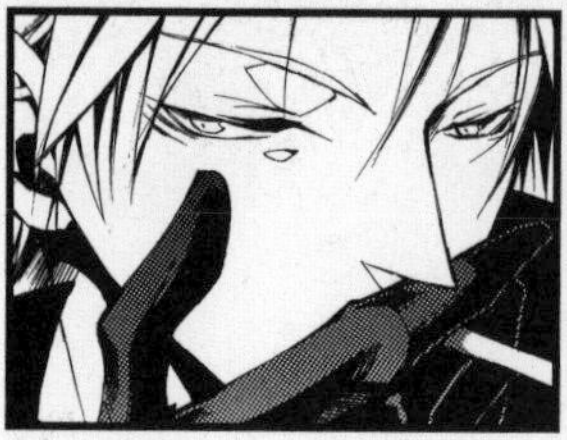

Frau

Bishop who saved Teito when he was fleeing from the academy and now watches over him. He is Zehel of the Seven Ghosts.

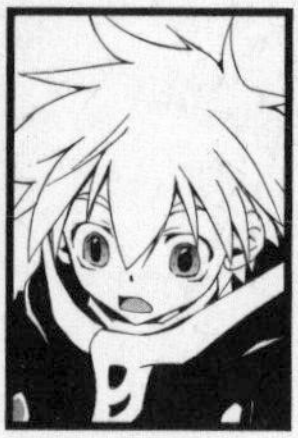

Capella

Child Teito saved from a slave trader.

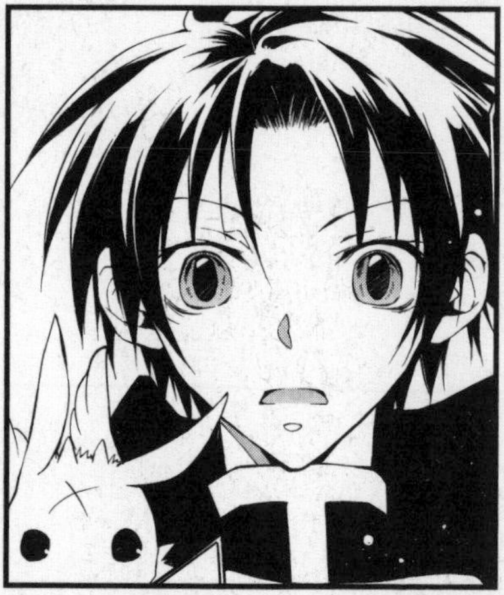

Teito Klein

Born a prince of Raggs, Teito was stripped of his memories and raised as a soldier by the military academy's chairman. He harbored the Eye of Mikael (an artifact said to bring either the world's salvation or destruction) in his right hand until the Black Hawks stole it. Currently Frau's apprentice.

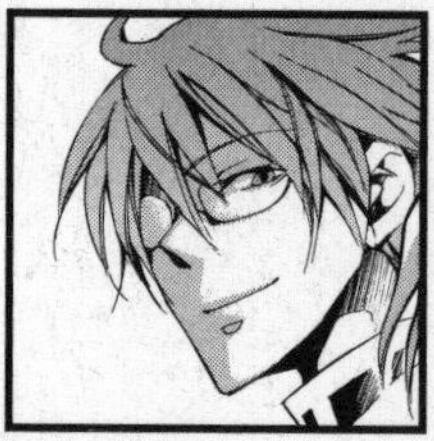

Castor

Bishop who can manipulate puppets. He watches over Teito and is Fest of the Seven Ghosts.

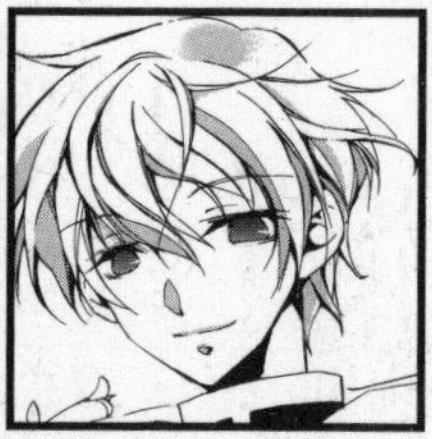

Labrador

Flower-loving bishop with the power of prophecy. One of the Seven Ghosts.

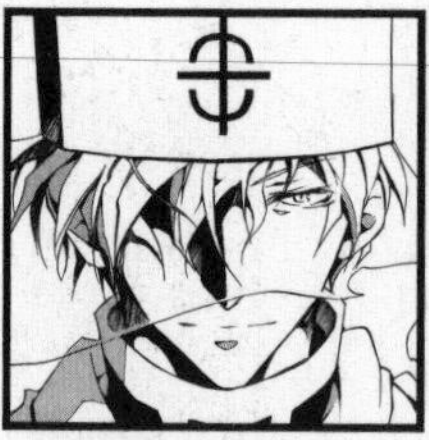

Ayanami

Imperial Army's Chief of Staff. Thief of the Eye of Mikael, and possibly responsible for the king of Raggs' death.

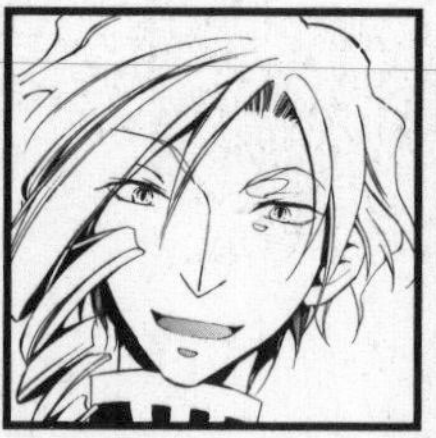

Lance

Bishop with no sense of direction who loves to travel. Head Proctor of the bishop examination.

Story

Teito is a student at the Barsburg Empire's military academy until the day he discovers that his father was the king of Raggs, the ruler of a kingdom the Barsburg Empire destroyed. Teito receives sanctuary from the Barsburg Church, but loses his best friend Mikage, who Ayanami controls like a puppet to get at Teito. As a first step in avenging Mikage's death, Teito becomes an apprentice bishop to obtain special privileges. He then embarks on a journey to the "Land of Seele," which holds the key to his past and the truth about the fall of Raggs. He gains his first Cursed Ticket at District 6's God House, then returns to his long lost homeland of District 5.

Kapitel.42
"Relikt"

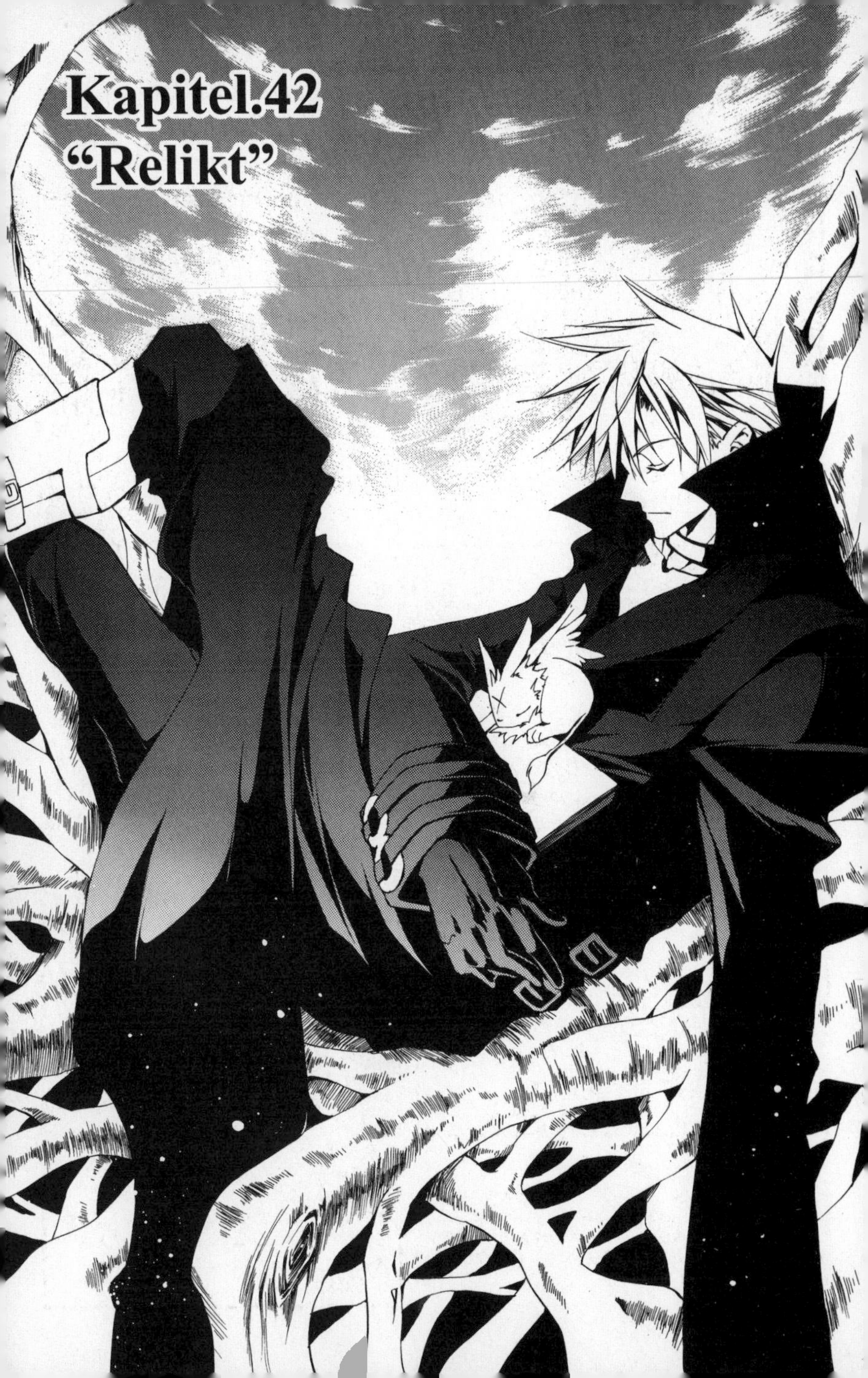

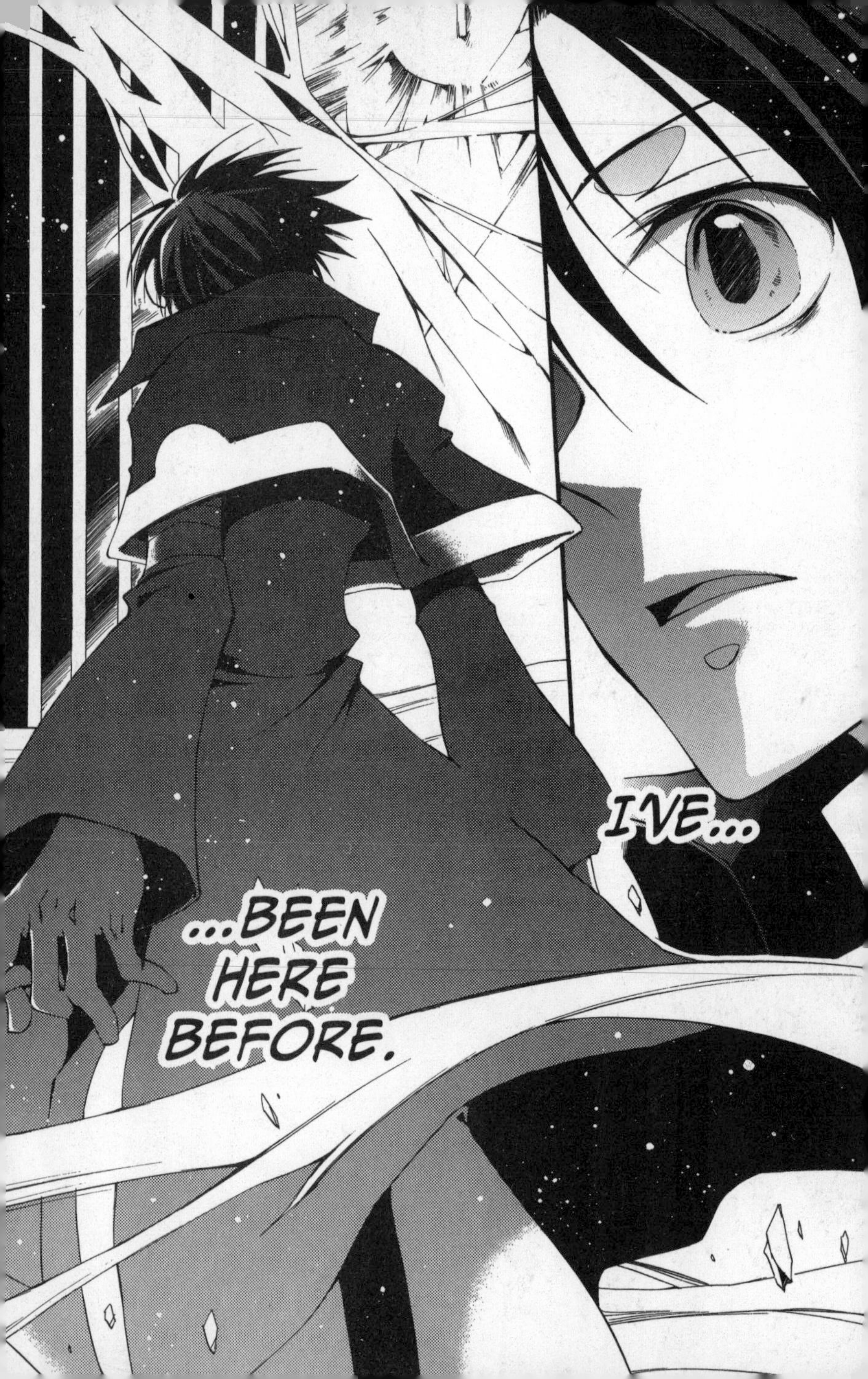
I'VE...
...BEEN HERE BEFORE.

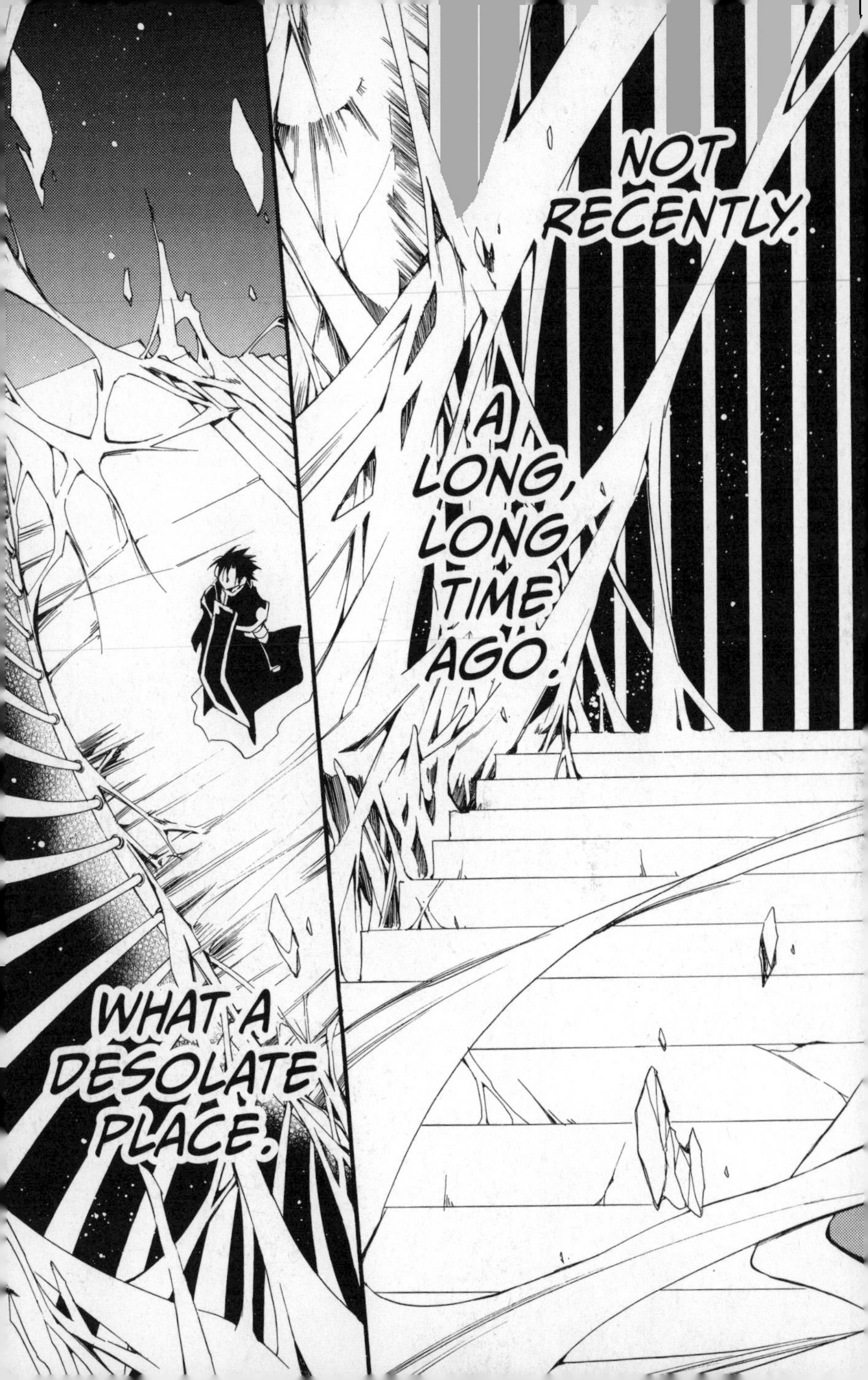
NOT RECENTLY.
A LONG, LONG TIME AGO.
WHAT A DESOLATE PLACE.

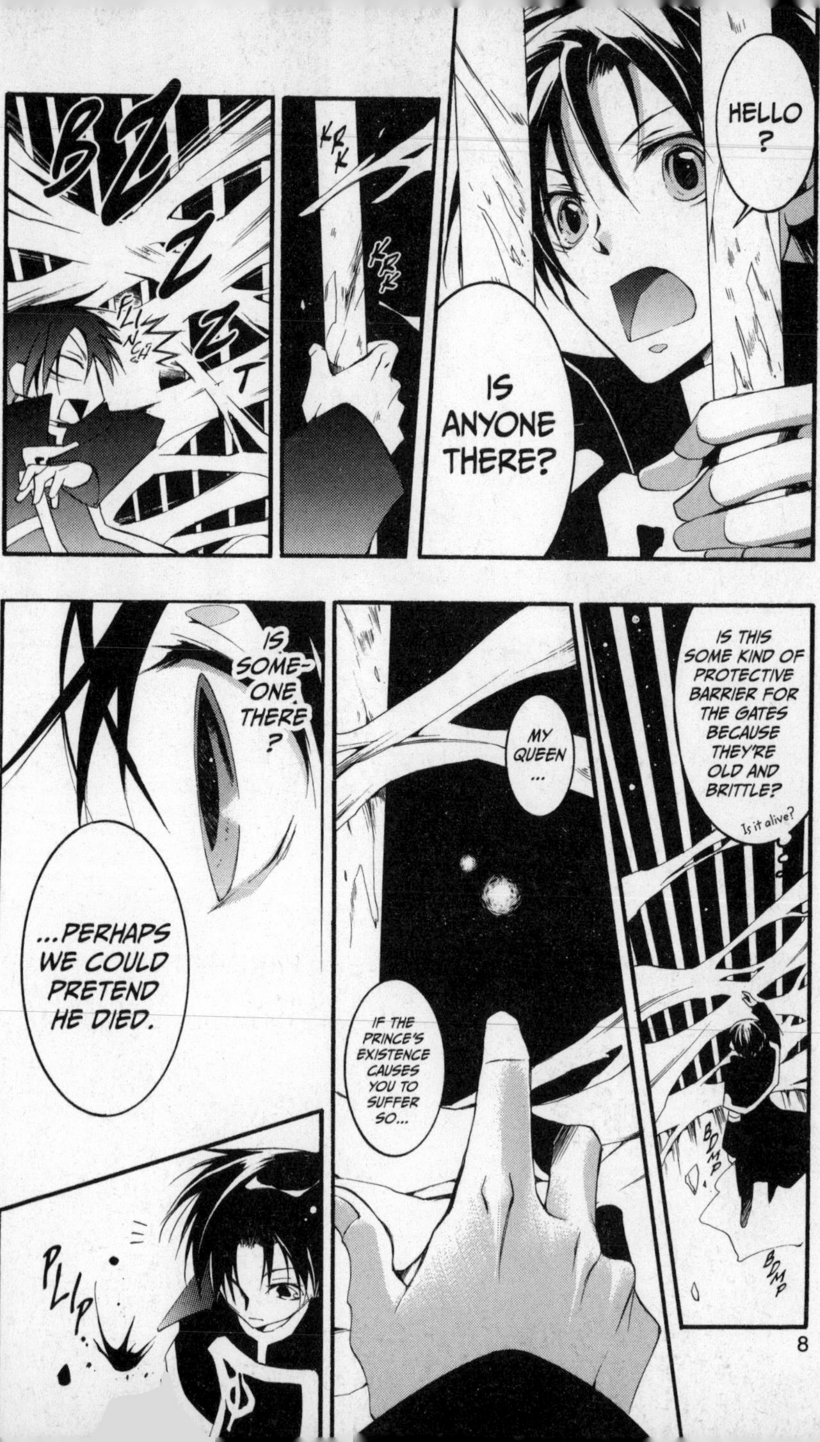
HELLO ?
IS ANYONE THERE?
KRK
KRK
BZZZT
FLINCH
IS THIS SOME KIND OF PROTECTIVE BARRIER FOR THE GATES BECAUSE THEY'RE OLD AND BRITTLE?
Is it alive?
BDMP
BDMP
MY QUEEN ...
IF THE PRINCE'S EXISTENCE CAUSES YOU TO SUFFER SO...
IS SOME-ONE THERE ?
...PERHAPS WE COULD PRETEND HE DIED.
PLIP

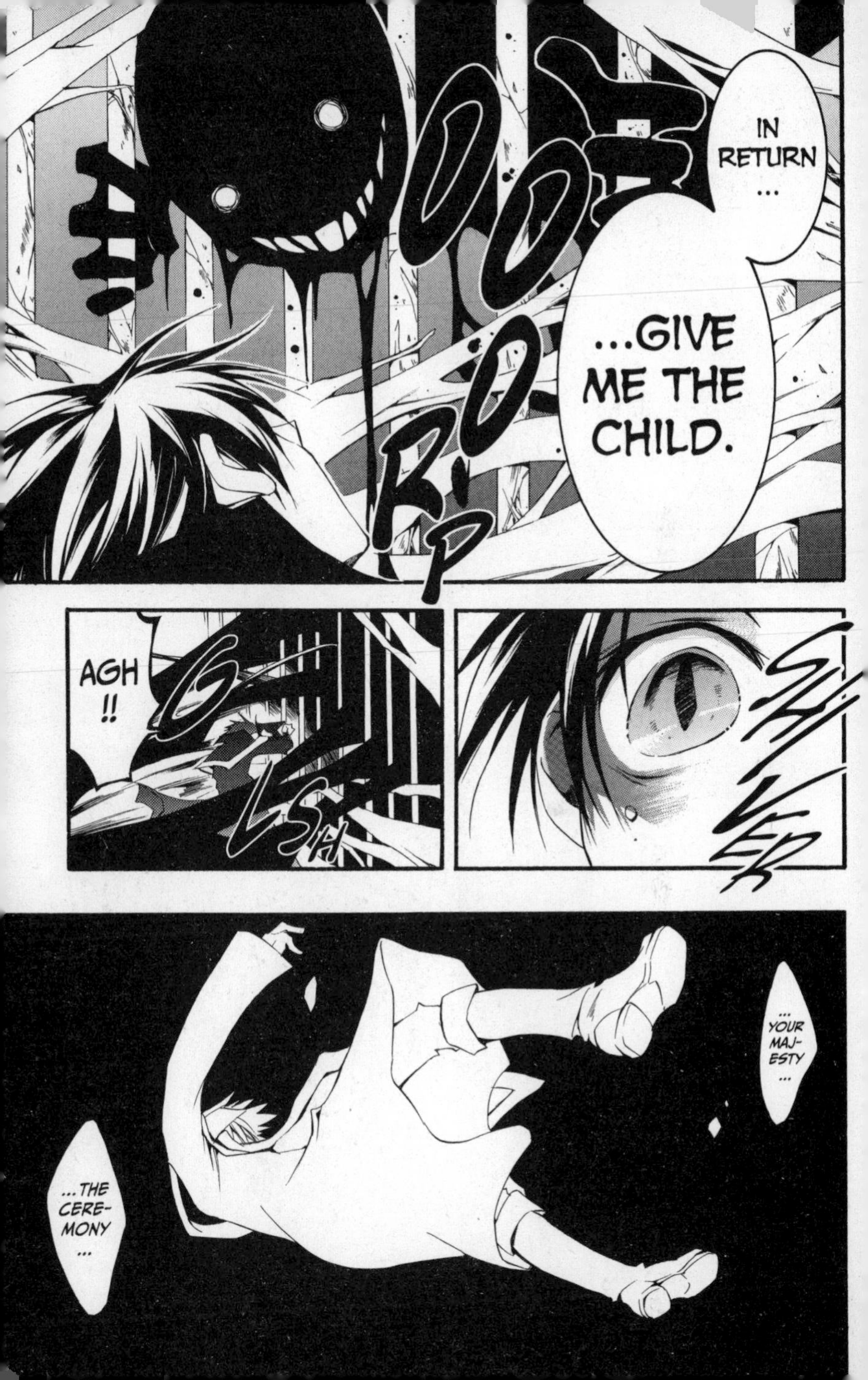
IN RETURN ...
...GIVE ME THE CHILD.
AGH !!
SHIVER
... YOUR MAJ-ESTY ...
...THE CERE-MONY ...

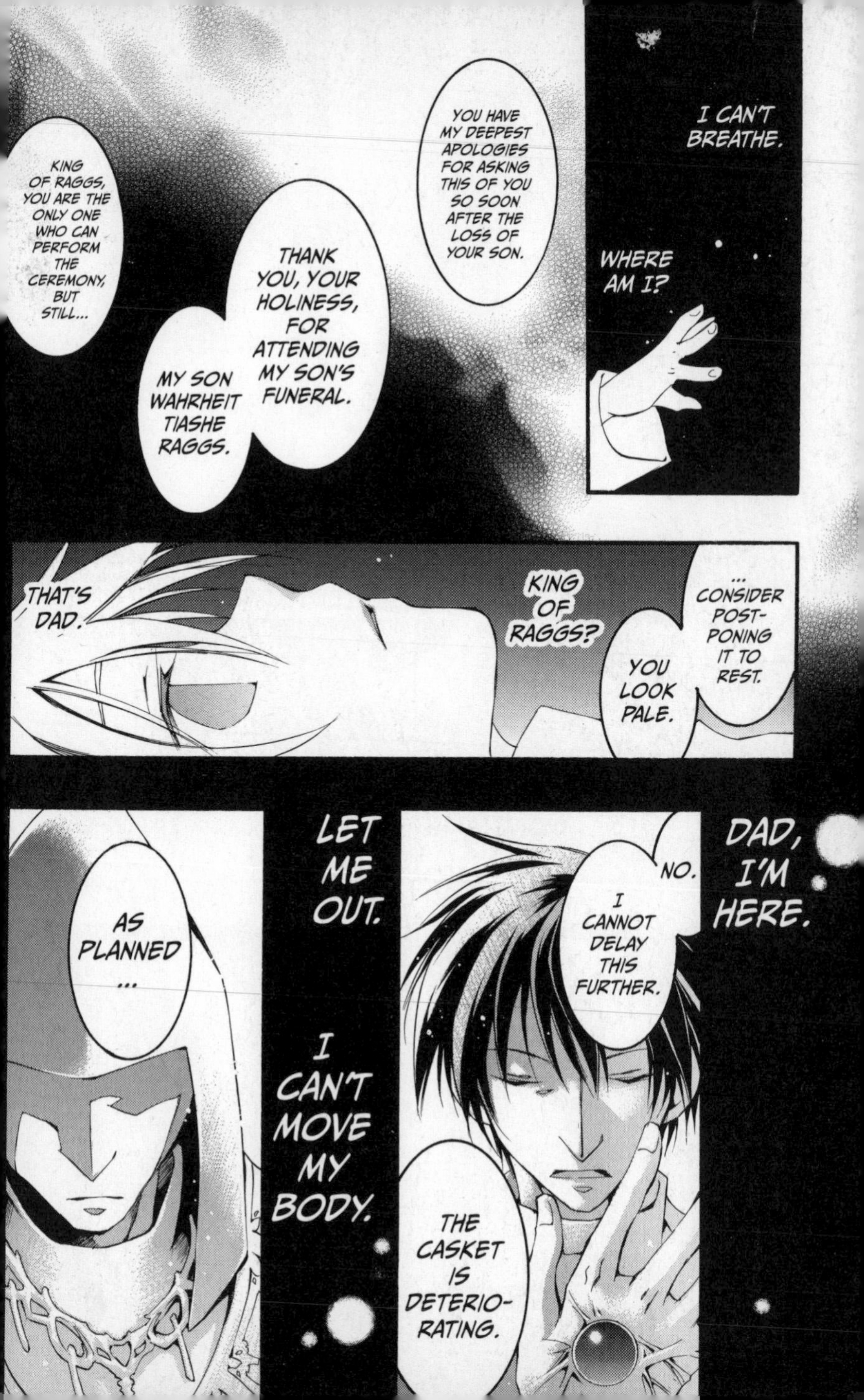
I CAN'T BREATHE.
WHERE AM I?
YOU HAVE MY DEEPEST APOLOGIES FOR ASKING THIS OF YOU SO SOON AFTER THE LOSS OF YOUR SON.
THANK YOU, YOUR HOLINESS, FOR ATTENDING MY SON'S FUNERAL.
MY SON WAHRHEIT TIASHE RAGGS.
KING OF RAGGS, YOU ARE THE ONLY ONE WHO CAN PERFORM THE CEREMONY, BUT STILL...
...CONSIDER POST-PONING IT TO REST.
YOU LOOK PALE.
KING OF RAGGS?
THAT'S DAD.
DAD, I'M HERE.
NO.
I CANNOT DELAY THIS FURTHER.
THE CASKET IS DETERIO-RATING.
LET ME OUT.
I CAN'T MOVE MY BODY.
AS PLANNED ...

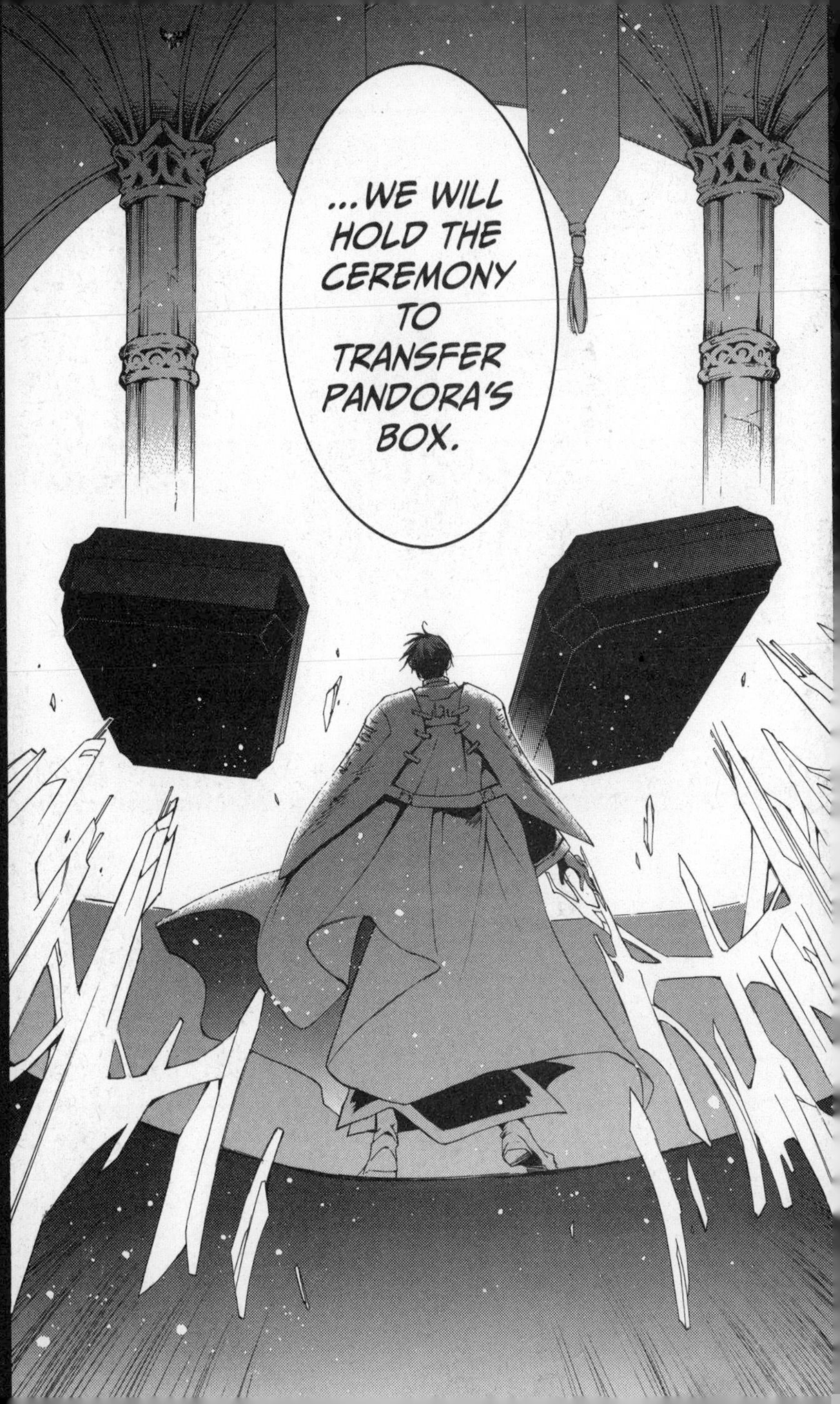
...WE WILL HOLD THE CEREMONY TO TRANSFER PANDORA'S BOX.

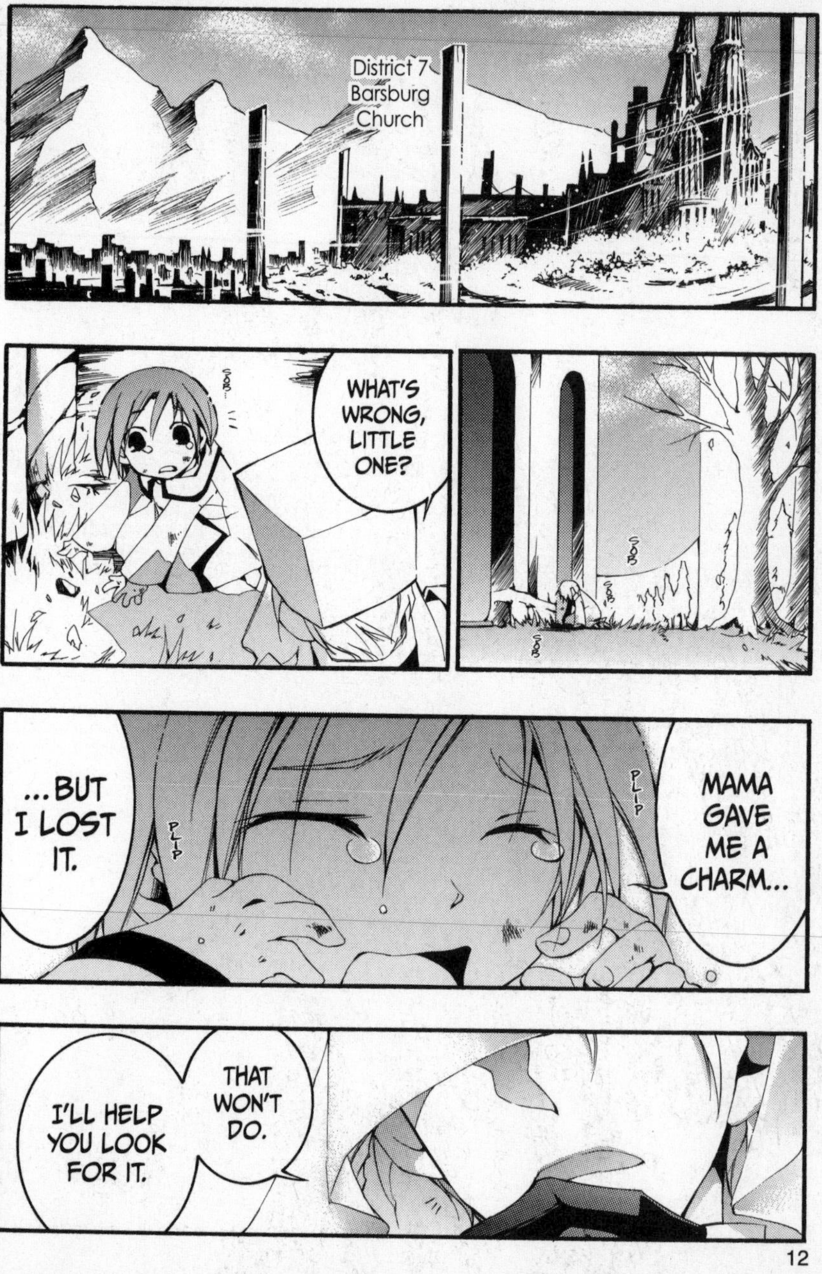
District 7
Barsburg
Church
SOB
SOB
SOB
SOB...
WHAT'S WRONG, LITTLE ONE?
MAMA GAVE ME A CHARM...
PLIP
PLIP
...BUT I LOST IT.
THAT WON'T DO.
I'LL HELP YOU LOOK FOR IT.

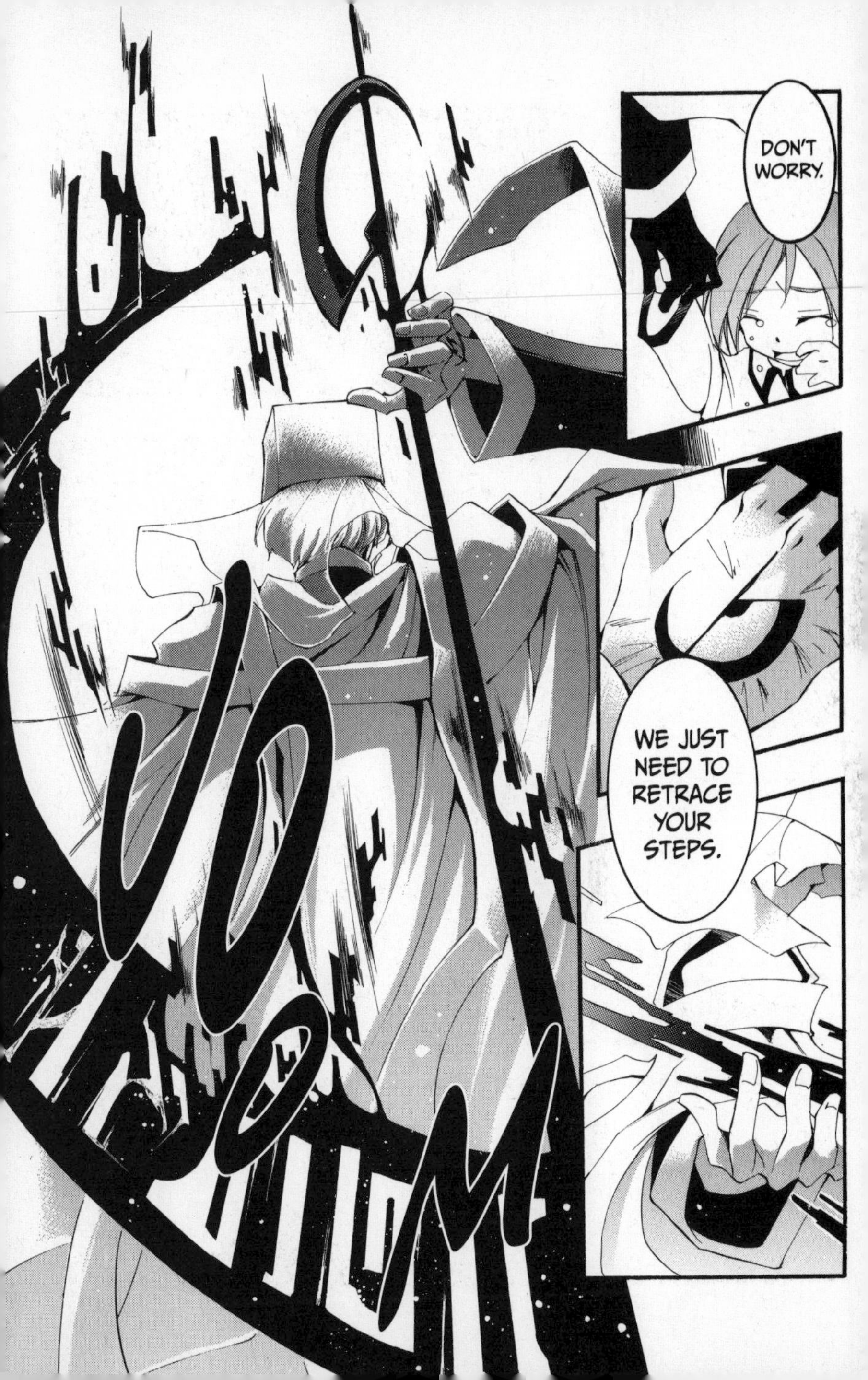
DON'T WORRY.
WE JUST NEED TO RETRACE YOUR STEPS.

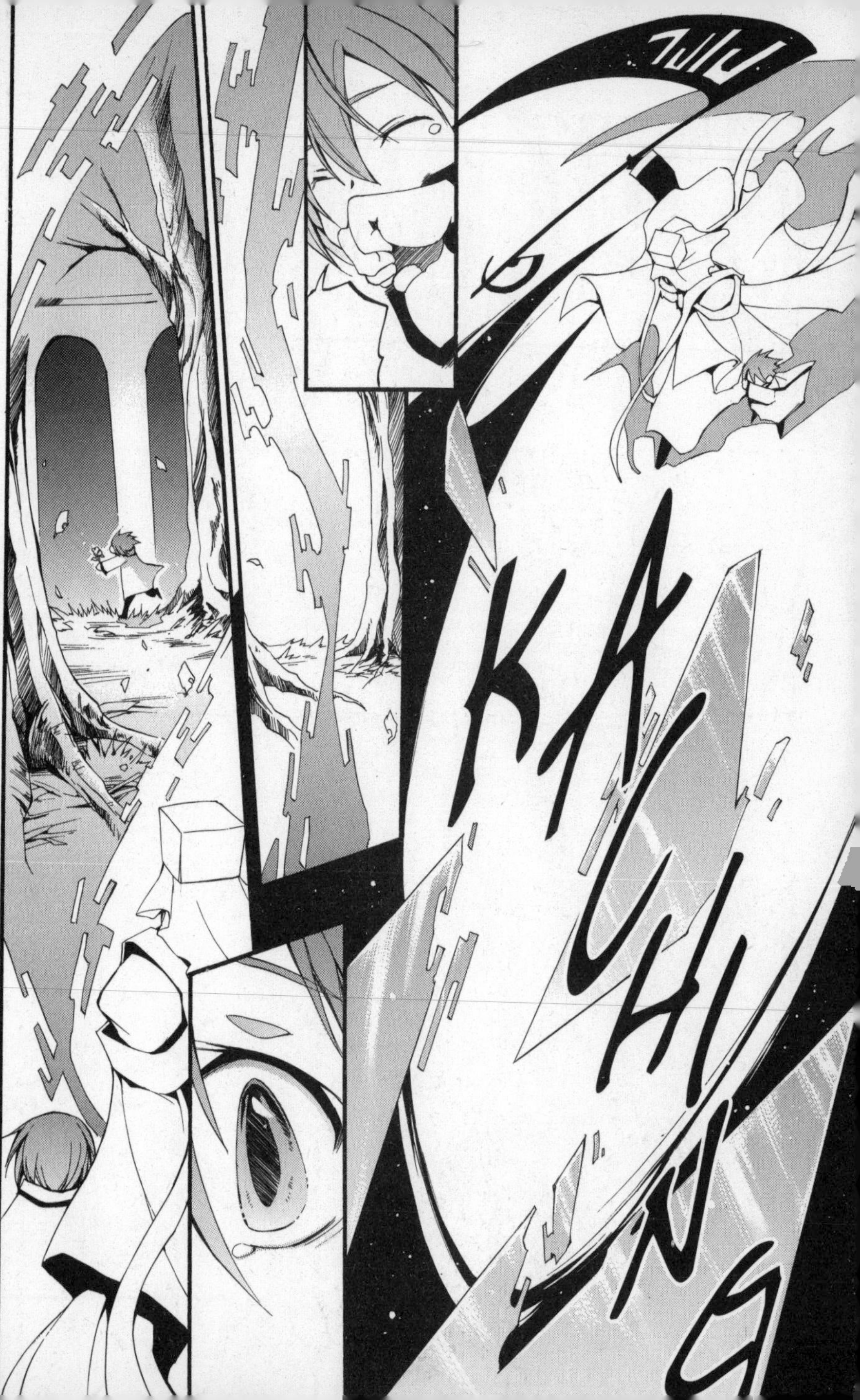
KACHNG

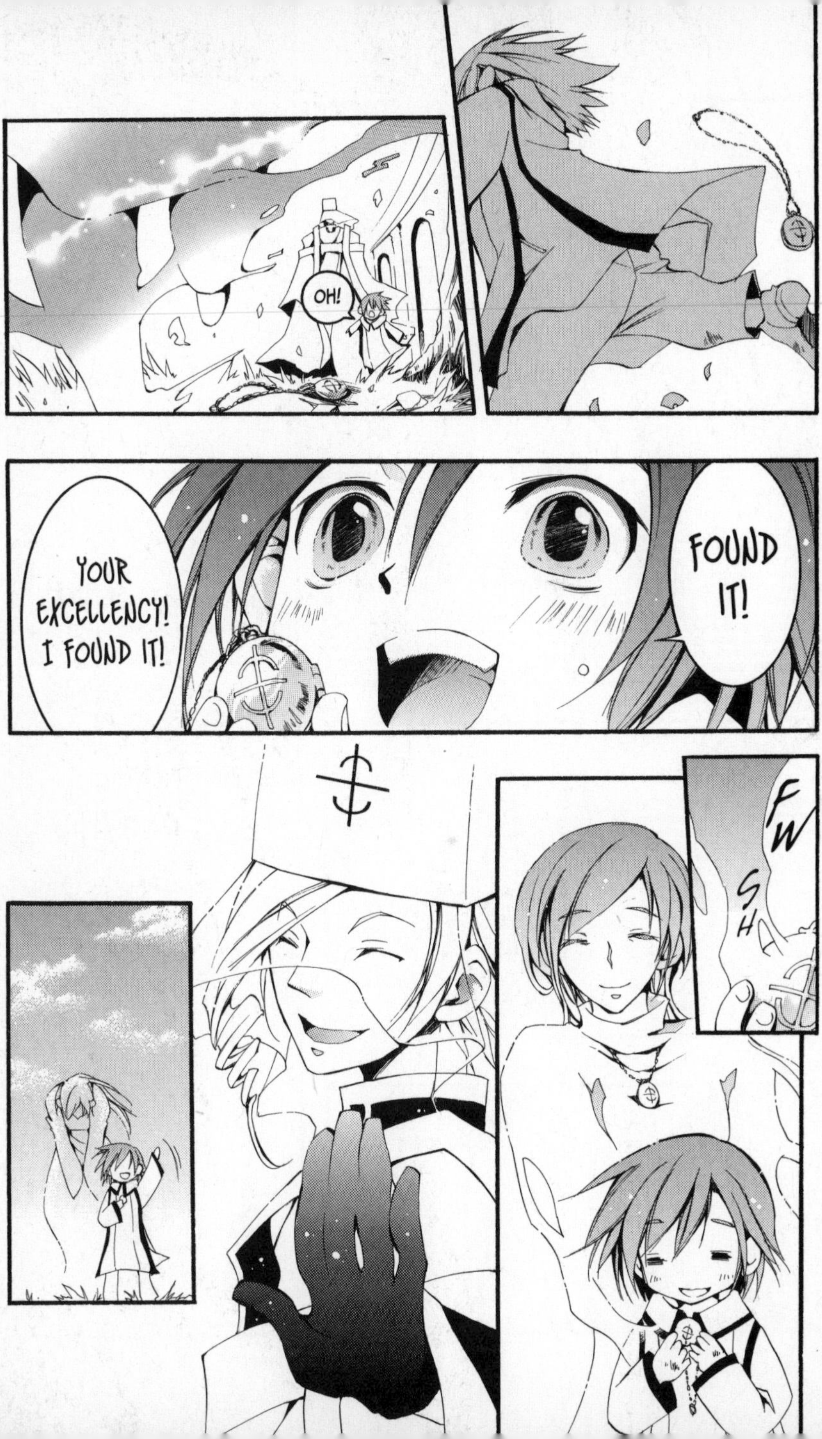
OH!
FOUND IT!
YOUR EXCELLENCY! I FOUND IT!
FWSH

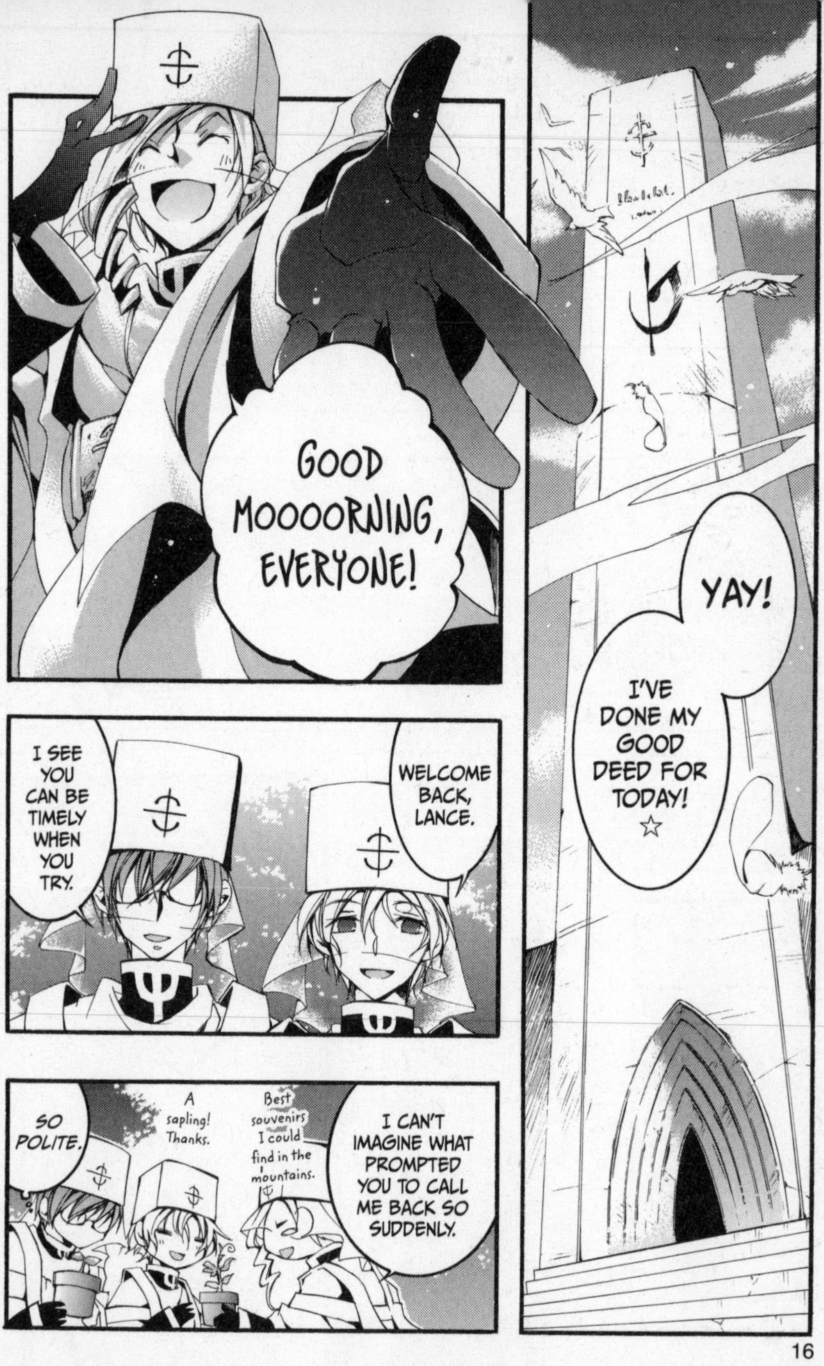
YAY!
I'VE DONE MY GOOD DEED FOR TODAY! ☆
GOOD MOOOORNING, EVERYONE!
WELCOME BACK, LANCE.
I SEE YOU CAN BE TIMELY WHEN YOU TRY.
I CAN'T IMAGINE WHAT PROMPTED YOU TO CALL ME BACK SO SUDDENLY.
Best souvenirs I could find in the mountains.
A sapling! Thanks.
SO POLITE.

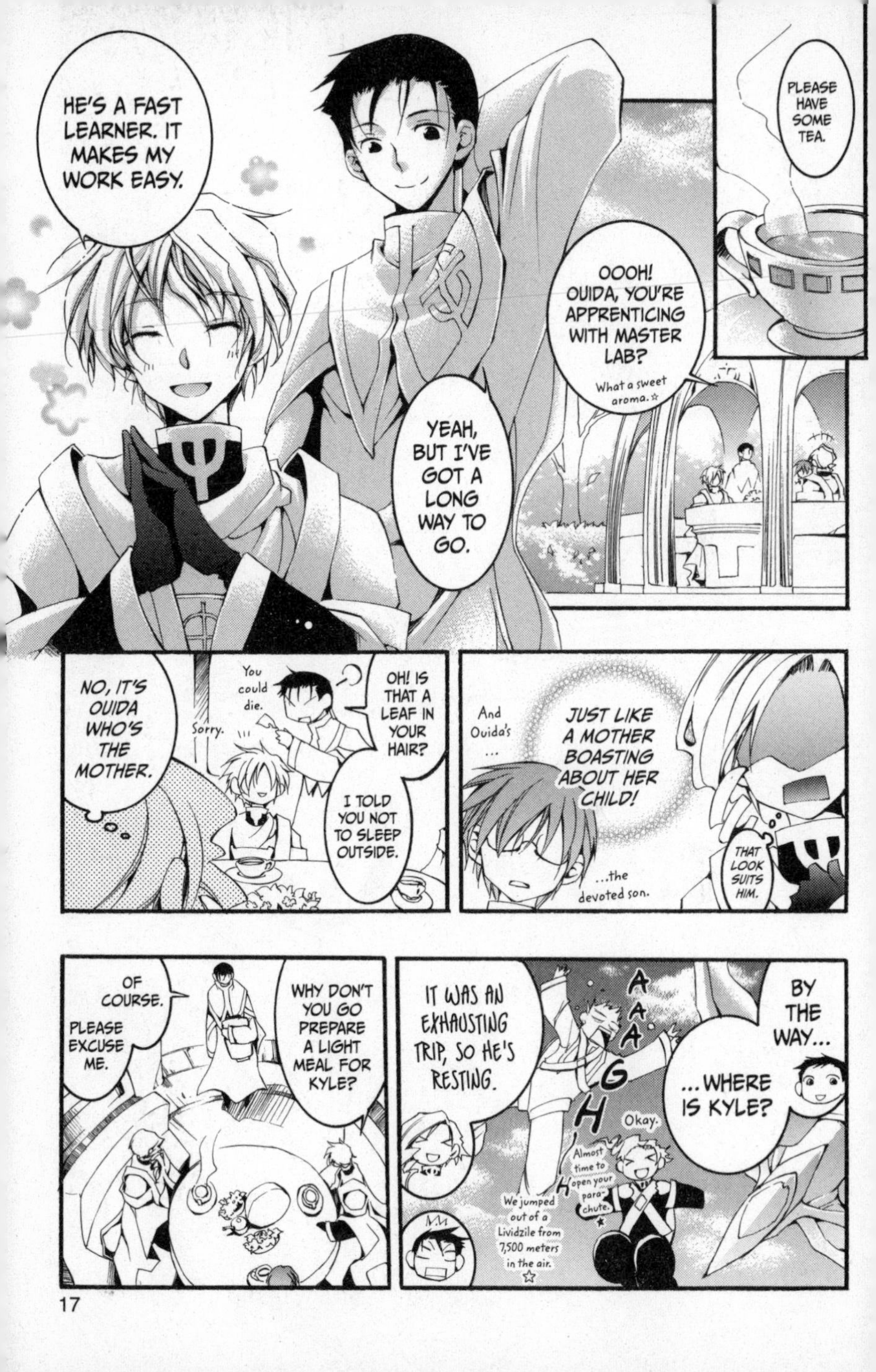
PLEASE HAVE SOME TEA.
OOOH! OUIDA, YOU'RE APPRENTICING WITH MASTER LAB?
What a sweet aroma.☆
YEAH, BUT I'VE GOT A LONG WAY TO GO.
HE'S A FAST LEARNER. IT MAKES MY WORK EASY.
JUST LIKE A MOTHER BOASTING ABOUT HER CHILD!
And Ouida's ...
...the devoted son.
THAT LOOK SUITS HIM.
OH! IS THAT A LEAF IN YOUR HAIR?
You could die.
Sorry.
I TOLD YOU NOT TO SLEEP OUTSIDE.
NO, IT'S OUIDA WHO'S THE MOTHER.
BY THE WAY...
...WHERE IS KYLE?
IT WAS AN EXHAUSTING TRIP, SO HE'S RESTING.
AAAGHH
Okay.
Almost time to open your para-chute.★
We jumped out of a Lividzile from 7,500 meters in the air.☆
WHY DON'T YOU GO PREPARE A LIGHT MEAL FOR KYLE?
OF COURSE.
PLEASE EXCUSE ME.

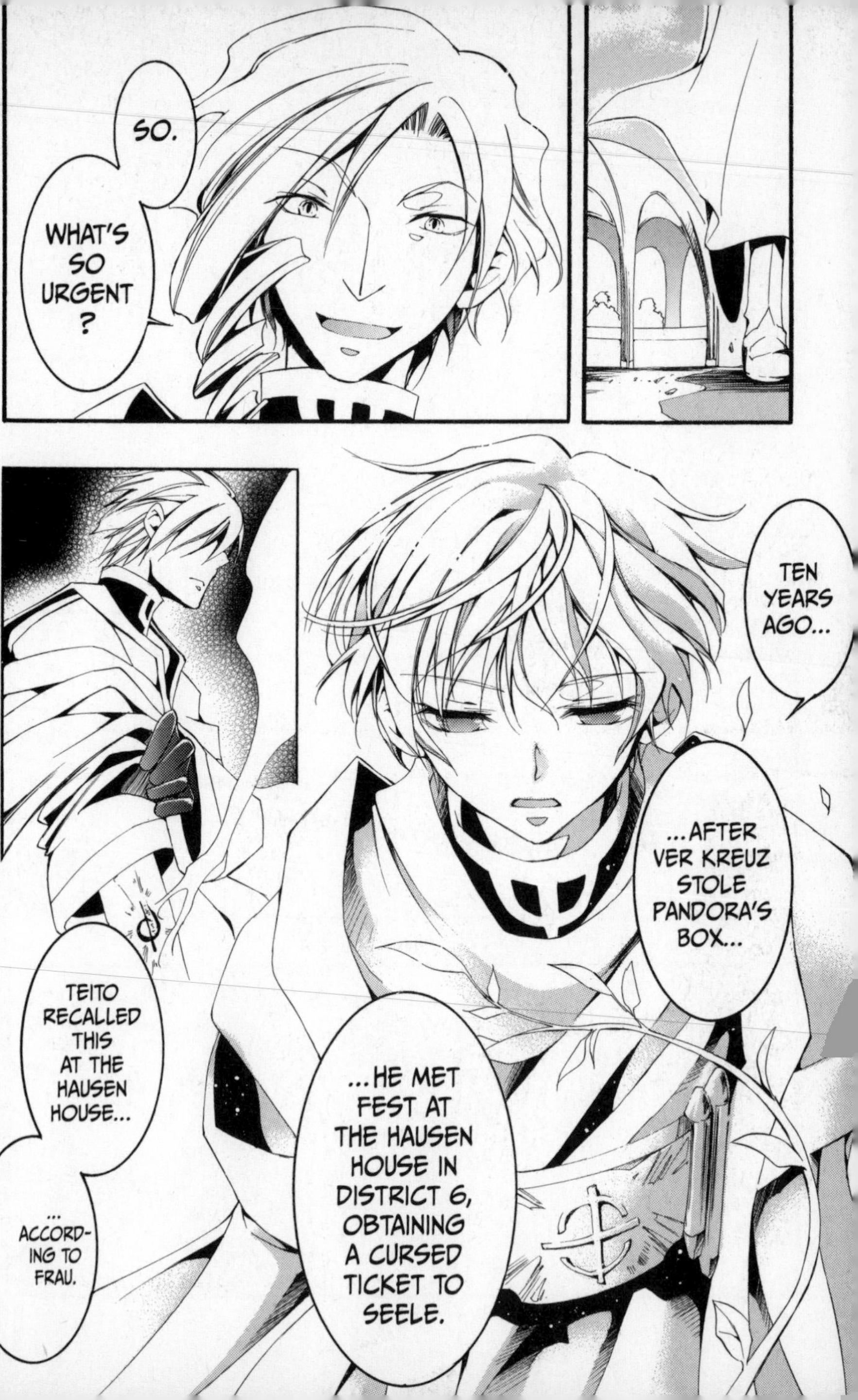
SO.
WHAT'S SO URGENT?
TEN YEARS AGO...
...AFTER VER KREUZ STOLE PANDORA'S BOX...
...HE MET FEST AT THE HAUSEN HOUSE IN DISTRICT 6, OBTAINING A CURSED TICKET TO SEELE.
TEITO RECALLED THIS AT THE HAUSEN HOUSE...
...ACCORDING TO FRAU.

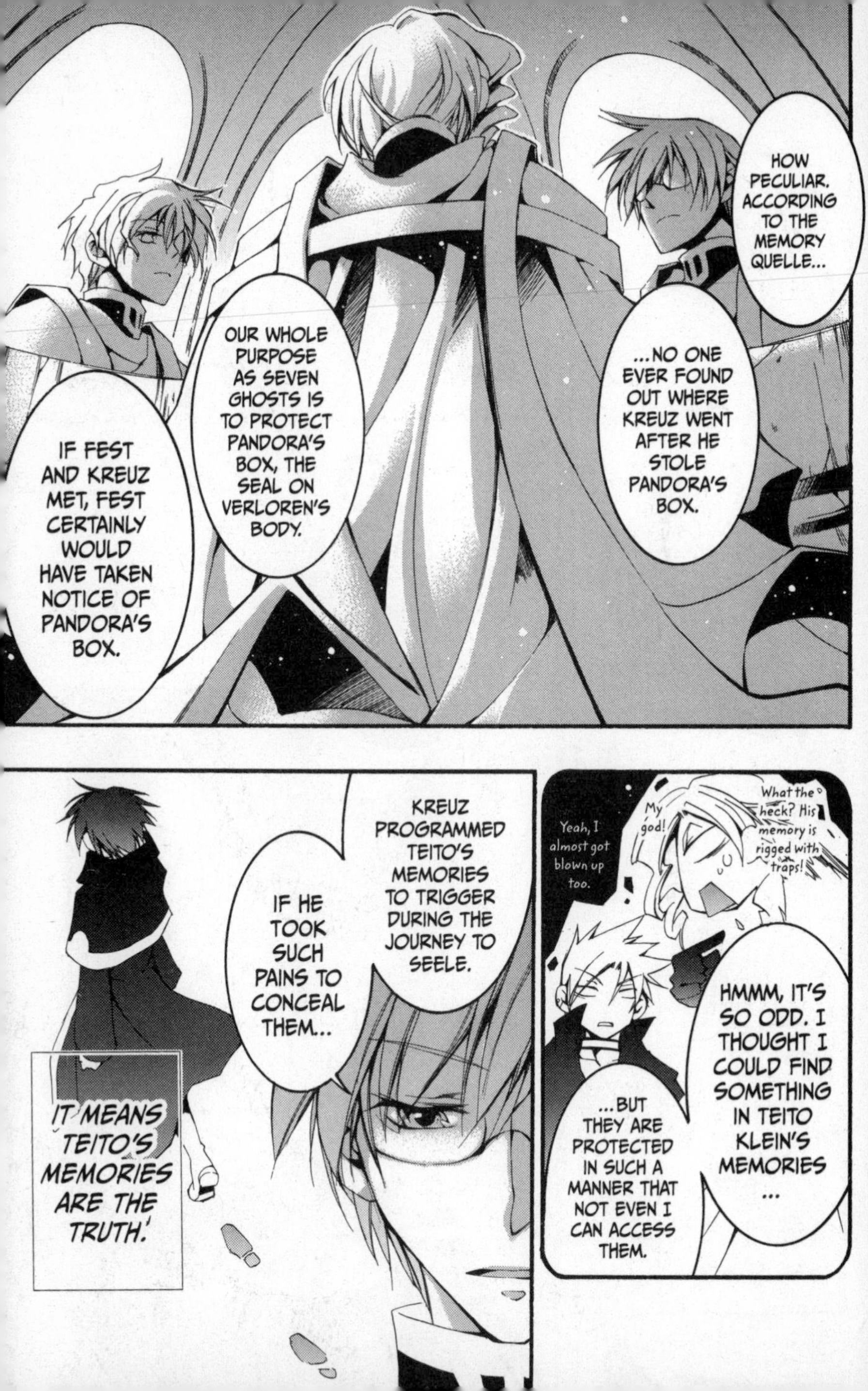
HOW PECULIAR. ACCORDING TO THE MEMORY QUELLE...
...NO ONE EVER FOUND OUT WHERE KREUZ WENT AFTER HE STOLE PANDORA'S BOX.
OUR WHOLE PURPOSE AS SEVEN GHOSTS IS TO PROTECT PANDORA'S BOX, THE SEAL ON VERLOREN'S BODY.
IF FEST AND KREUZ MET, FEST CERTAINLY WOULD HAVE TAKEN NOTICE OF PANDORA'S BOX.
What the heck? His memory is rigged with traps!
My god!
Yeah, I almost got blown up too.
HMMM, IT'S SO ODD. I THOUGHT I COULD FIND SOMETHING IN TEITO KLEIN'S MEMORIES ...
...BUT THEY ARE PROTECTED IN SUCH A MANNER THAT NOT EVEN I CAN ACCESS THEM.
KREUZ PROGRAMMED TEITO'S MEMORIES TO TRIGGER DURING THE JOURNEY TO SEELE.
IF HE TOOK SUCH PAINS TO CONCEAL THEM...
IT MEANS TEITO'S MEMORIES ARE THE TRUTH.'

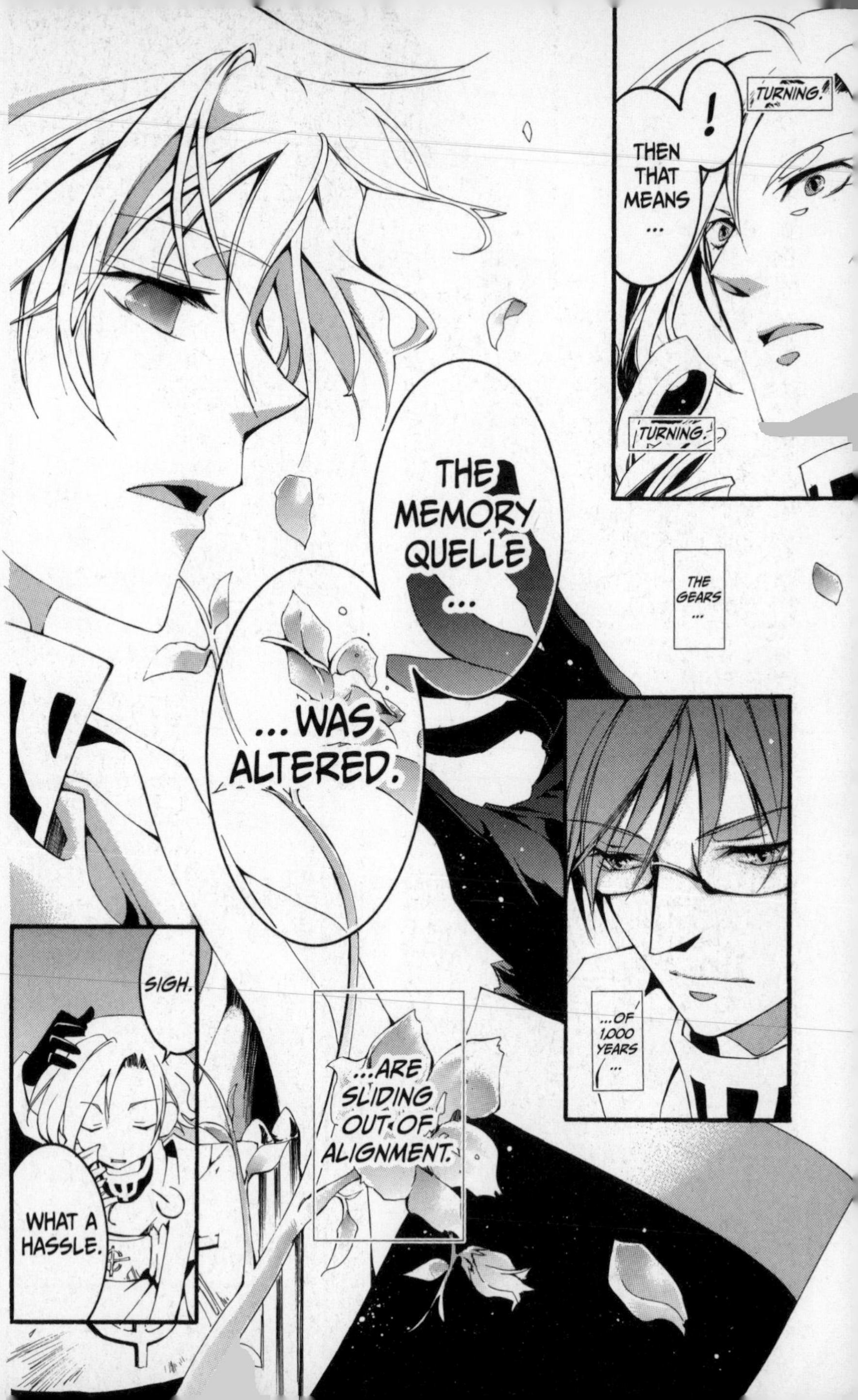
!
TURNING.
THEN THAT MEANS ...
TURNING.
THE MEMORY QUELLE ...
... WAS ALTERED.
THE GEARS ...
...OF 1,000 YEARS ...
...ARE SLIDING OUT OF ALIGNMENT.
SIGH.
WHAT A HASSLE.

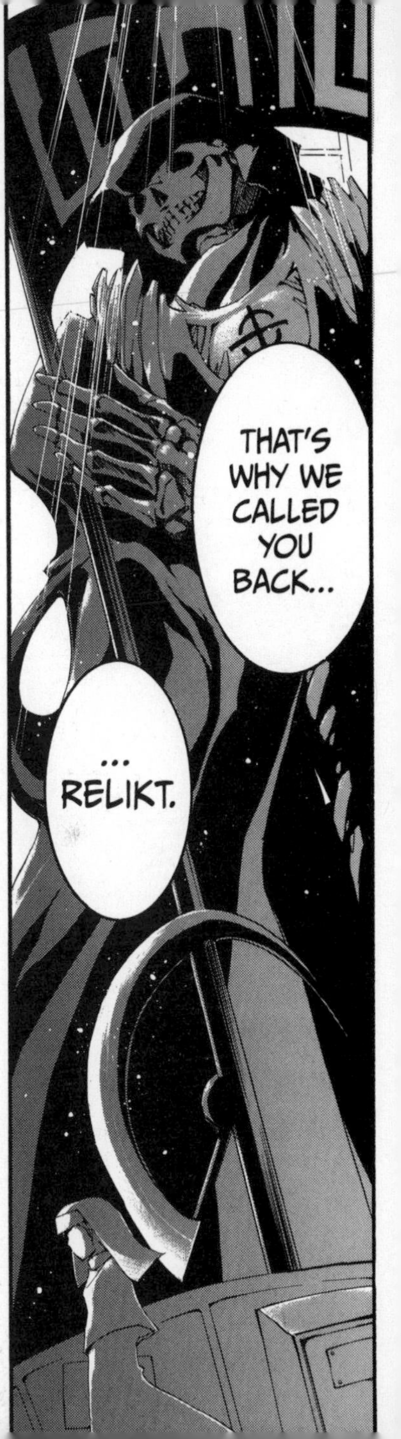
THAT'S WHY WE CALLED YOU BACK...
... RELIKT.

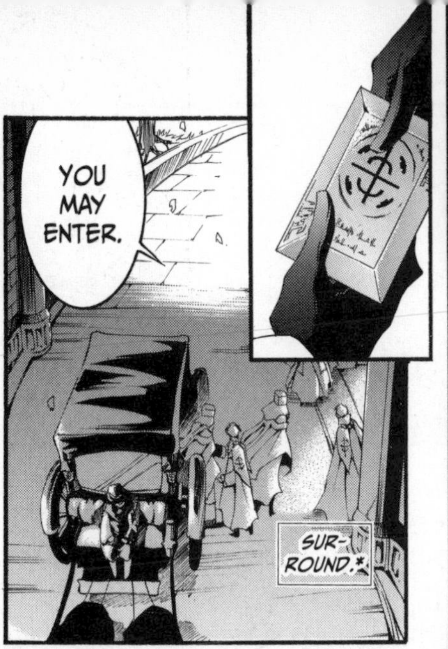
YOU MAY ENTER.
SUR-ROUND.*

*Chant from "Kagome Kagome," a Japanese children's game similar to "Ring Around the Rosie" or "Duck, Duck Goose"

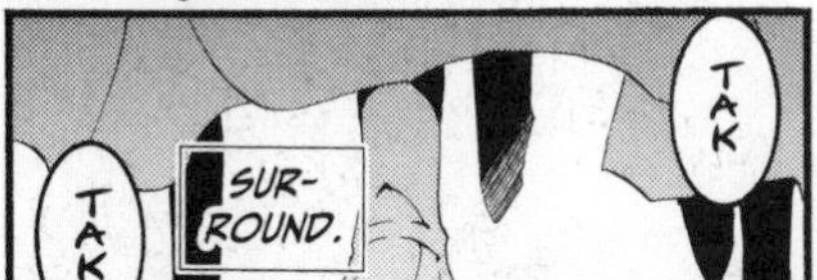
TAK
SUR-ROUND.
TAK

Traditional lyrics: Kagome kagome (surround, surround) / The bird in the cage / When will it come out / In the evening of dawn / The crane and turtle slipped / Who is behind you

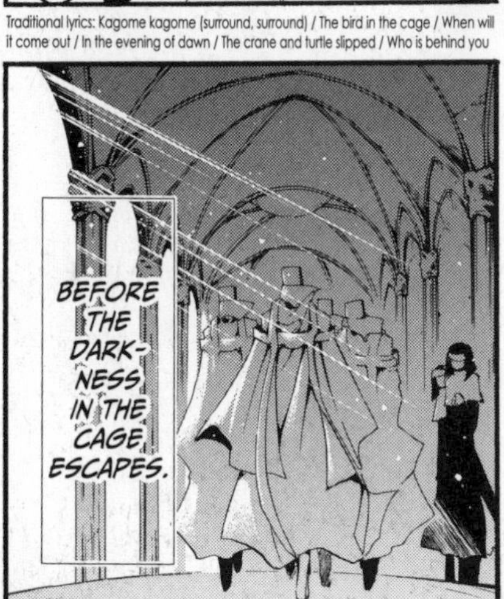
BEFORE THE DARKNESS IN THE CAGE ESCAPES.

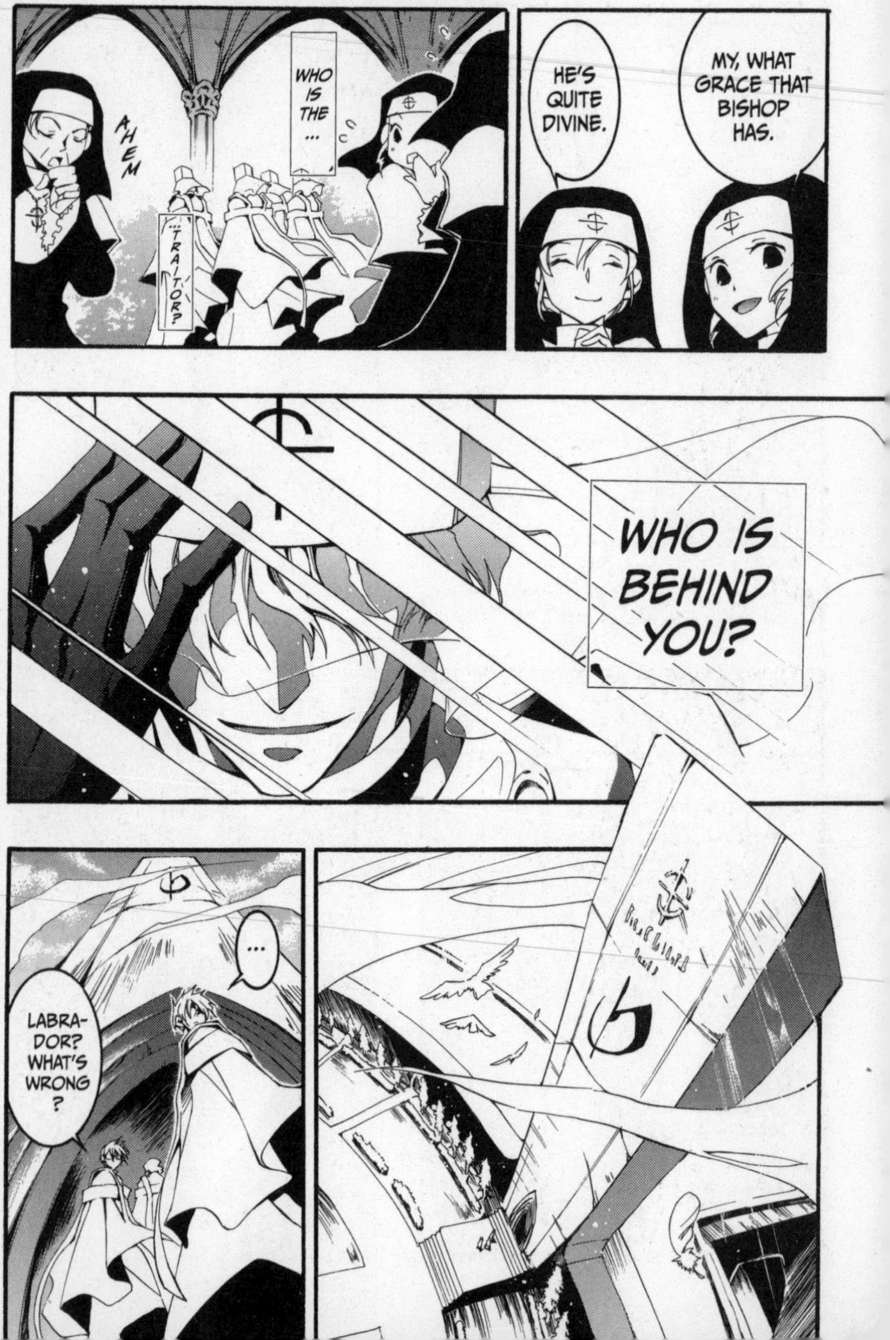
MY, WHAT GRACE THAT BISHOP HAS.
HE'S QUITE DIVINE.
WHO IS THE ...
...TRAITOR?
AHEM
WHO IS BEHIND YOU?
...
LABRADOR? WHAT'S WRONG?

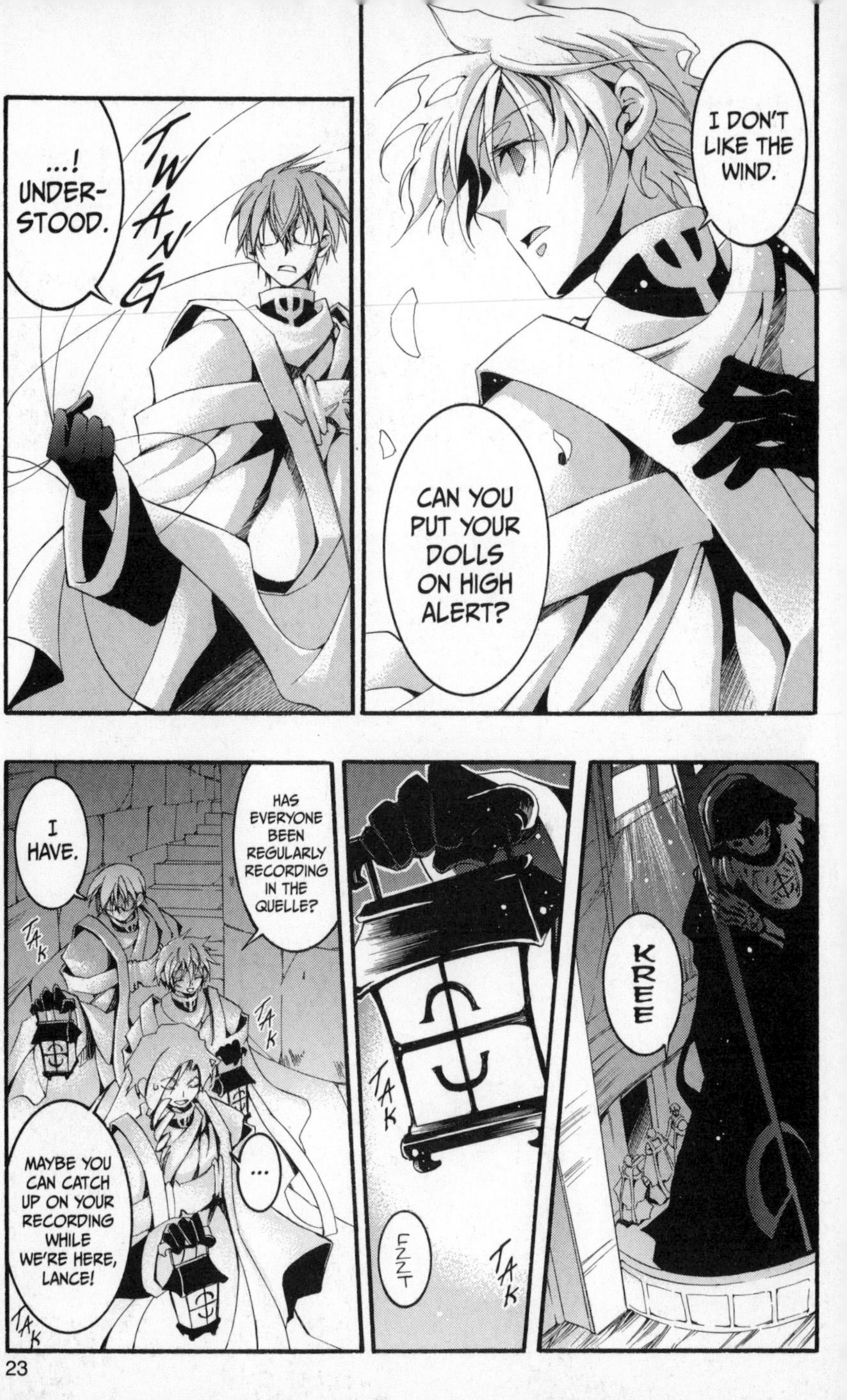
I DON'T LIKE THE WIND.
CAN YOU PUT YOUR DOLLS ON HIGH ALERT?
...! UNDER-STOOD.
TWANG
KREE
TAK
FZZT
TAK
HAS EVERYONE BEEN REGULARLY RECORDING IN THE QUELLE?
I HAVE.
TAK
TAK
...
MAYBE YOU CAN CATCH UP ON YOUR RECORDING WHILE WE'RE HERE, LANCE!
TAK

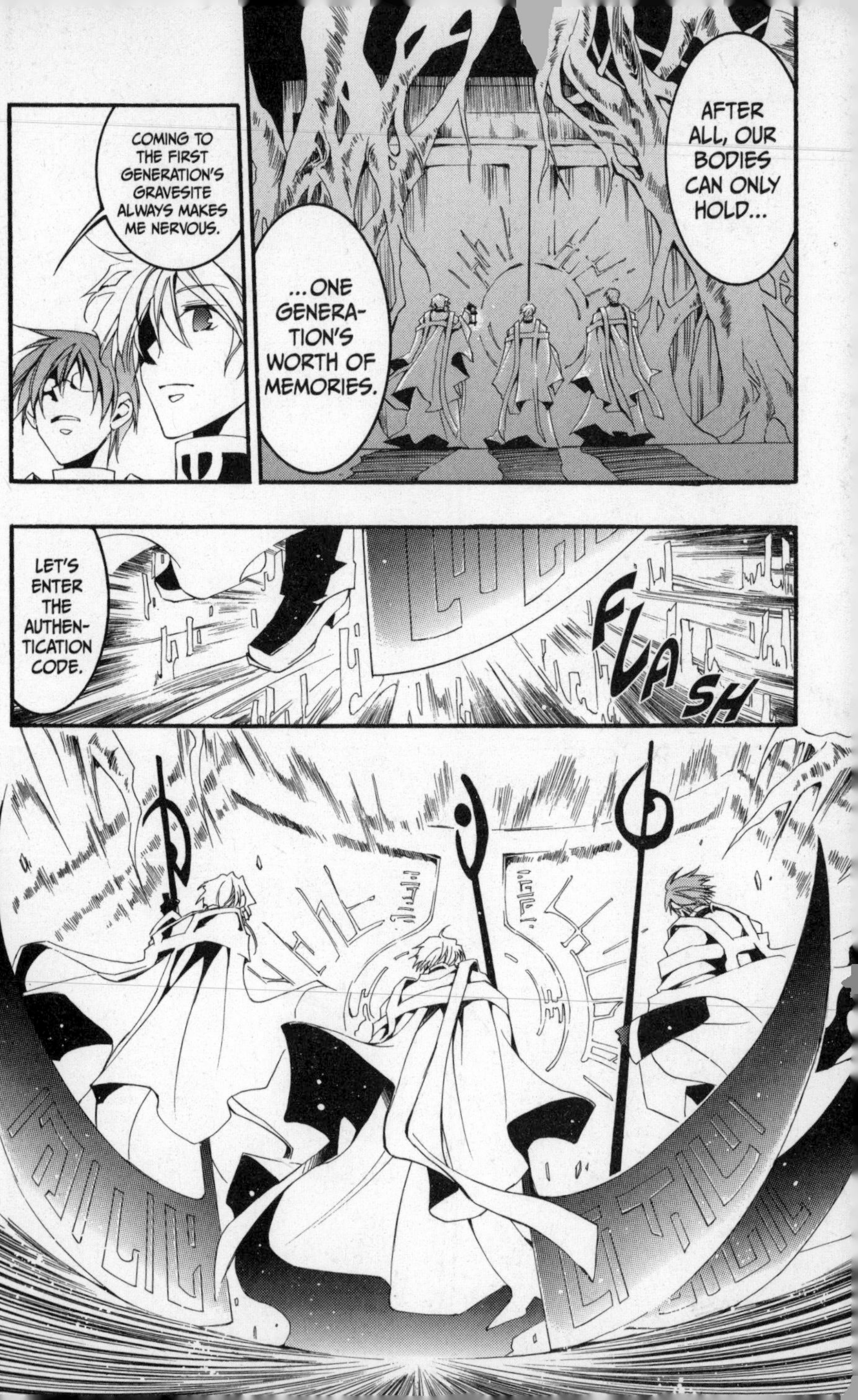
AFTER ALL, OUR BODIES CAN ONLY HOLD...
...ONE GENERATION'S WORTH OF MEMORIES.
COMING TO THE FIRST GENERATION'S GRAVESITE ALWAYS MAKES ME NERVOUS.
FLASH
LET'S ENTER THE AUTHENTICATION CODE.

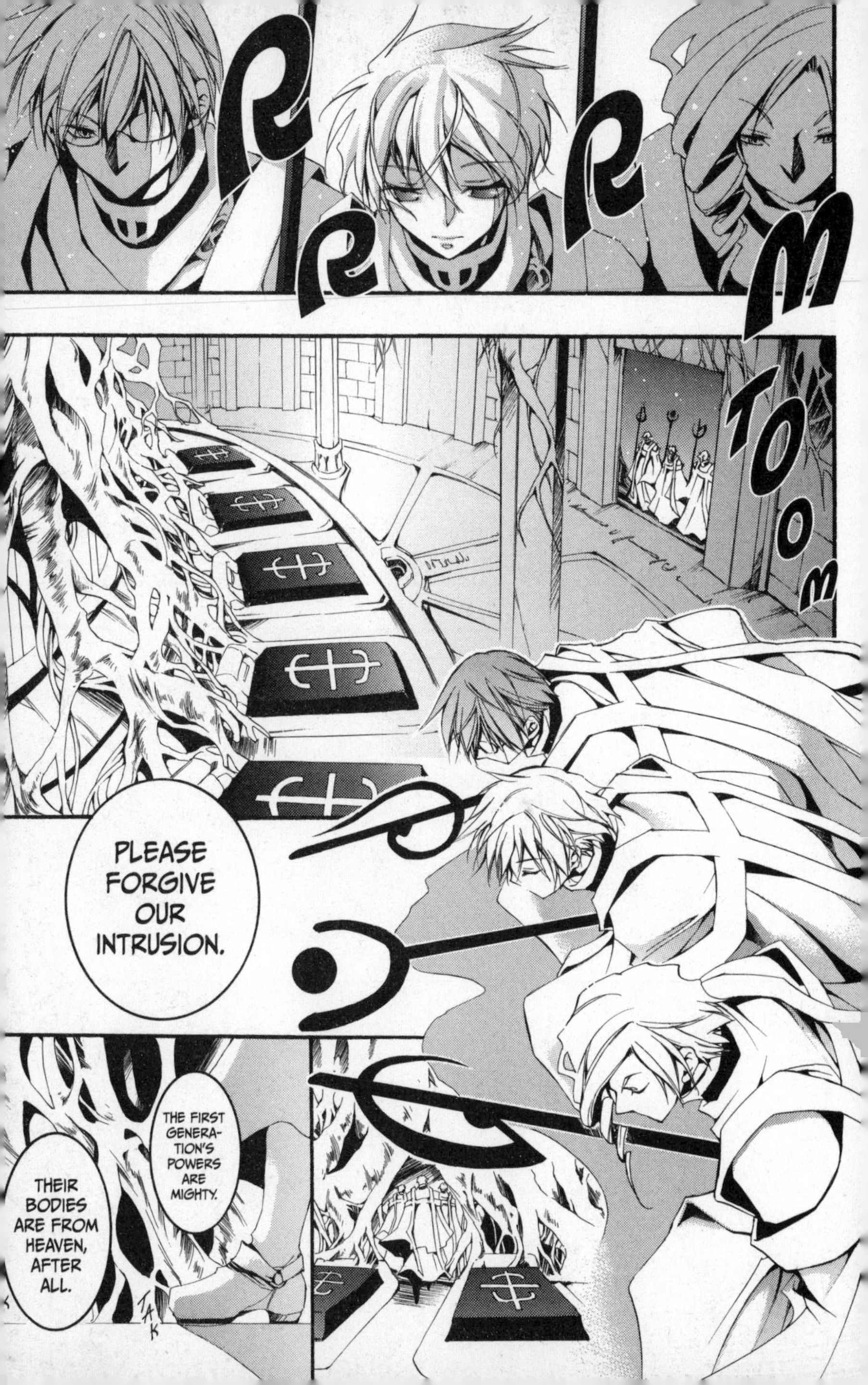
RRRRRM
TOOOM
PLEASE FORGIVE OUR INTRUSION.
THE FIRST GENERATION'S POWERS ARE MIGHTY.
THEIR BODIES ARE FROM HEAVEN, AFTER ALL.
TAK

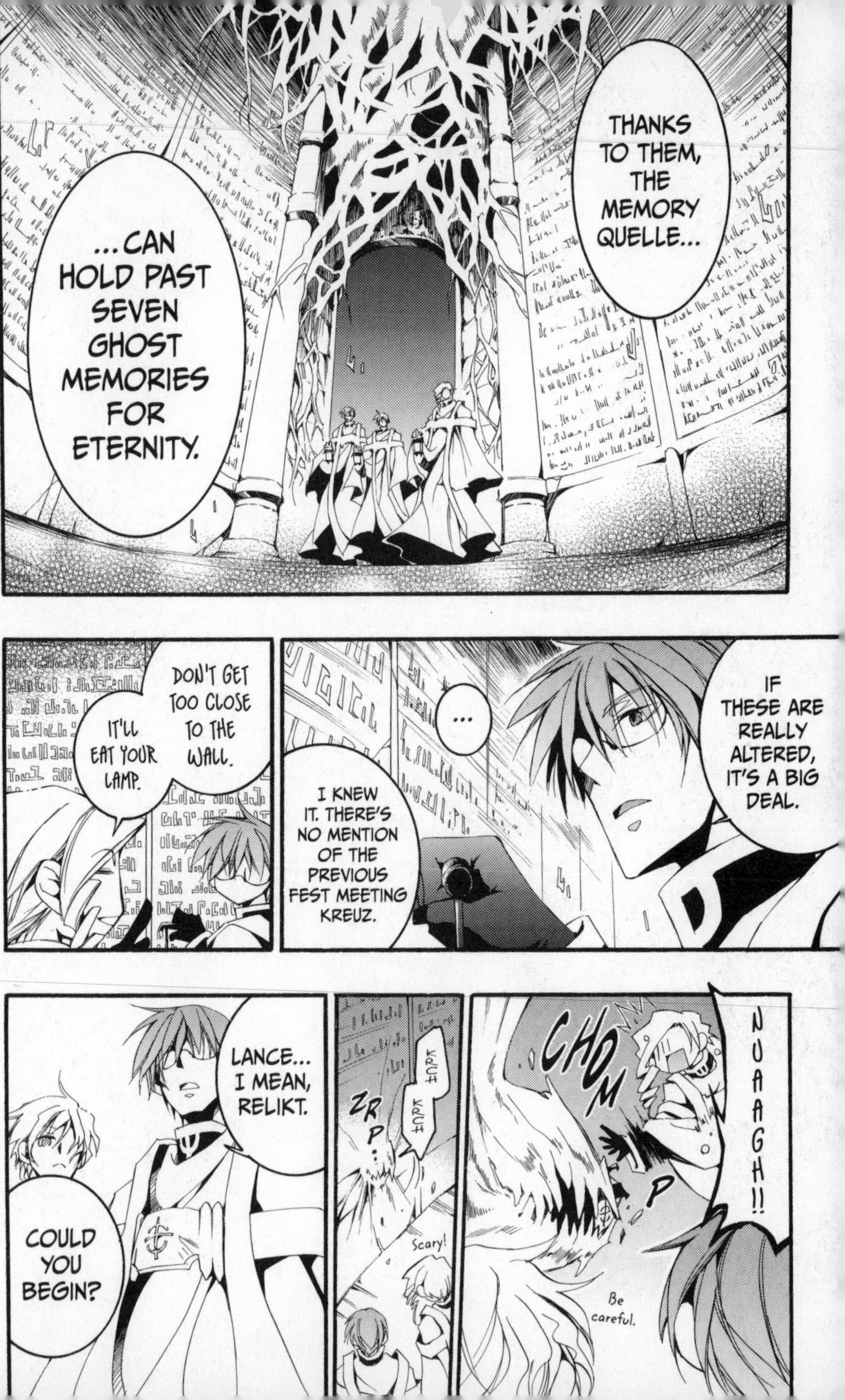
THANKS TO THEM, THE MEMORY QUELLE...
...CAN HOLD PAST SEVEN GHOST MEMORIES FOR ETERNITY.
IF THESE ARE REALLY ALTERED, IT'S A BIG DEAL.
...
I KNEW IT. THERE'S NO MENTION OF THE PREVIOUS FEST MEETING KREUZ.
DON'T GET TOO CLOSE TO THE WALL.
IT'LL EAT YOUR LAMP.
NUAAGH!!
CHOMP
Be careful.
KRCH KRCH
ZRP...
Scary!
LANCE... I MEAN, RELIKT.
COULD YOU BEGIN?

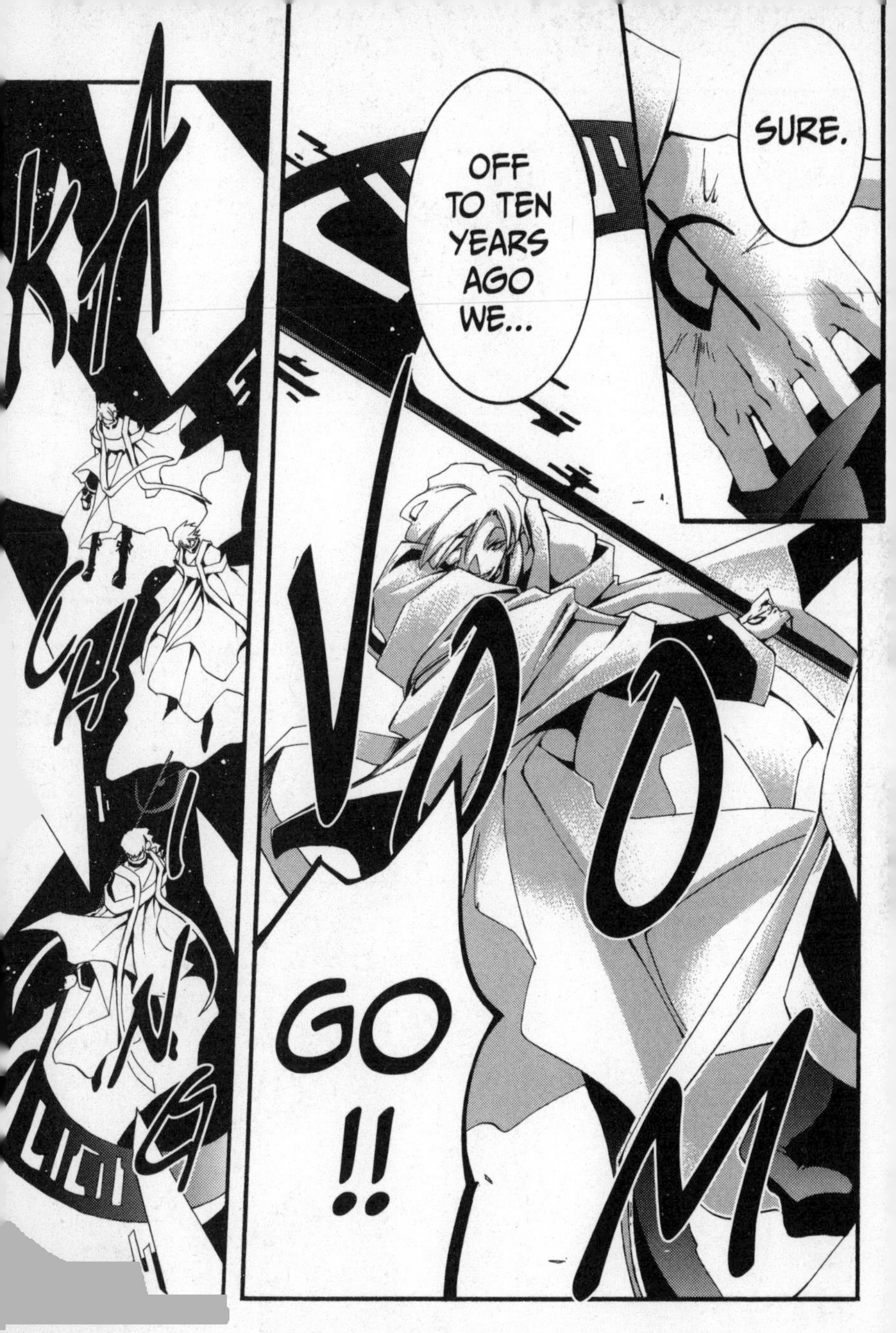
SURE.
OFF TO TEN YEARS AGO WE...
VOOM
GO!!
KACHING

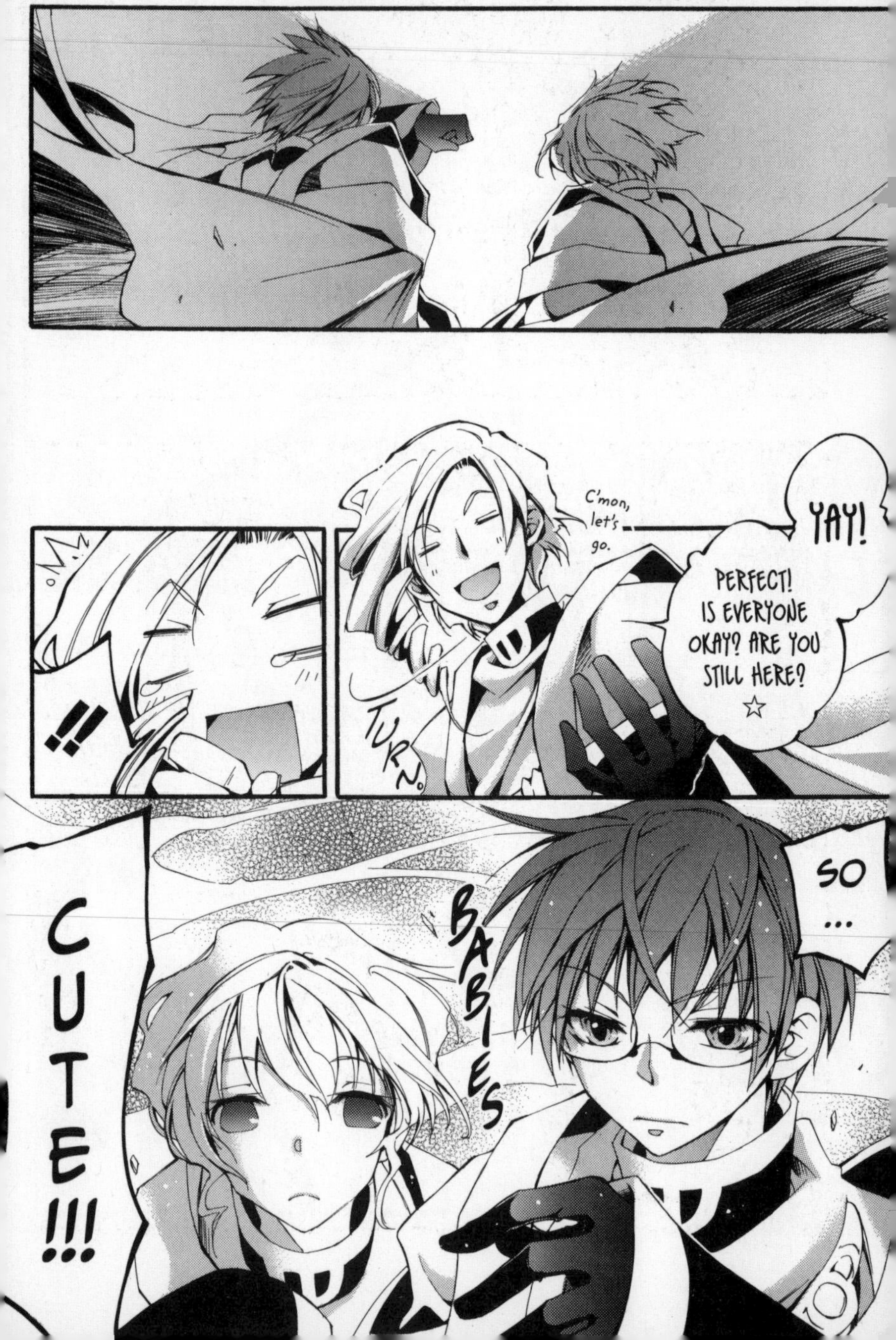
YAY!
PERFECT! IS EVERYONE OKAY? ARE YOU STILL HERE? ☆
C'mon, let's go.
TURN
!!
SO ...
BABIES
CUTE!!!

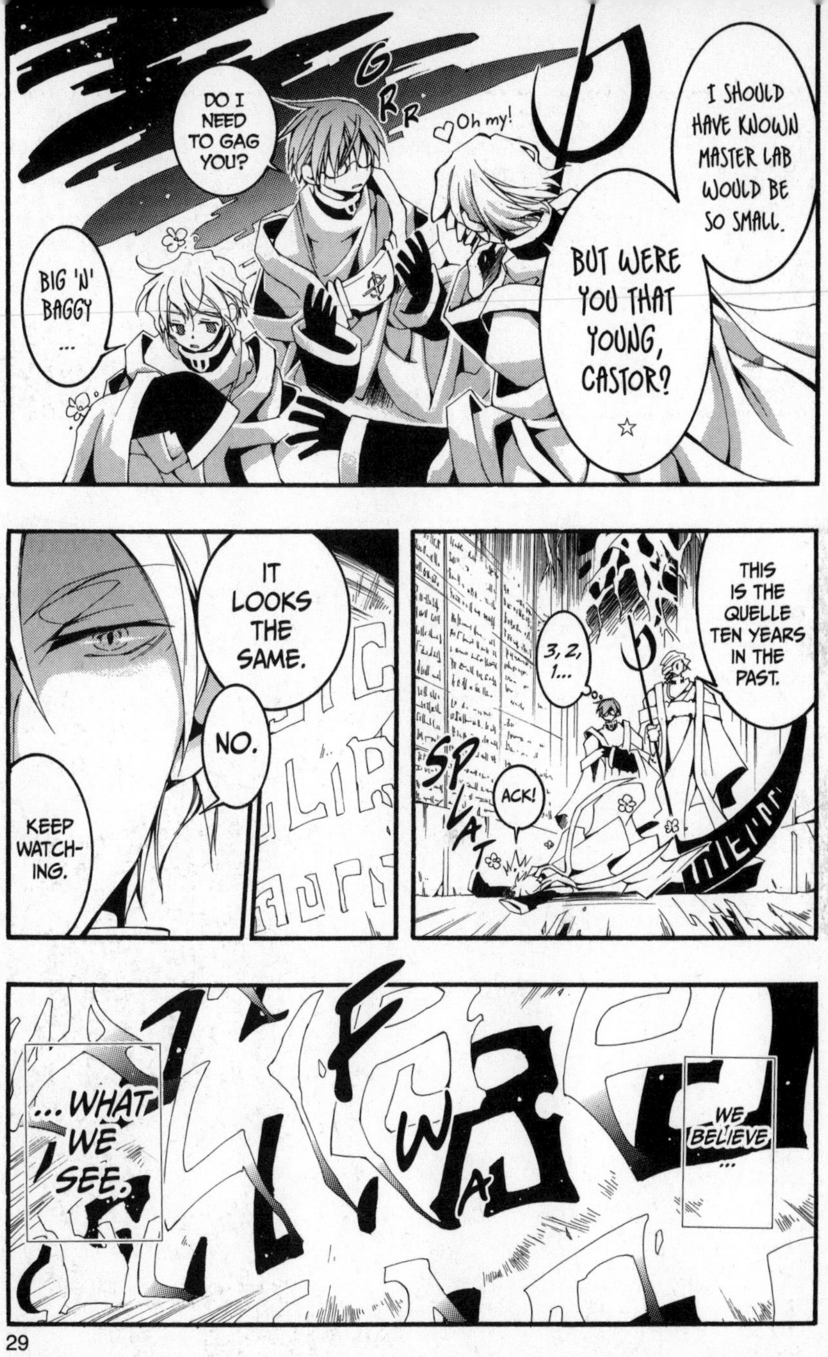

I SHOULD HAVE KNOWN MASTER LAB WOULD BE SO SMALL.
BUT WERE YOU THAT YOUNG, CASTOR? ☆
Oh my!
GRR
DO I NEED TO GAG YOU?
BIG 'N' BAGGY ...
THIS IS THE QUELLE TEN YEARS IN THE PAST.
3, 2, 1...
ACK!
SPLAT
IT LOOKS THE SAME.
NO.
KEEP WATCHING.
WE BELIEVE ...
FWA
... WHAT WE SEE.

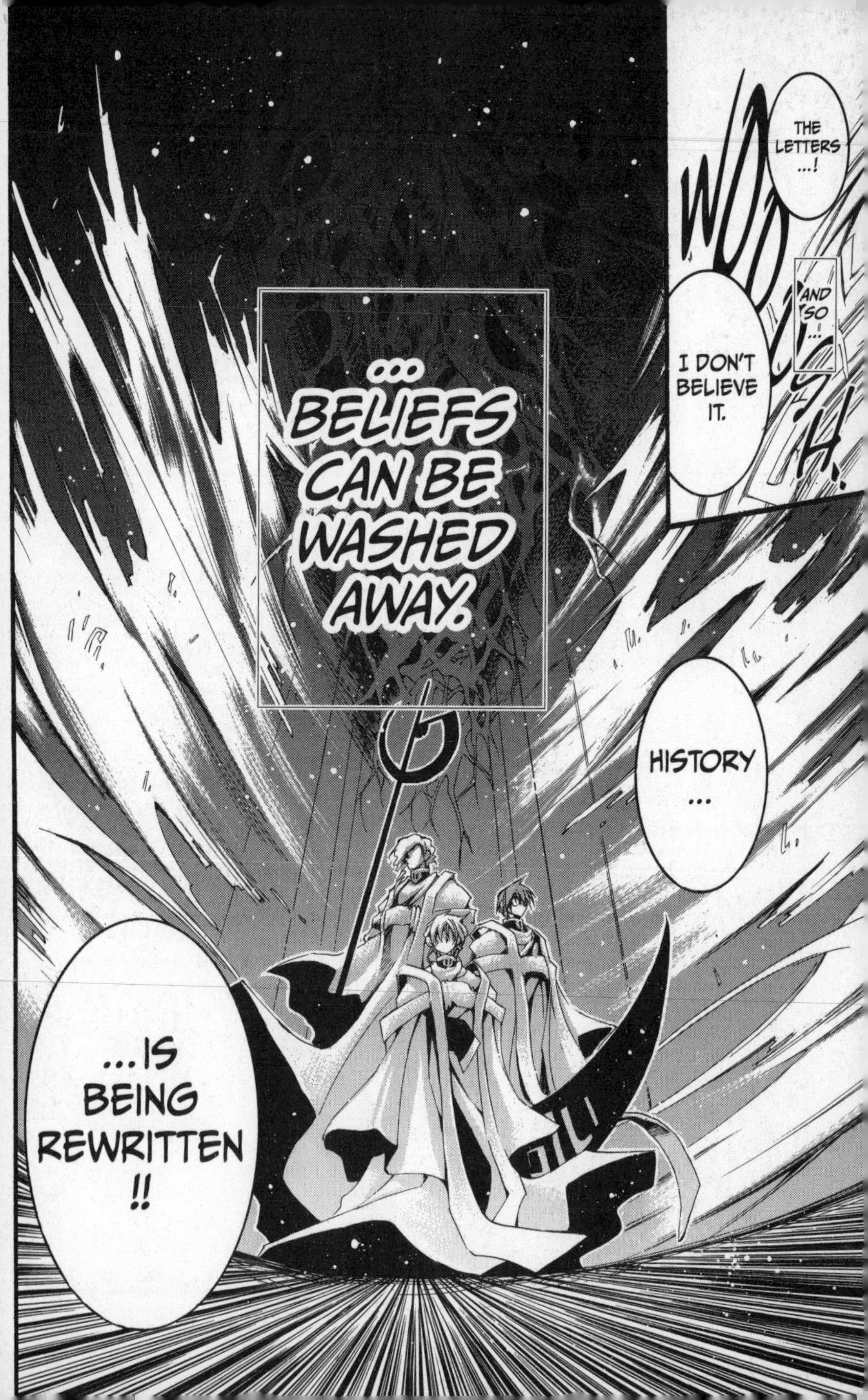
THE LETTERS ...!
AND SO ...
I DON'T BELIEVE IT.
...BELIEFS CAN BE WASHED AWAY.
HISTORY ...
...IS BEING REWRITTEN !!

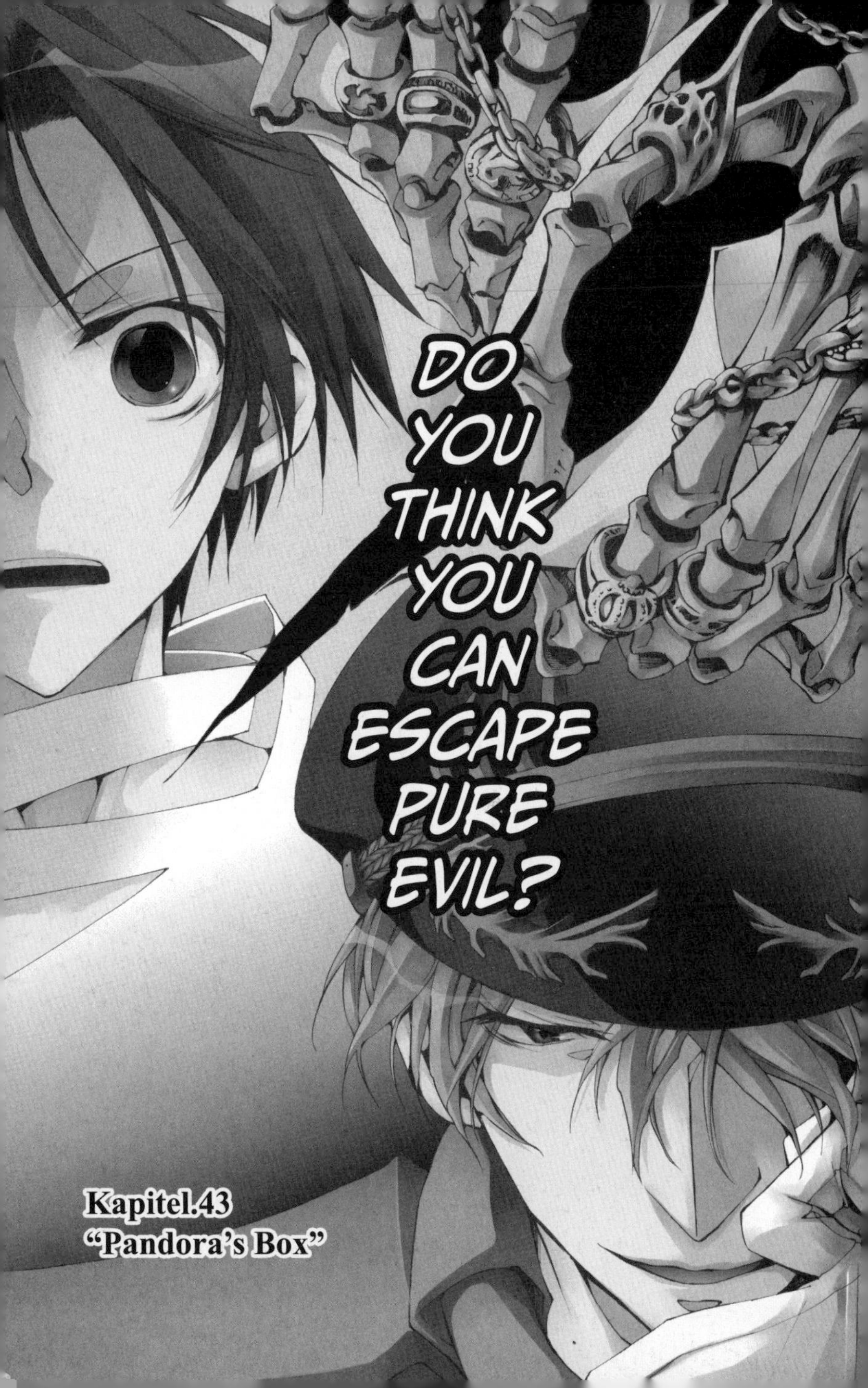
DO YOU THINK YOU CAN ESCAPE PURE EVIL?
Kapitel.43
"Pandora's Box"

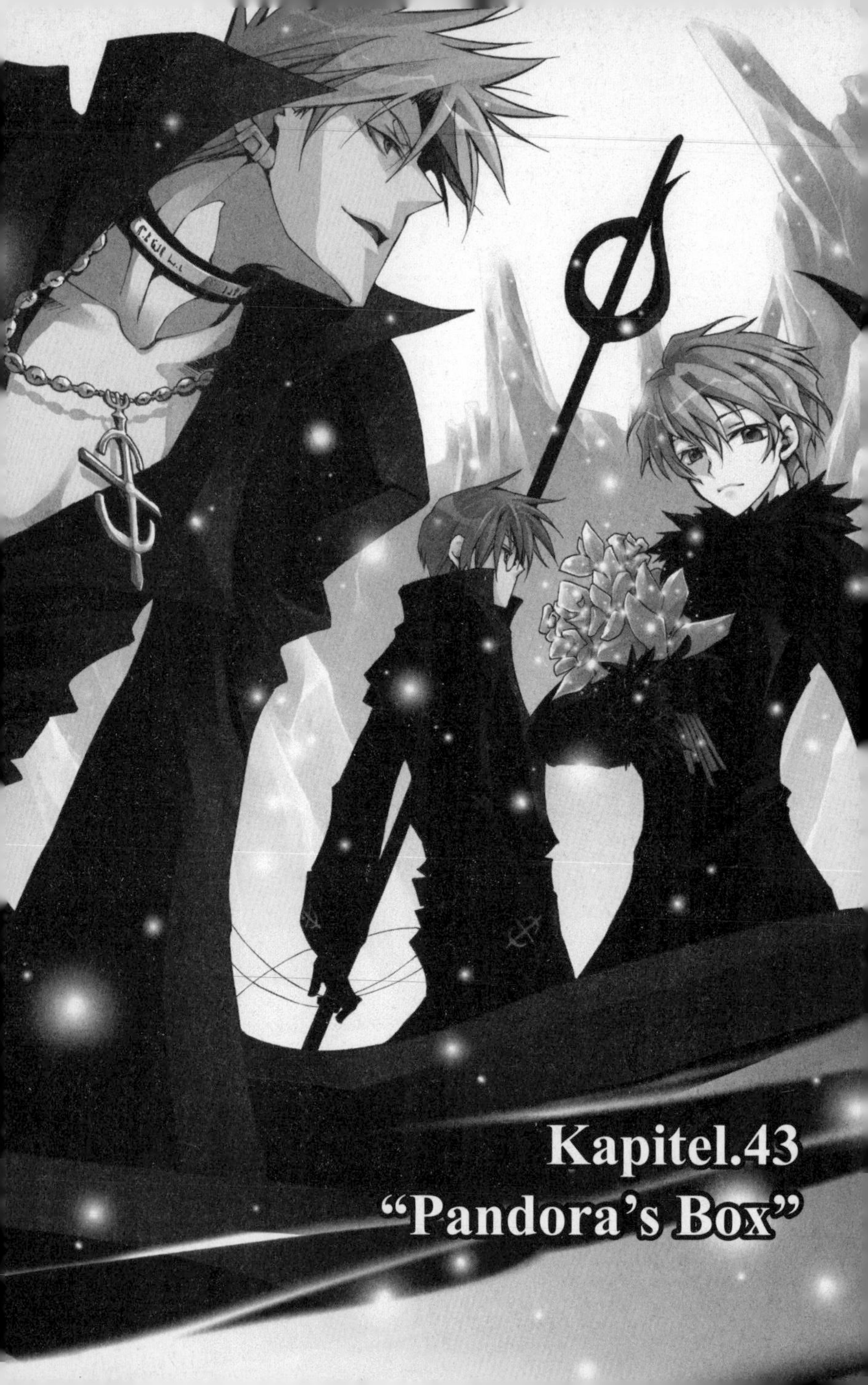
Kapitel.43
“Pandora’s Box”

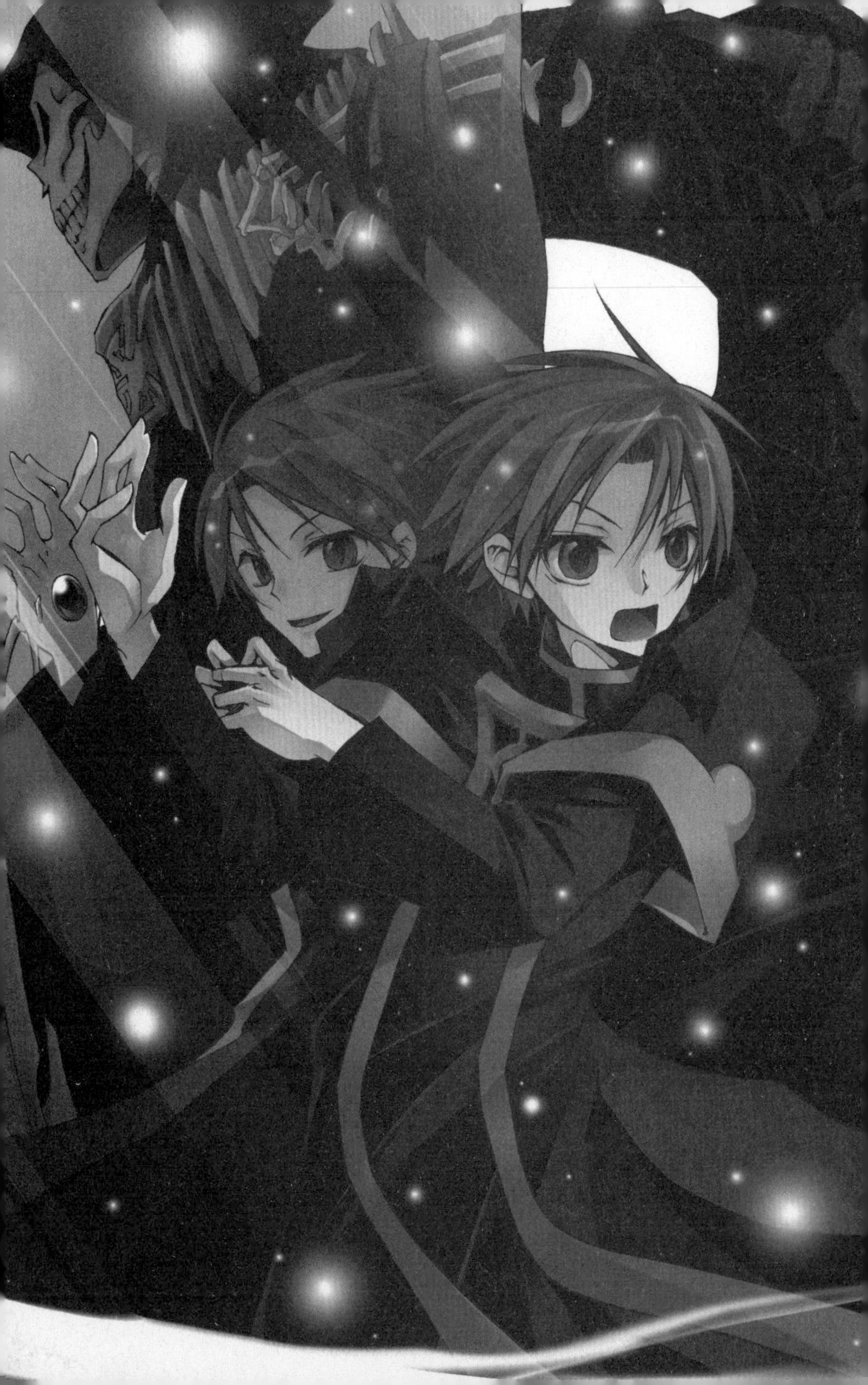

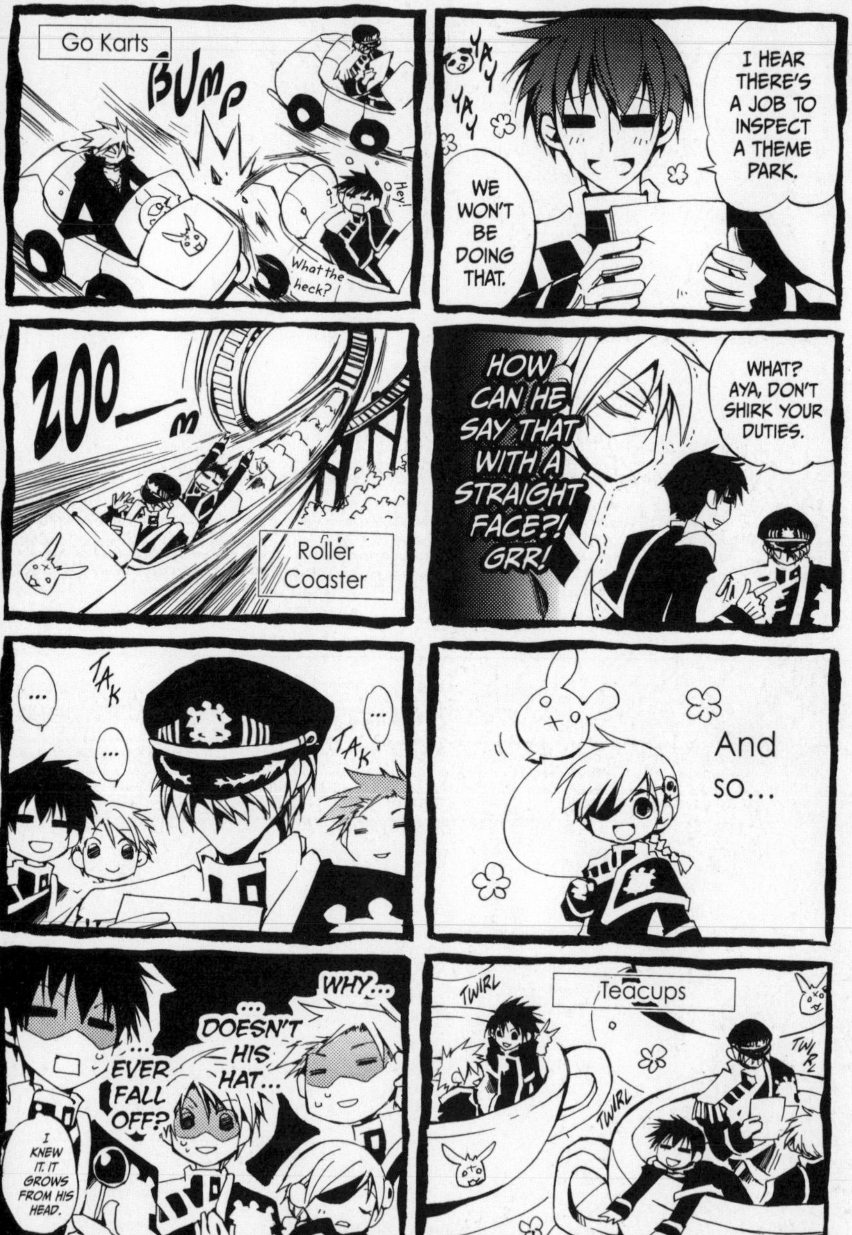
I HEAR THERE'S A JOB TO INSPECT A THEME PARK.
YAY YAY
WE WON'T BE DOING THAT.
Go Karts
BUMP
Hey!
What the heck?
WHAT? AYA, DON'T SHIRK YOUR DUTIES.
HOW CAN HE SAY THAT WITH A STRAIGHT FACE?! GRR!
ZOOO—m
Roller Coaster
And so...
...
TAK
...
...
TAK
Teacups
TWIRL
TWIRL
TWIRL
WHY...
...DOESN'T HIS HAT...
...EVER FALL OFF?
I KNEW IT. IT GROWS FROM HIS HEAD.

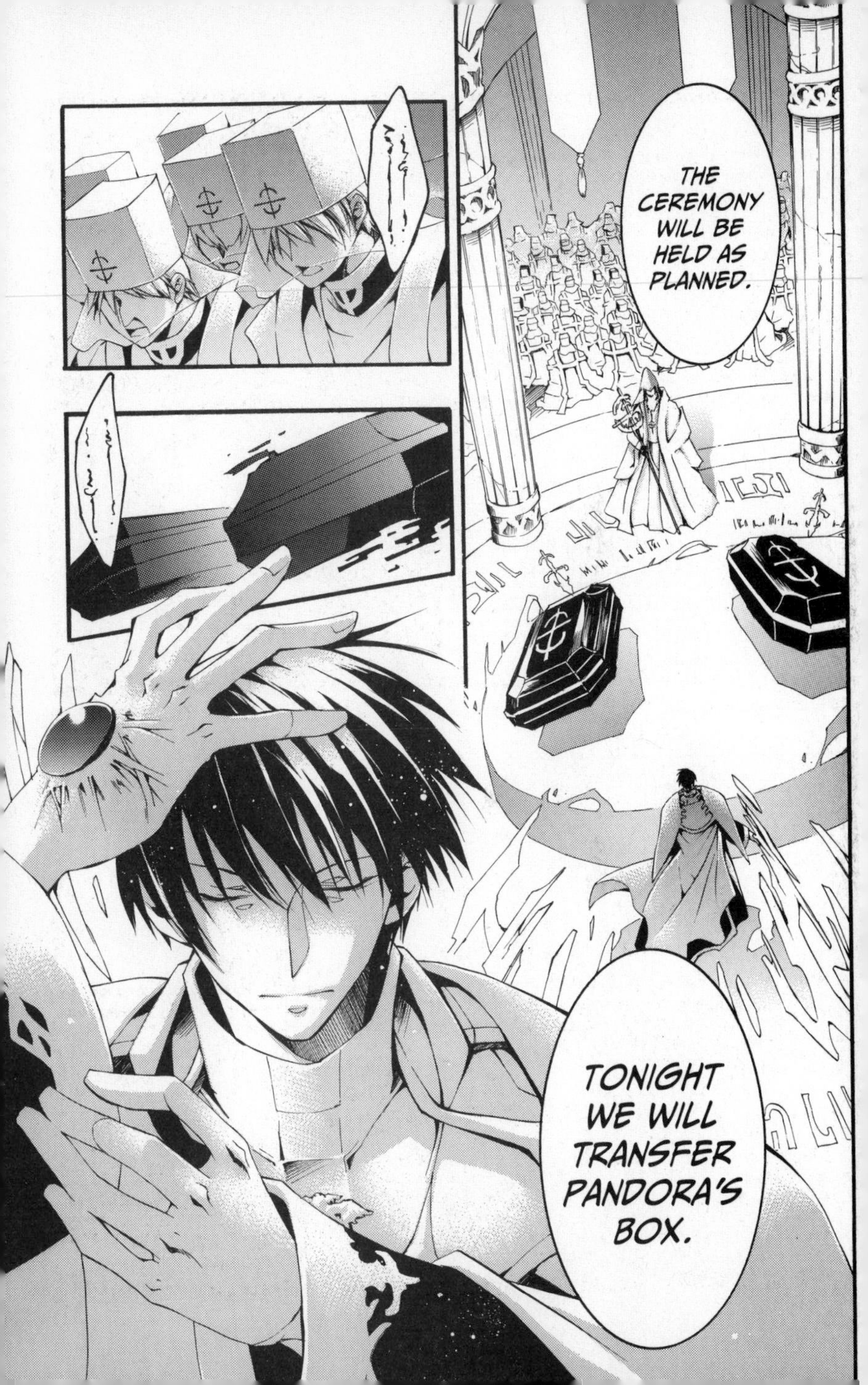
THE CEREMONY WILL BE HELD AS PLANNED.
TONIGHT WE WILL TRANSFER PANDORA'S BOX.

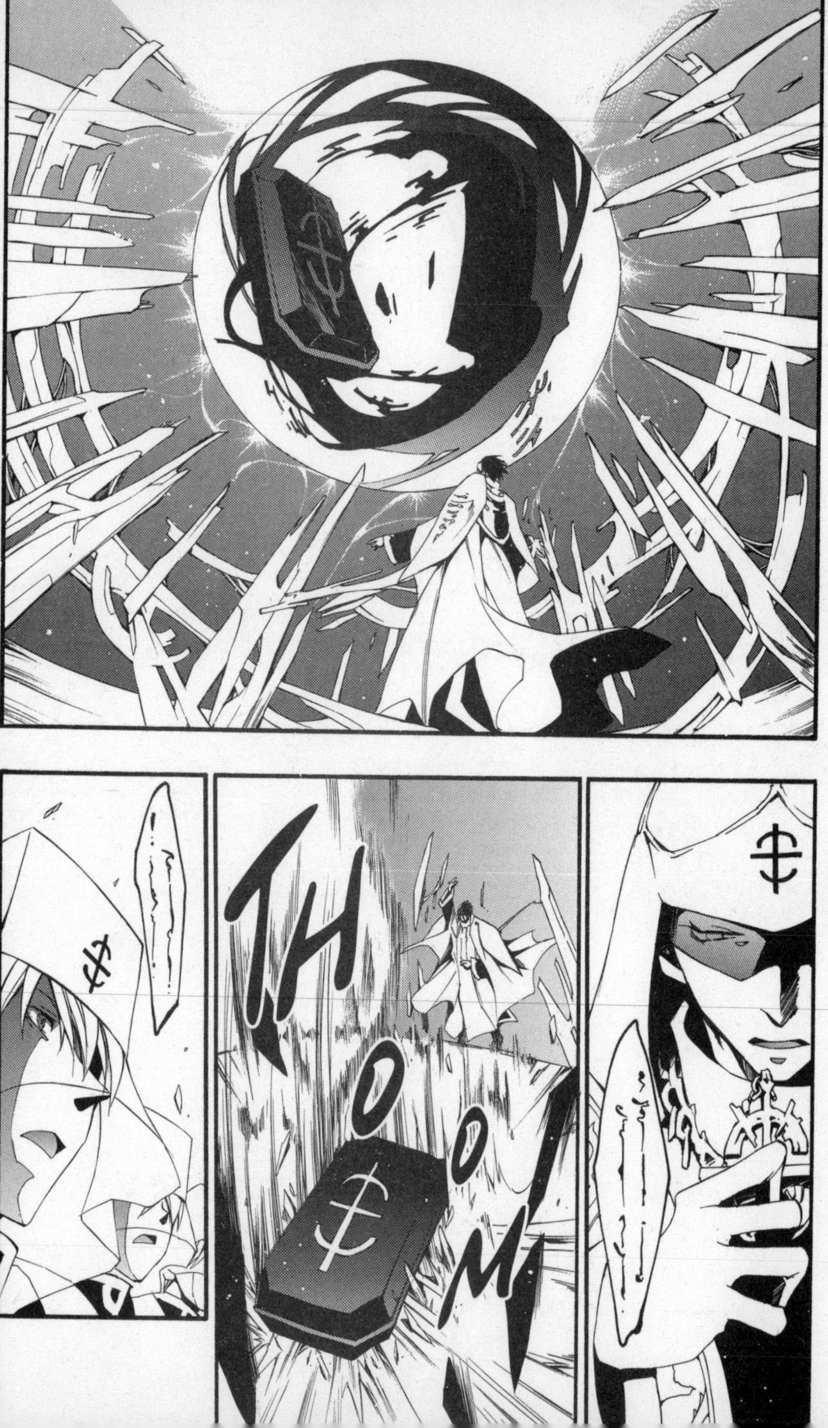
......
THOOOM
...!

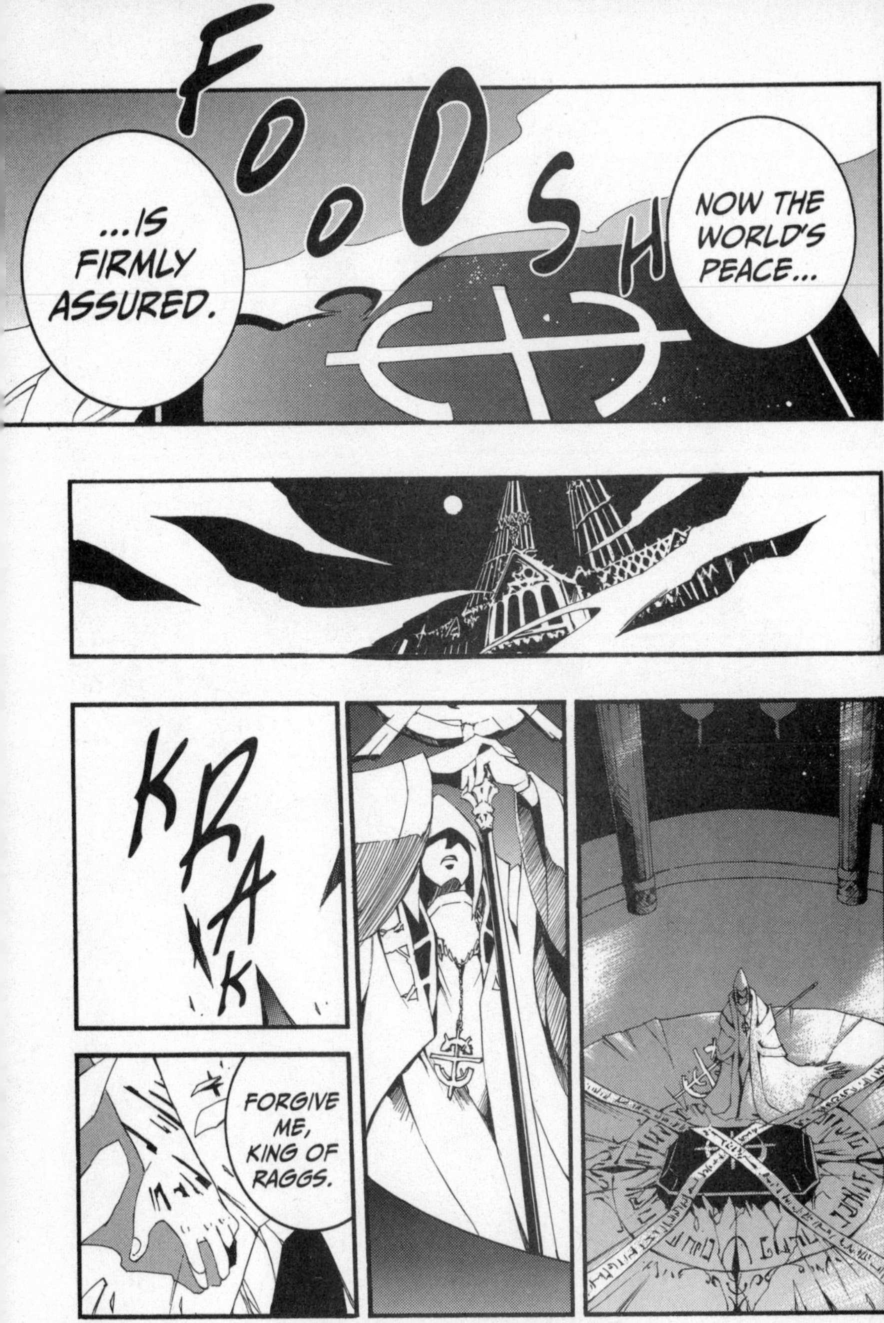
NOW THE WORLD'S PEACE...
FOOOSH
...IS FIRMLY ASSURED.
KRAKK
FORGIVE ME, KING OF RAGGS.

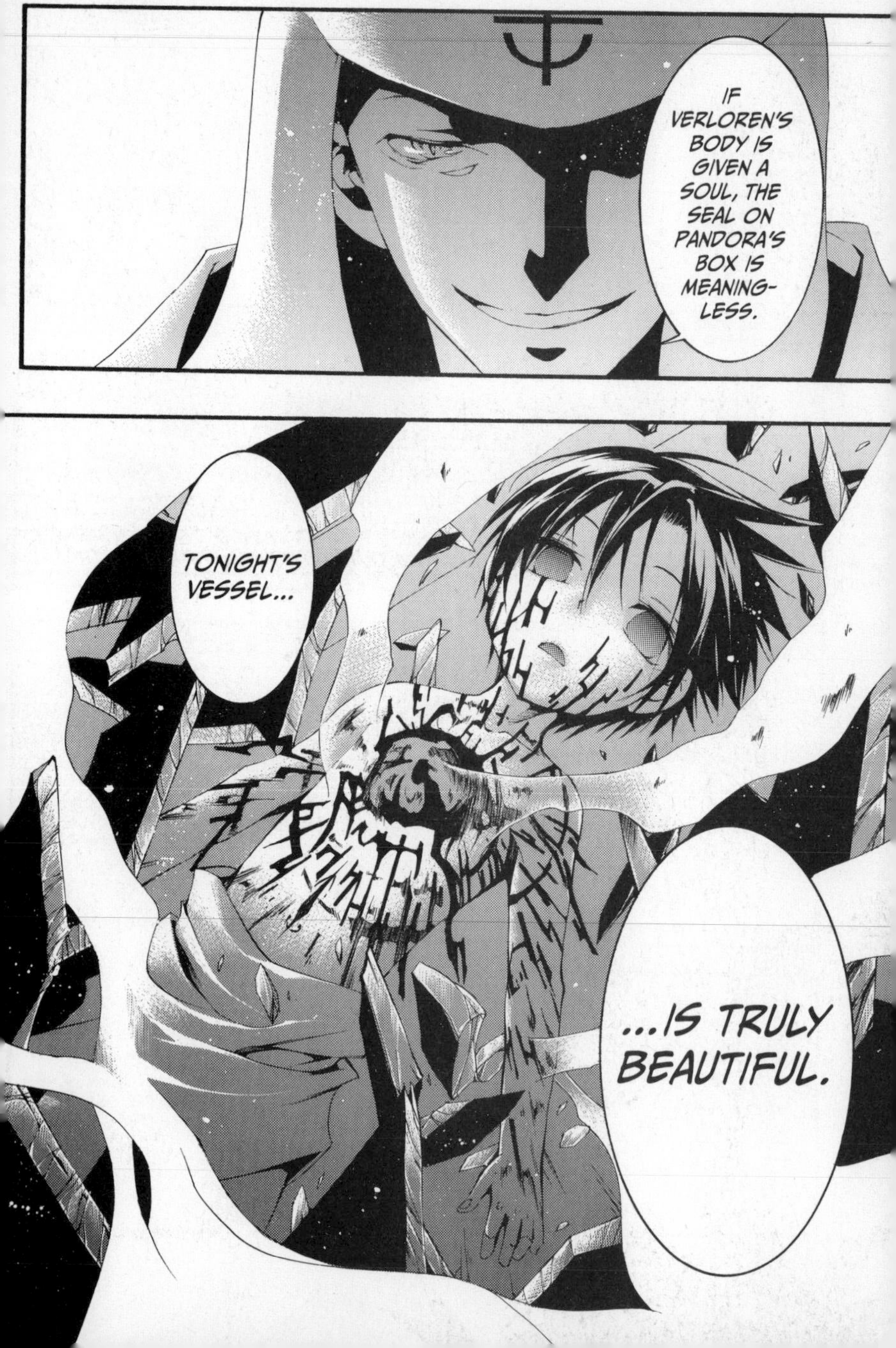
IF VERLOREN'S BODY IS GIVEN A SOUL, THE SEAL ON PANDORA'S BOX IS MEANING-LESS.
TONIGHT'S VESSEL...
...IS TRULY BEAUTIFUL.

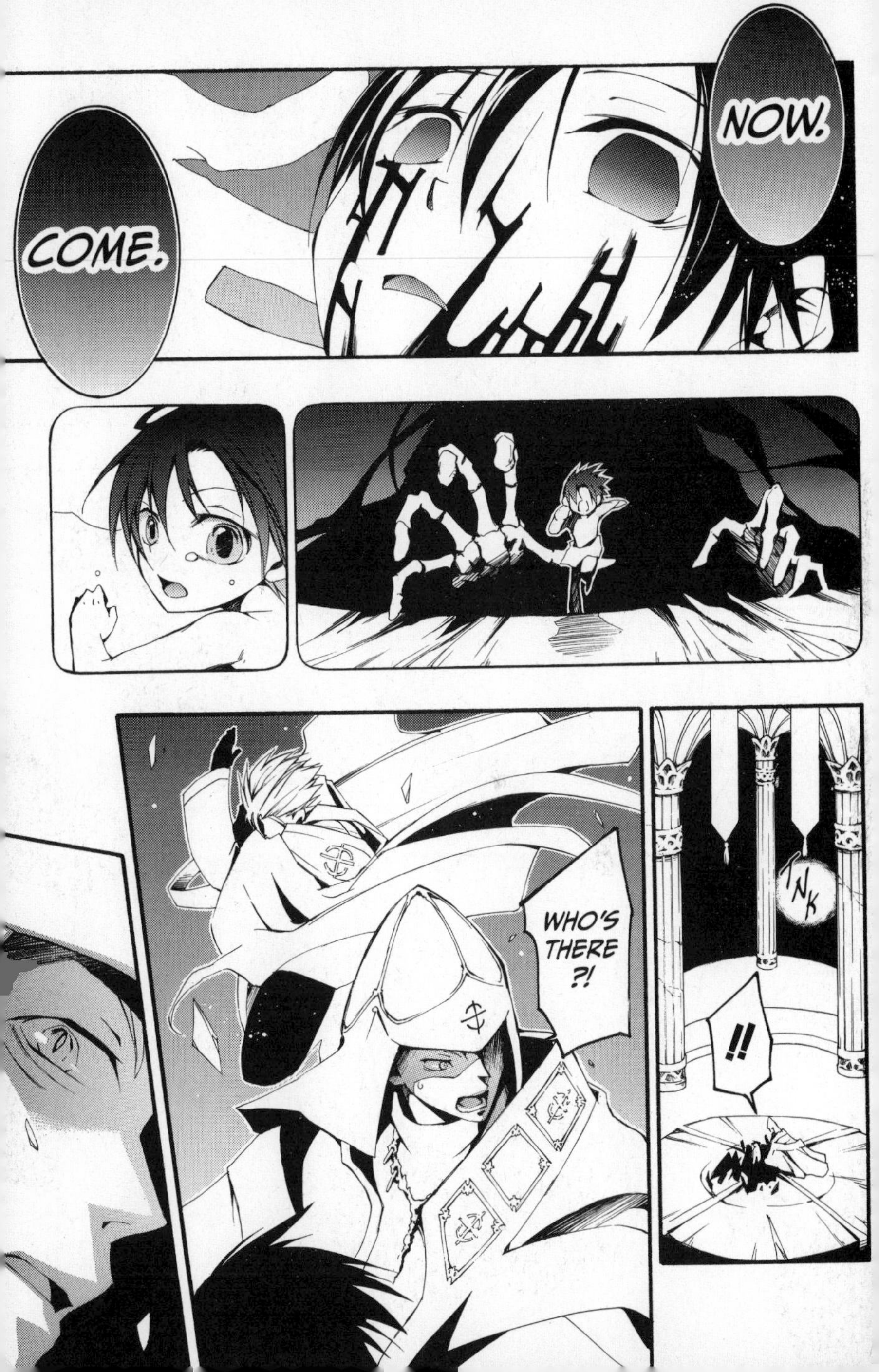
NOW.
COME.
TINK
!!
WHO'S THERE ?!

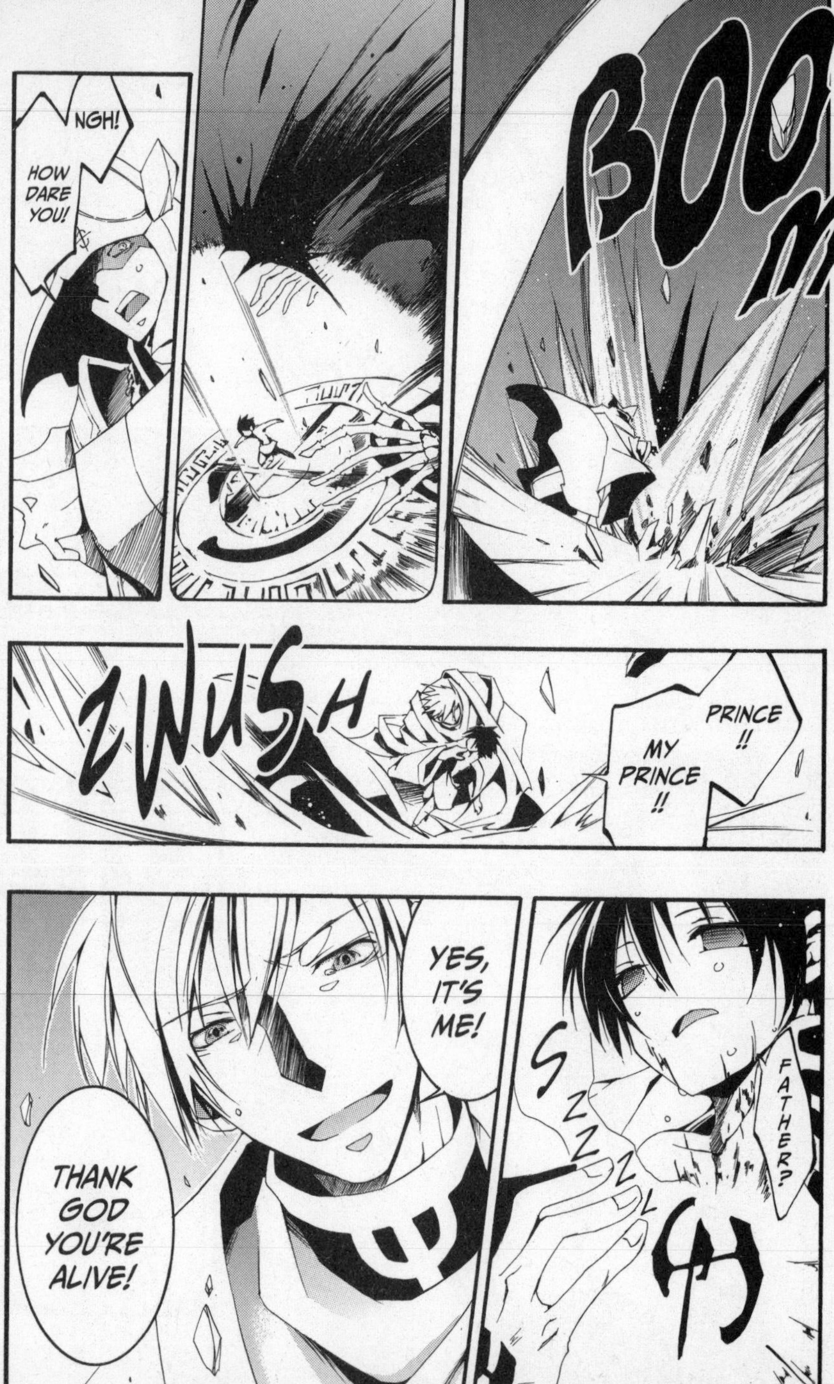
BOOM
NGH!
HOW DARE YOU!
PRINCE!!
MY PRINCE!!
ZWUSH
FATHER?
SZZZL
YES, IT'S ME!
THANK GOD YOU'RE ALIVE!

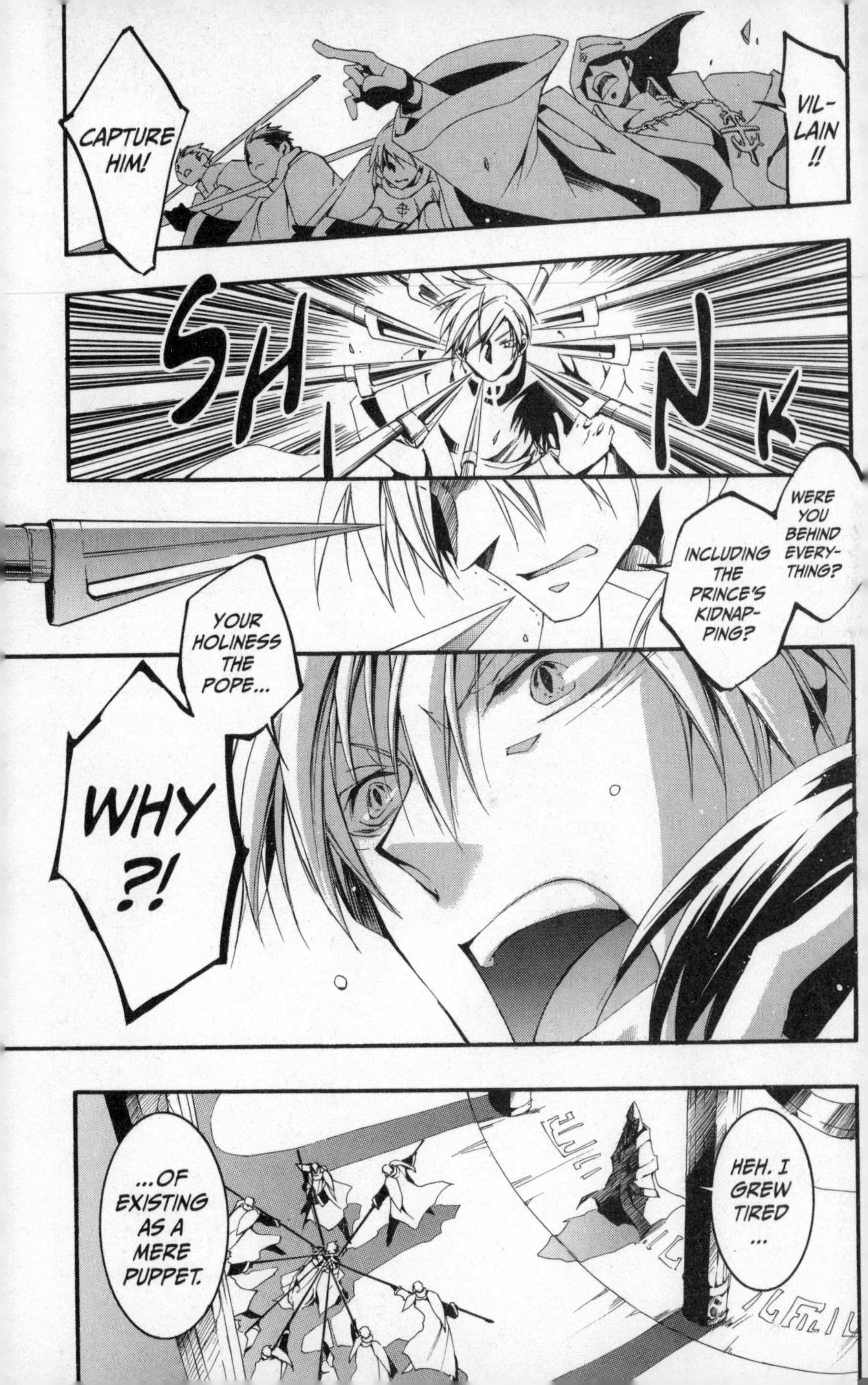
VIL-LAIN!!
CAPTURE HIM!
SHHNK
WERE YOU BEHIND EVERYTHING?
INCLUDING THE PRINCE'S KIDNAPPING?
YOUR HOLINESS THE POPE...
WHY?!
HEH. I GREW TIRED...
...OF EXISTING AS A MERE PUPPET.

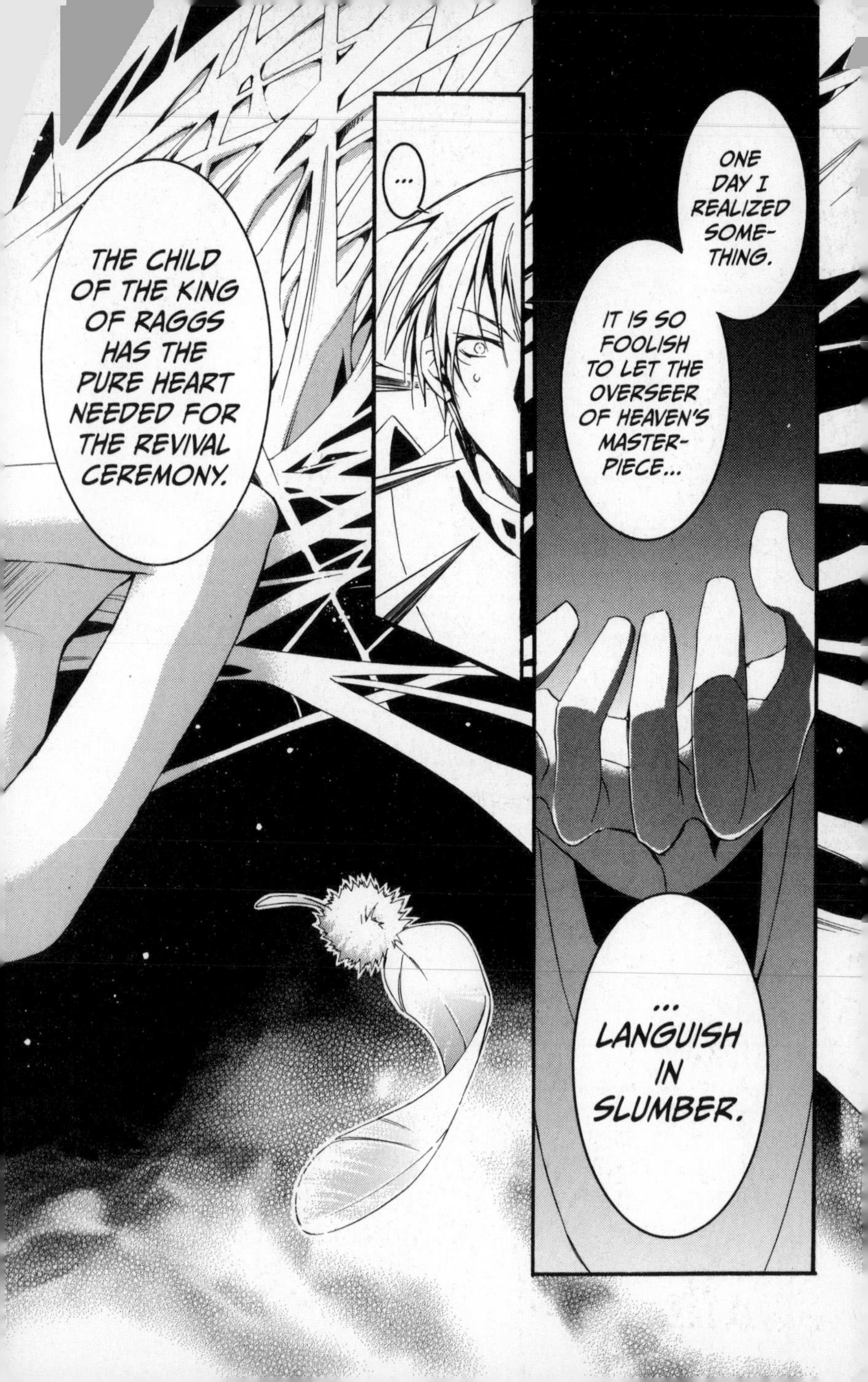
ONE DAY I REALIZED SOME-THING.
IT IS SO FOOLISH TO LET THE OVERSEER OF HEAVEN'S MASTER-PIECE...
...LANGUISH IN SLUMBER.
...
THE CHILD OF THE KING OF RAGGS HAS THE PURE HEART NEEDED FOR THE REVIVAL CEREMONY.

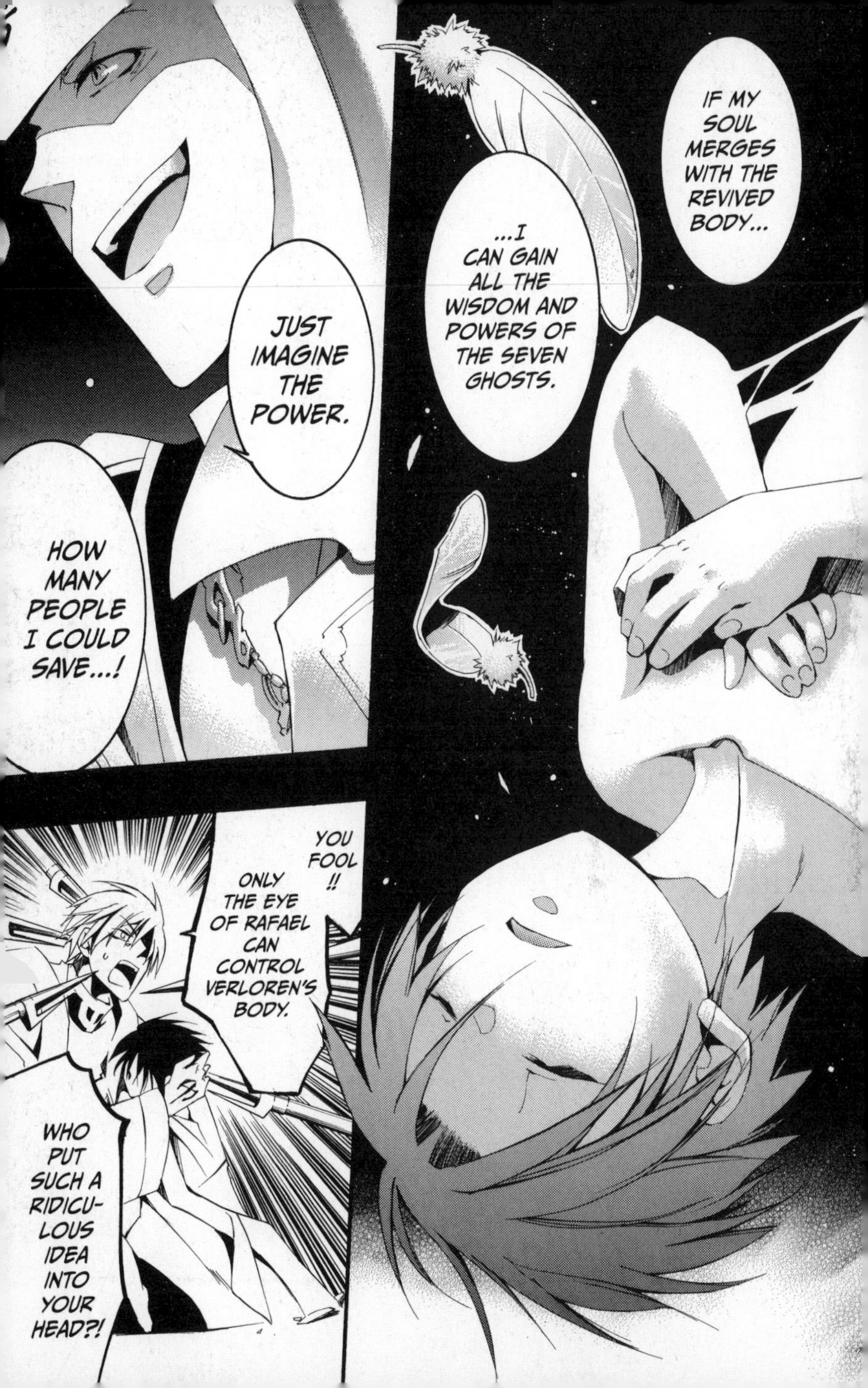
IF MY SOUL MERGES WITH THE REVIVED BODY...
...I CAN GAIN ALL THE WISDOM AND POWERS OF THE SEVEN GHOSTS.
JUST IMAGINE THE POWER.
HOW MANY PEOPLE I COULD SAVE...!
YOU FOOL !!
ONLY THE EYE OF RAFAEL CAN CONTROL VERLOREN'S BODY.
WHO PUT SUCH A RIDICU-LOUS IDEA INTO YOUR HEAD?!

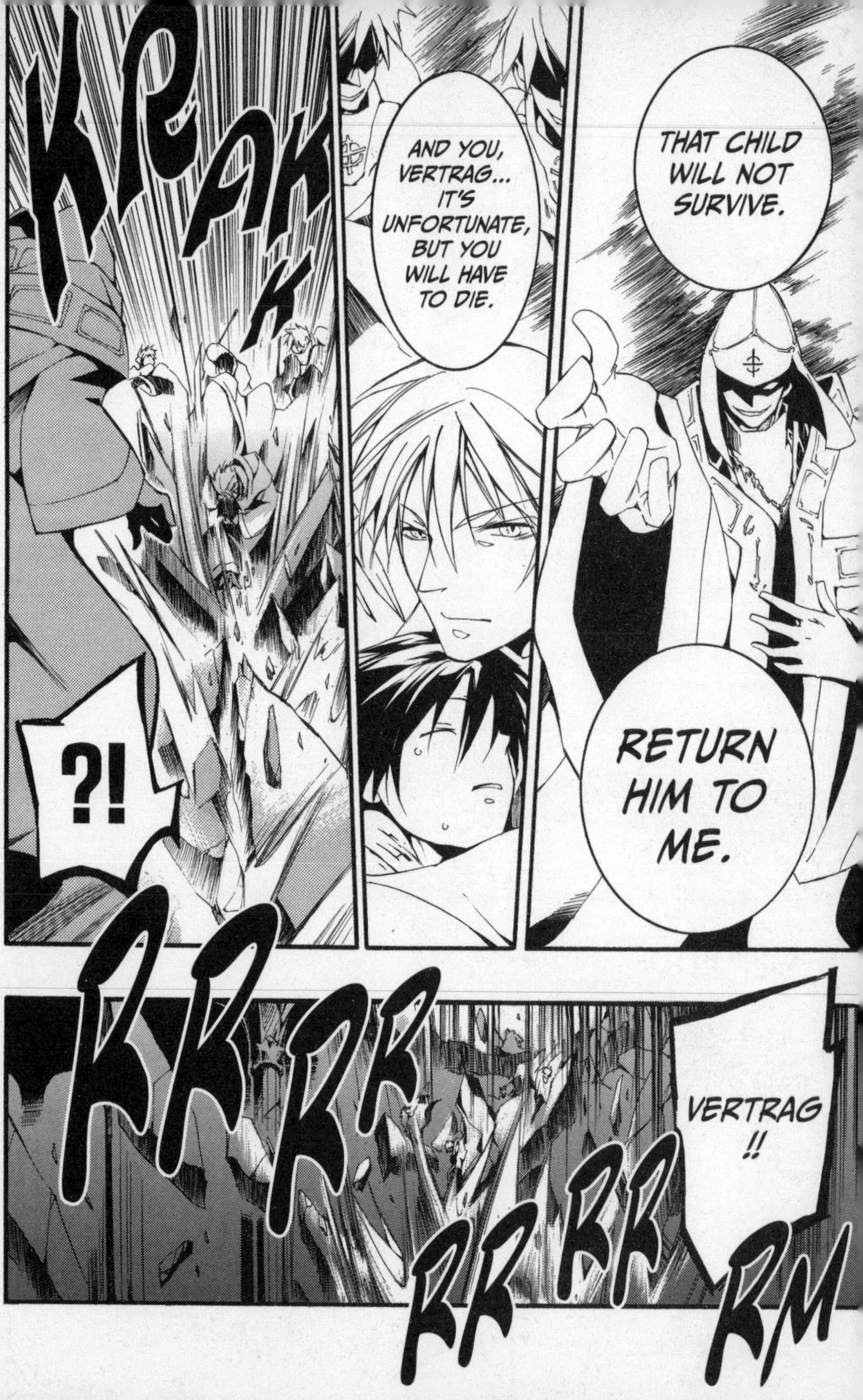
THAT CHILD WILL NOT SURVIVE.
RETURN HIM TO ME.
AND YOU, VERTRAG... IT'S UNFORTUNATE, BUT YOU WILL HAVE TO DIE.
KREAKK
?!
VERTRAG !!
RRRRRRRRRRM

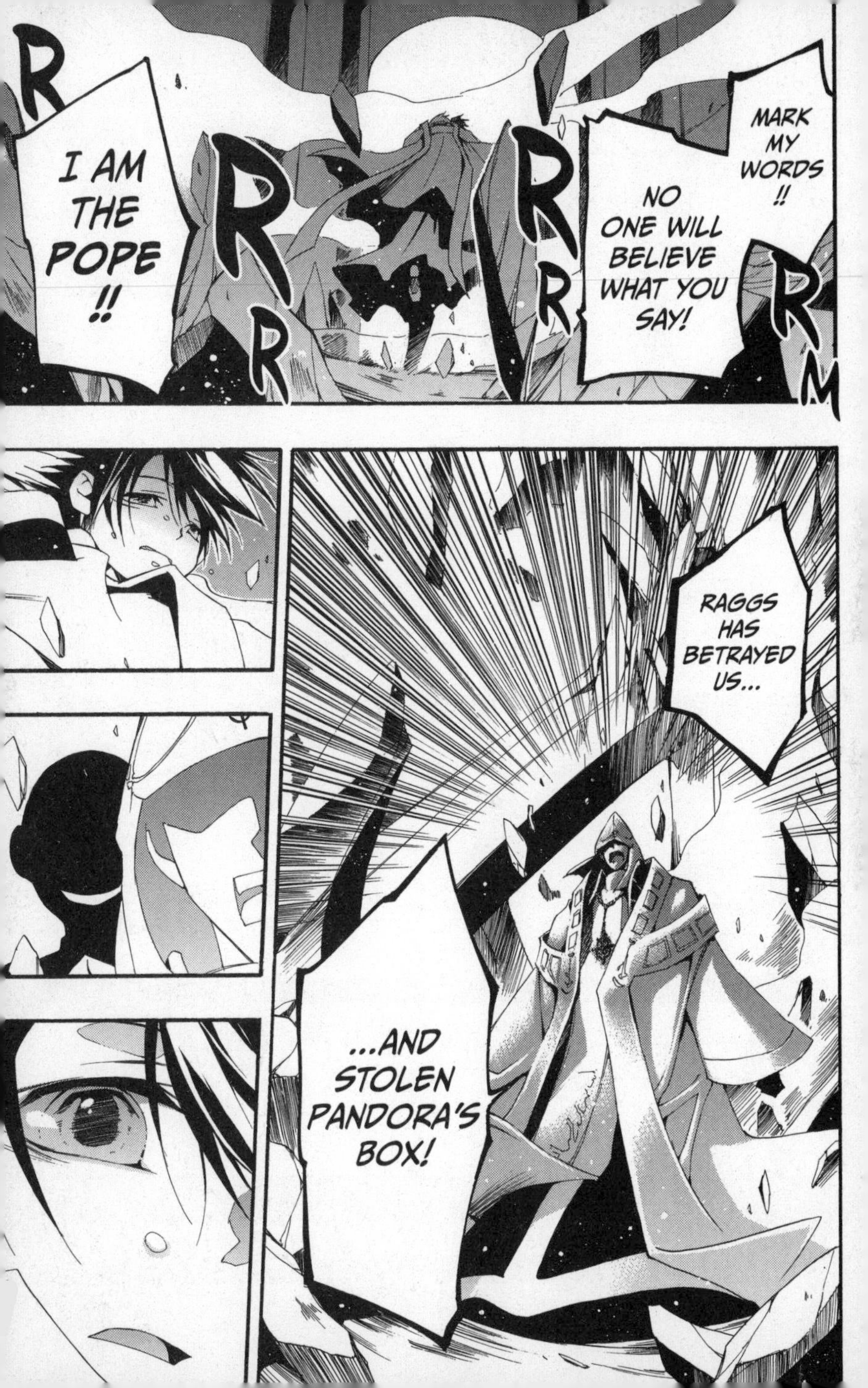
MARK MY WORDS!!
NO ONE WILL BELIEVE WHAT YOU SAY!
I AM THE POPE!!
RRRRRRM
RAGGS HAS BETRAYED US...
...AND STOLEN PANDORA'S BOX!

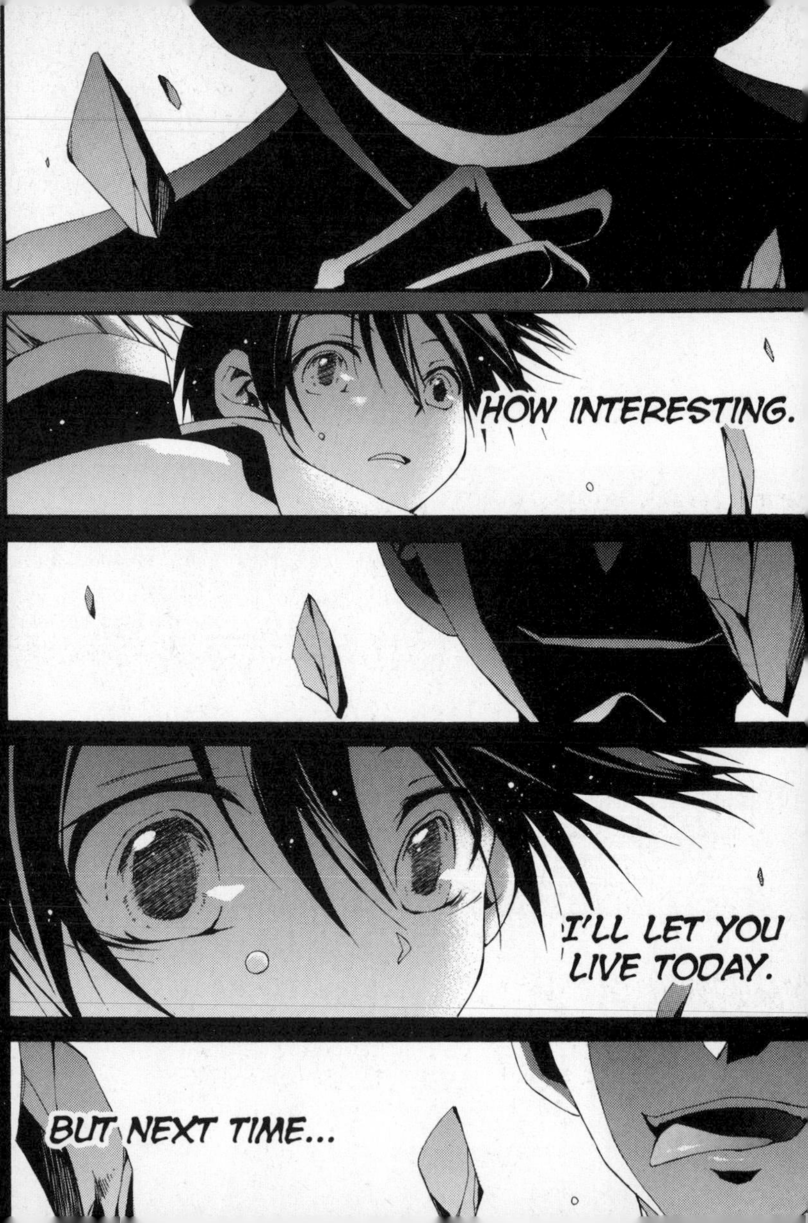
HOW INTERESTING.
I'LL LET YOU LIVE TODAY.
BUT NEXT TIME...

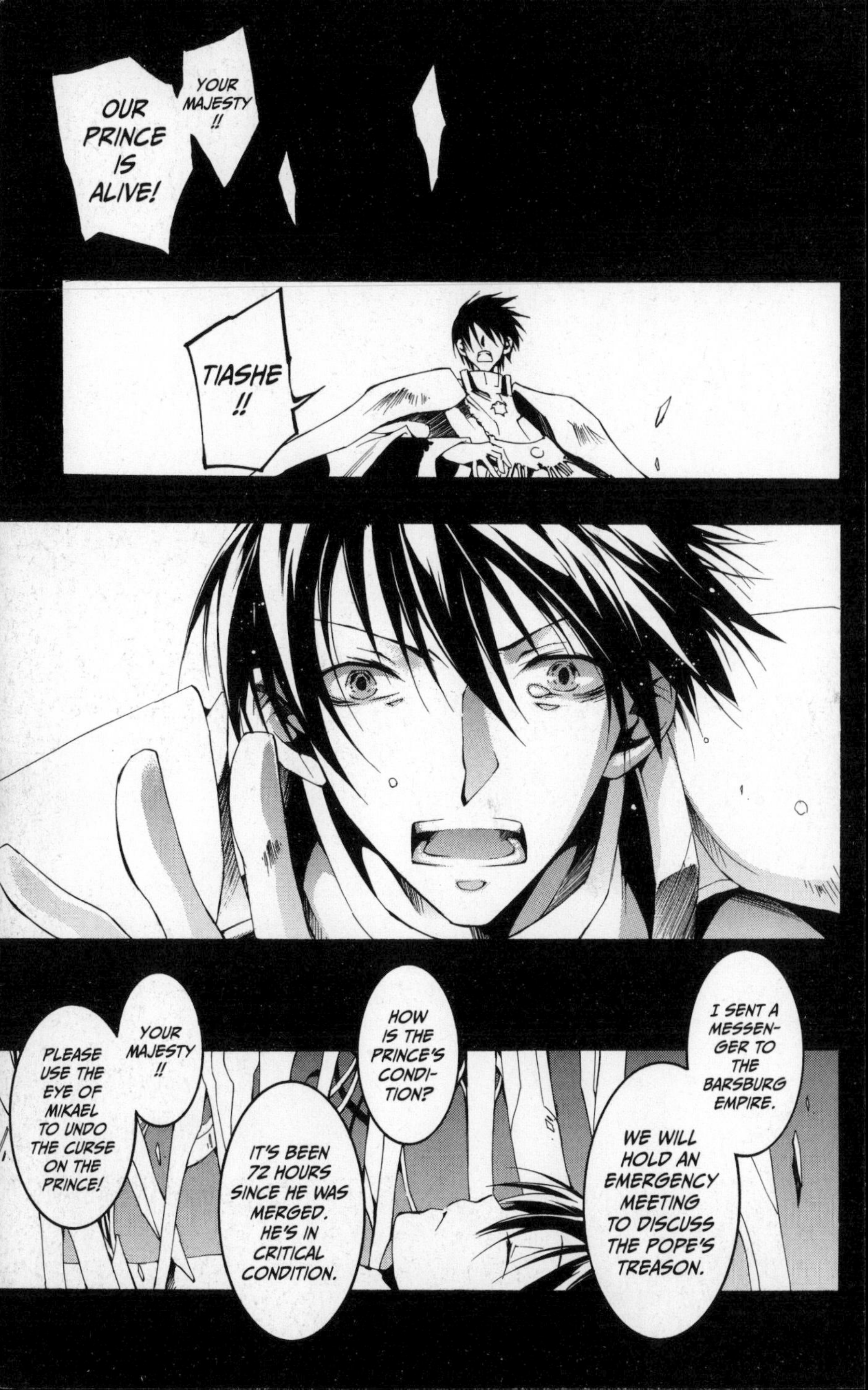
YOUR MAJESTY !!
OUR PRINCE IS ALIVE!
TIASHE !!
I SENT A MESSENGER TO THE BARSBURG EMPIRE.
WE WILL HOLD AN EMERGENCY MEETING TO DISCUSS THE POPE'S TREASON.
HOW IS THE PRINCE'S CONDITION?
IT'S BEEN 72 HOURS SINCE HE WAS MERGED. HE'S IN CRITICAL CONDITION.
YOUR MAJESTY !!
PLEASE USE THE EYE OF MIKAEL TO UNDO THE CURSE ON THE PRINCE!

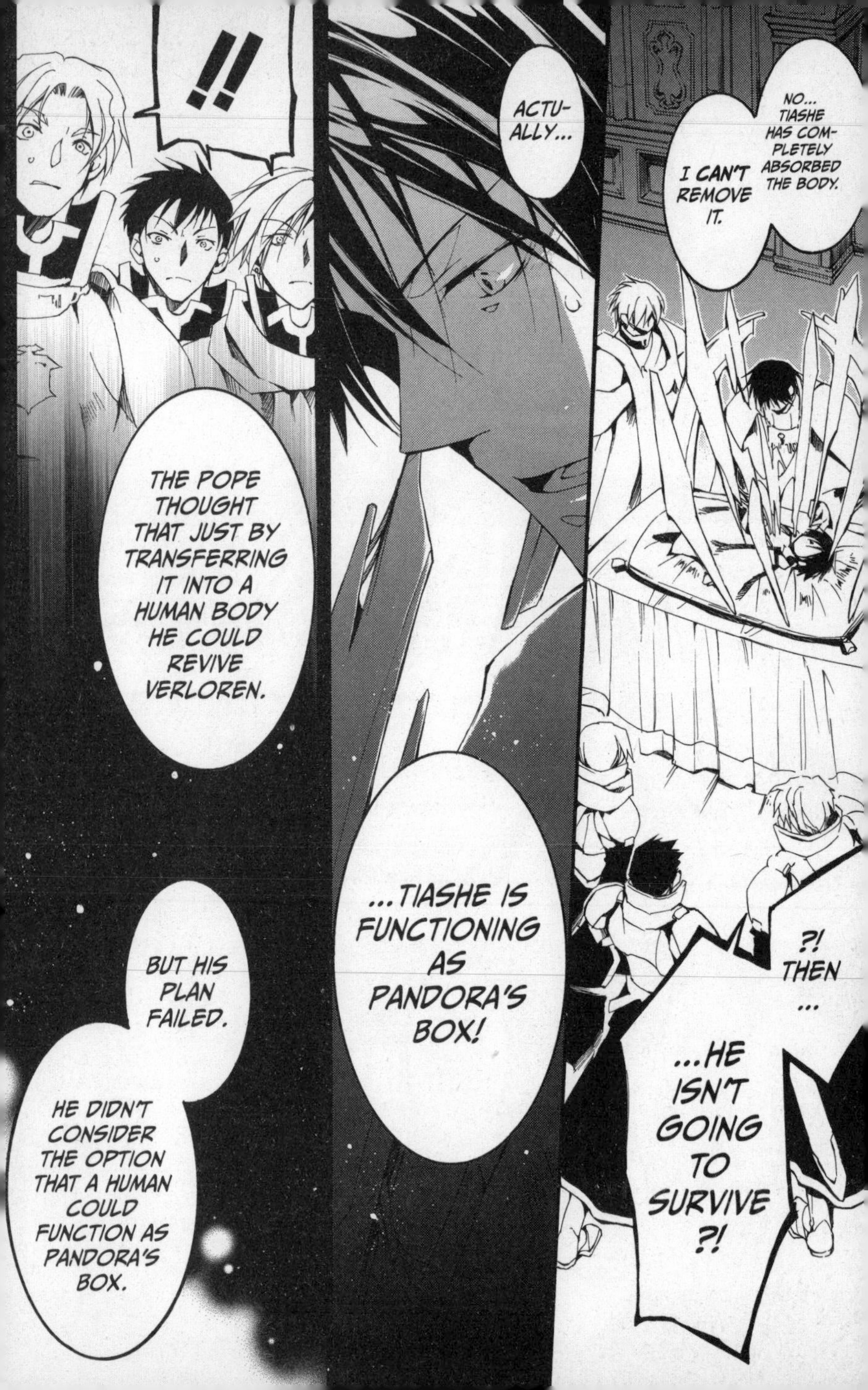
NO... TIASHE HAS COMPLETELY ABSORBED THE BODY.
I CAN'T REMOVE IT.
?! THEN ...
...HE ISN'T GOING TO SURVIVE ?!
ACTUALLY...
...TIASHE IS FUNCTIONING AS PANDORA'S BOX!
!!
THE POPE THOUGHT THAT JUST BY TRANSFERRING IT INTO A HUMAN BODY HE COULD REVIVE VERLOREN.
BUT HIS PLAN FAILED.
HE DIDN'T CONSIDER THE OPTION THAT A HUMAN COULD FUNCTION AS PANDORA'S BOX.

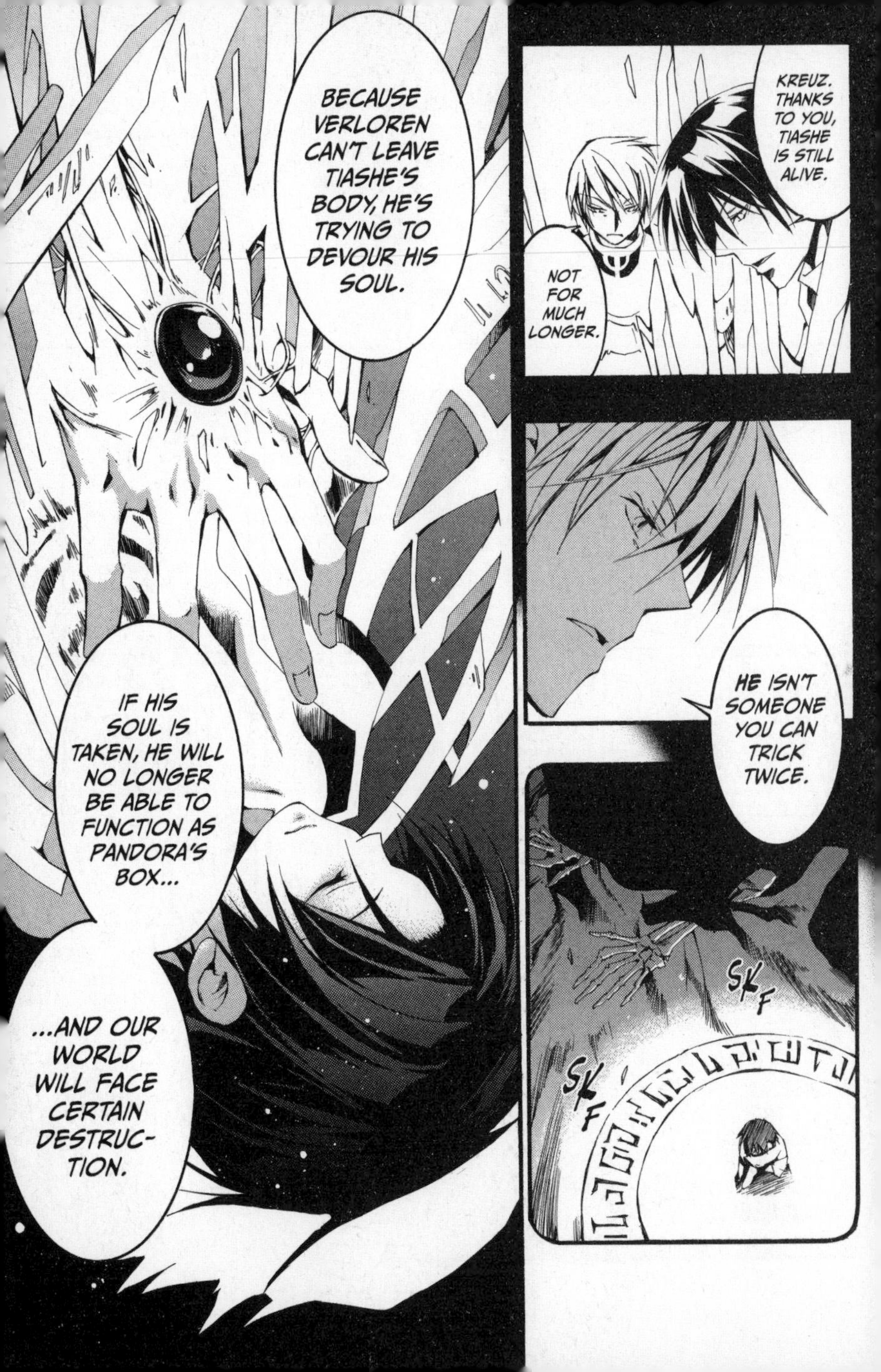
KREUZ. THANKS TO YOU, TIASHE IS STILL ALIVE.
NOT FOR MUCH LONGER.
HE ISN'T SOMEONE YOU CAN TRICK TWICE.
SKF
SKF
BECAUSE VERLOREN CAN'T LEAVE TIASHE'S BODY, HE'S TRYING TO DEVOUR HIS SOUL.
IF HIS SOUL IS TAKEN, HE WILL NO LONGER BE ABLE TO FUNCTION AS PANDORA'S BOX...
...AND OUR WORLD WILL FACE CERTAIN DESTRUC-TION.

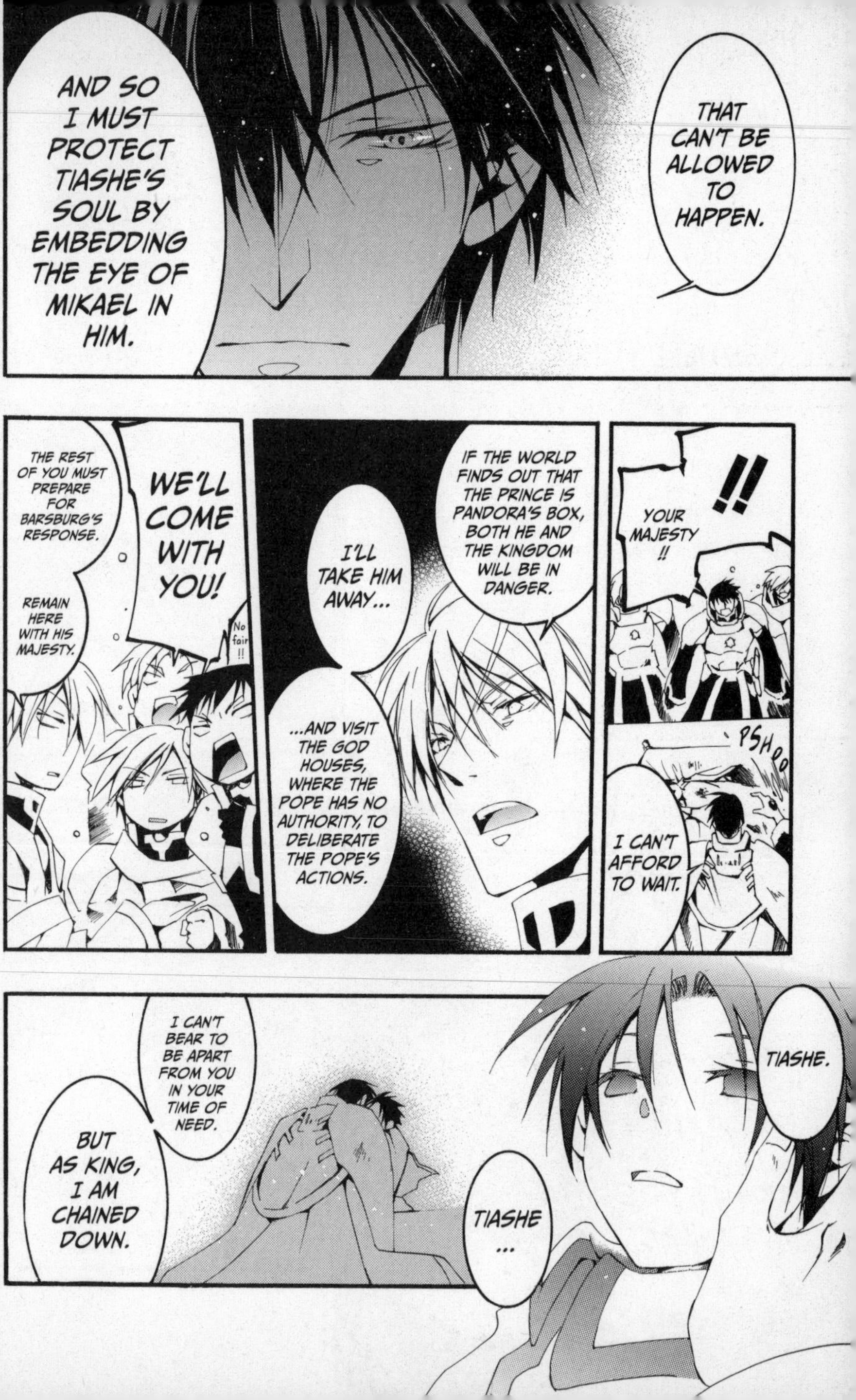
THAT CAN'T BE ALLOWED TO HAPPEN.
AND SO I MUST PROTECT TIASHE'S SOUL BY EMBEDDING THE EYE OF MIKAEL IN HIM.
!!
YOUR MAJESTY !!
PSHOO
I CAN'T AFFORD TO WAIT.
IF THE WORLD FINDS OUT THAT THE PRINCE IS PANDORA'S BOX, BOTH HE AND THE KINGDOM WILL BE IN DANGER.
I'LL TAKE HIM AWAY...
...AND VISIT THE GOD HOUSES, WHERE THE POPE HAS NO AUTHORITY, TO DELIBERATE THE POPE'S ACTIONS.
WE'LL COME WITH YOU!
No fair !!
THE REST OF YOU MUST PREPARE FOR BARSBURG'S RESPONSE.
REMAIN HERE WITH HIS MAJESTY.
TIASHE.
TIASHE ...
I CAN'T BEAR TO BE APART FROM YOU IN YOUR TIME OF NEED.
BUT AS KING, I AM CHAINED DOWN.

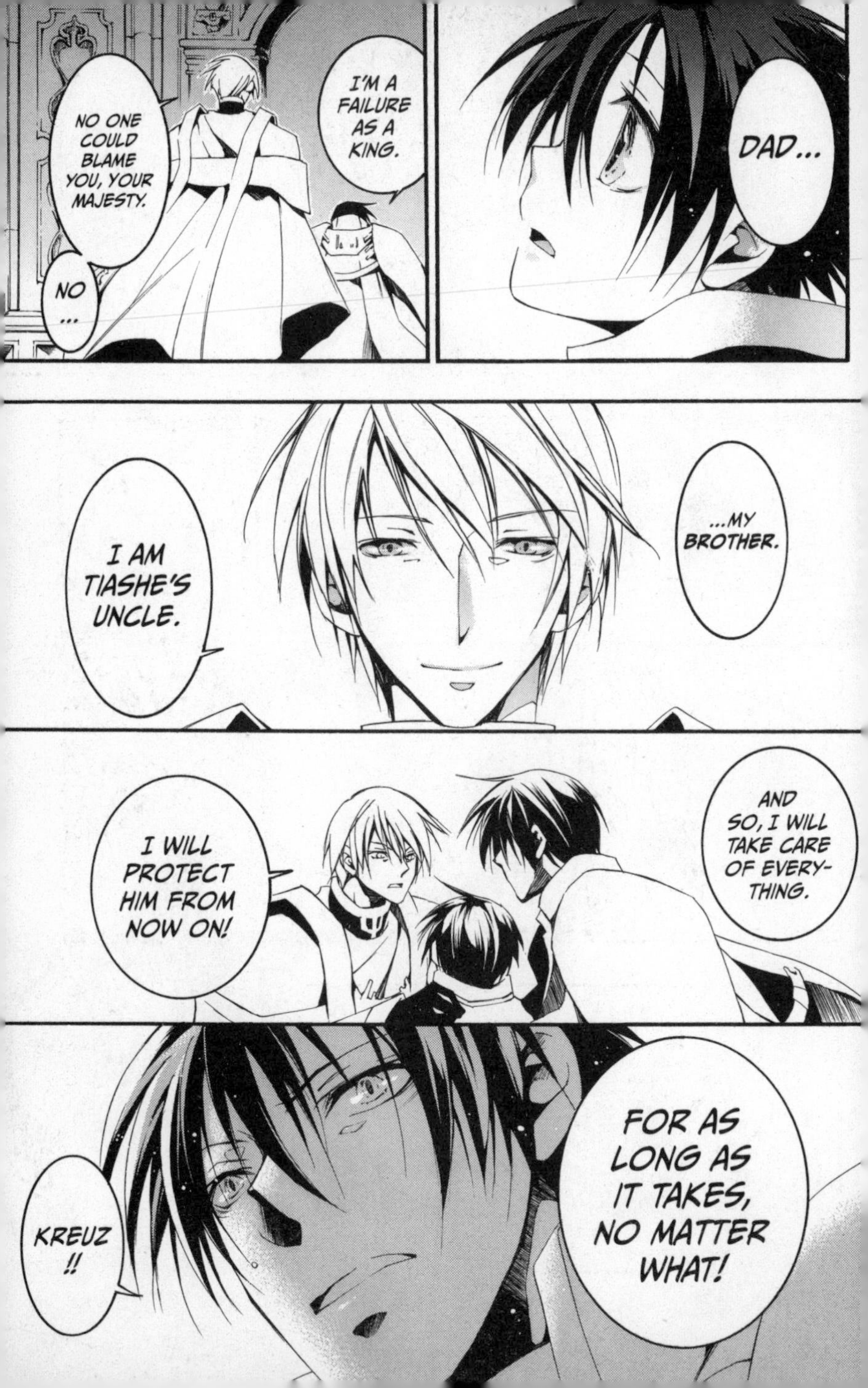
DAD...
I'M A FAILURE AS A KING.
NO ONE COULD BLAME YOU, YOUR MAJESTY.
NO ...
...MY BROTHER.
I AM TIASHE'S UNCLE.
AND SO, I WILL TAKE CARE OF EVERY-THING.
I WILL PROTECT HIM FROM NOW ON!
FOR AS LONG AS IT TAKES, NO MATTER WHAT!
KREUZ !!

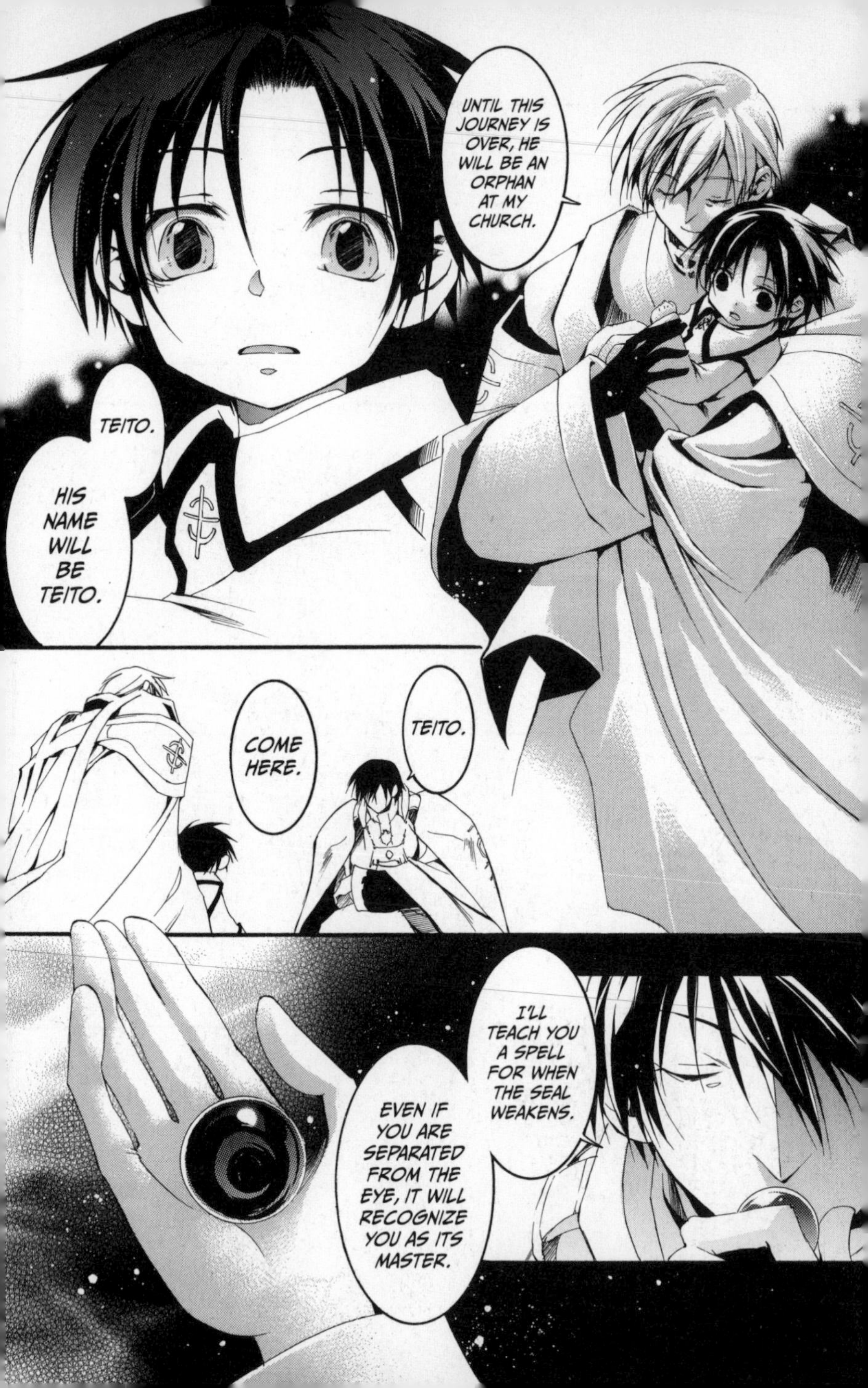
UNTIL THIS JOURNEY IS OVER, HE WILL BE AN ORPHAN AT MY CHURCH.
TEITO.
HIS NAME WILL BE TEITO.
TEITO.
COME HERE.
I'LL TEACH YOU A SPELL FOR WHEN THE SEAL WEAKENS.
EVEN IF YOU ARE SEPARATED FROM THE EYE, IT WILL RECOGNIZE YOU AS ITS MASTER.

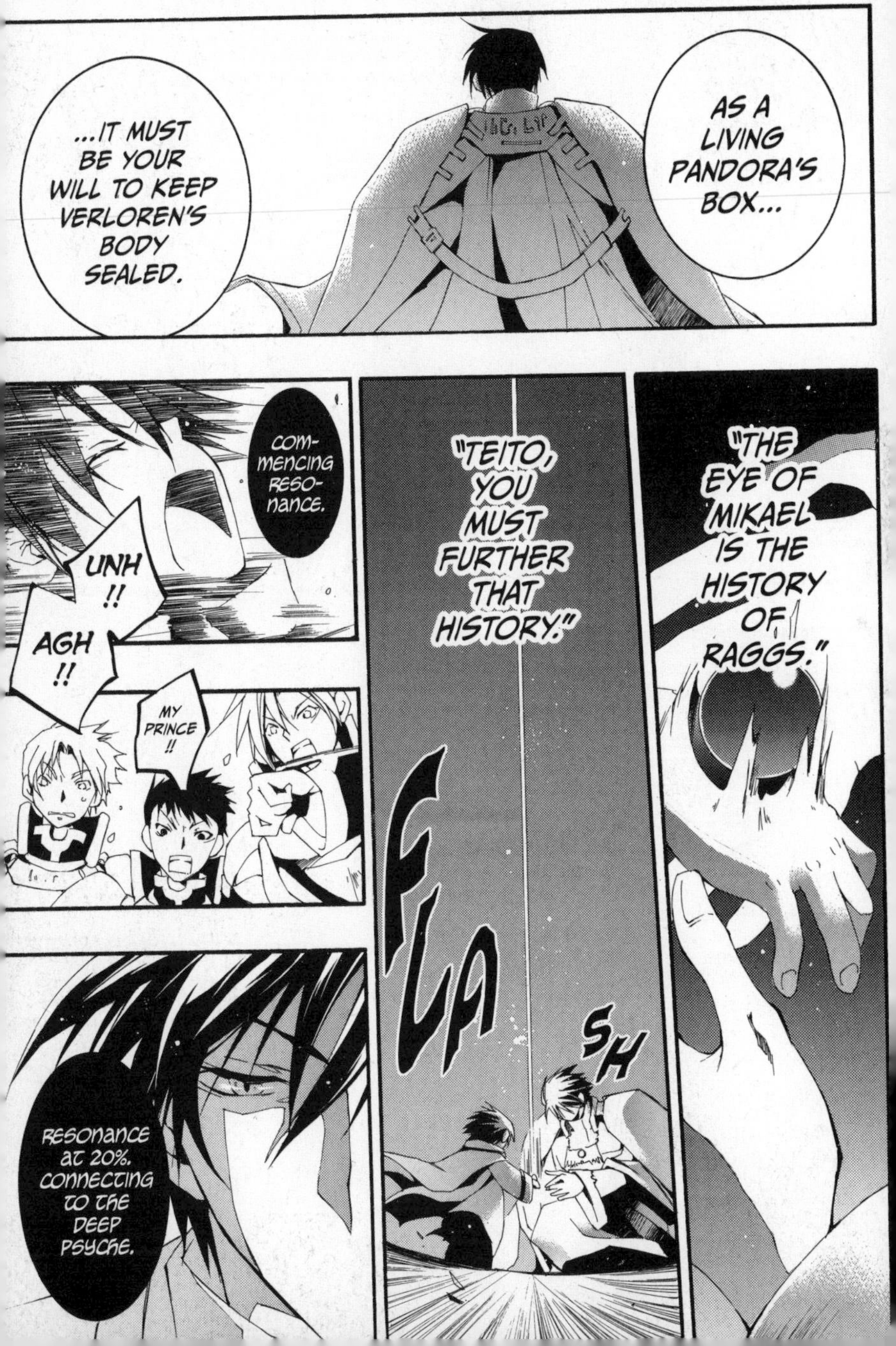
AS A LIVING PANDORA'S BOX...
...IT MUST BE YOUR WILL TO KEEP VERLOREN'S BODY SEALED.
"THE EYE OF MIKAEL IS THE HISTORY OF RAGGS."
"TEITO, YOU MUST FURTHER THAT HISTORY."
FLASH
COM-MENCING RESO-NANCE.
UNH!!
AGH!!
MY PRINCE!!
RESONANCE AT 20%. CONNECTING TO THE DEEP PSYCHE.

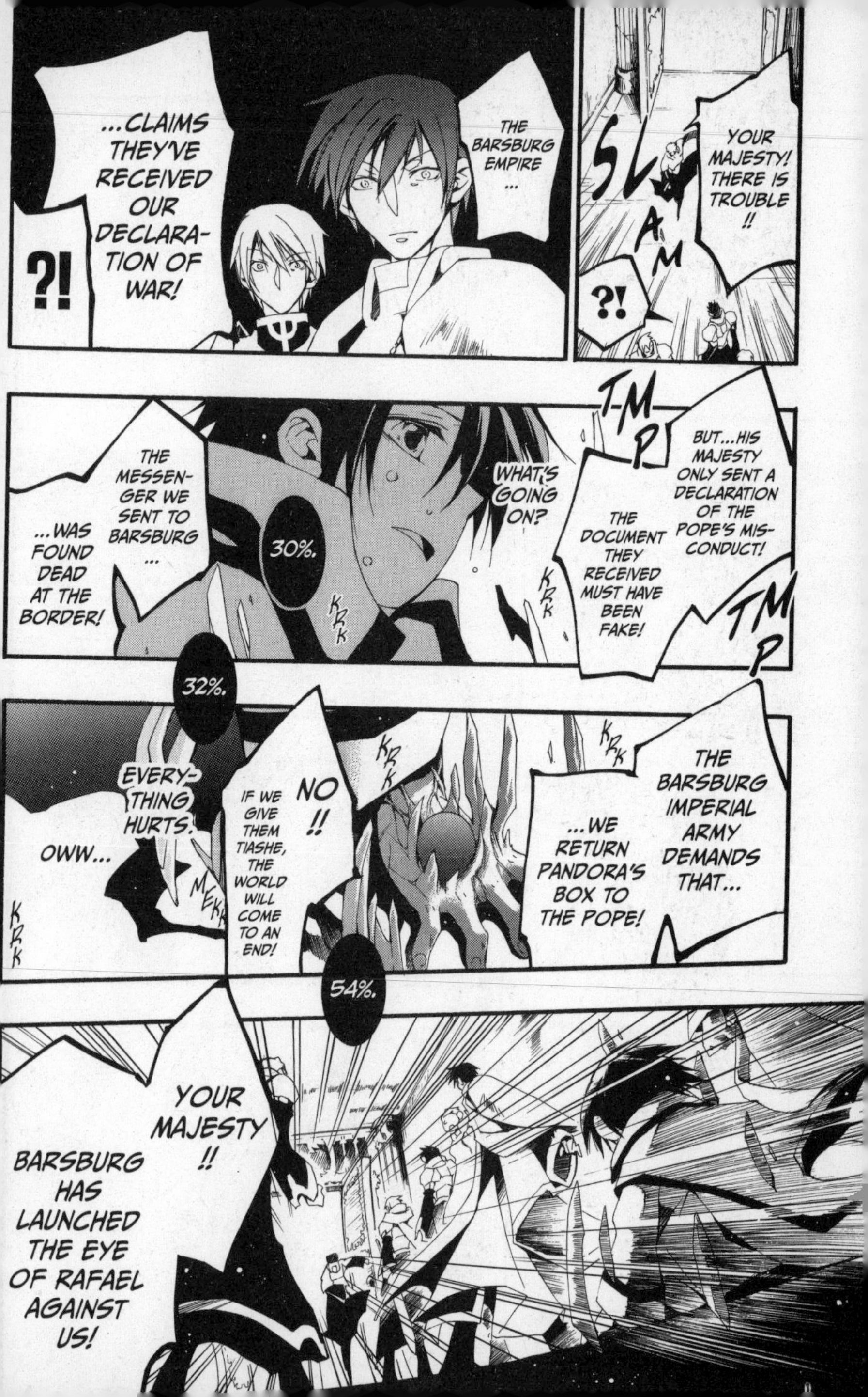
SLAM
YOUR MAJESTY! THERE IS TROUBLE !!
?!
THE BARSBURG EMPIRE ...
...CLAIMS THEY'VE RECEIVED OUR DECLARATION OF WAR!
?!
T-M-P
BUT...HIS MAJESTY ONLY SENT A DECLARATION OF THE POPE'S MISCONDUCT!
THE DOCUMENT THEY RECEIVED MUST HAVE BEEN FAKE!
TMP
KRK
WHAT'S GOING ON?
30%.
KRK
THE MESSENGER WE SENT TO BARSBURG ...
...WAS FOUND DEAD AT THE BORDER!
32%.
THE BARSBURG IMPERIAL ARMY DEMANDS THAT...
...WE RETURN PANDORA'S BOX TO THE POPE!
KRK
KRK
NO !!
IF WE GIVE THEM TIASHE, THE WORLD WILL COME TO AN END!
EVERYTHING HURTS.
OWW...
MEKK
KRK
54%.
YOUR MAJESTY !!
BARSBURG HAS LAUNCHED THE EYE OF RAFAEL AGAINST US!

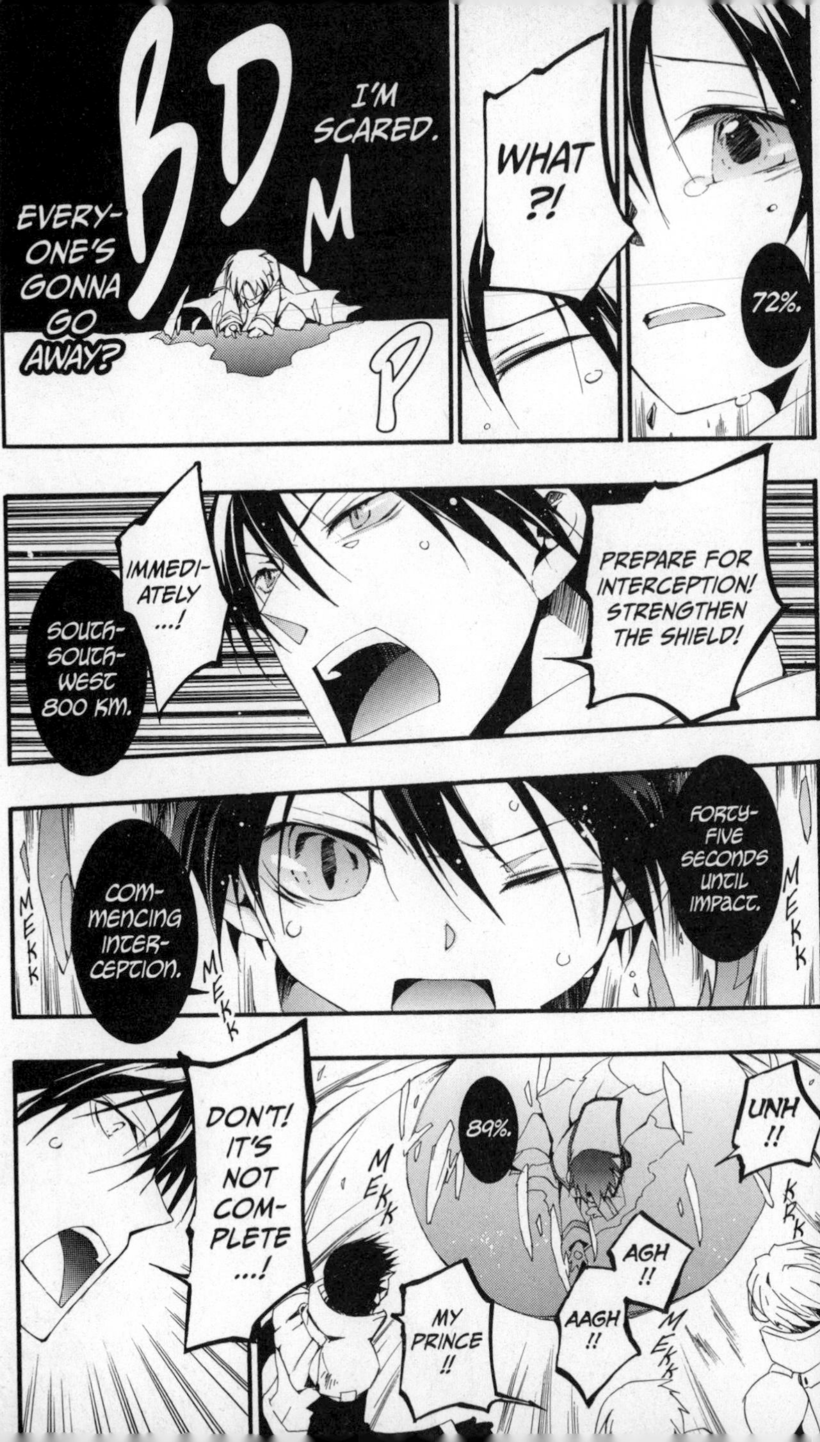
72%.
WHAT ?!
I'M SCARED.
BDMP
EVERYONE'S GONNA GO AWAY?
PREPARE FOR INTERCEPTION! STRENGTHEN THE SHIELD!
IMMEDIATELY ...!
SOUTH-SOUTHWEST 800 KM.
FORTY-FIVE SECONDS UNTIL IMPACT.
MEKK
COMMENCING INTERCEPTION.
MEKK
MEKK
UNH !!
KRK
89%.
MEKK
DON'T! IT'S NOT COMPLETE ...!
AGH !!
AAGH !!
MEKK
MY PRINCE !!

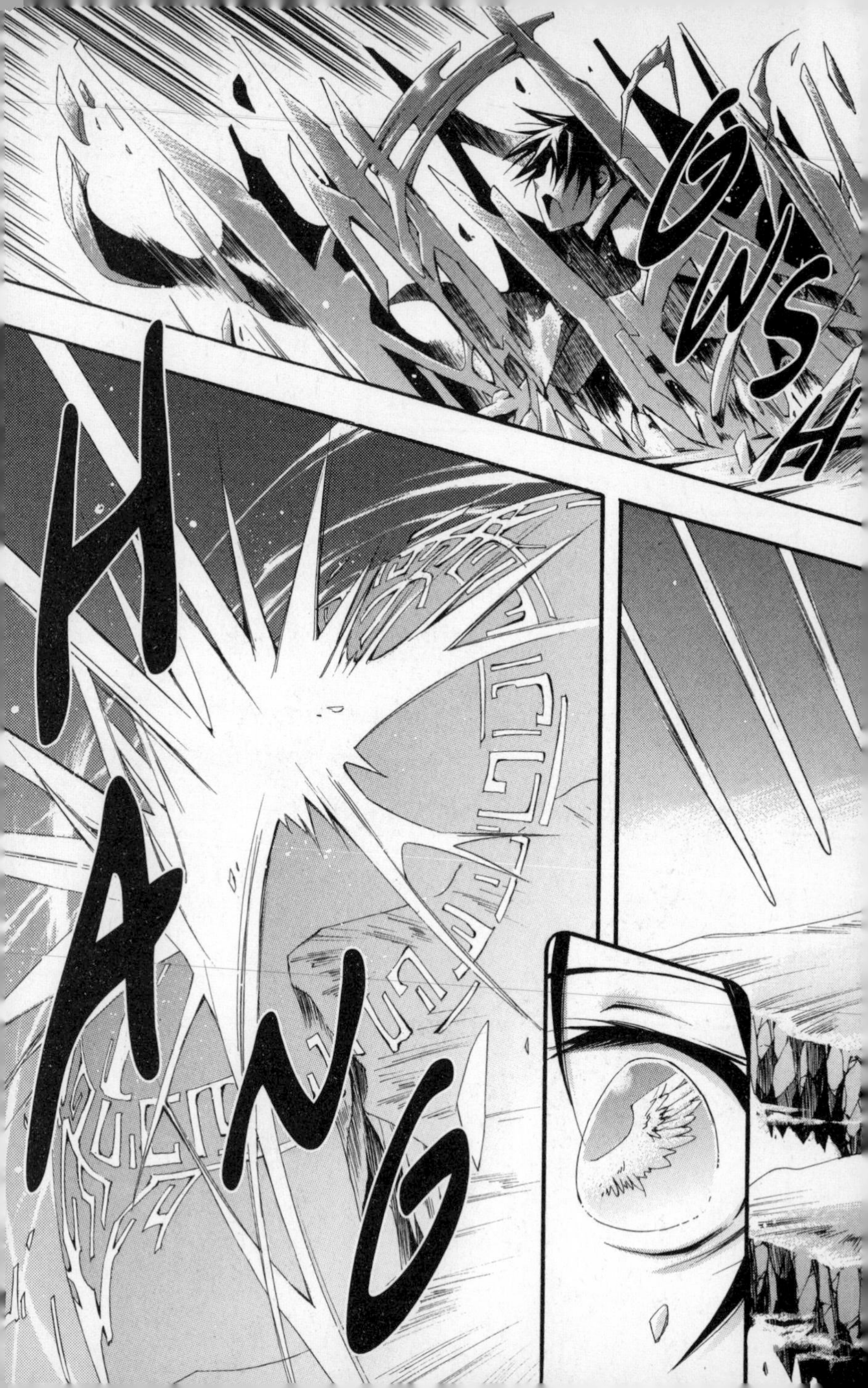
GWSH
HANG

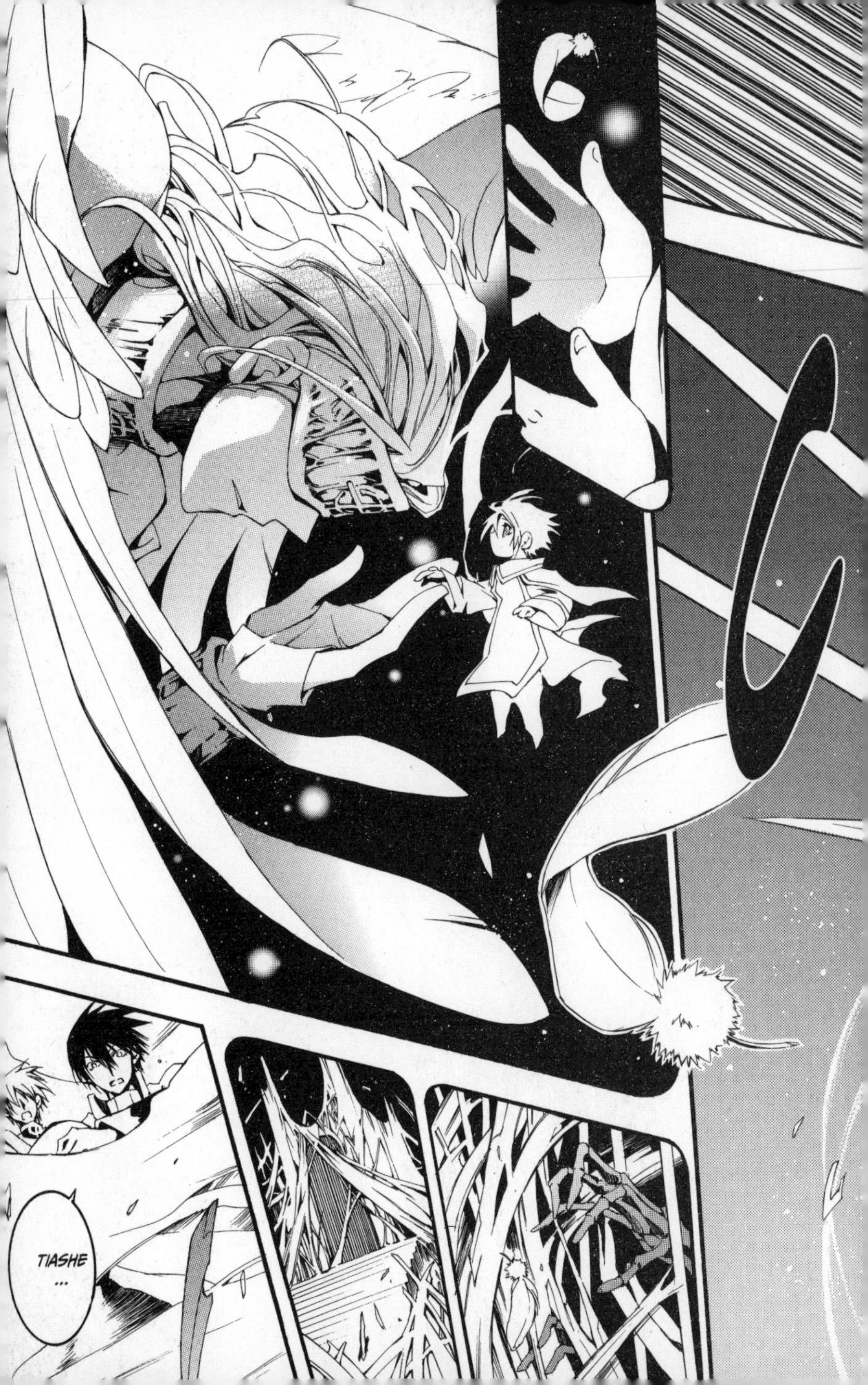
TIASHE ...

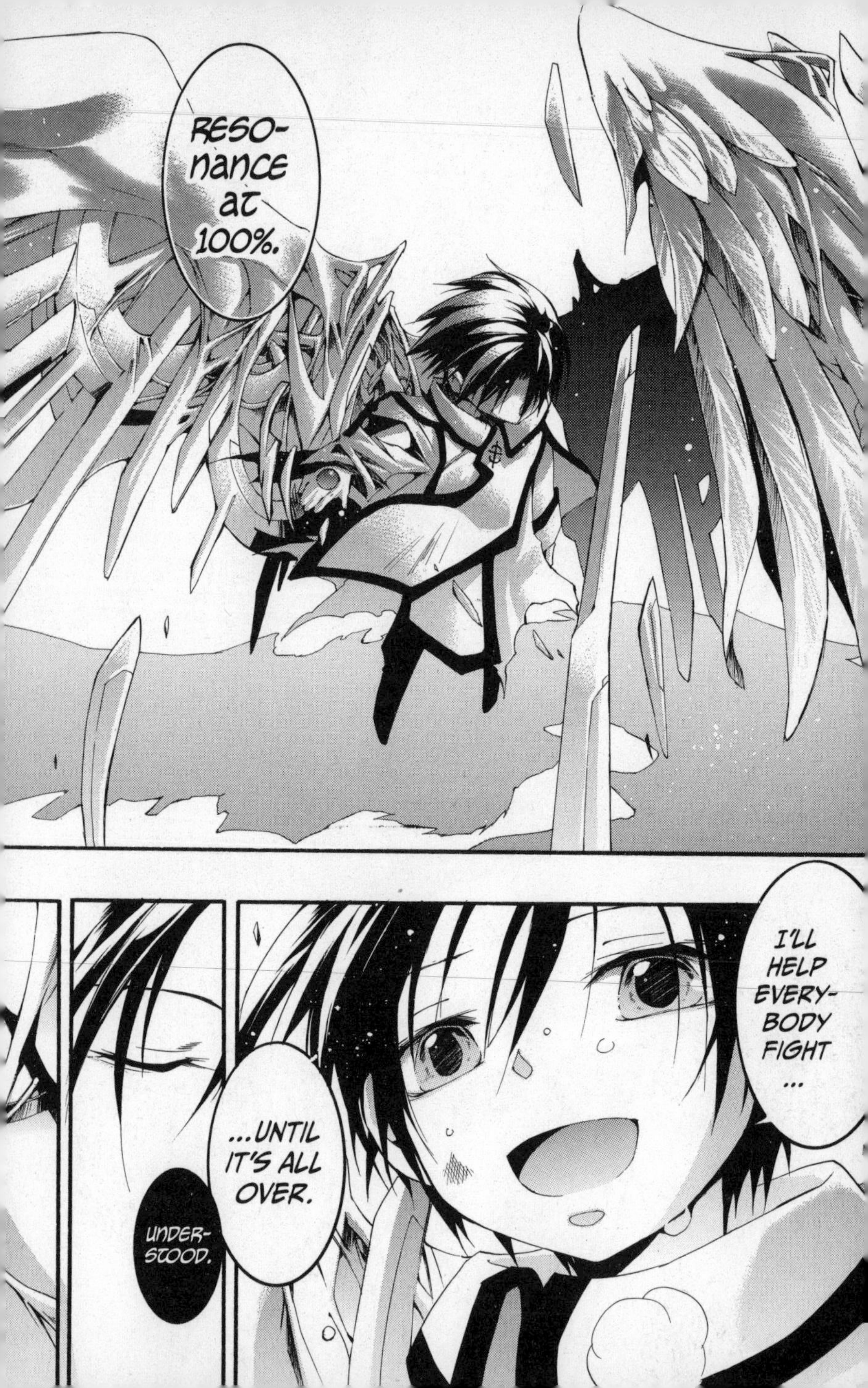
RESO-nance at 100%.
I'LL HELP EVERY-BODY FIGHT...
...UNTIL IT'S ALL OVER.
UNDER-STOOD.

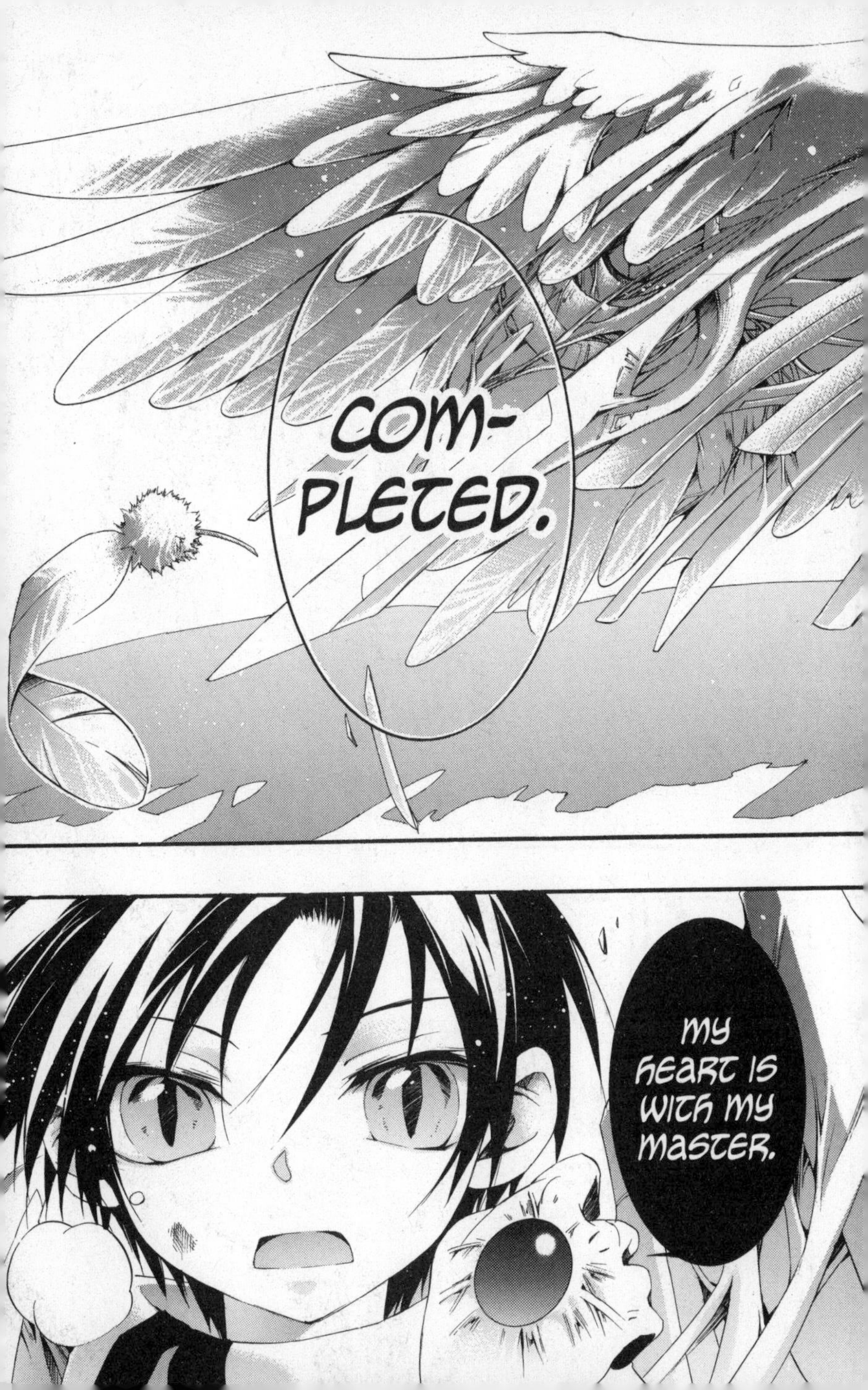
COM-
PLETED.
MY HEART IS WITH MY MASTER.

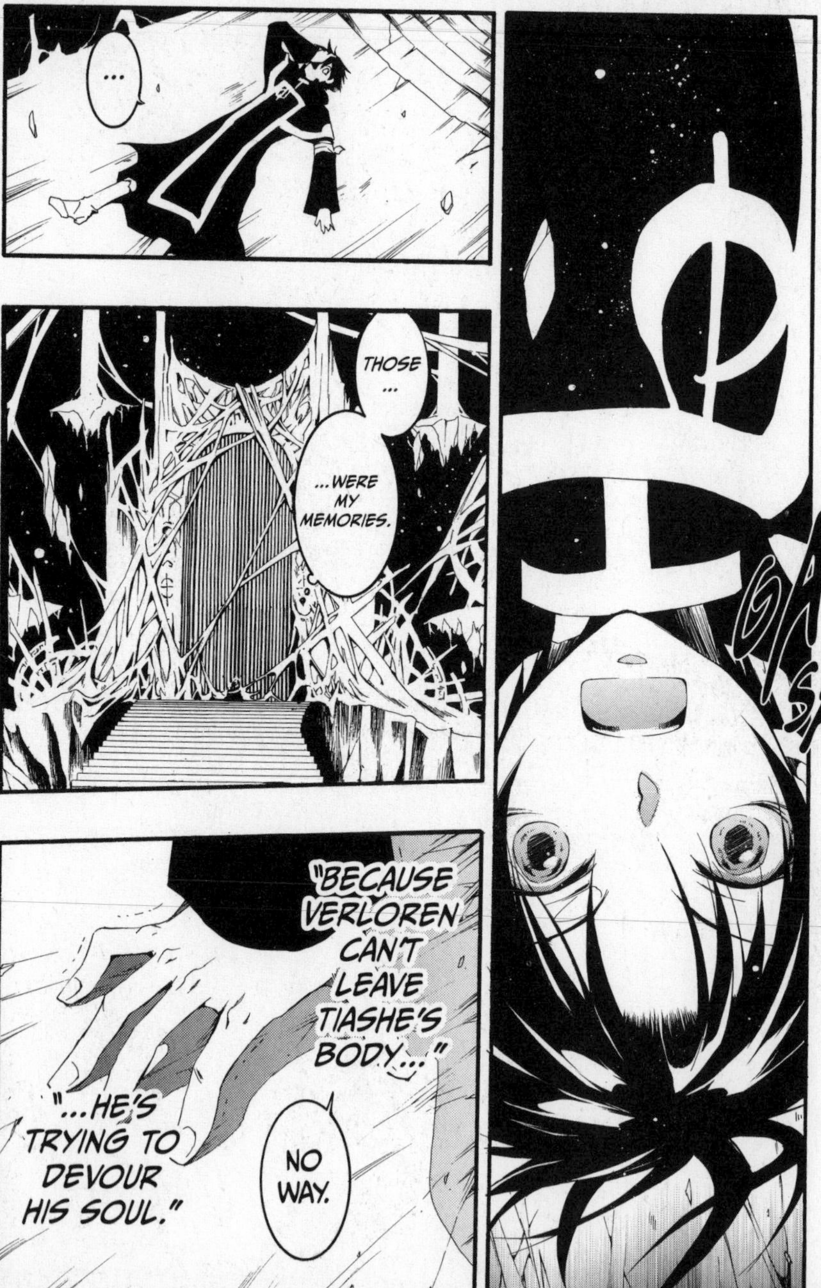
GASP
...
THOSE ...
...WERE MY MEMORIES.
"BECAUSE VERLOREN CAN'T LEAVE TIASHE'S BODY..."
"...HE'S TRYING TO DEVOUR HIS SOUL."
NO WAY.

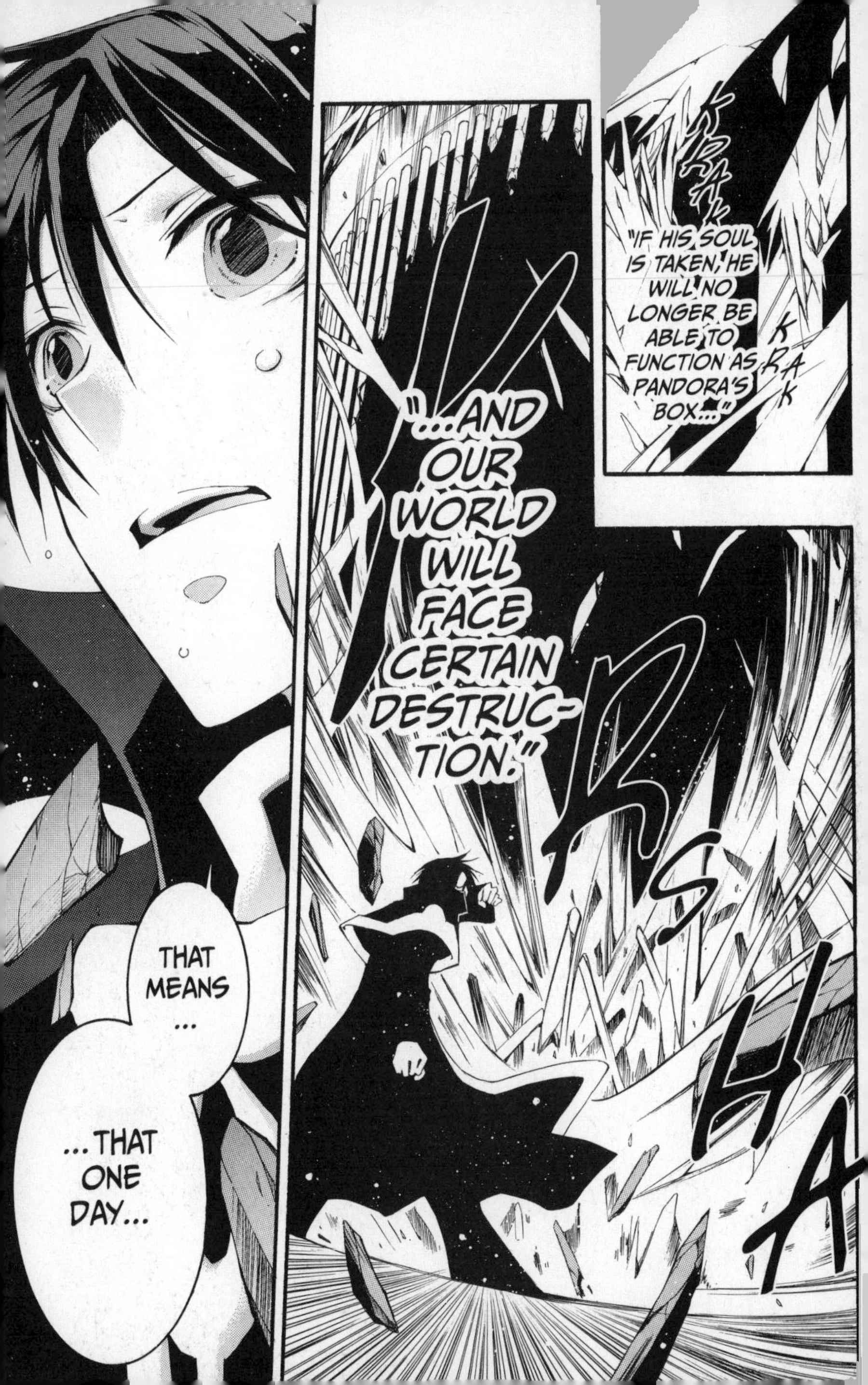
KRAK
"IF HIS SOUL IS TAKEN, HE WILL NO LONGER BE ABLE TO FUNCTION AS PANDORA'S BOX..."
KRAK
"...AND OUR WORLD WILL FACE CERTAIN DESTRUCTION."
THAT MEANS ...
...THAT ONE DAY...

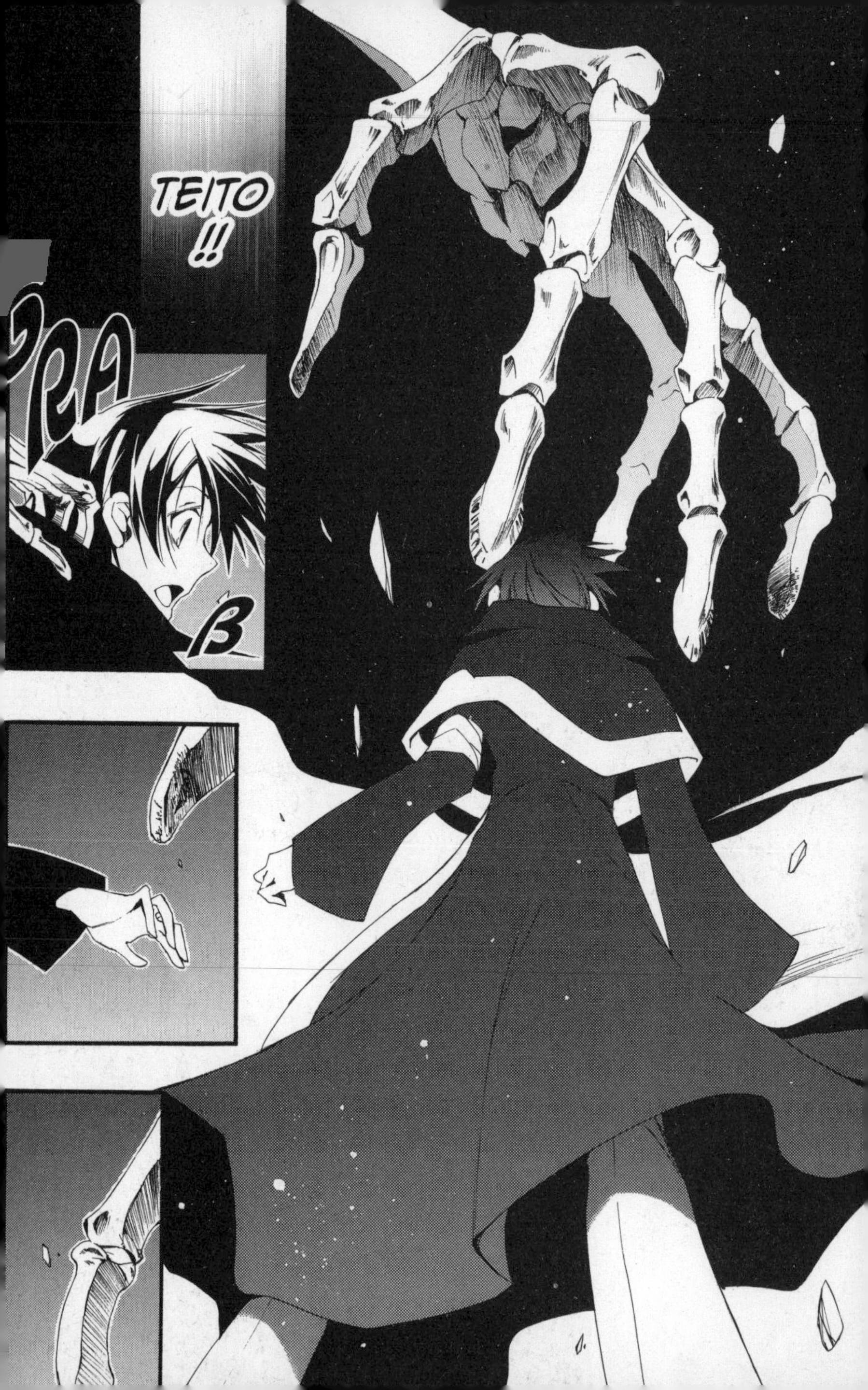
TEITO!!
GRA
β

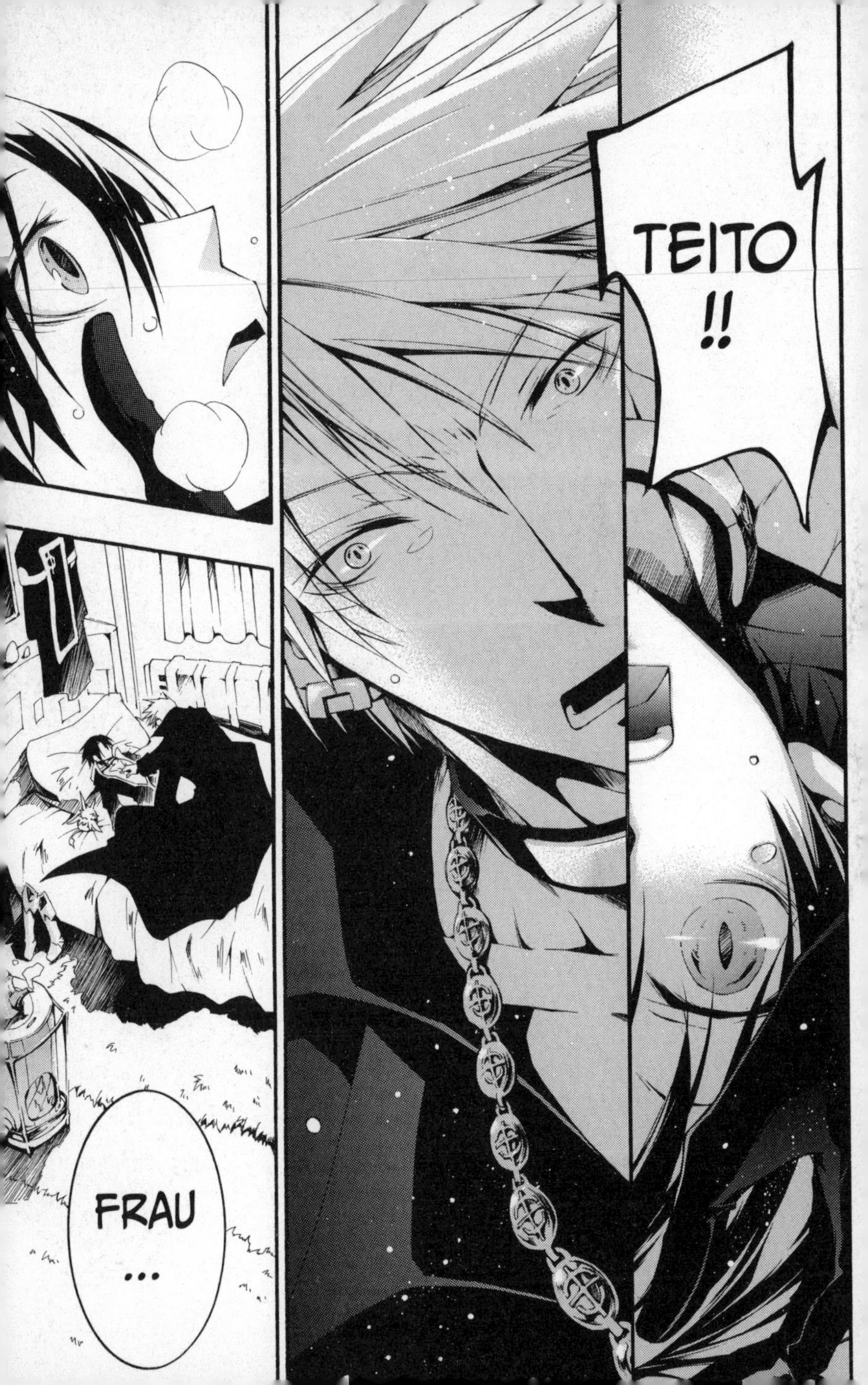
TEITO !!
FRAU ...

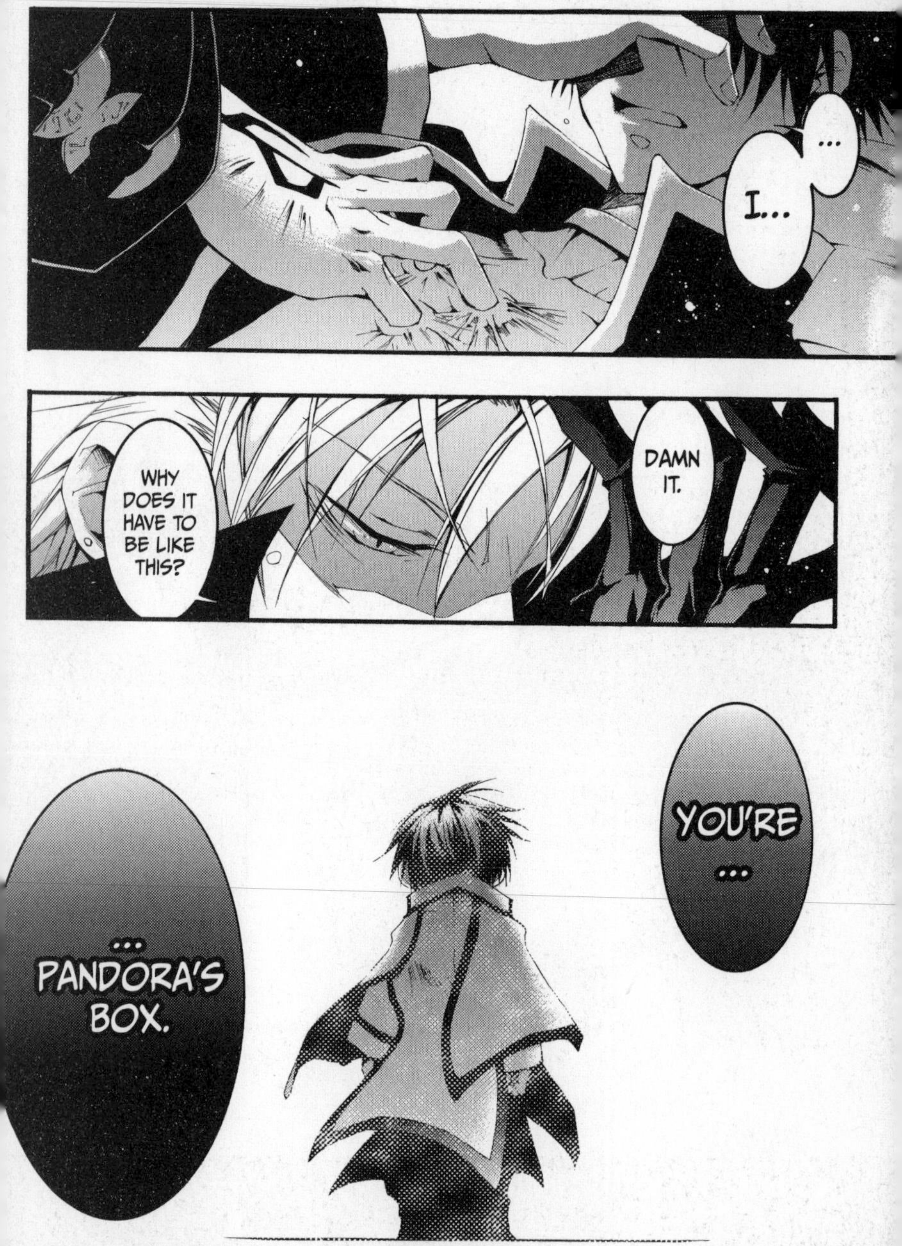
...
I...
DAMN IT.
WHY DOES IT HAVE TO BE LIKE THIS?
YOU'RE ...
... PANDORA'S BOX.

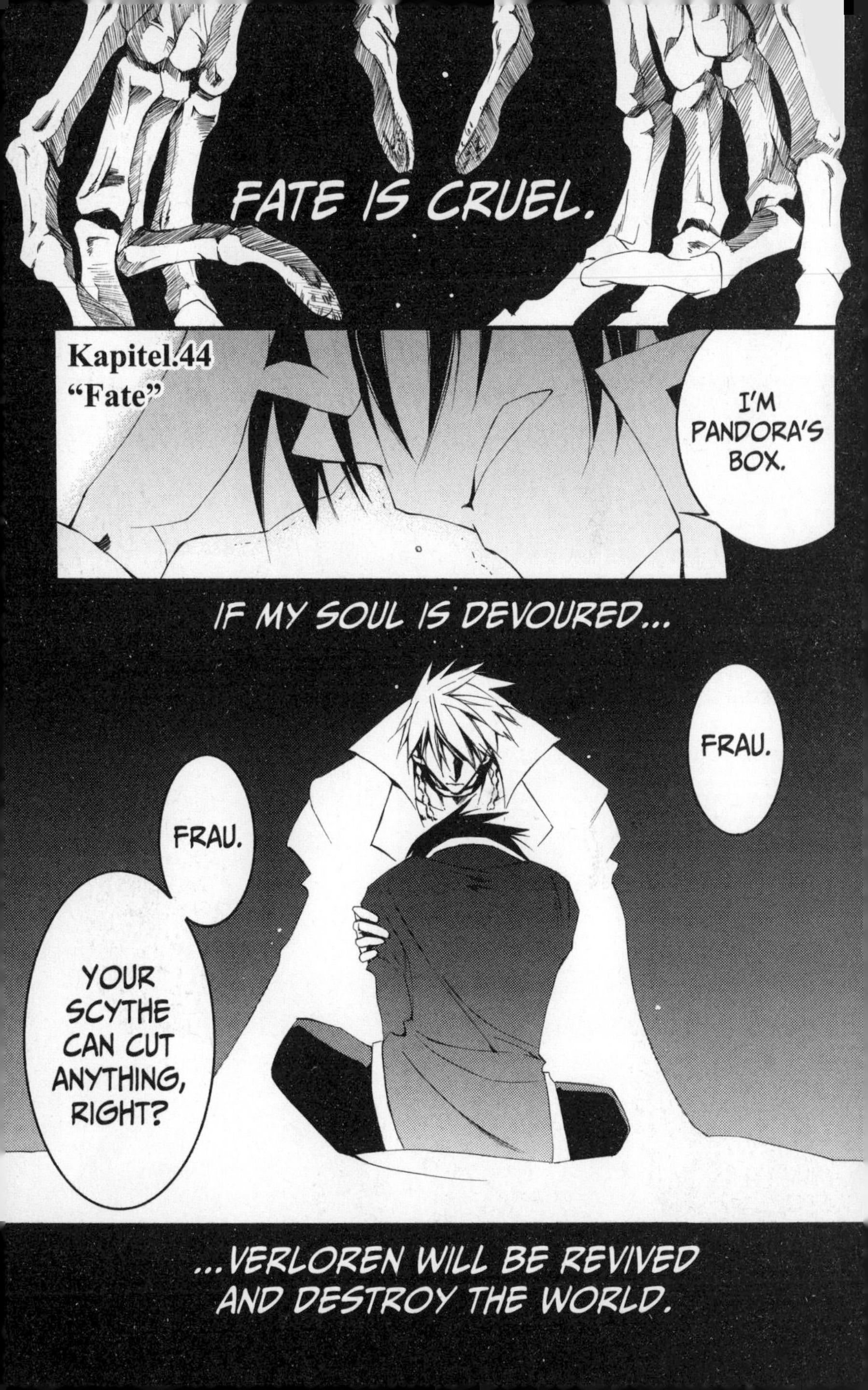
FATE IS CRUEL.
I'M PANDORA'S BOX.
Kapitel.44 "Fate"
IF MY SOUL IS DEVOURED...
FRAU.
FRAU.
YOUR SCYTHE CAN CUT ANYTHING, RIGHT?
...VERLOREN WILL BE REVIVED AND DESTROY THE WORLD.

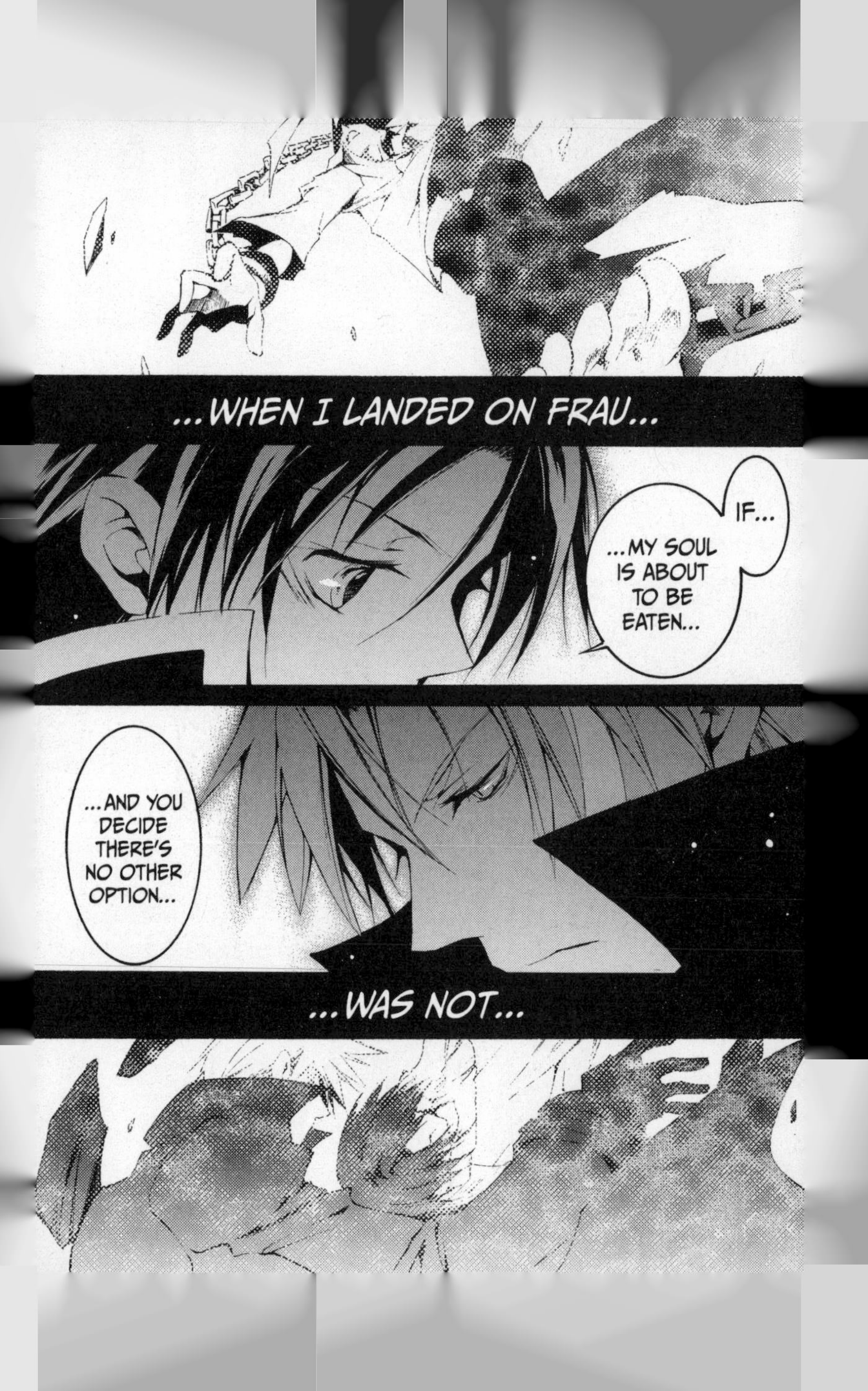
...WHEN I LANDED ON FRAU...
IF...
...MY SOUL IS ABOUT TO BE EATEN...
...AND YOU DECIDE THERE'S NO OTHER OPTION...
...WAS NOT...

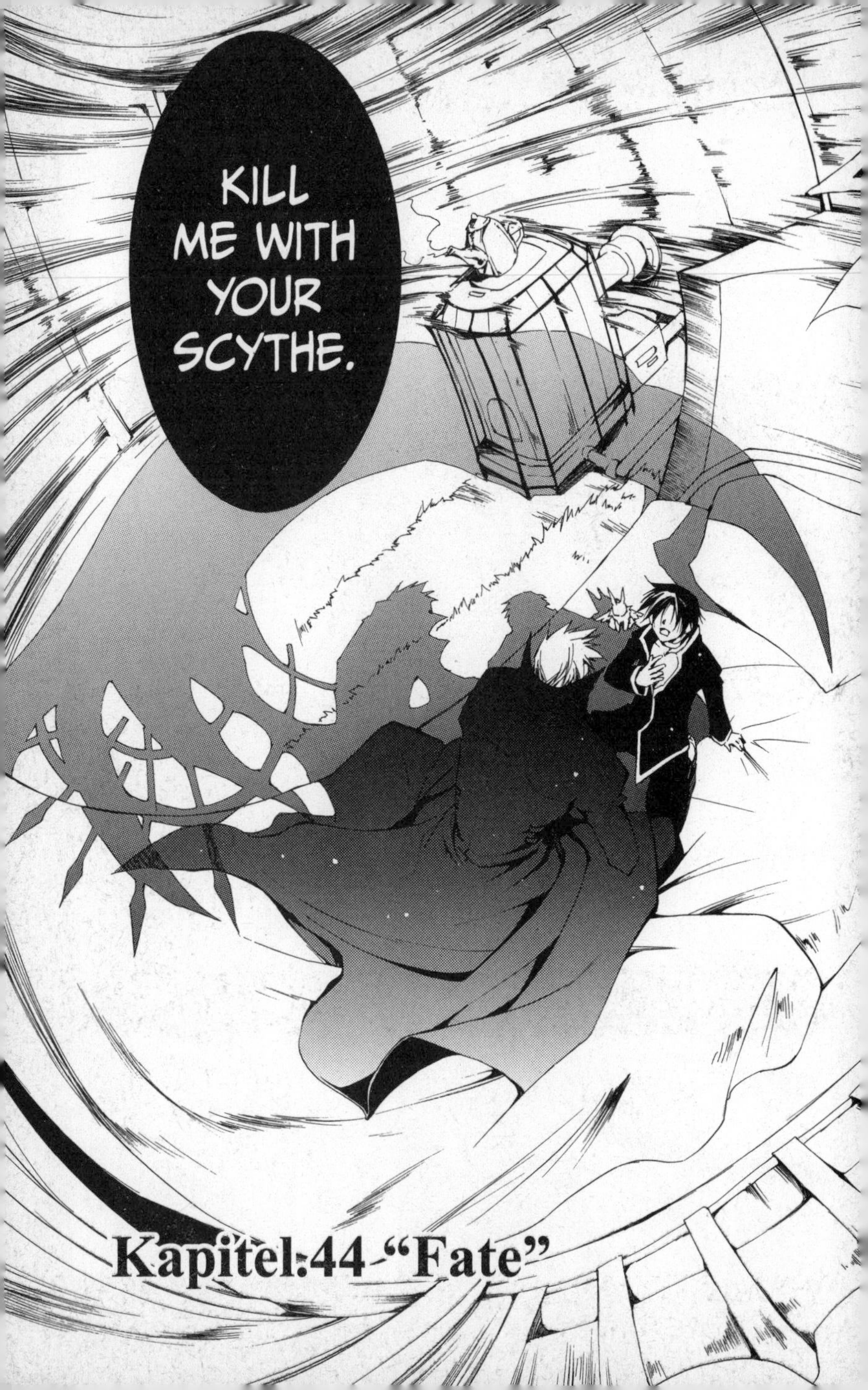
KILL ME WITH YOUR SCYTHE.

Kapitel:44 "Fate"

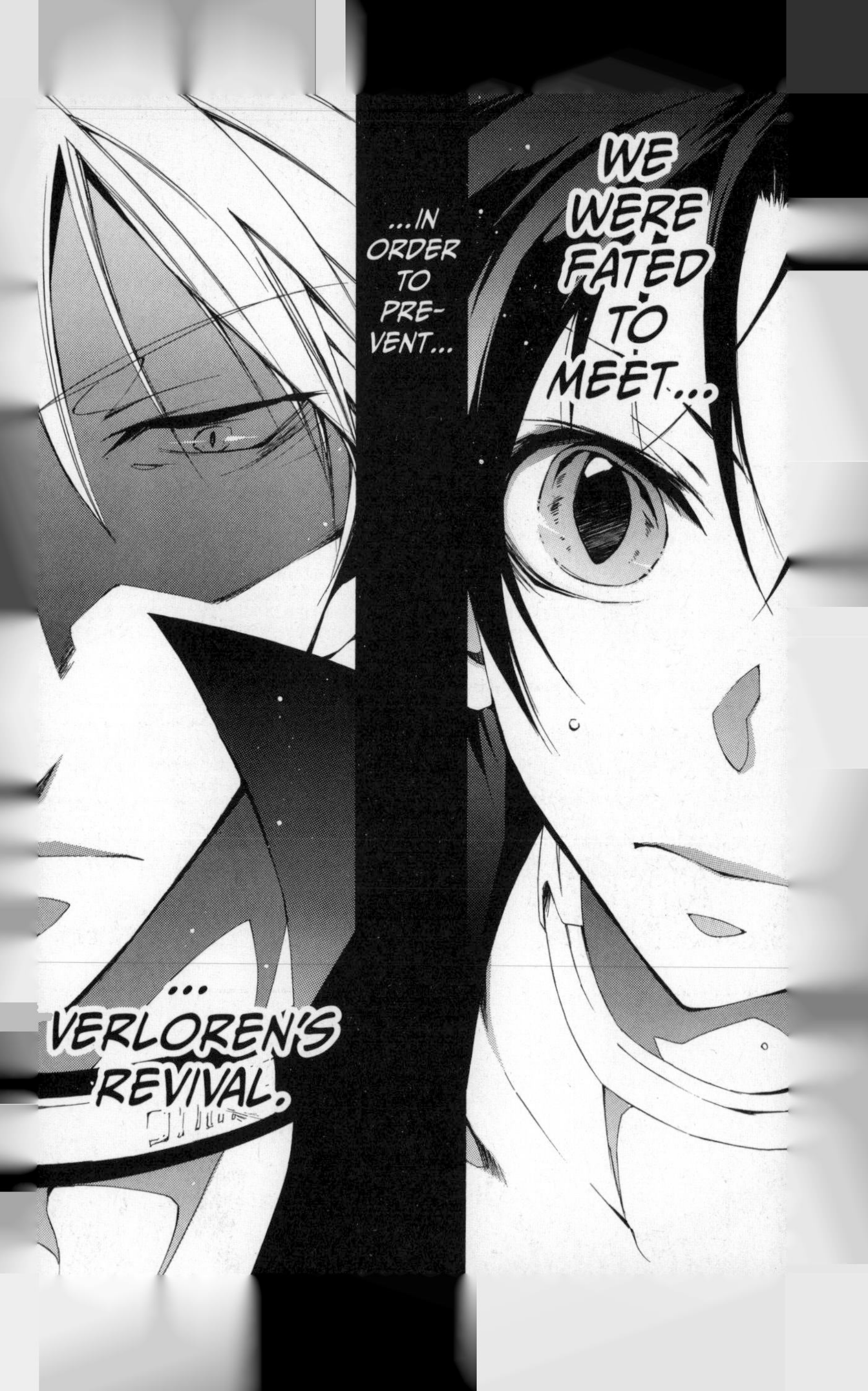
WE WERE FATED TO MEET...
...IN ORDER TO PRE-VENT...
...VERLOREN'S REVIVAL.

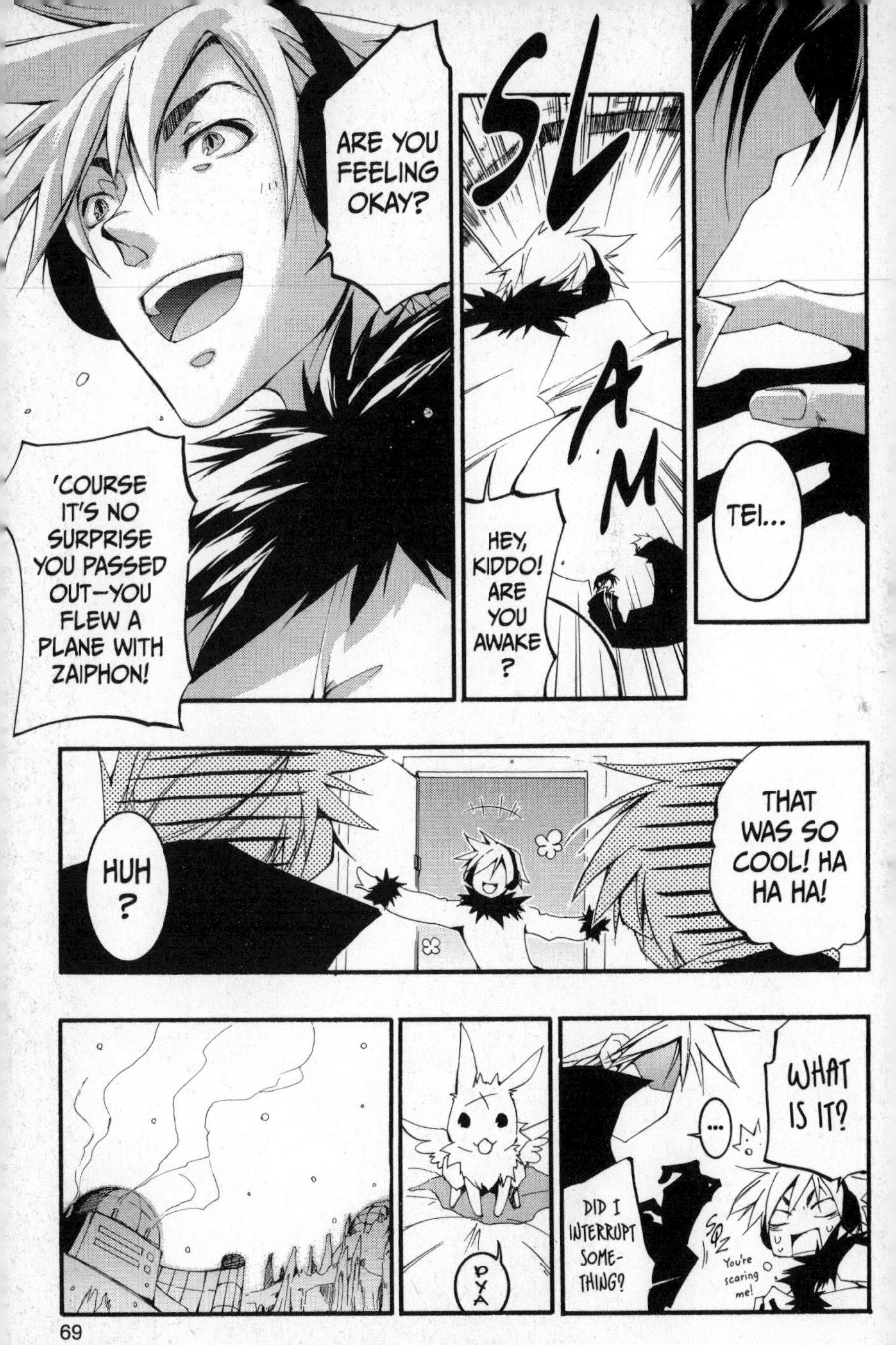
TEI...
SLAM
HEY, KIDDO! ARE YOU AWAKE?
ARE YOU FEELING OKAY?
'COURSE IT'S NO SURPRISE YOU PASSED OUT—YOU FLEW A PLANE WITH ZAIPHON!
THAT WAS SO COOL! HA HA HA!
HUH?
WHAT IS IT?
...
DID I INTERRUPT SOME-THING?
You're scaring me!
PYA

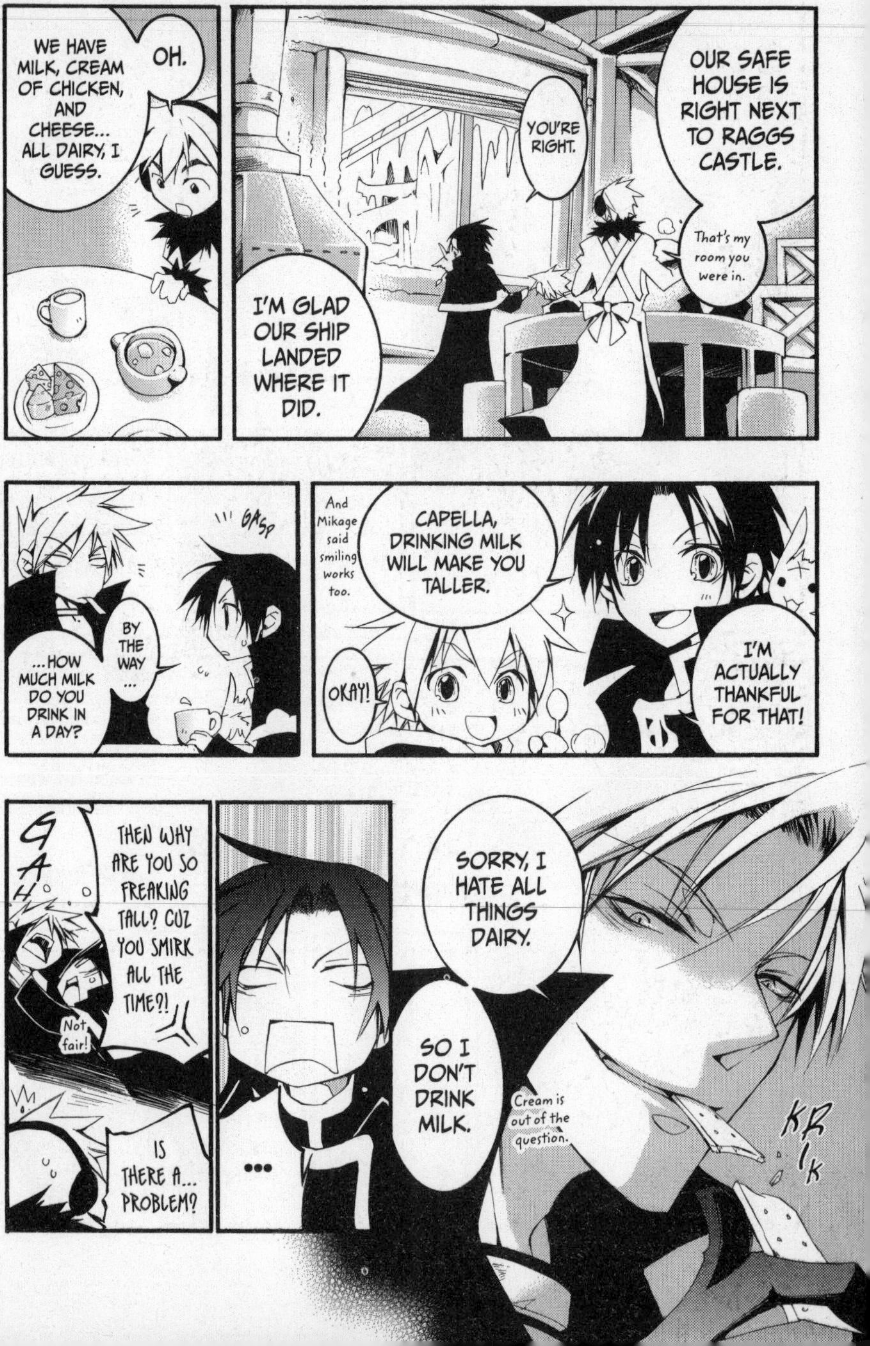
OUR SAFE HOUSE IS RIGHT NEXT TO RAGGS CASTLE.
That's my room you were in.
YOU'RE RIGHT.
I'M GLAD OUR SHIP LANDED WHERE IT DID.
OH.
WE HAVE MILK, CREAM OF CHICKEN, AND CHEESE... ALL DAIRY, I GUESS.
CAPELLA, DRINKING MILK WILL MAKE YOU TALLER.
And Mikage said smiling works too.
I'M ACTUALLY THANKFUL FOR THAT!
OKAY!
GASP
BY THE WAY...
...HOW MUCH MILK DO YOU DRINK IN A DAY?
SORRY, I HATE ALL THINGS DAIRY.
SO I DON'T DRINK MILK.
Cream is out of the question.
KRIK
...
GAH
THEN WHY ARE YOU SO FREAKING TALL? CUZ YOU SMIRK ALL THE TIME?!
Not fair!
IS THERE A... PROBLEM?

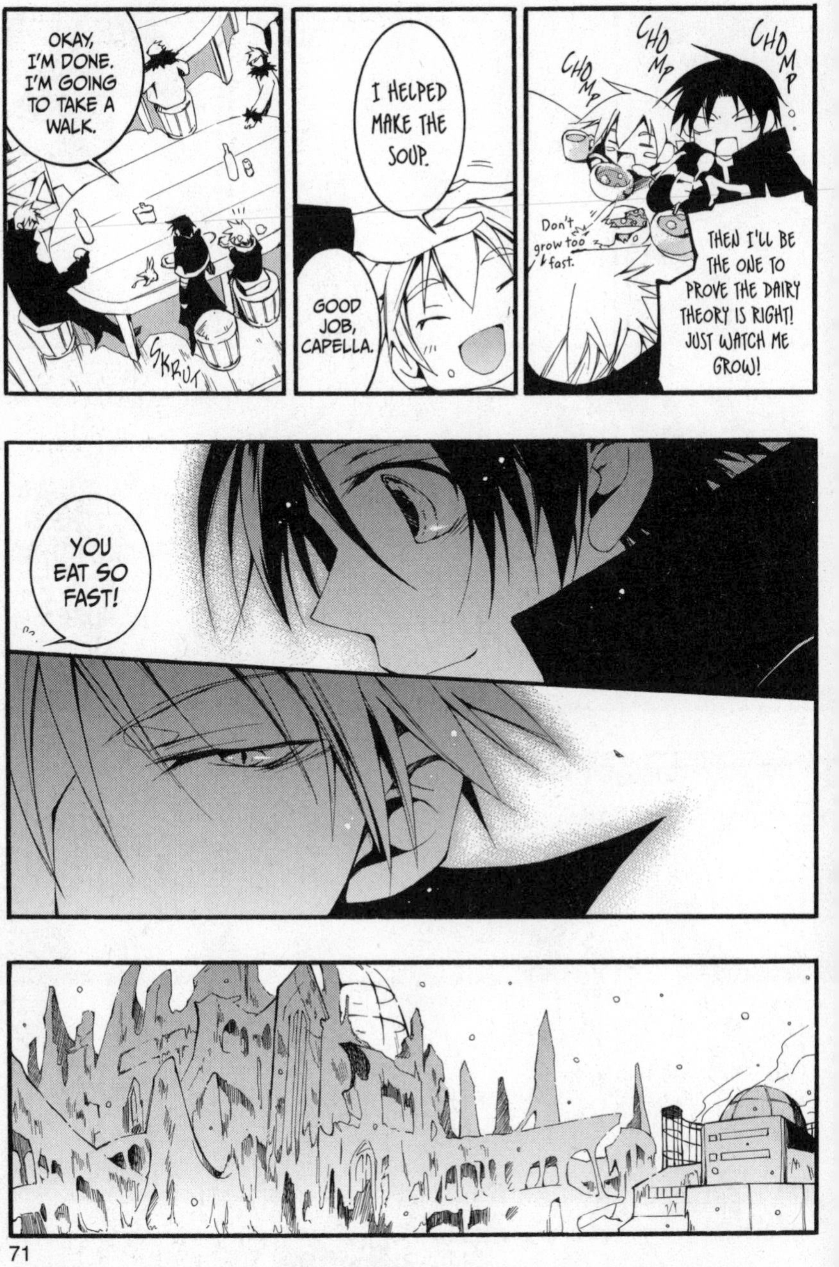
CHOMP
CHOMP
CHOMP
THEN I'LL BE THE ONE TO PROVE THE DAIRY THEORY IS RIGHT! JUST WATCH ME GROW!
Don't grow too fast.
I HELPED MAKE THE SOUP.
GOOD JOB, CAPELLA.
OKAY, I'M DONE. I'M GOING TO TAKE A WALK.
SKRUT
YOU EAT SO FAST!

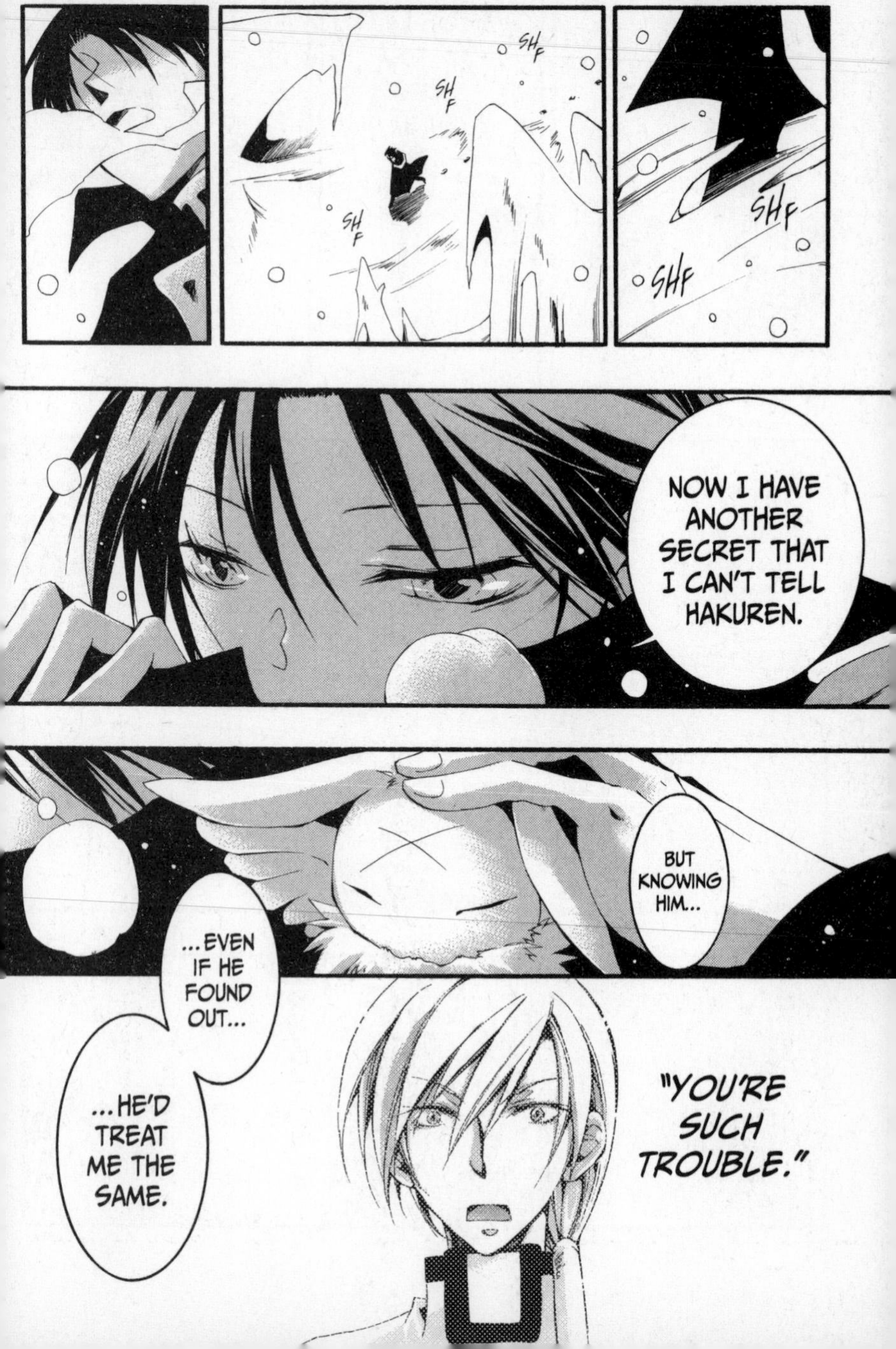
SHF
SHF
SHF
SHF
SHF
NOW I HAVE ANOTHER SECRET THAT I CAN'T TELL HAKUREN.
BUT KNOWING HIM...
...EVEN IF HE FOUND OUT...
...HE'D TREAT ME THE SAME.
"YOU'RE SUCH TROUBLE."

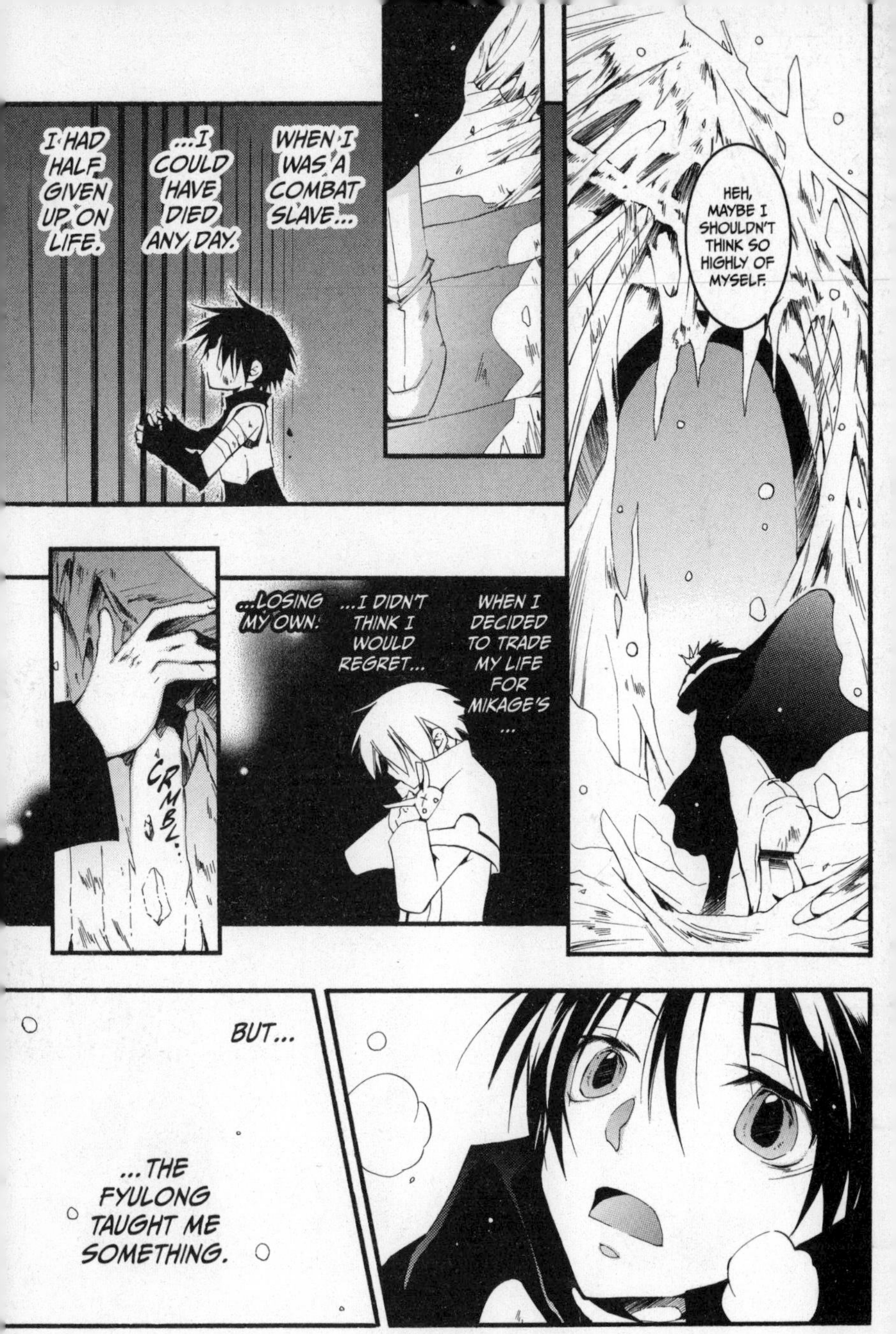
HEH, MAYBE I SHOULDN'T THINK SO HIGHLY OF MYSELF.
WHEN I WAS A COMBAT SLAVE...
...I COULD HAVE DIED ANY DAY.
I HAD HALF GIVEN UP ON LIFE.
WHEN I DECIDED TO TRADE MY LIFE FOR MIKAGE'S...
...I DIDN'T THINK I WOULD REGRET...
...LOSING MY OWN.
CRMBL...
BUT...
...THE FYULONG TAUGHT ME SOMETHING.

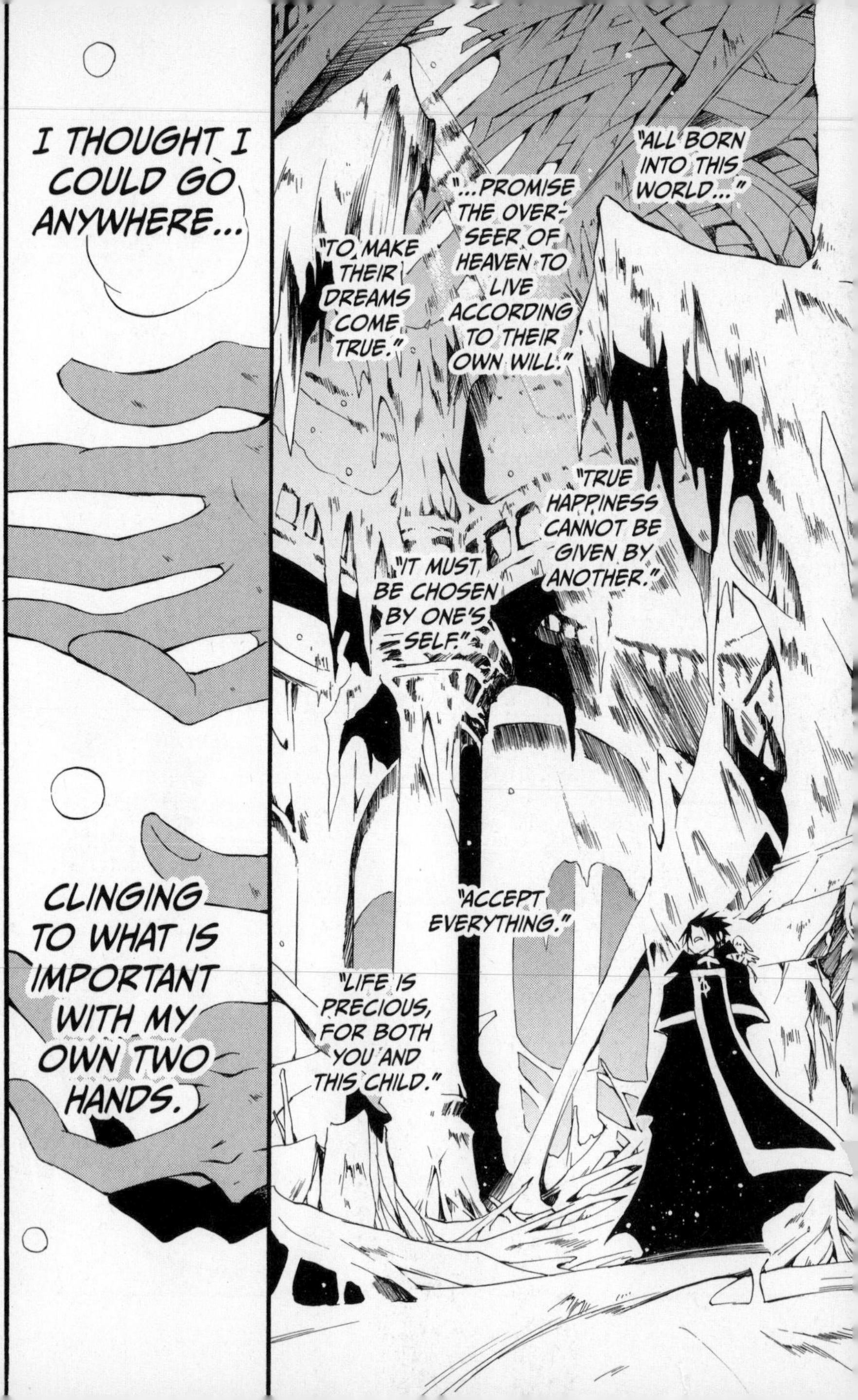
"ALL BORN INTO THIS WORLD..."
"...PROMISE THE OVER-SEER OF HEAVEN TO LIVE ACCORDING TO THEIR OWN WILL."
"TO MAKE THEIR DREAMS COME TRUE."
"TRUE HAPPINESS CANNOT BE GIVEN BY ANOTHER."
"IT MUST BE CHOSEN BY ONE'S SELF."
"ACCEPT EVERYTHING."
"LIFE IS PRECIOUS, FOR BOTH YOU AND THIS CHILD."
I THOUGHT I COULD GO ANYWHERE...
CLINGING TO WHAT IS IMPORTANT WITH MY OWN TWO HANDS.

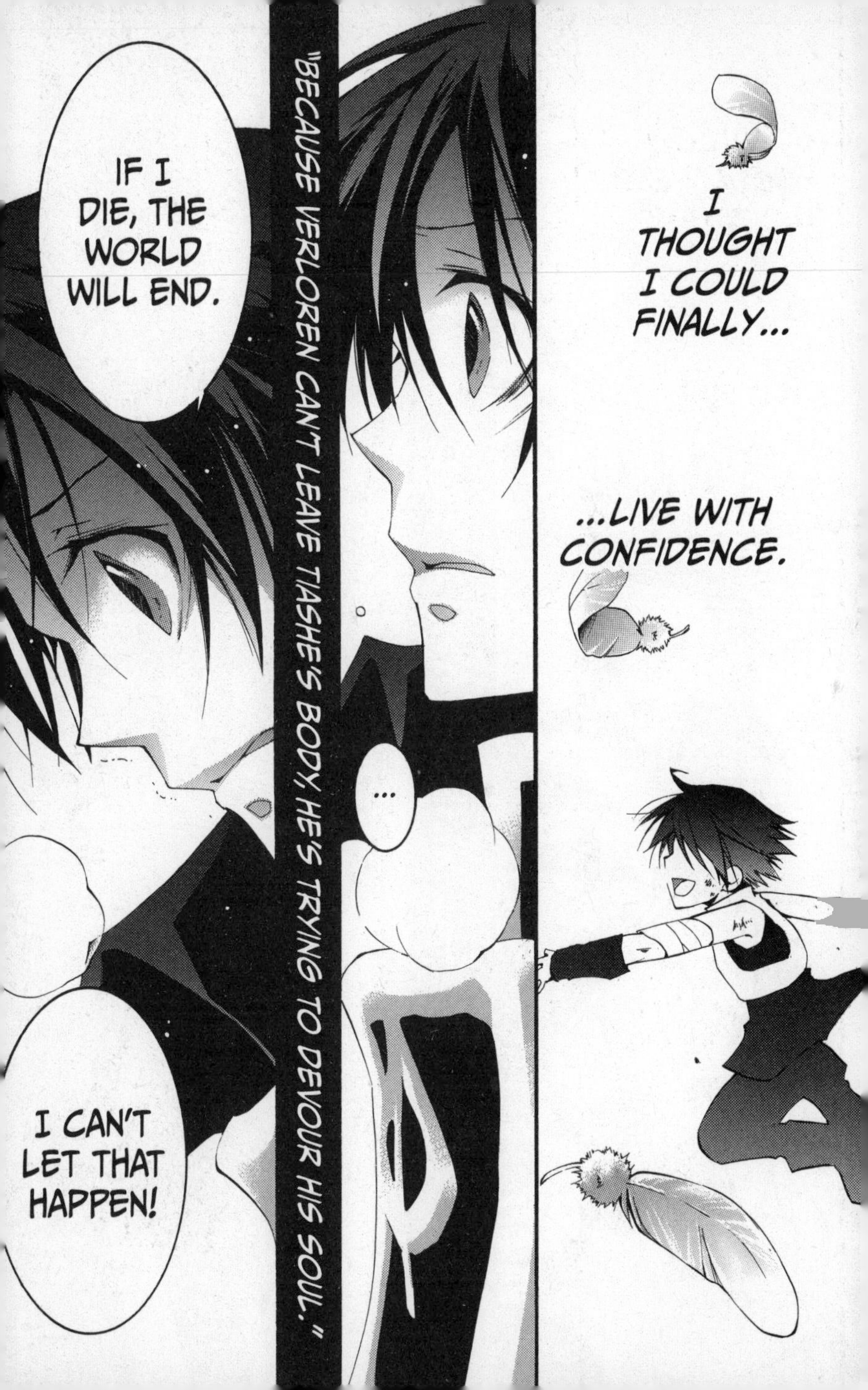
I THOUGHT I COULD FINALLY...
...LIVE WITH CONFIDENCE.
"BECAUSE VERLOREN CAN'T LEAVE TIASHE'S BODY, HE'S TRYING TO DEVOUR HIS SOUL."
...
IF I DIE, THE WORLD WILL END.
I CAN'T LET THAT HAPPEN!

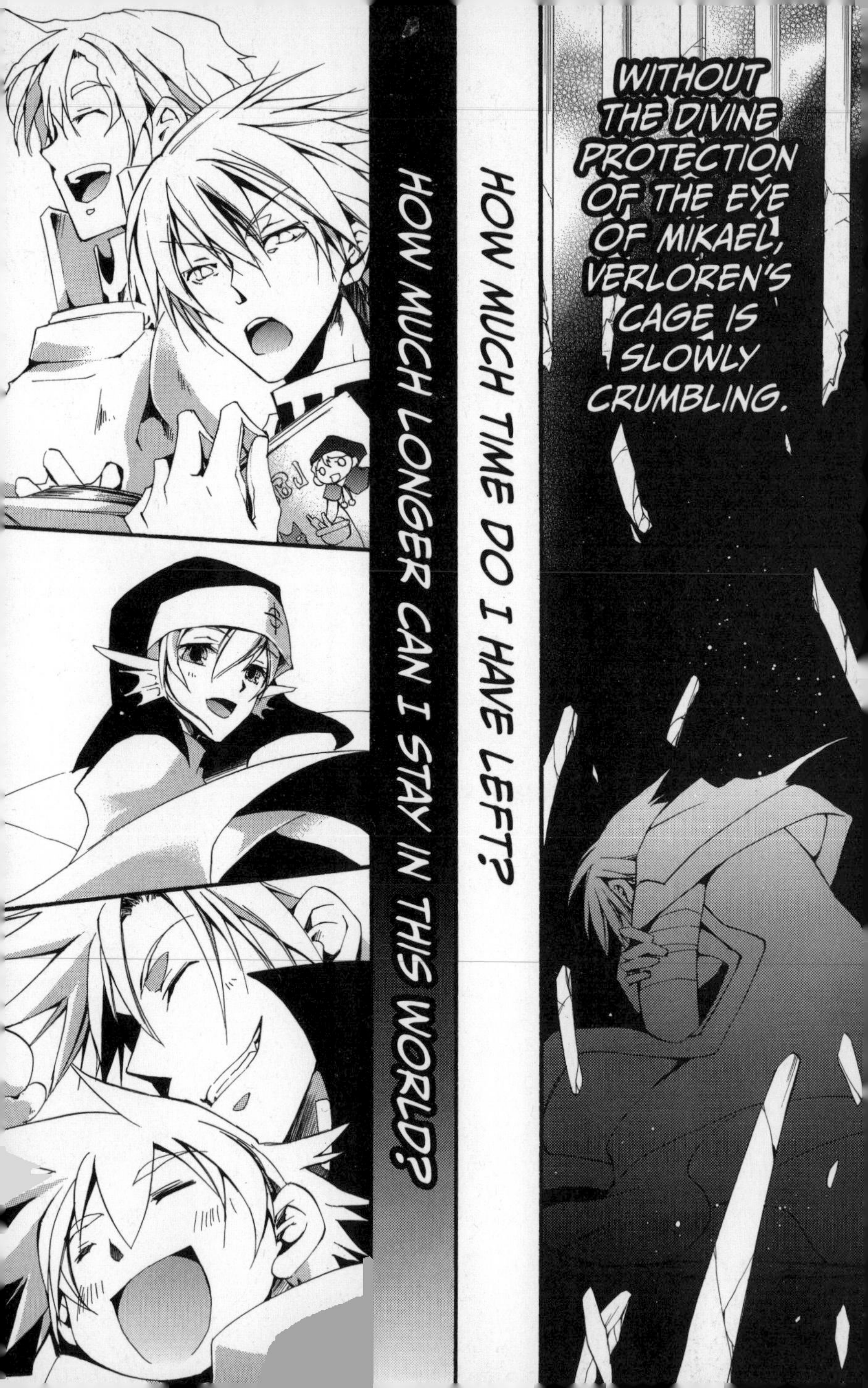
WITHOUT THE DIVINE PROTECTION OF THE EYE OF MIKAEL, VERLOREN'S CAGE IS SLOWLY CRUMBLING.
HOW MUCH TIME DO I HAVE LEFT?
HOW MUCH LONGER CAN I STAY IN THIS WORLD?

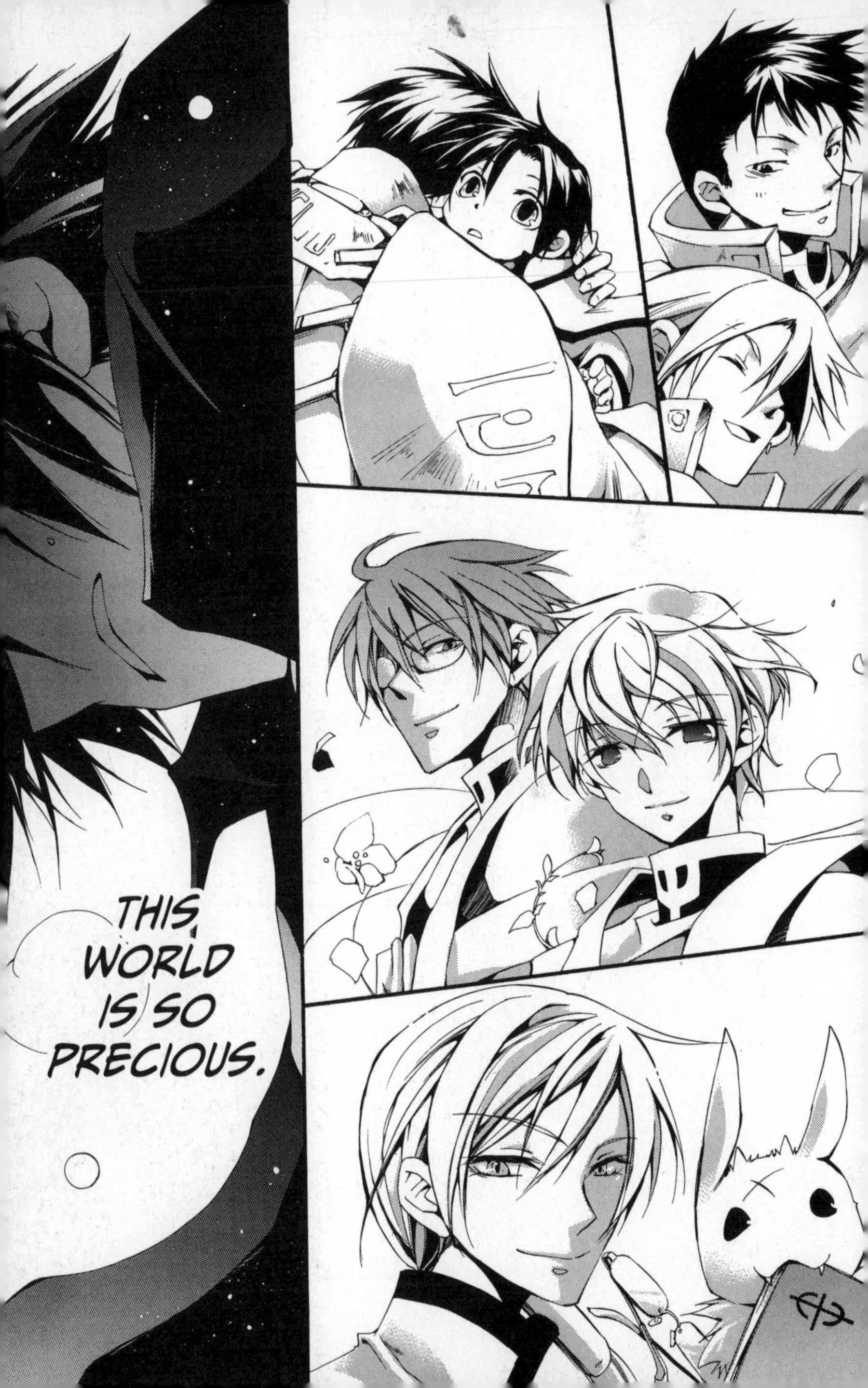
THIS WORLD IS SO PRECIOUS.

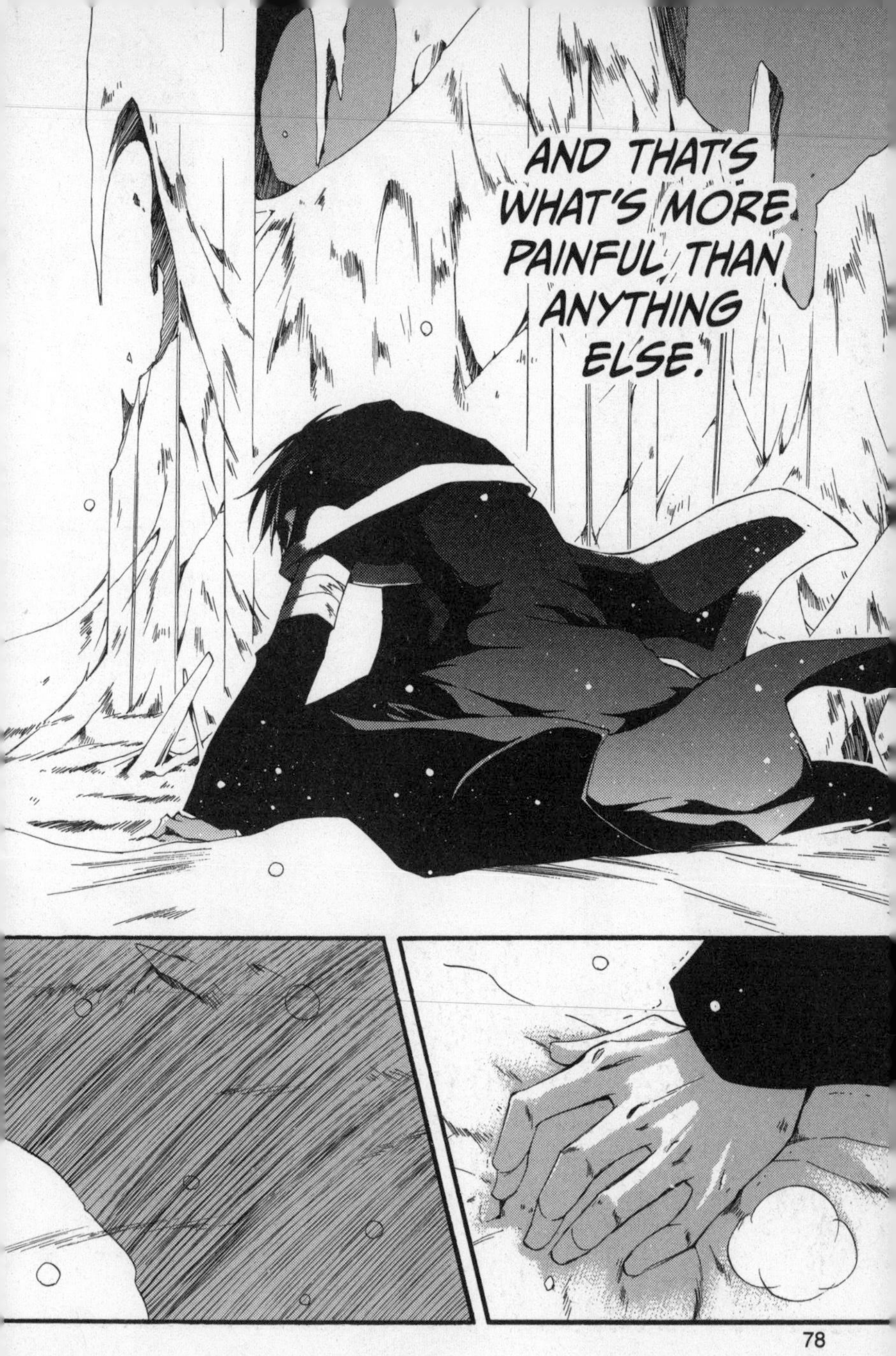
AND THAT'S WHAT'S MORE PAINFUL THAN ANYTHING ELSE.

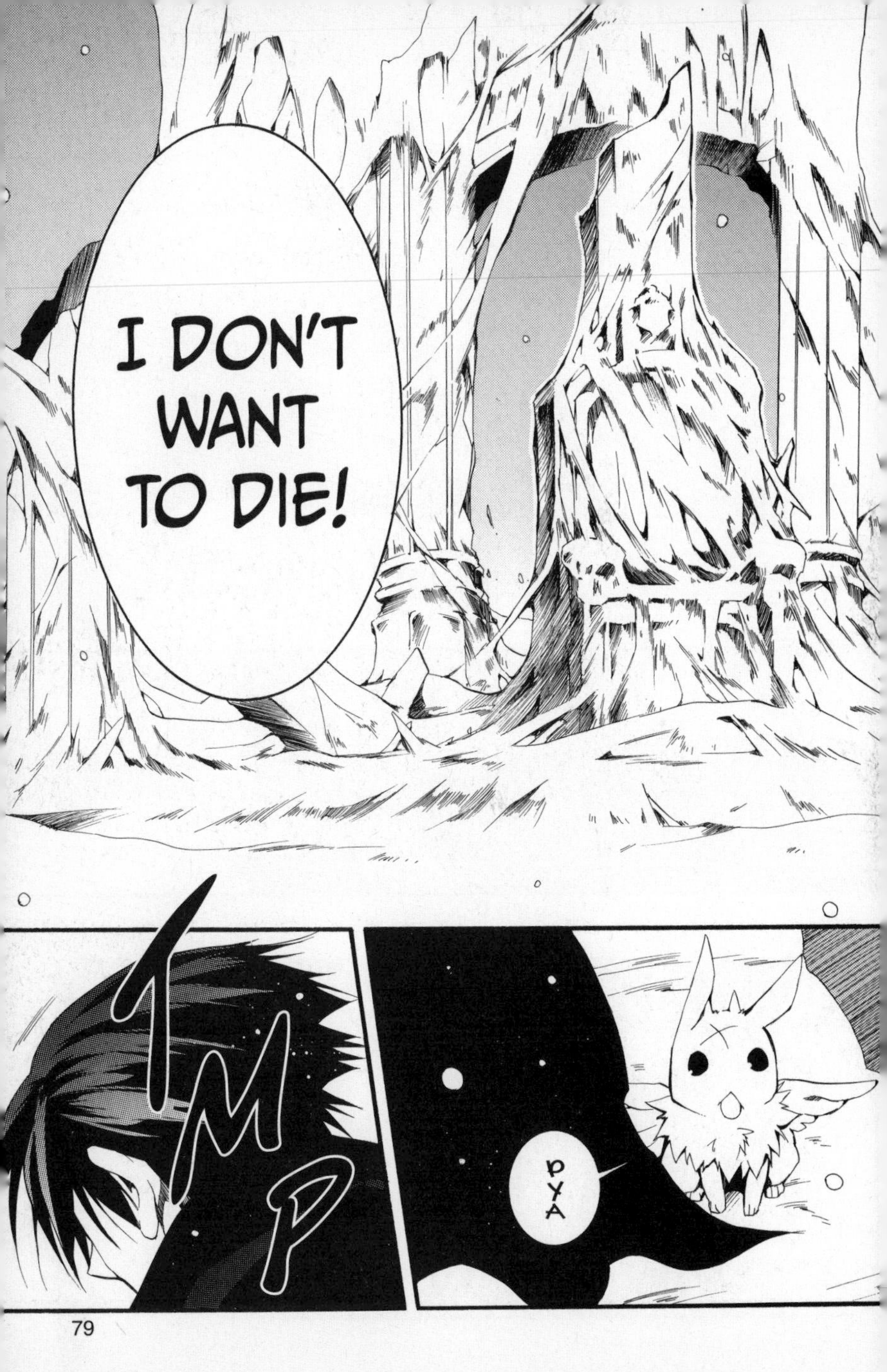
I DON'T WANT TO DIE!
PYA
TMP

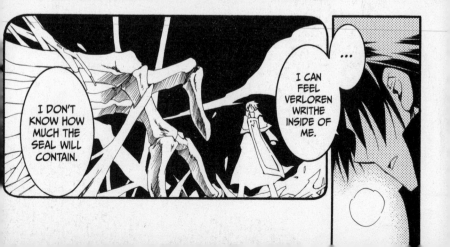

I CAN FEEL VERLOREN WRITHE INSIDE OF ME.

...

I DON'T KNOW HOW MUCH THE SEAL WILL CONTAIN.

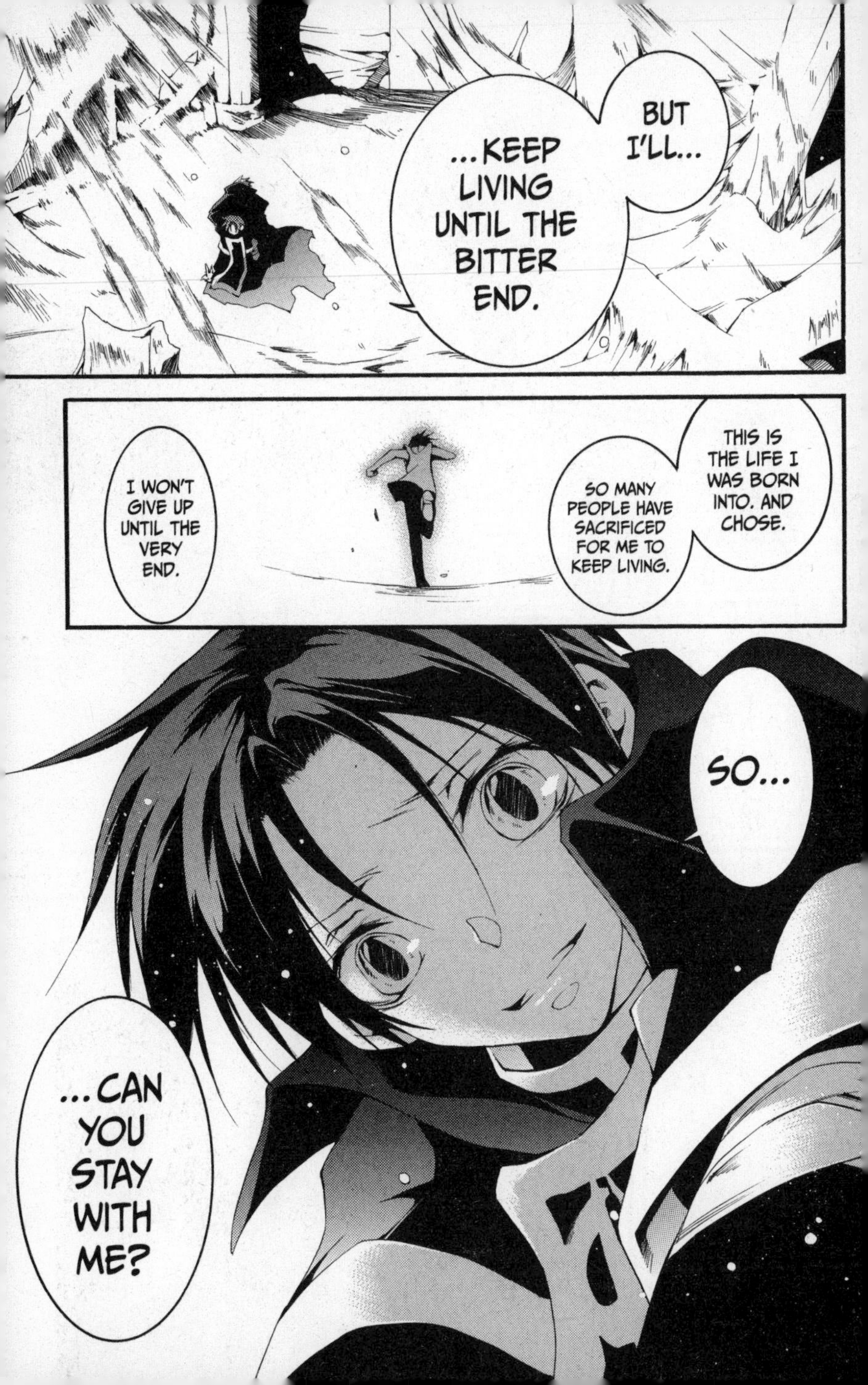
BUT I'LL...
...KEEP LIVING UNTIL THE BITTER END.
THIS IS THE LIFE I WAS BORN INTO. AND CHOSE.
SO MANY PEOPLE HAVE SACRIFICED FOR ME TO KEEP LIVING.
I WON'T GIVE UP UNTIL THE VERY END.
SO...
...CAN YOU STAY WITH ME?

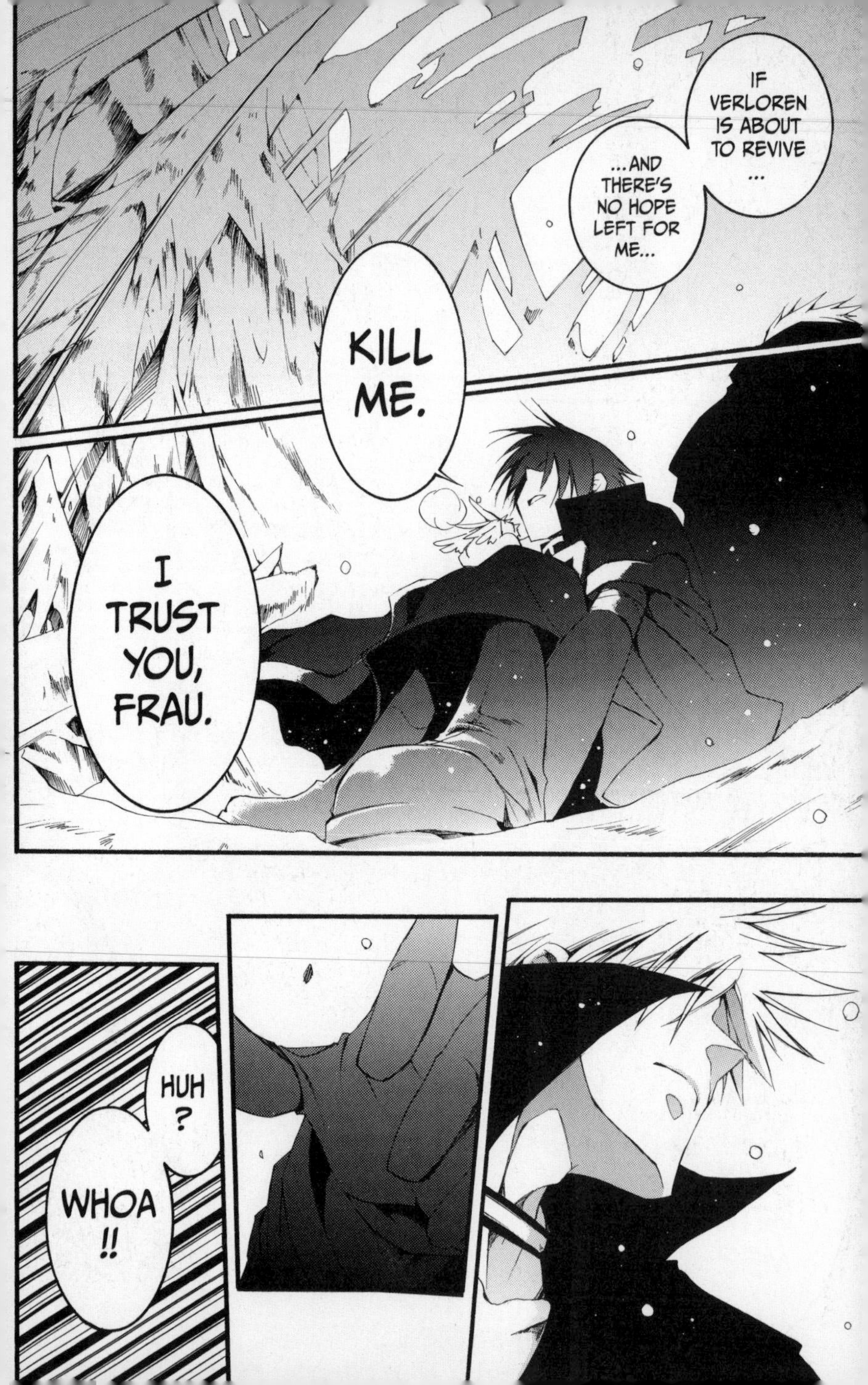
IF VERLOREN IS ABOUT TO REVIVE ...
...AND THERE'S NO HOPE LEFT FOR ME...
KILL ME.
I TRUST YOU, FRAU.
HUH ?
WHOA !!

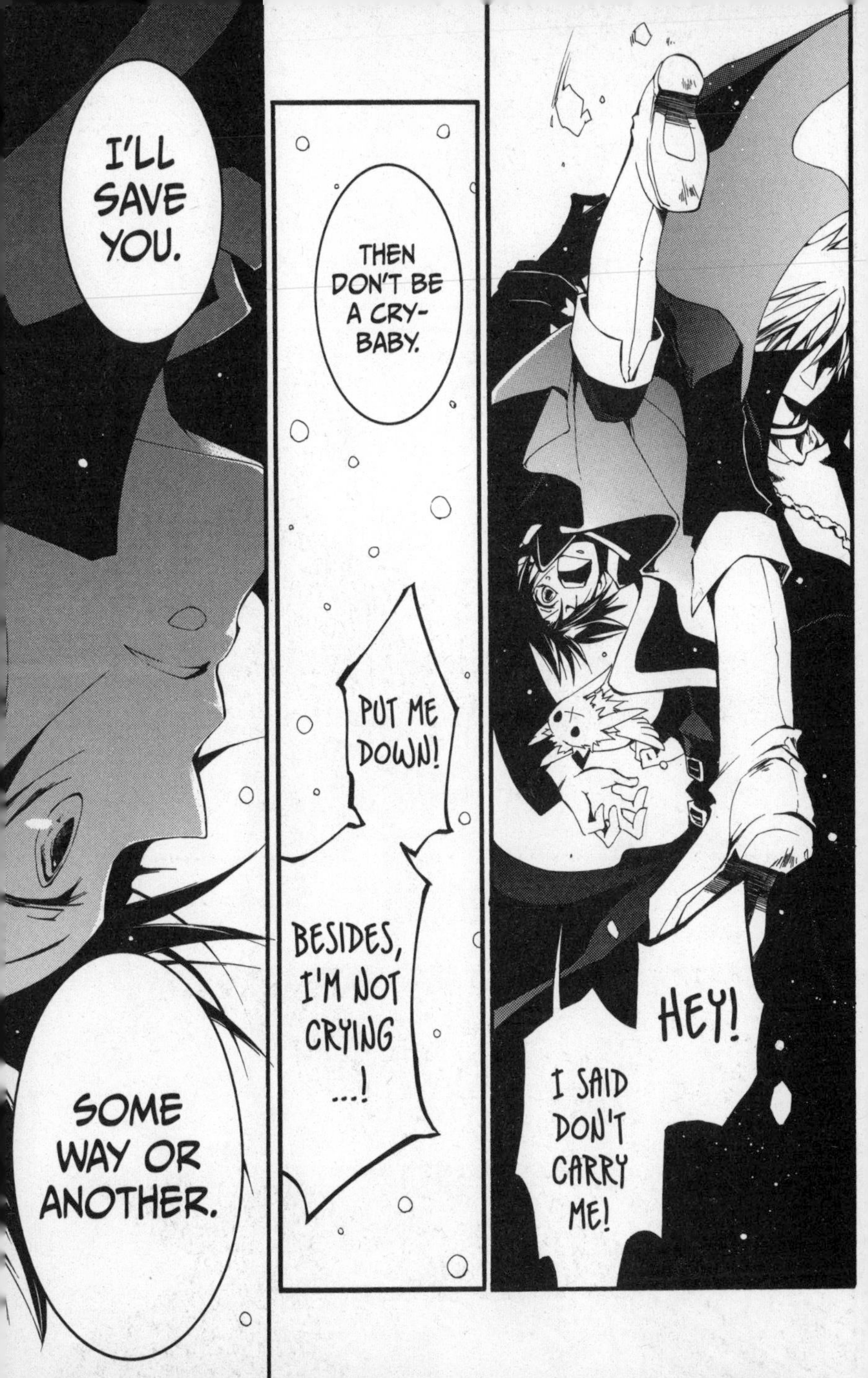
HEY!
I SAID DON'T CARRY ME!
THEN DON'T BE A CRY-BABY.
PUT ME DOWN!
BESIDES, I'M NOT CRYING ...!
I'LL SAVE YOU.
SOME WAY OR ANOTHER.

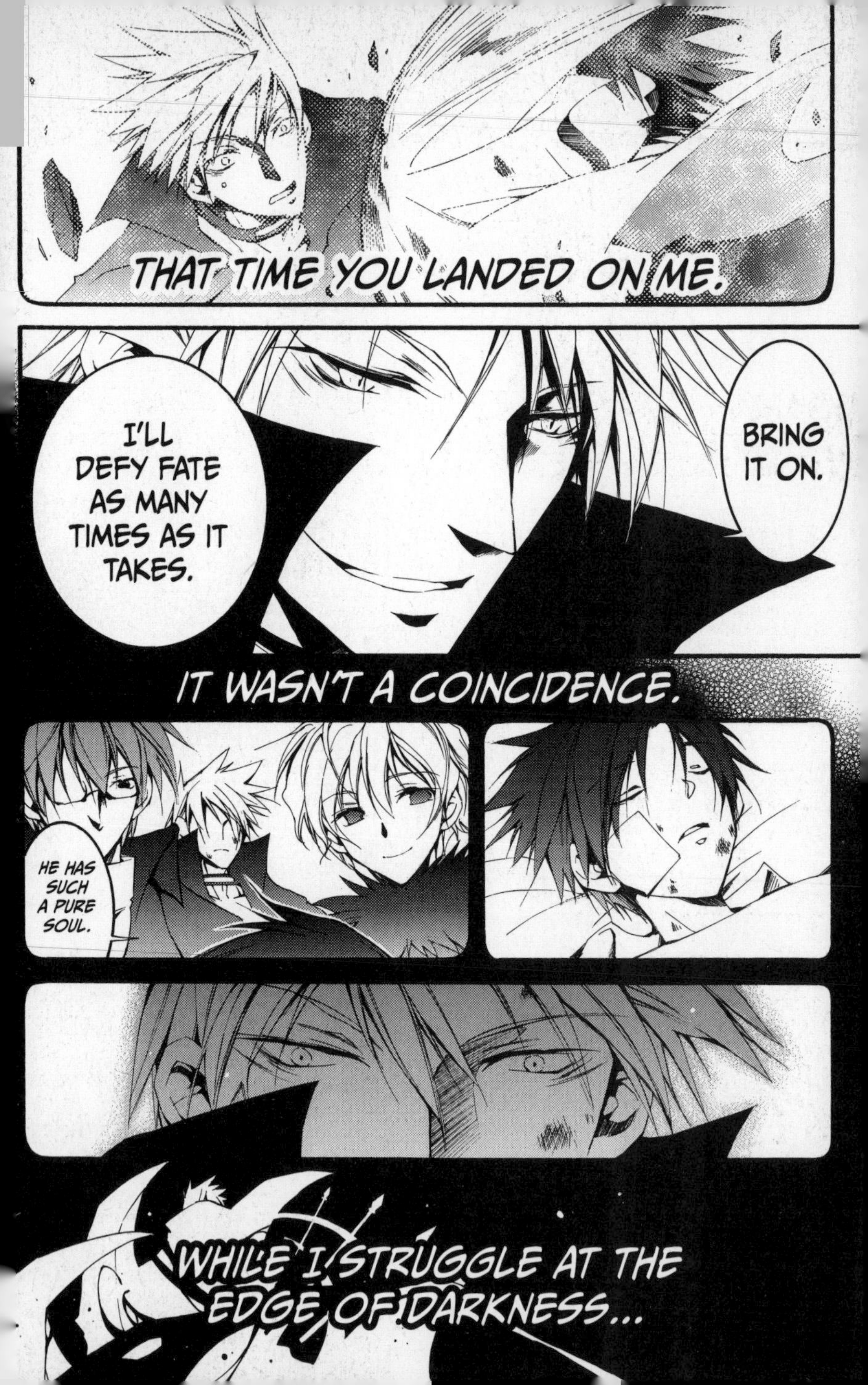
THAT TIME YOU LANDED ON ME.
BRING IT ON.
I'LL DEFY FATE AS MANY TIMES AS IT TAKES.
IT WASN'T A COINCIDENCE.
HE HAS SUCH A PURE SOUL.
WHILE I STRUGGLE AT THE EDGE OF DARKNESS...

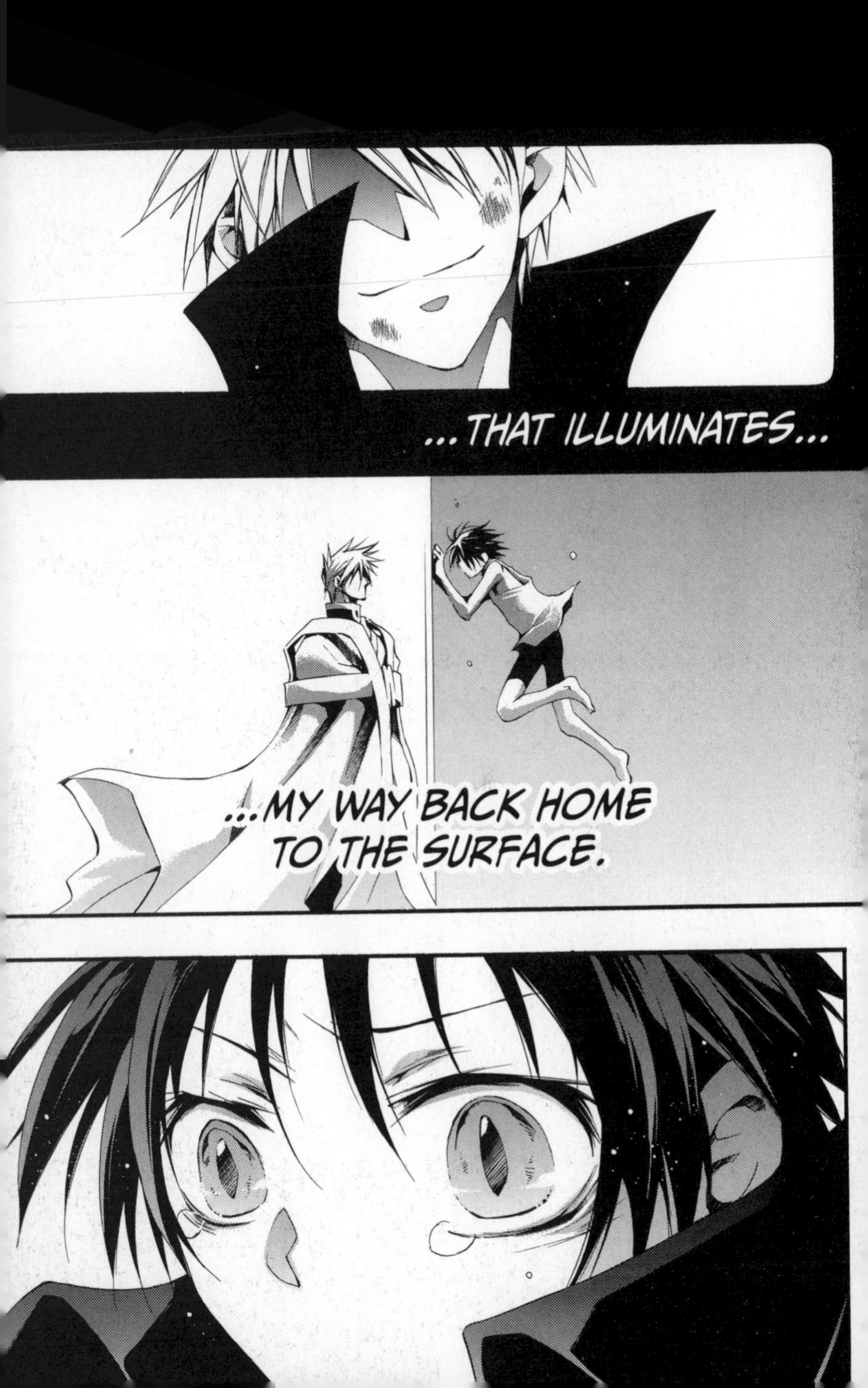
...THAT ILLUMINATES...
...MY WAY BACK HOME TO THE SURFACE.

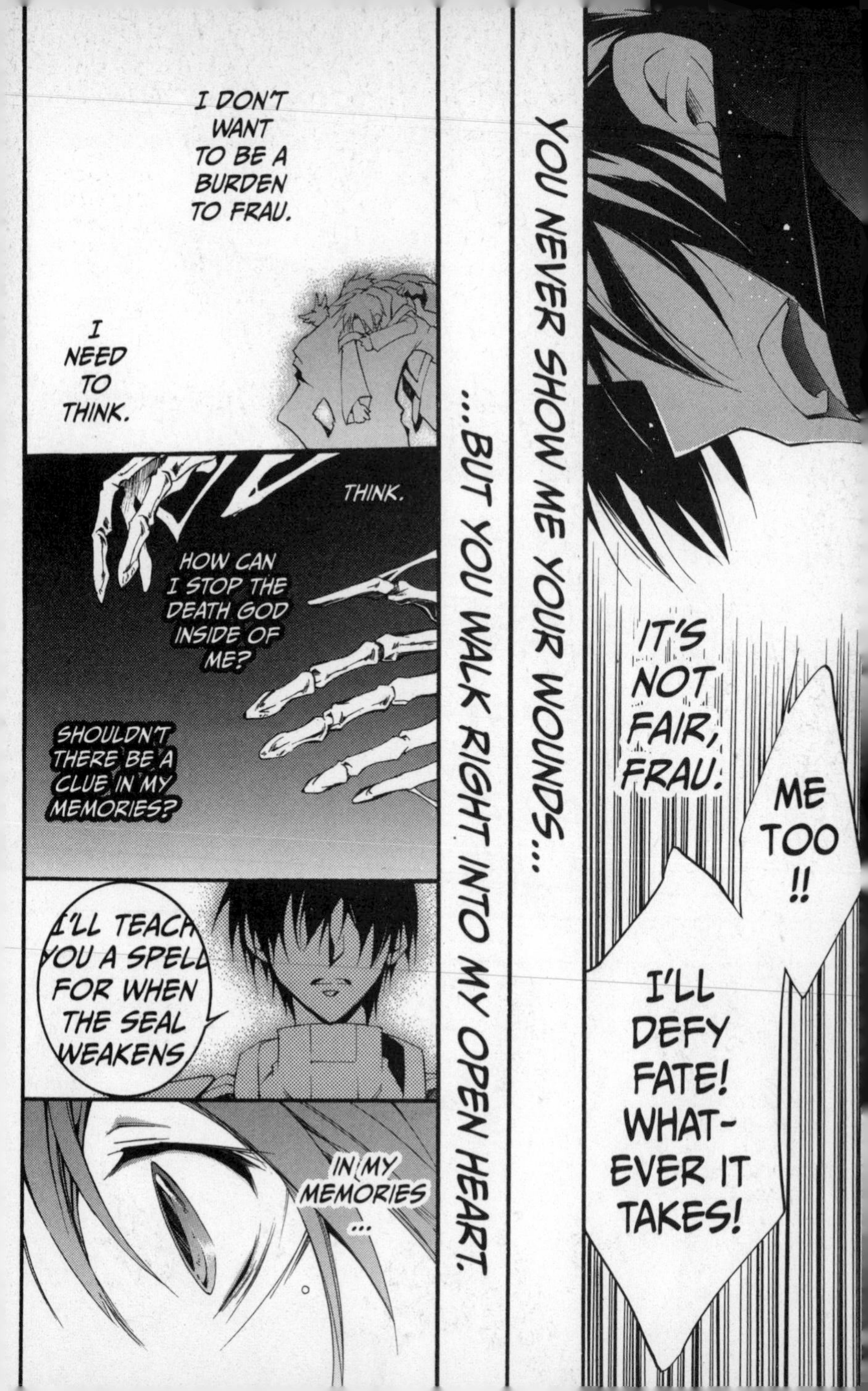
IT'S NOT FAIR, FRAU.
ME TOO!!
I'LL DEFY FATE! WHATEVER IT TAKES!
YOU NEVER SHOW ME YOUR WOUNDS...
...BUT YOU WALK RIGHT INTO MY OPEN HEART.
I DON'T WANT TO BE A BURDEN TO FRAU.
I NEED TO THINK.
THINK.
HOW CAN I STOP THE DEATH GOD INSIDE OF ME?
SHOULDN'T THERE BE A CLUE IN MY MEMORIES?
I'LL TEACH YOU A SPELL FOR WHEN THE SEAL WEAKENS
IN MY MEMORIES...

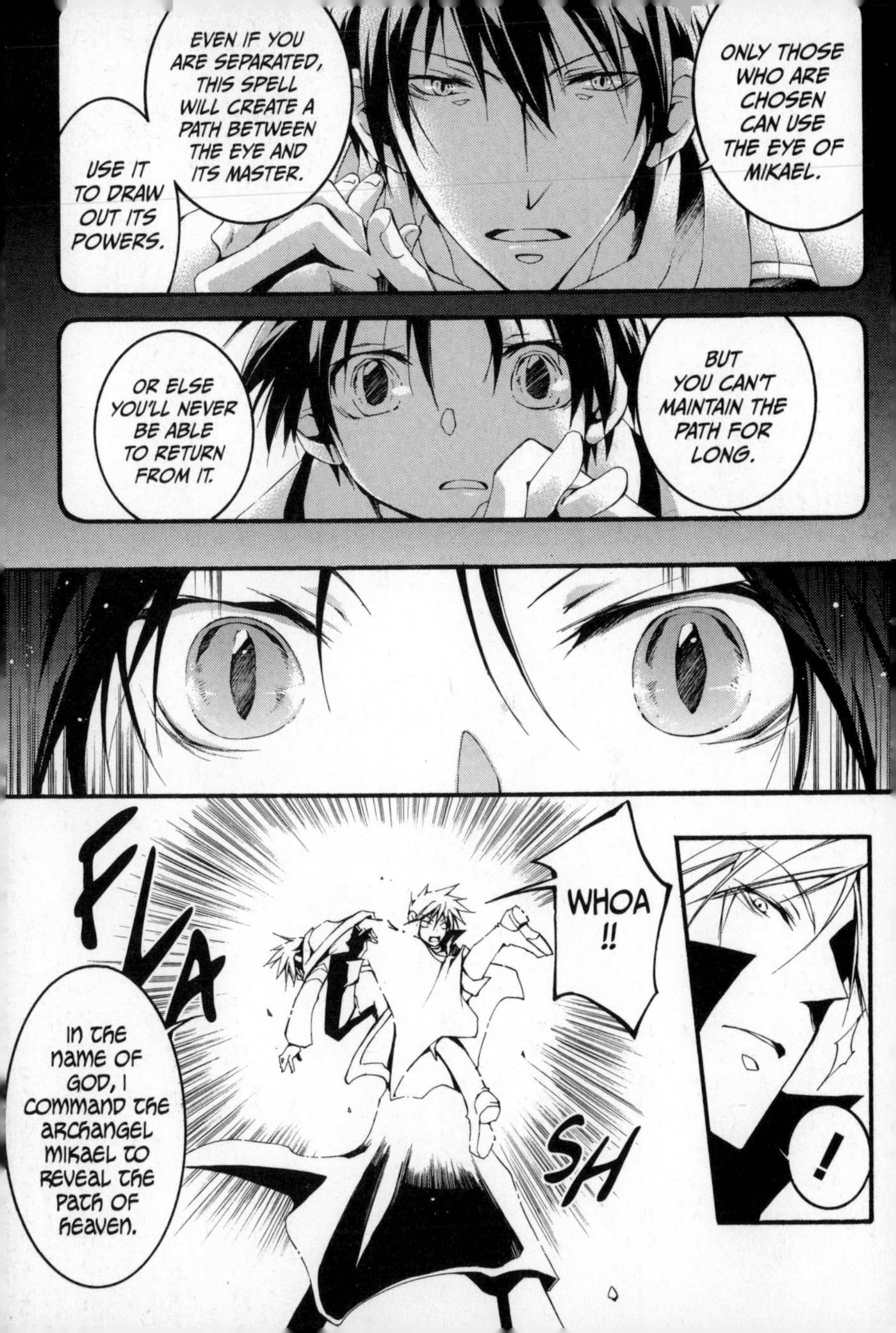
ONLY THOSE WHO ARE CHOSEN CAN USE THE EYE OF MIKAEL.
EVEN IF YOU ARE SEPARATED, THIS SPELL WILL CREATE A PATH BETWEEN THE EYE AND ITS MASTER.
USE IT TO DRAW OUT ITS POWERS.
BUT YOU CAN'T MAINTAIN THE PATH FOR LONG.
OR ELSE YOU'LL NEVER BE ABLE TO RETURN FROM IT.
!
WHOA !!
FLASH
IN THE NAME OF GOD, I COMMAND THE ARCHANGEL MIKAEL TO REVEAL THE PATH OF HEAVEN.

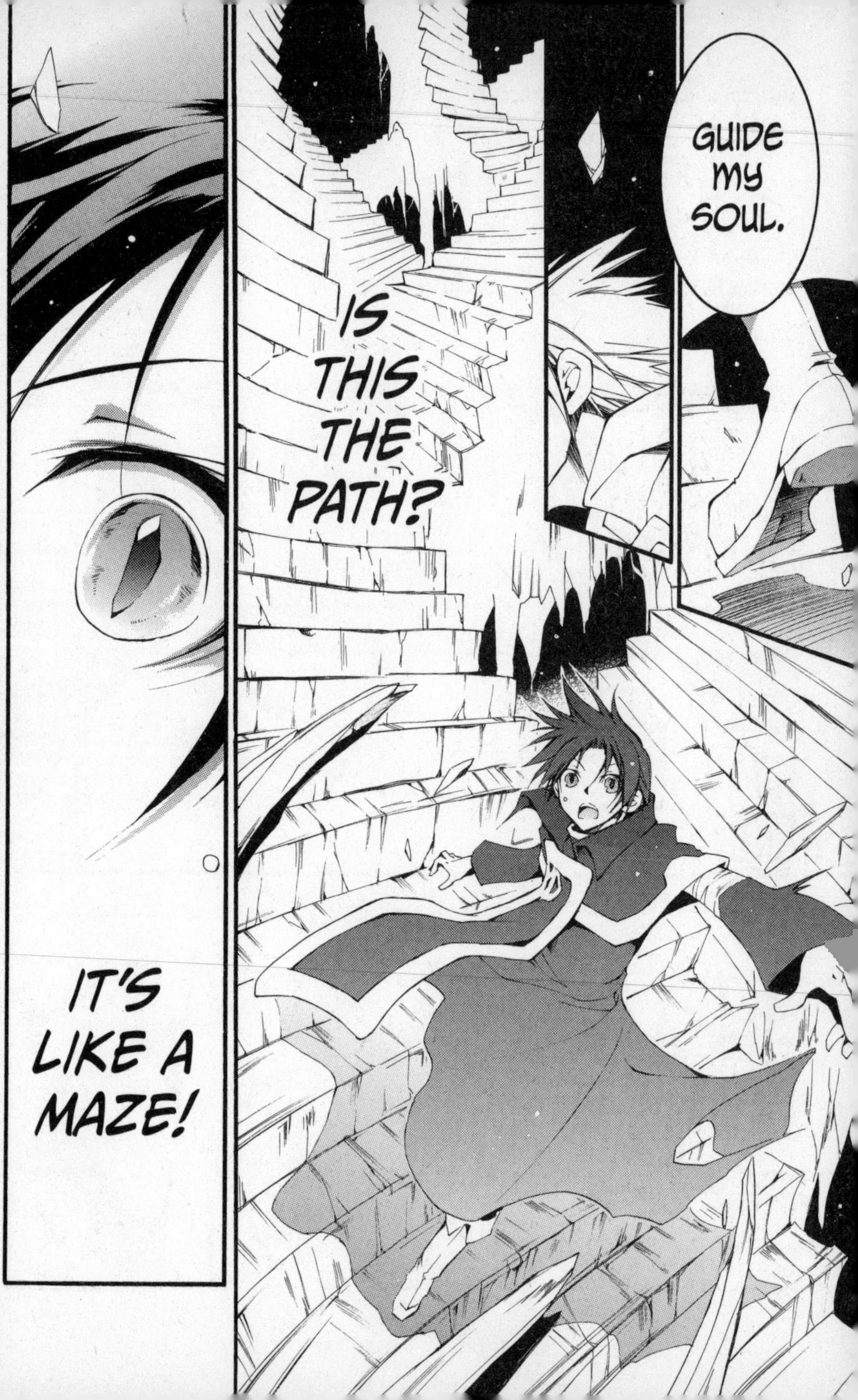
GUIDE MY SOUL.
IS THIS THE PATH?
IT'S LIKE A MAZE!

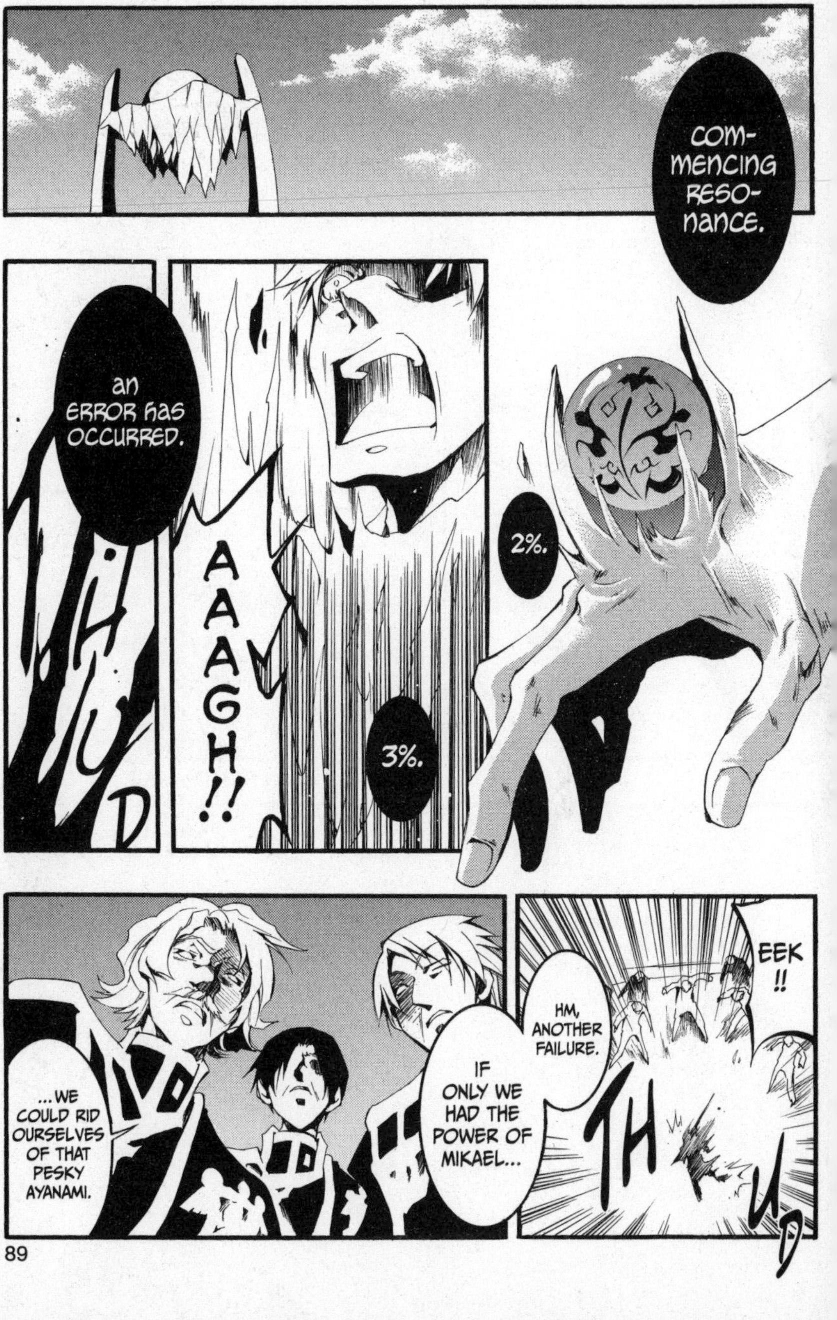
COMMENCING RESONANCE.
2%.
3%.
AAAGH!!
an ERROR has OCCURRED.
THUD
EEK!!
THUD
HM, ANOTHER FAILURE.
IF ONLY WE HAD THE POWER OF MIKAEL...
...WE COULD RID OURSELVES OF THAT PESKY AYANAMI.

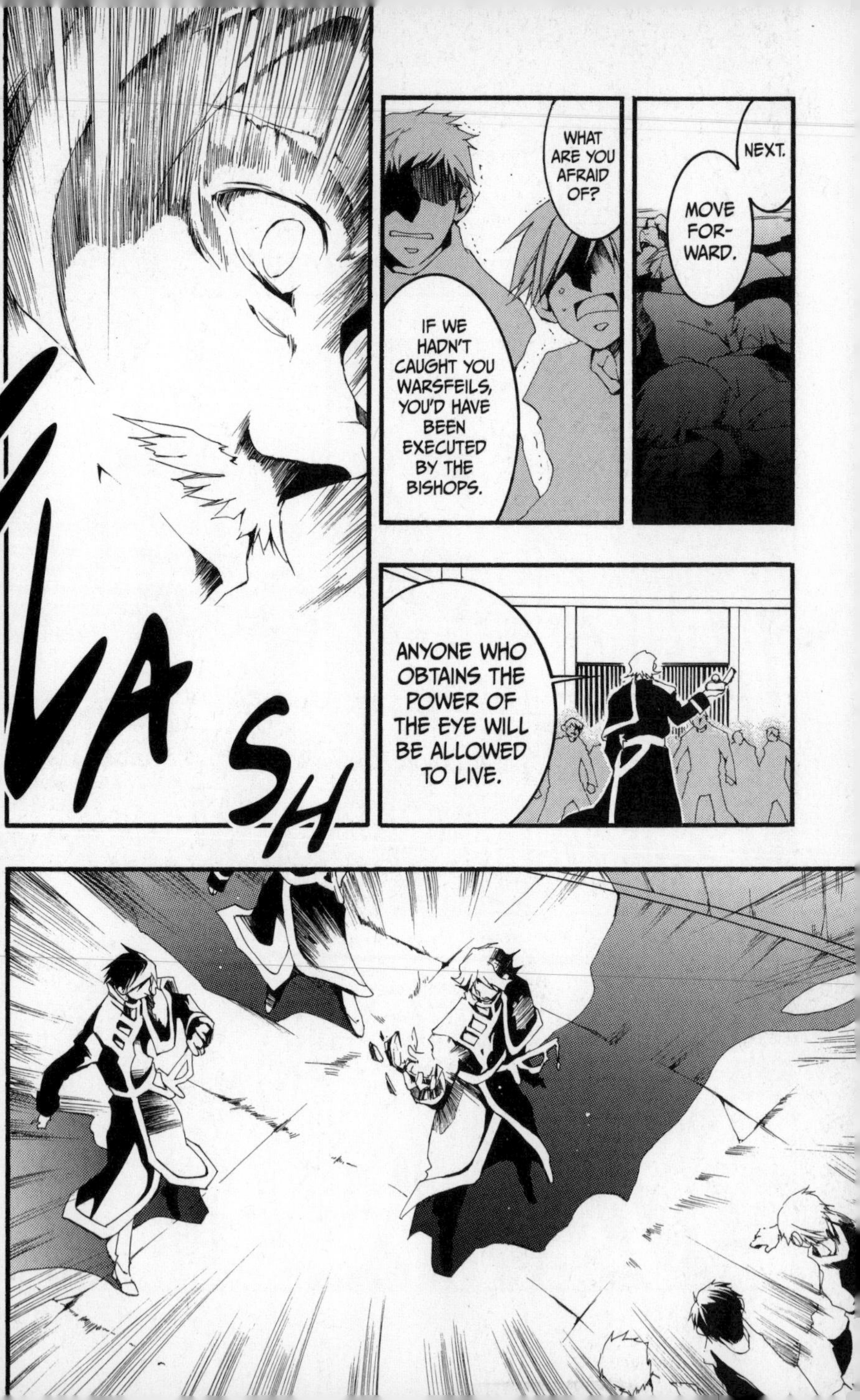
NEXT.
MOVE FOR-WARD.
WHAT ARE YOU AFRAID OF?
IF WE HADN'T CAUGHT YOU WARSFEILS, YOU'D HAVE BEEN EXECUTED BY THE BISHOPS.
ANYONE WHO OBTAINS THE POWER OF THE EYE WILL BE ALLOWED TO LIVE.

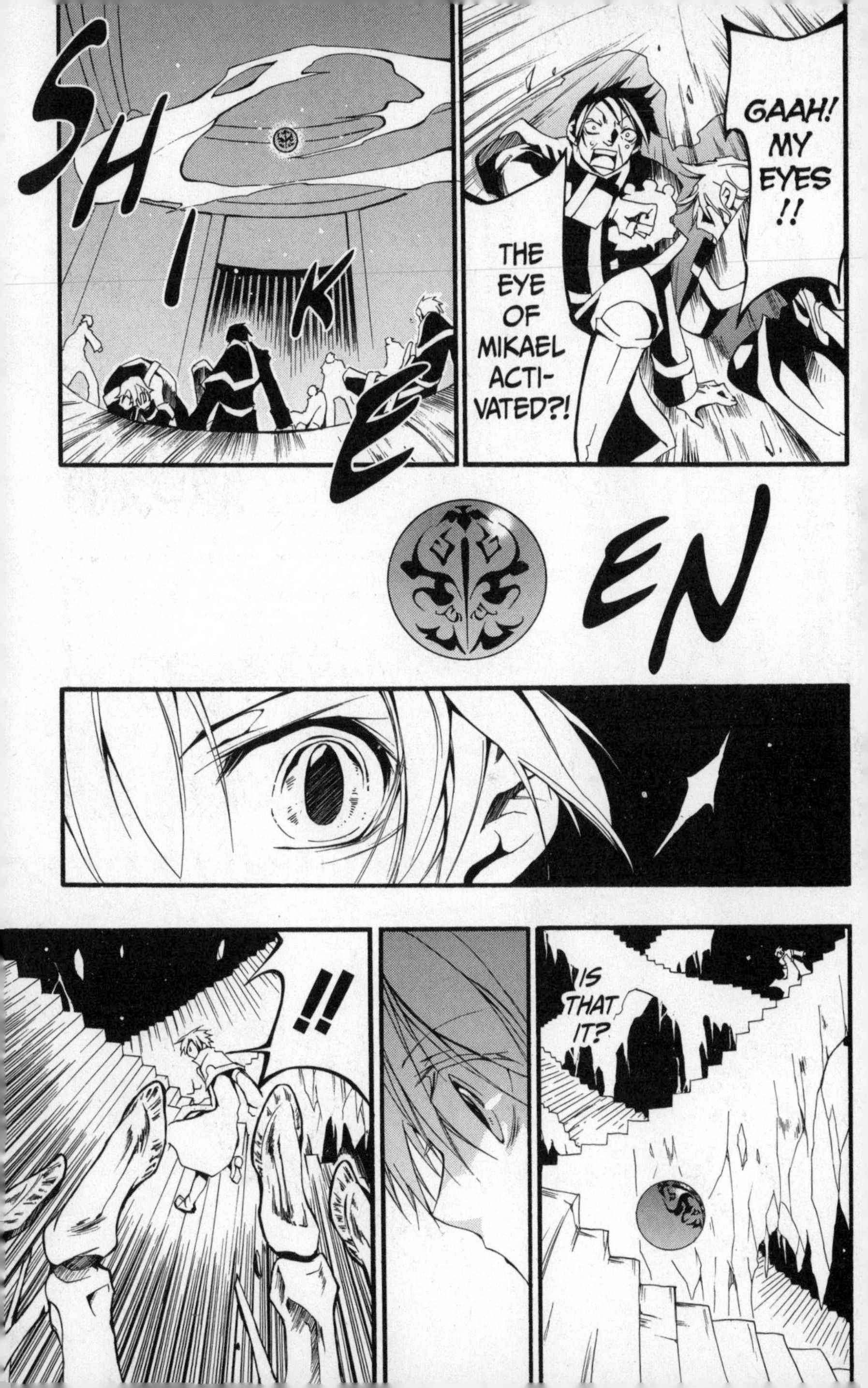
GAAH! MY EYES!!
THE EYE OF MIKAEL ACTI-VATED?!
SHIKEEN
IS THAT IT?
!!

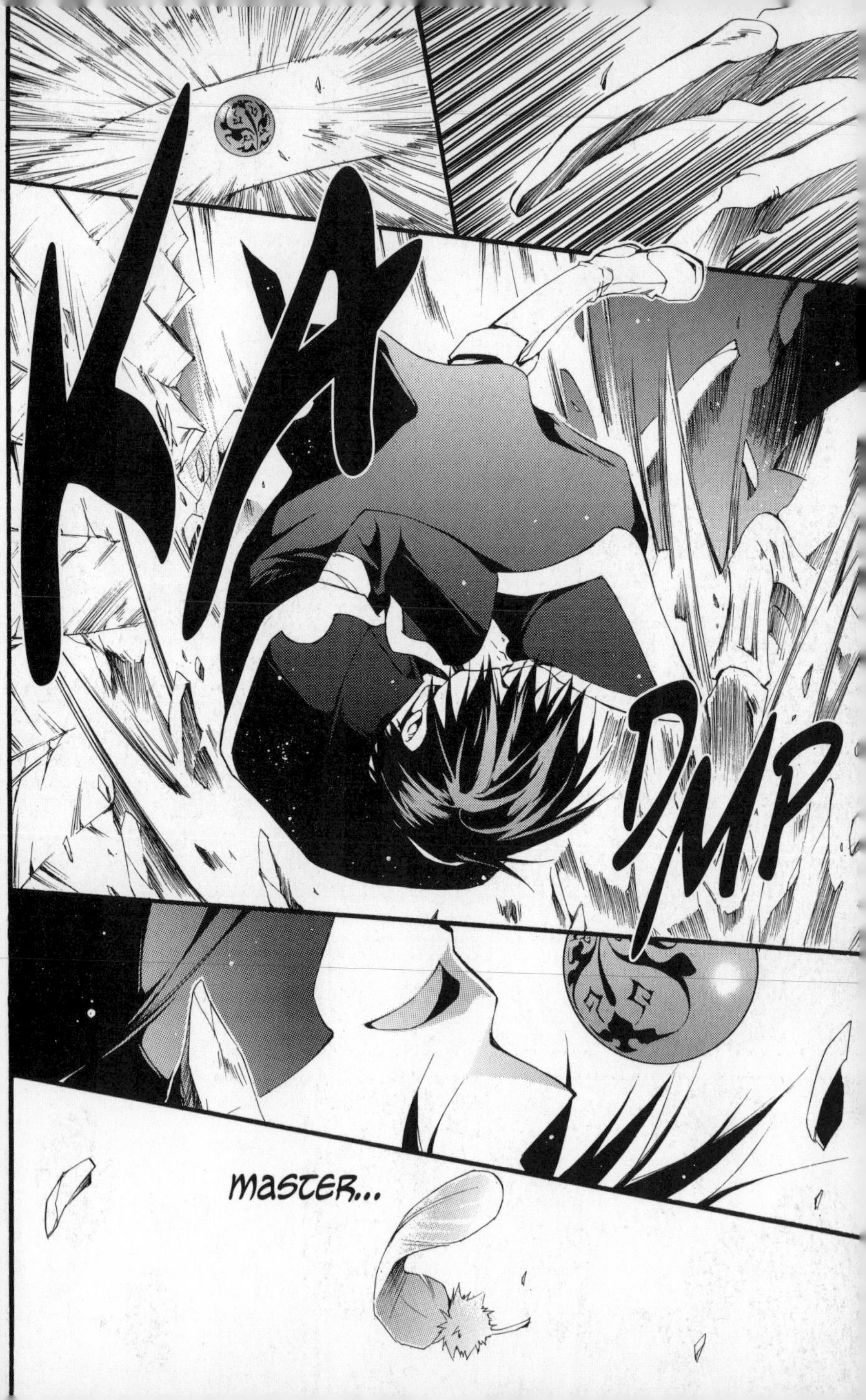
KA
DMP
MASTER...

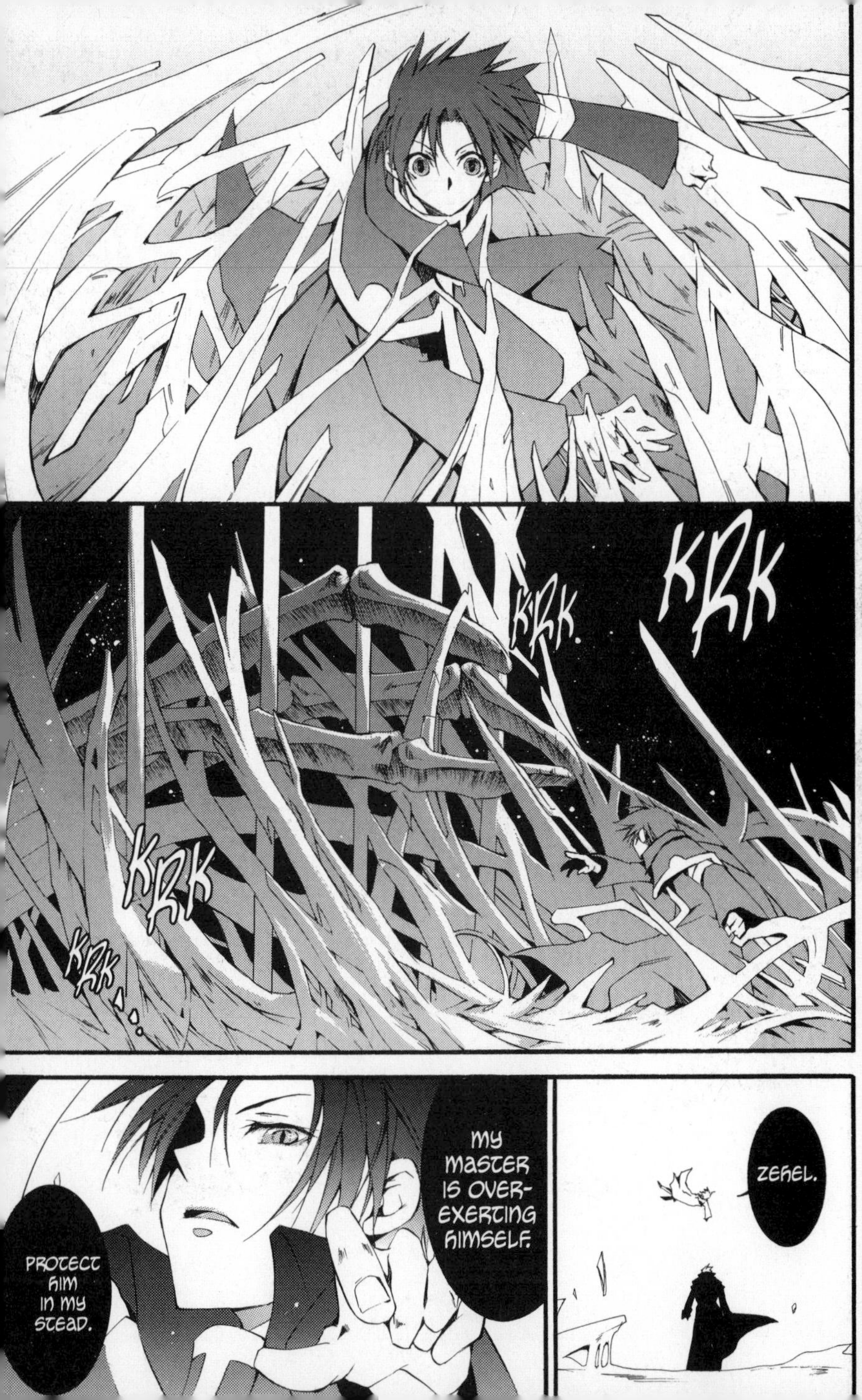
KRK
KRK.
KRK
KRK...
ZEHEL.
MY MASTER IS OVER-EXERTING HIMSELF.
PROTECT HIM IN MY STEAD.

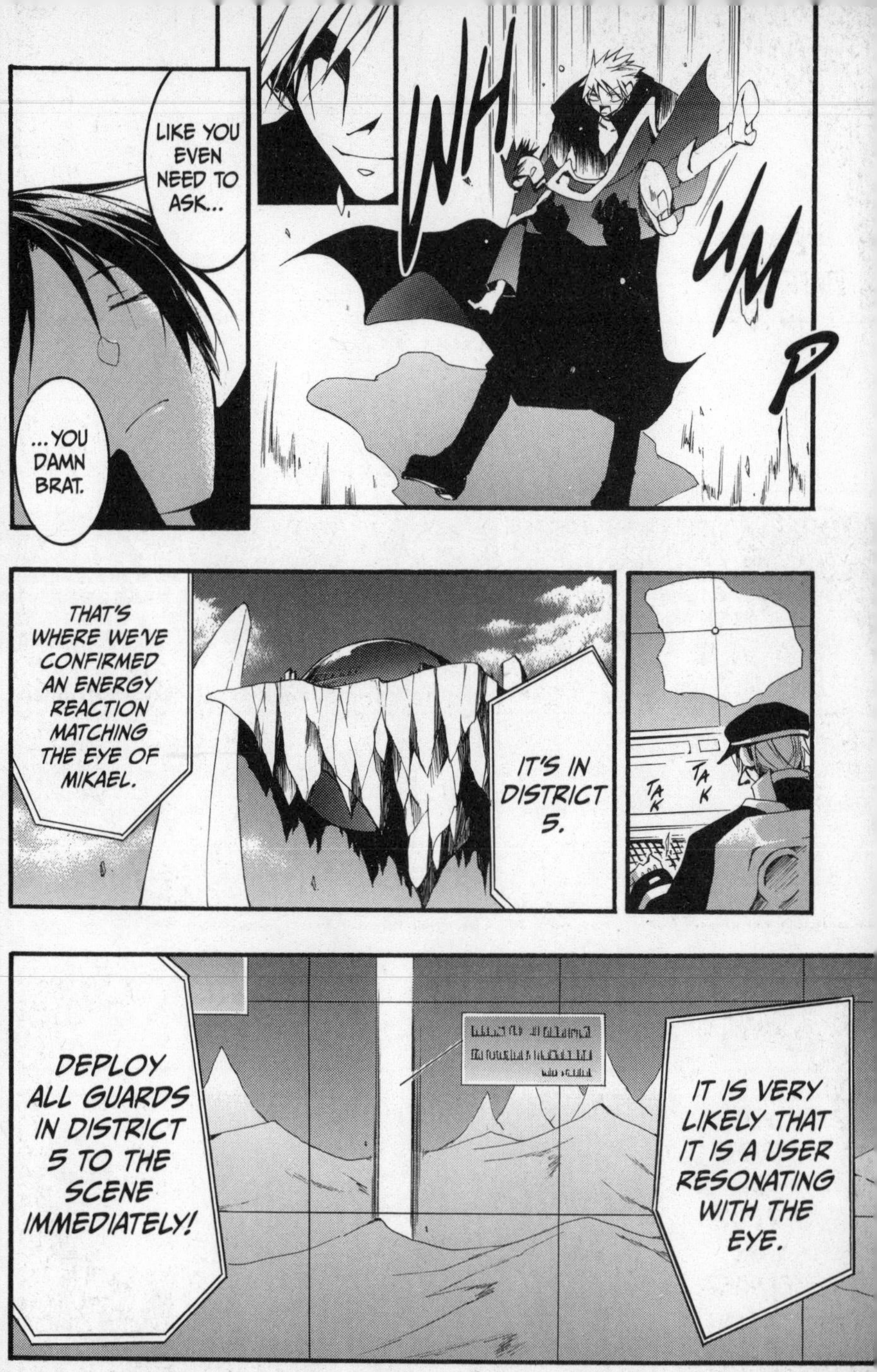
WHUMP
LIKE YOU EVEN NEED TO ASK...
...YOU DAMN BRAT.
TAK TAK
IT'S IN DISTRICT 5.
THAT'S WHERE WE'VE CONFIRMED AN ENERGY REACTION MATCHING THE EYE OF MIKAEL.
IT IS VERY LIKELY THAT IT IS A USER RESONATING WITH THE EYE.
DEPLOY ALL GUARDS IN DISTRICT 5 TO THE SCENE IMMEDIATELY!

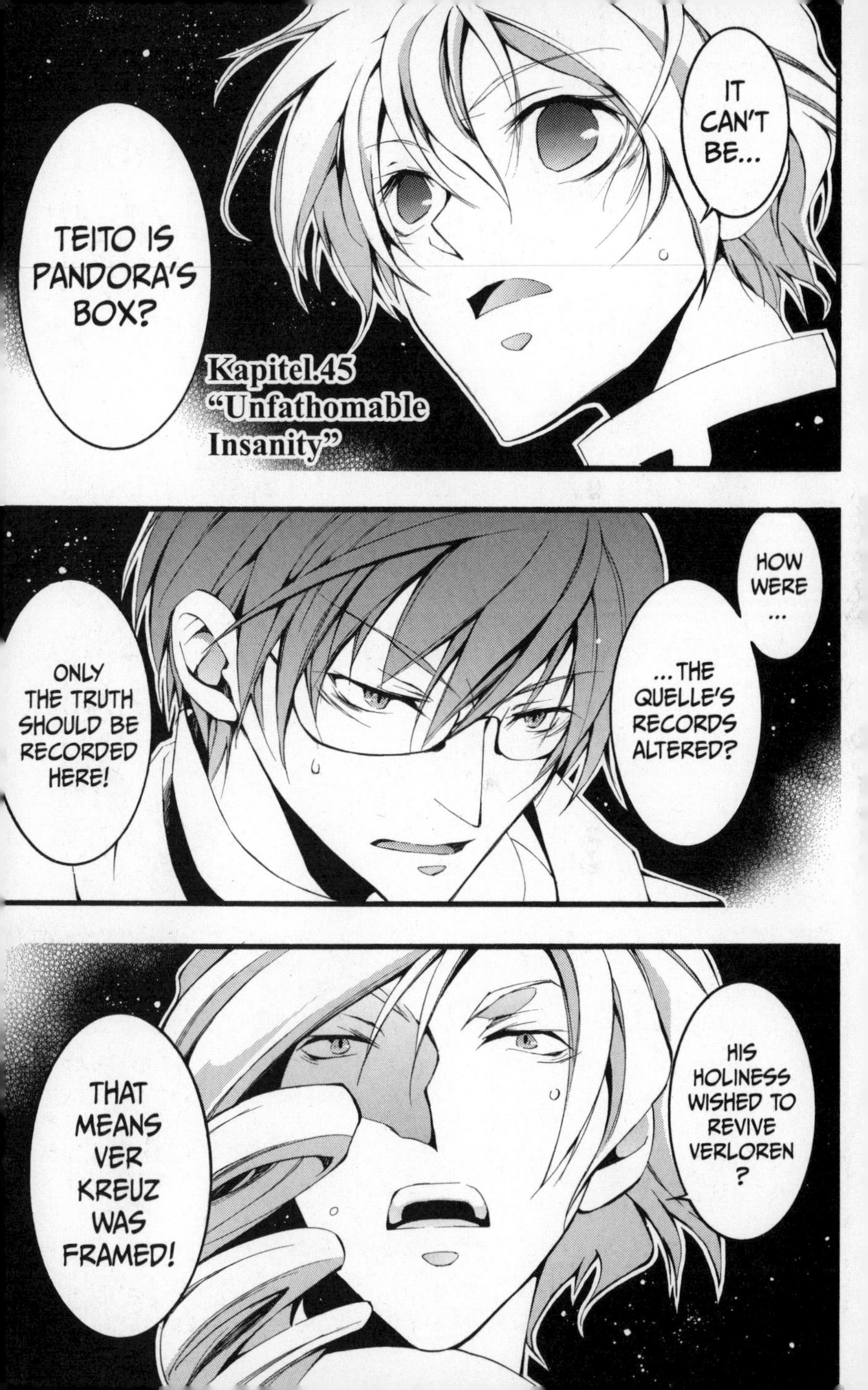
IT CAN'T BE...
TEITO IS PANDORA'S BOX?
Kapitel.45 "Unfathomable Insanity"
HOW WERE ...
...THE QUELLE'S RECORDS ALTERED?
ONLY THE TRUTH SHOULD BE RECORDED HERE!
HIS HOLINESS WISHED TO REVIVE VERLOREN ?
THAT MEANS VER KREUZ WAS FRAMED!

Kapitel.45
"Unfathomable Insanity"

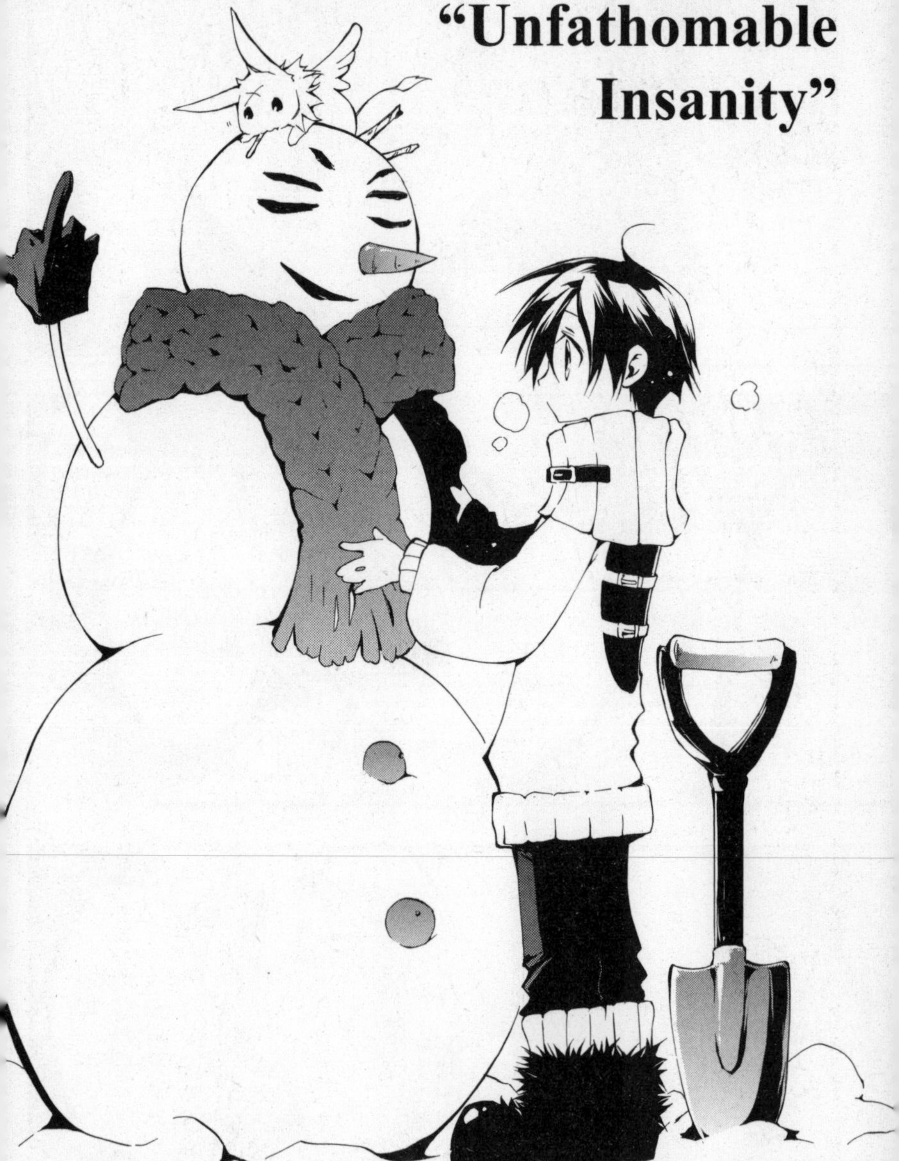

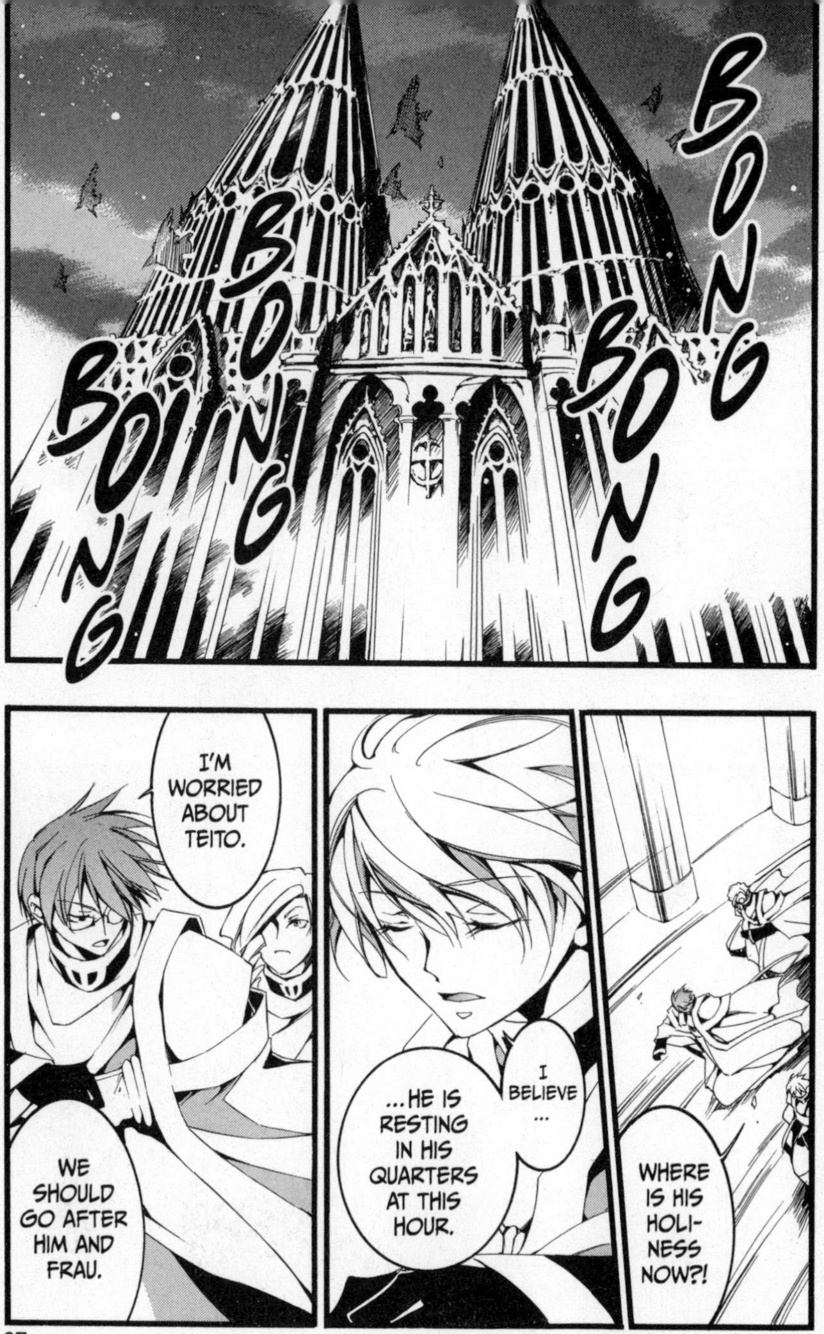
BONG
BONG
BONG
BONG
WHERE IS HIS HOLI-NESS NOW?!
I BELIEVE ...
...HE IS RESTING IN HIS QUARTERS AT THIS HOUR.
I'M WORRIED ABOUT TEITO.
WE SHOULD GO AFTER HIM AND FRAU.

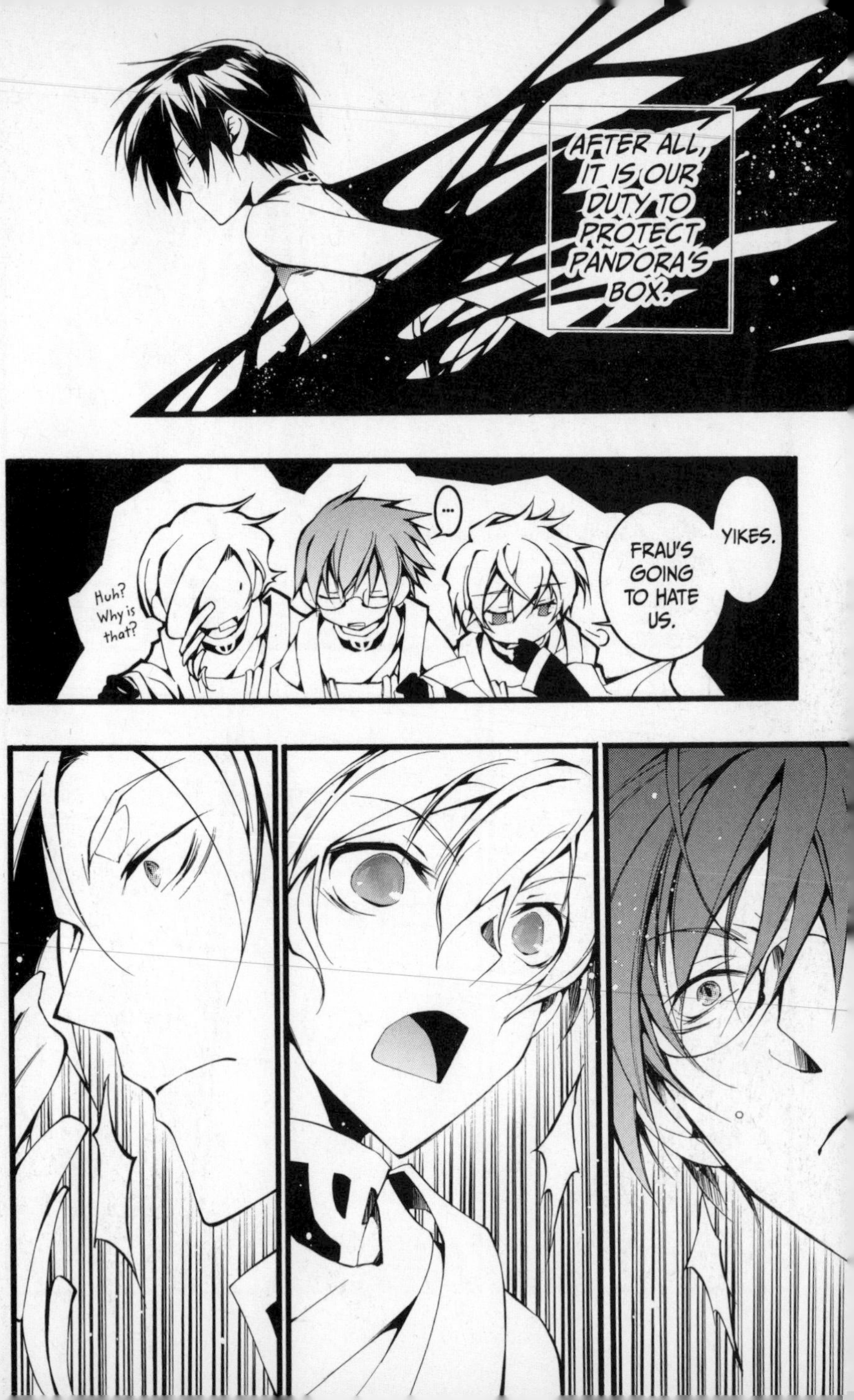
AFTER ALL, IT IS OUR DUTY TO PROTECT PANDORA'S BOX.
YIKES.
FRAU'S GOING TO HATE US.
...
Huh? Why is that?

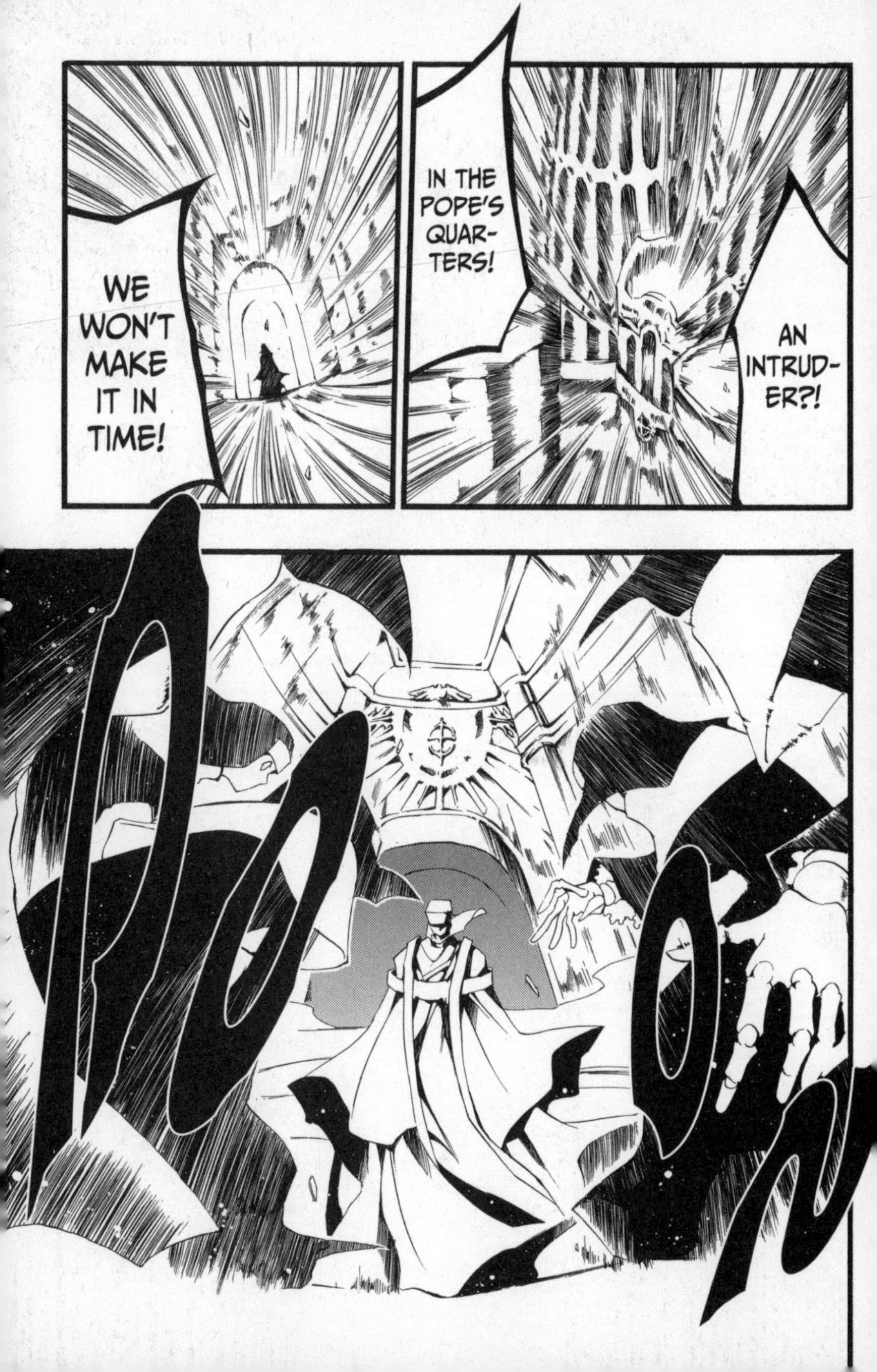
AN INTRUDER?!
IN THE POPE'S QUARTERS!
WE WON'T MAKE IT IN TIME!

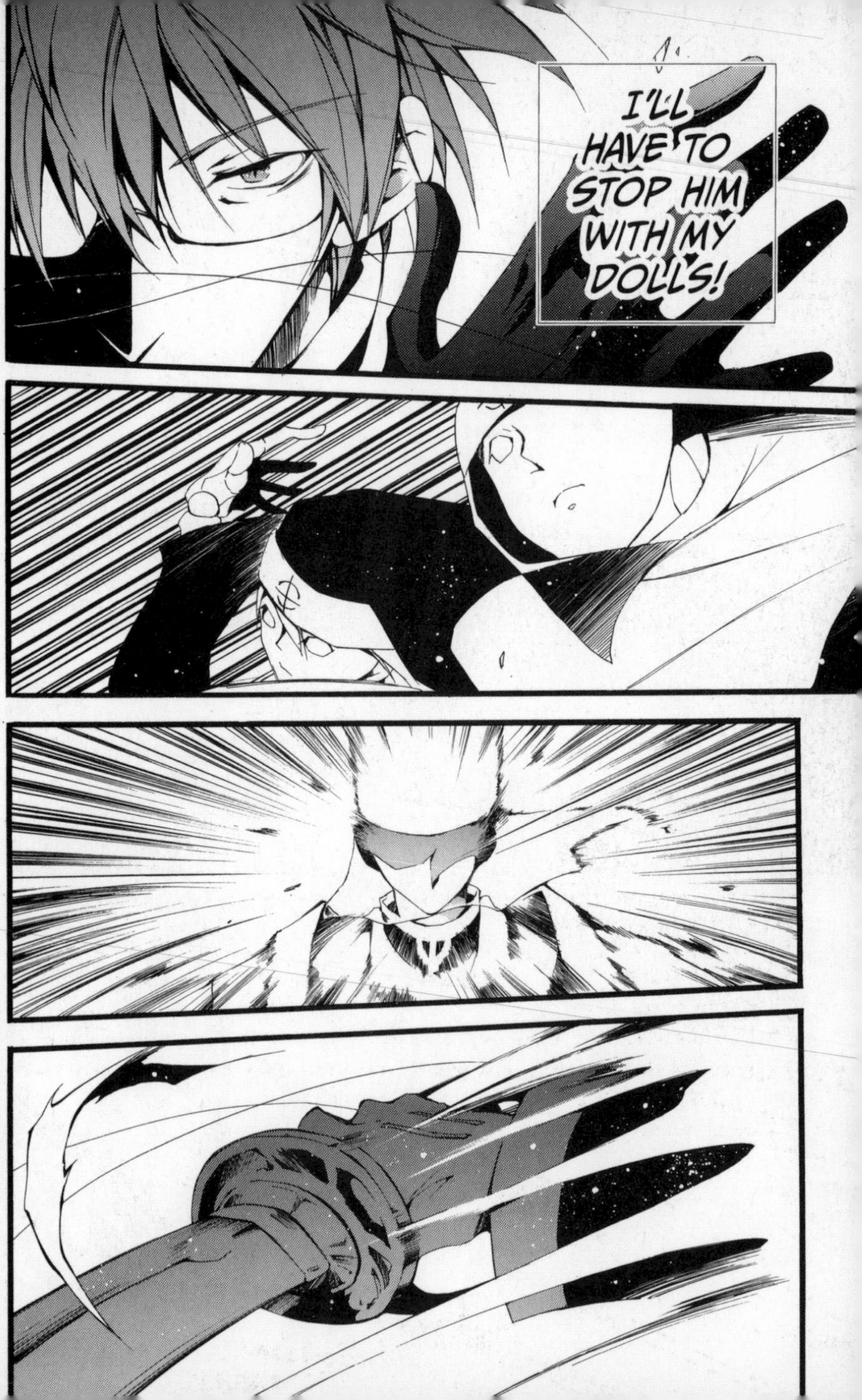
I'LL HAVE TO STOP HIM WITH MY DOLLS!

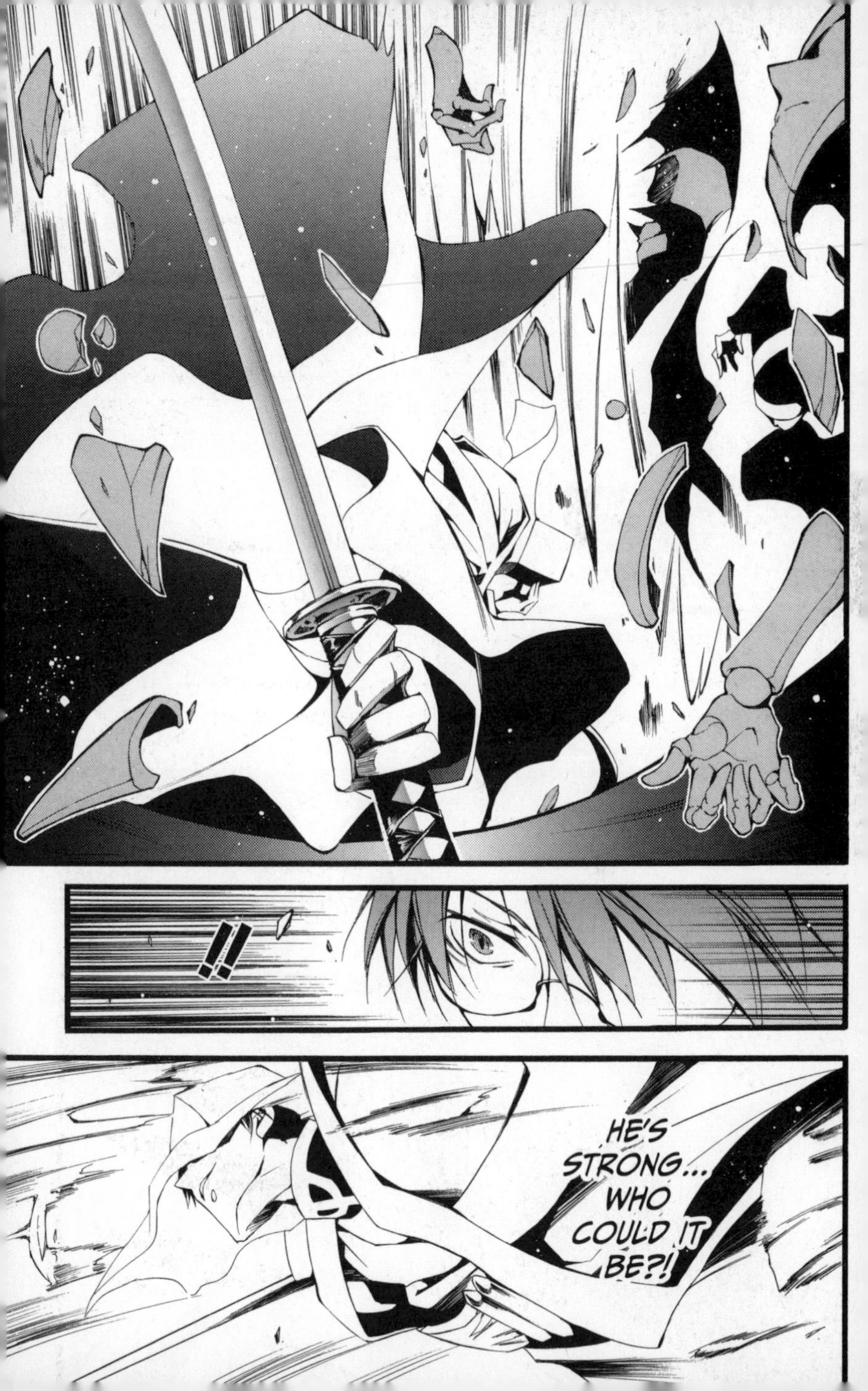
!!
HE'S STRONG... WHO COULD IT BE?!

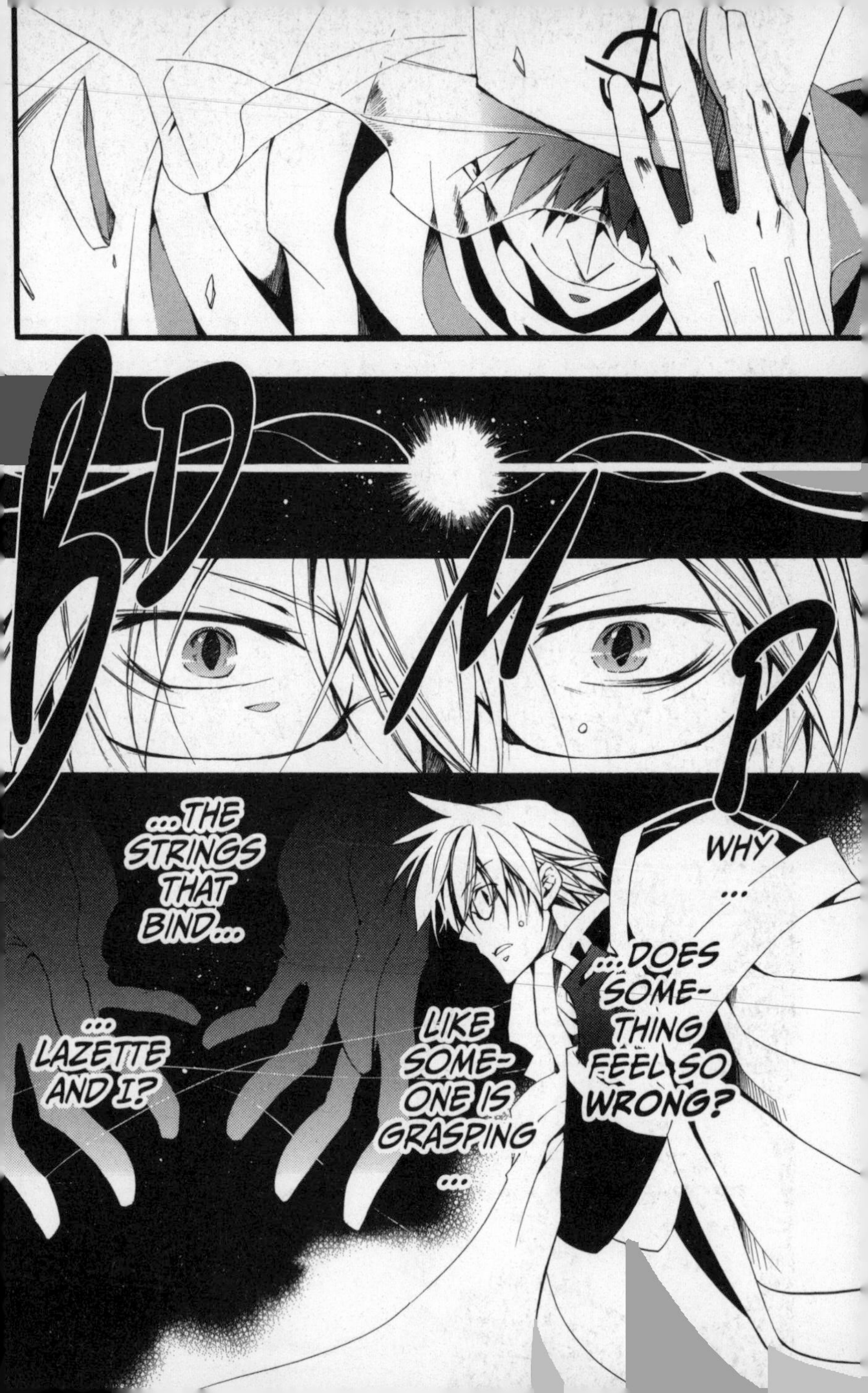
BDMP
WHY...
...DOES SOMETHING FEEL SO WRONG?
LIKE SOMEONE IS GRASPING...
...THE STRINGS THAT BIND...
...LAZETTE AND I?

FEST
...

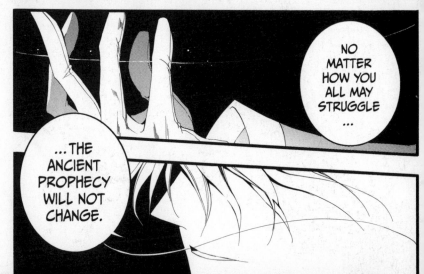

NO MATTER HOW YOU ALL MAY STRUGGLE
...

...THE ANCIENT PROPHECY WILL NOT CHANGE.

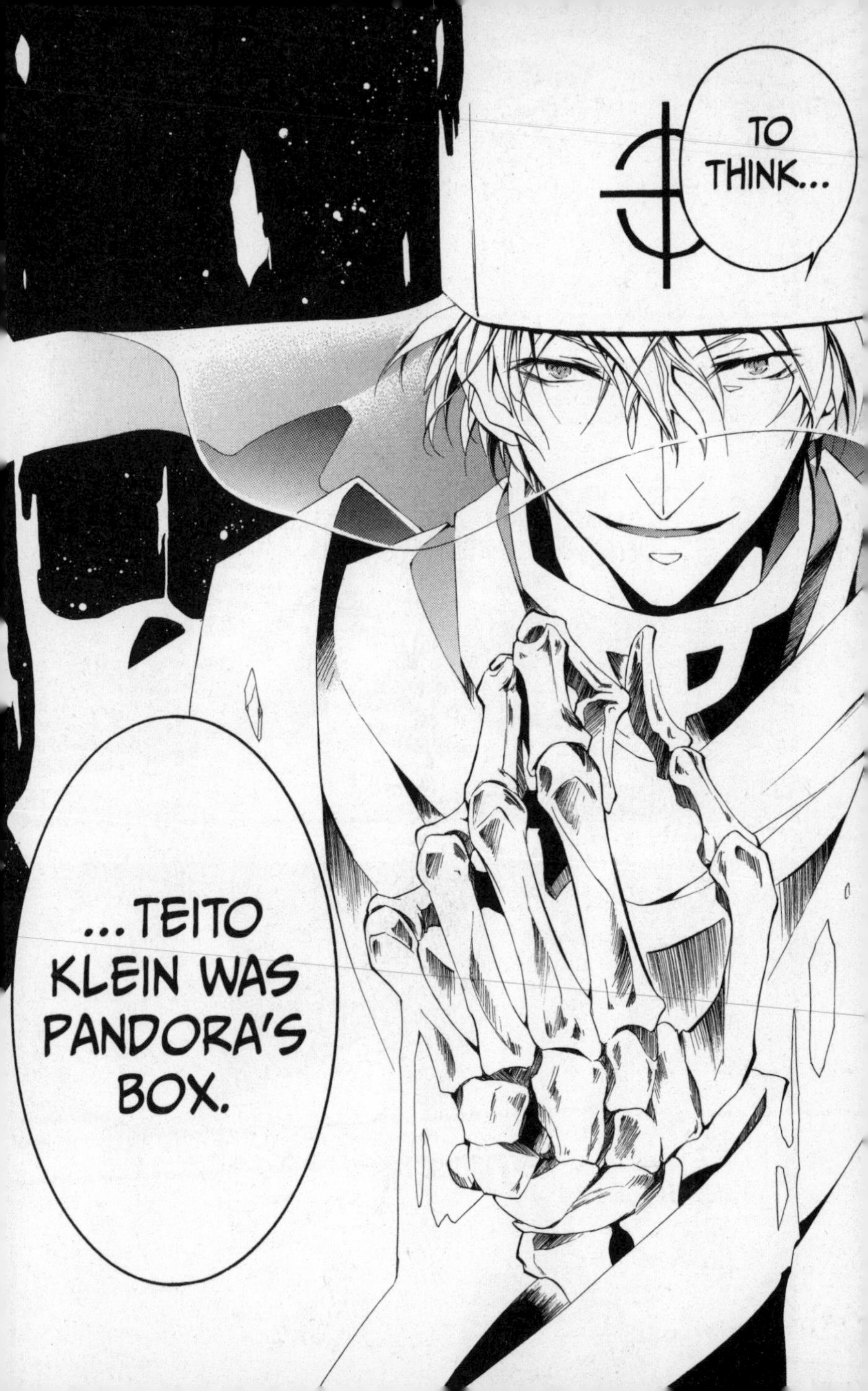
TO THINK...
...TEITO KLEIN WAS PANDORA'S BOX.

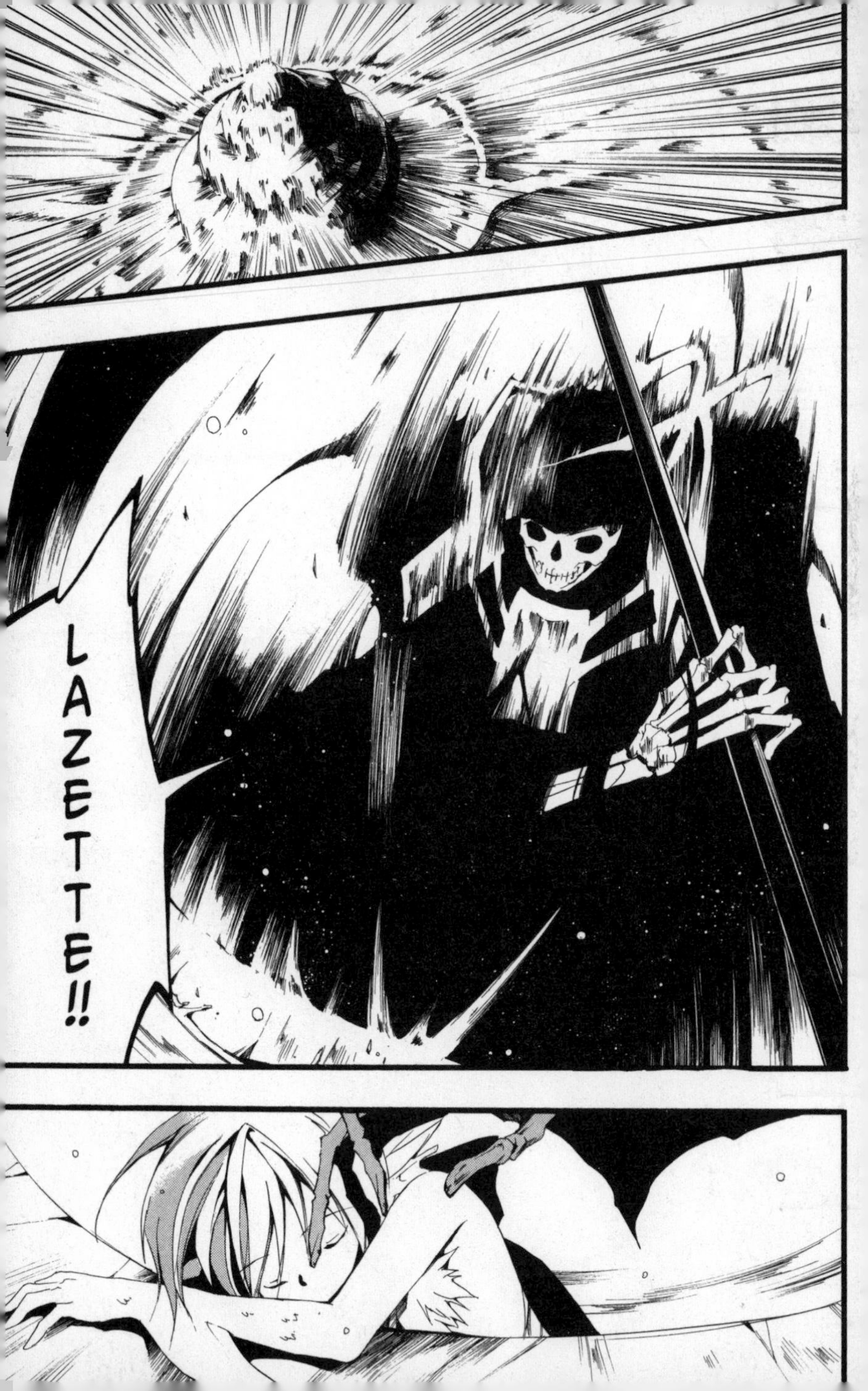
LAZETTE!!

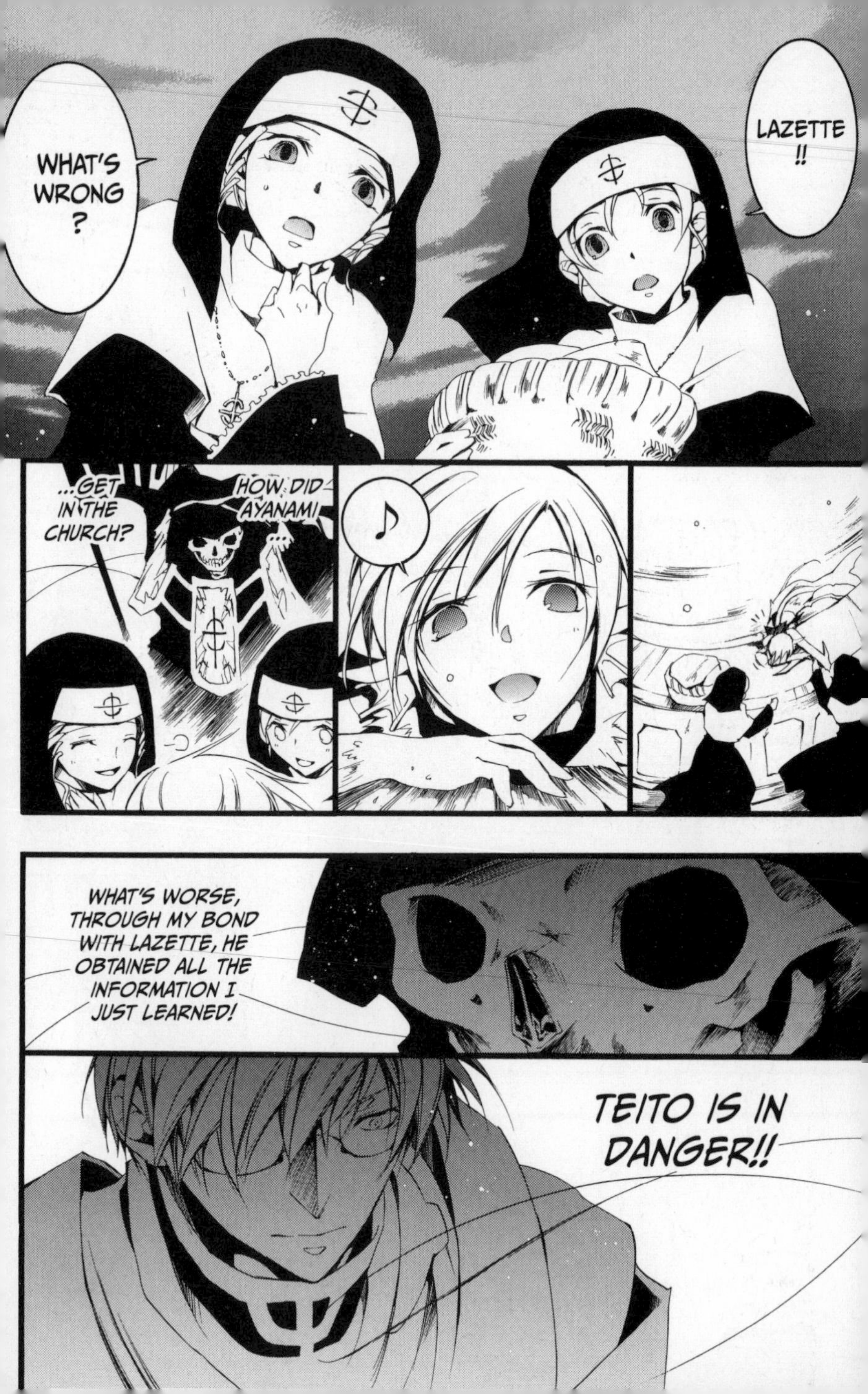
LAZETTE !!
WHAT'S WRONG ?
♪
HOW DID AYANAMI
...GET IN THE CHURCH?
WHAT'S WORSE, THROUGH MY BOND WITH LAZETTE, HE OBTAINED ALL THE INFORMATION I JUST LEARNED!
TEITO IS IN DANGER!!

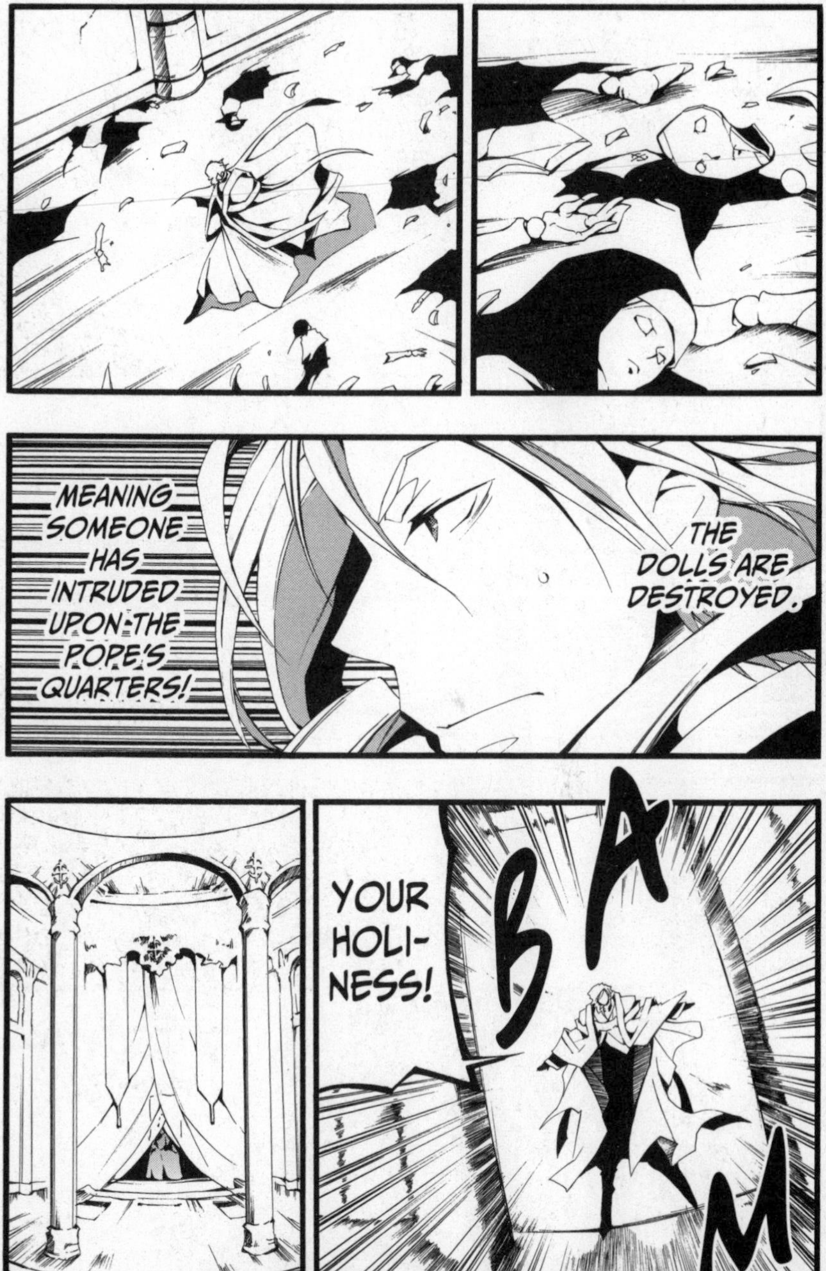
THE DOLLS ARE DESTROYED.
MEANING SOMEONE HAS INTRUDED UPON THE POPE'S QUARTERS!
BAM
YOUR HOLINESS!

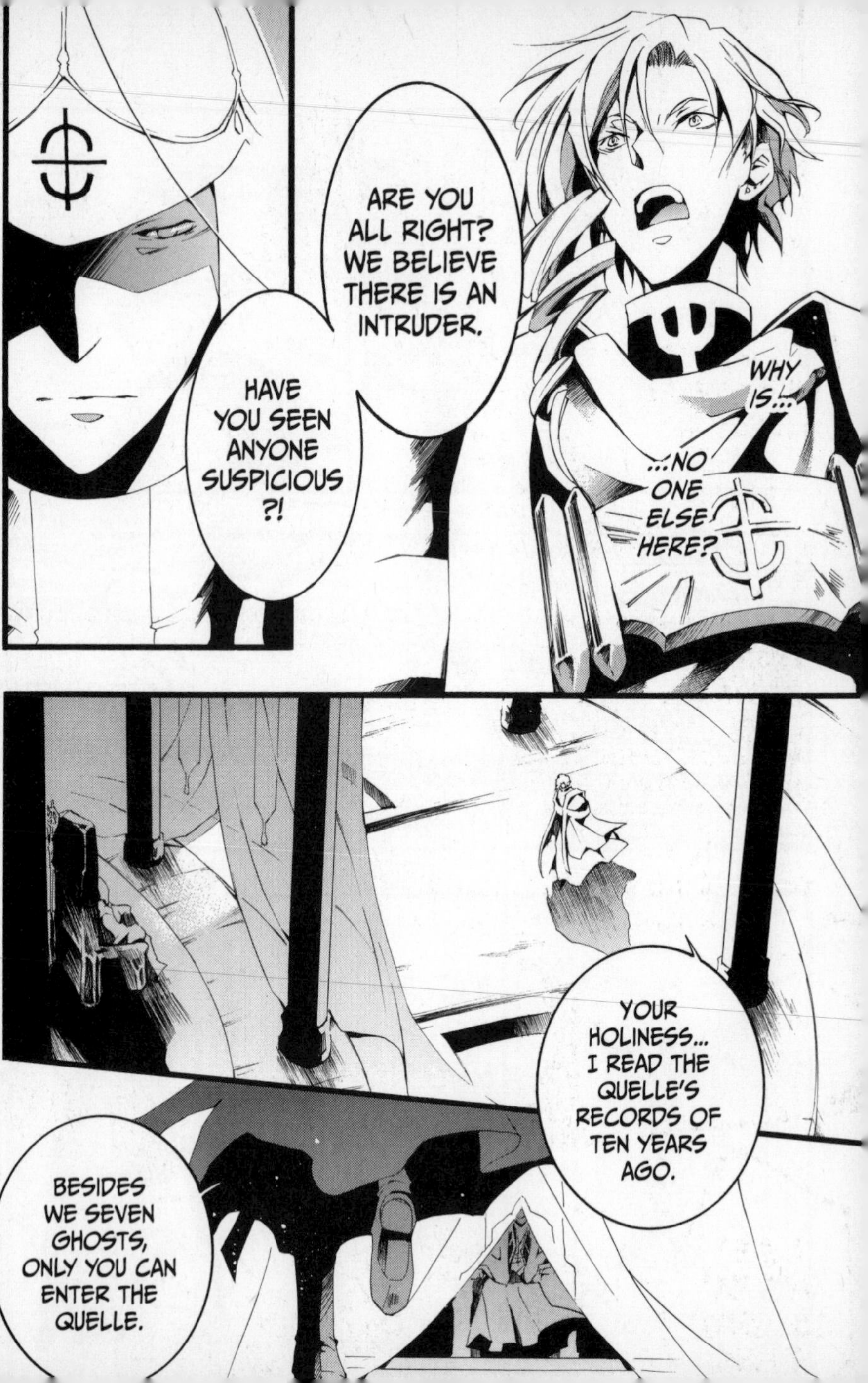
WHY IS...
...NO ONE ELSE HERE?
ARE YOU ALL RIGHT? WE BELIEVE THERE IS AN INTRUDER.
HAVE YOU SEEN ANYONE SUSPICIOUS ?!
YOUR HOLINESS... I READ THE QUELLE'S RECORDS OF TEN YEARS AGO.
BESIDES WE SEVEN GHOSTS, ONLY YOU CAN ENTER THE QUELLE.

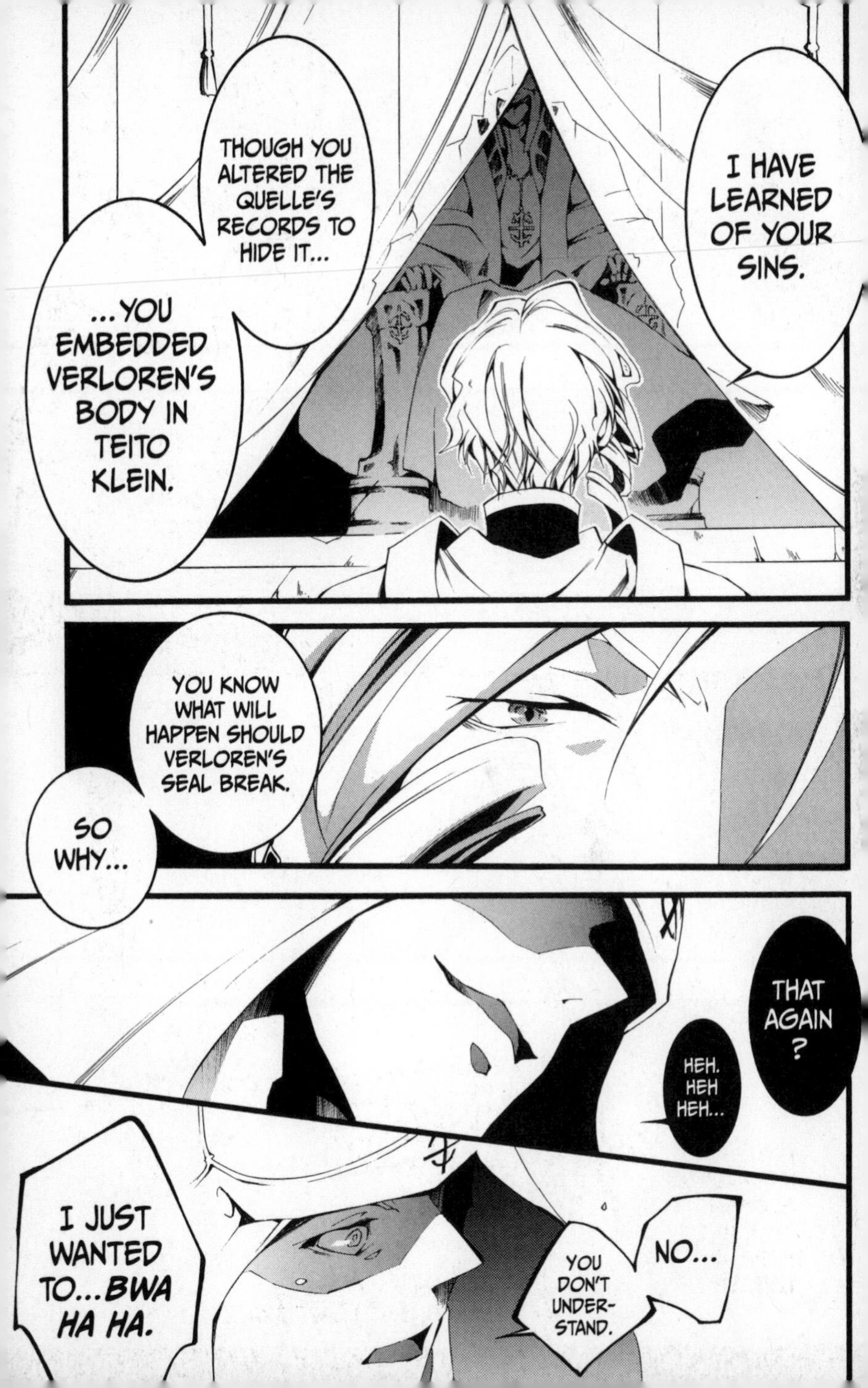
I HAVE LEARNED OF YOUR SINS.
THOUGH YOU ALTERED THE QUELLE'S RECORDS TO HIDE IT...
...YOU EMBEDDED VERLOREN'S BODY IN TEITO KLEIN.
YOU KNOW WHAT WILL HAPPEN SHOULD VERLOREN'S SEAL BREAK.
SO WHY...
THAT AGAIN?
HEH. HEH HEH...
NO...
YOU DON'T UNDER-STAND.
I JUST WANTED TO...*BWA HA HA.*

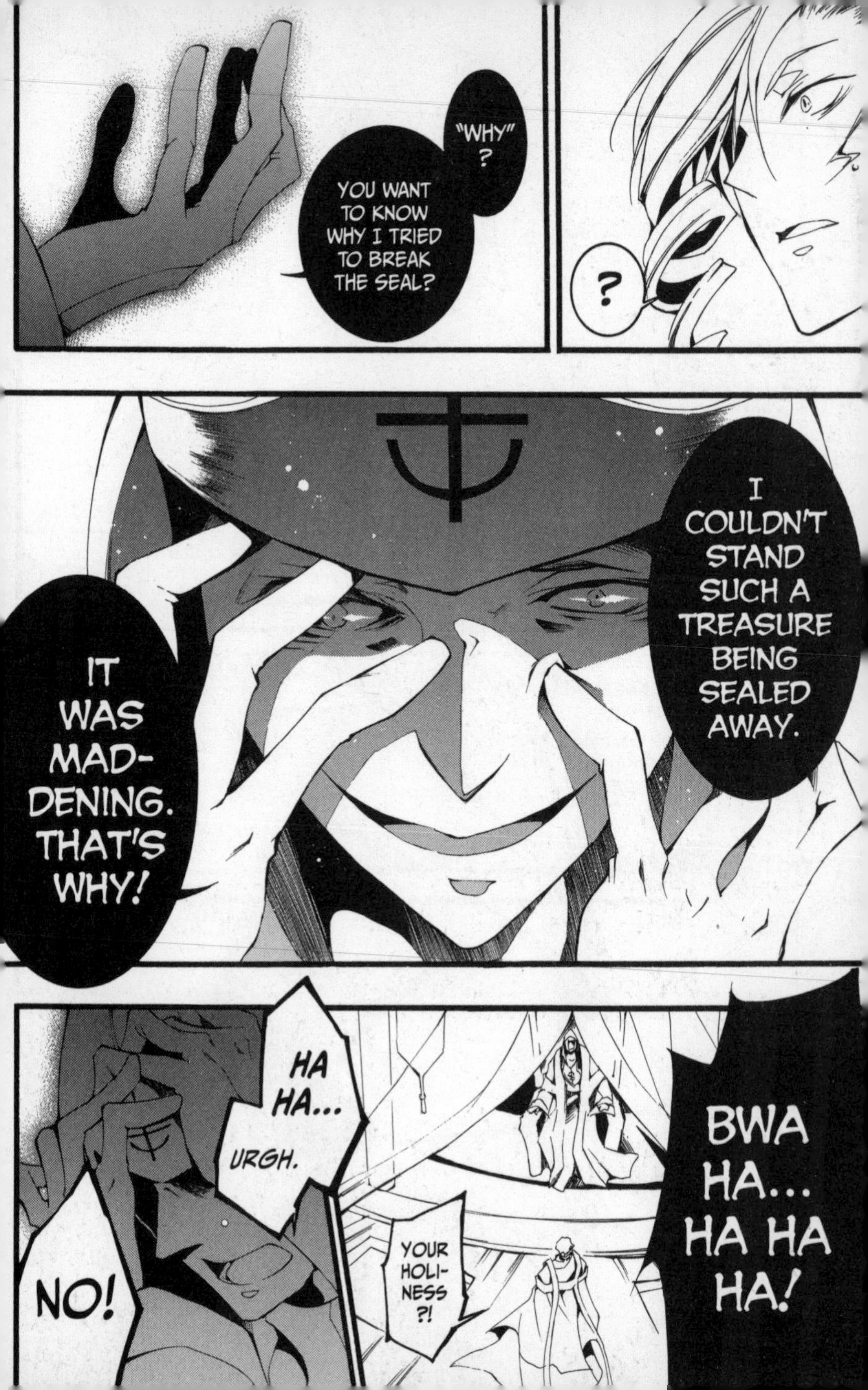
?
"WHY" ?
YOU WANT TO KNOW WHY I TRIED TO BREAK THE SEAL?
I COULDN'T STAND SUCH A TREASURE BEING SEALED AWAY.
IT WAS MAD-DENING. THAT'S WHY!
BWA HA... HA HA HA!
YOUR HOLI-NESS ?!
HA HA...
URGH.
NO!

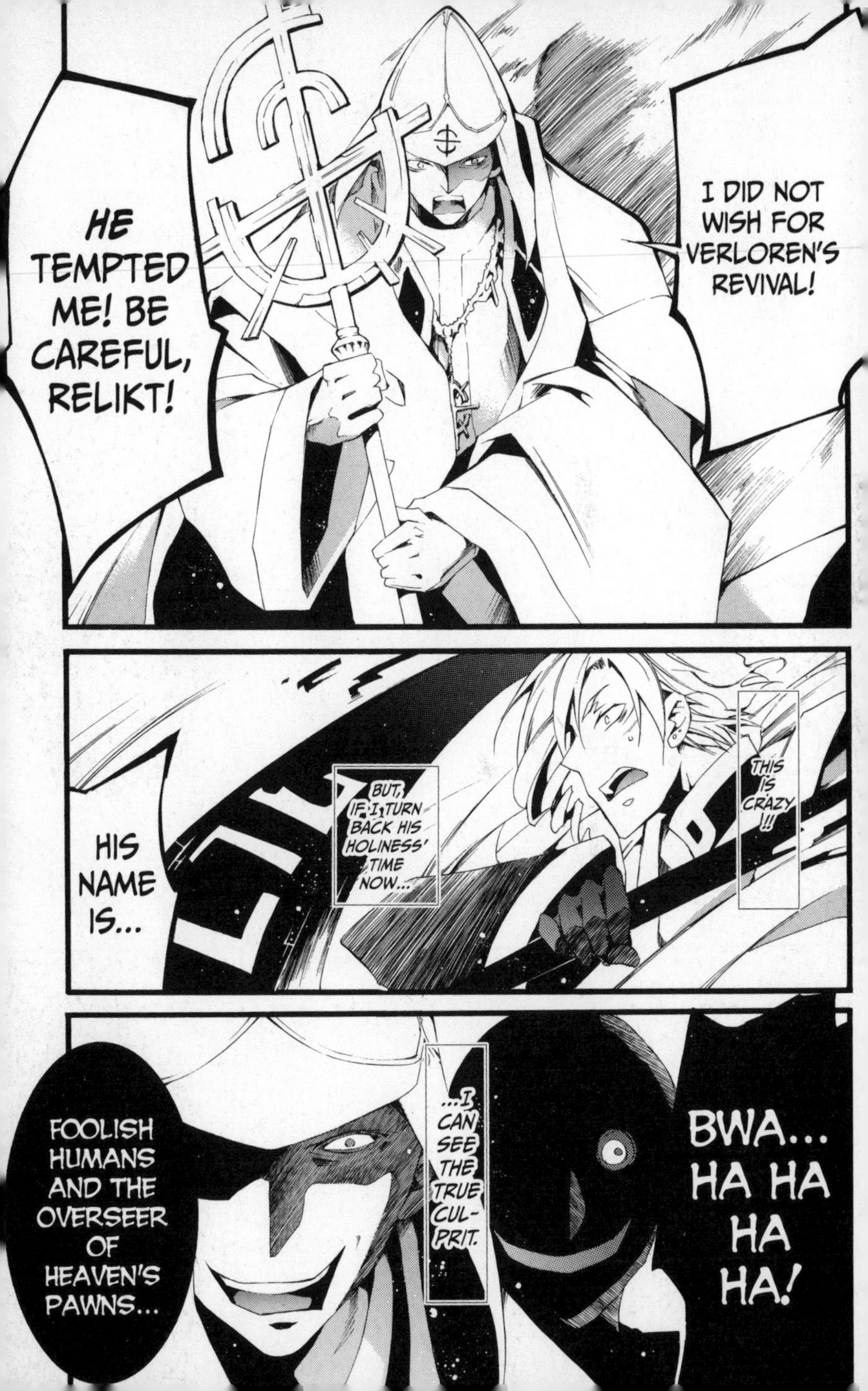
I DID NOT WISH FOR VERLOREN'S REVIVAL!
HE TEMPTED ME! BE CAREFUL, RELIKT!
THIS IS CRAZY!!
BUT, IF I TURN BACK HIS HOLINESS' TIME NOW...
HIS NAME IS...
BWA... HA HA HA HA HA!
...I CAN SEE THE TRUE CUL-PRIT.
FOOLISH HUMANS AND THE OVERSEER OF HEAVEN'S PAWNS...

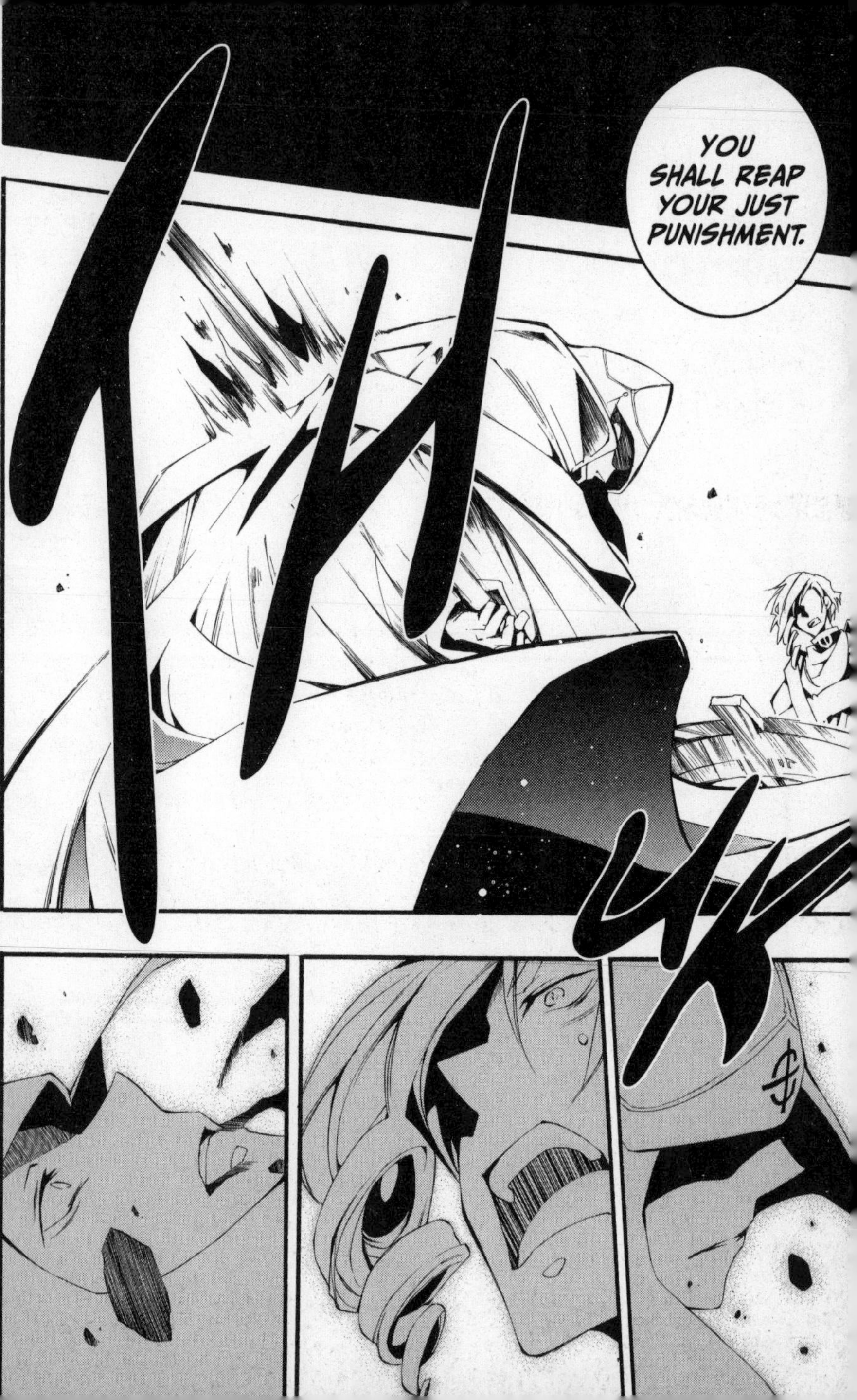
YOU SHALL REAP YOUR JUST PUNISHMENT.

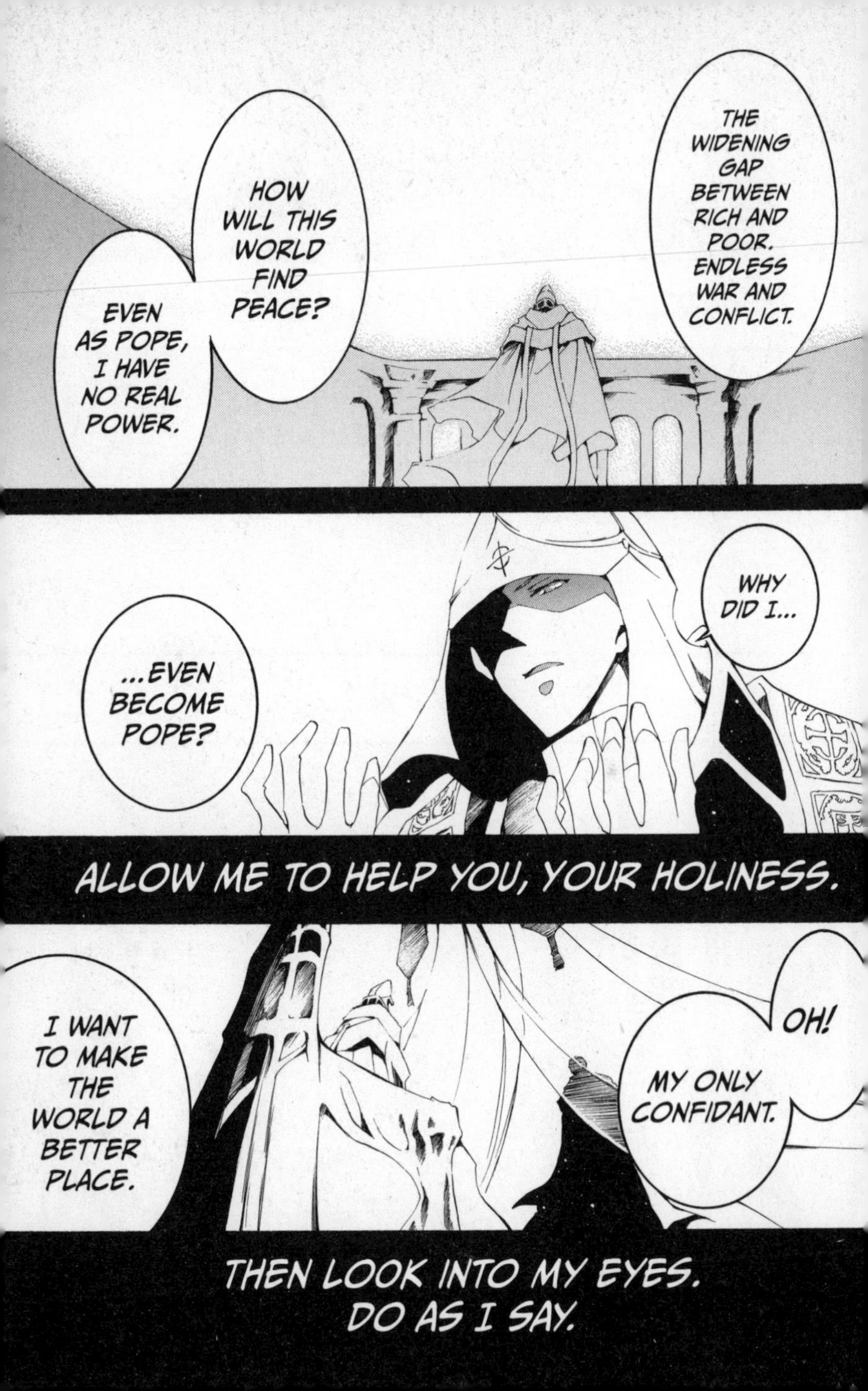
THE WIDENING GAP BETWEEN RICH AND POOR. ENDLESS WAR AND CONFLICT.
HOW WILL THIS WORLD FIND PEACE?
EVEN AS POPE, I HAVE NO REAL POWER.
WHY DID I...
...EVEN BECOME POPE?
ALLOW ME TO HELP YOU, YOUR HOLINESS.
OH!
MY ONLY CONFIDANT.
I WANT TO MAKE THE WORLD A BETTER PLACE.
THEN LOOK INTO MY EYES.
DO AS I SAY.

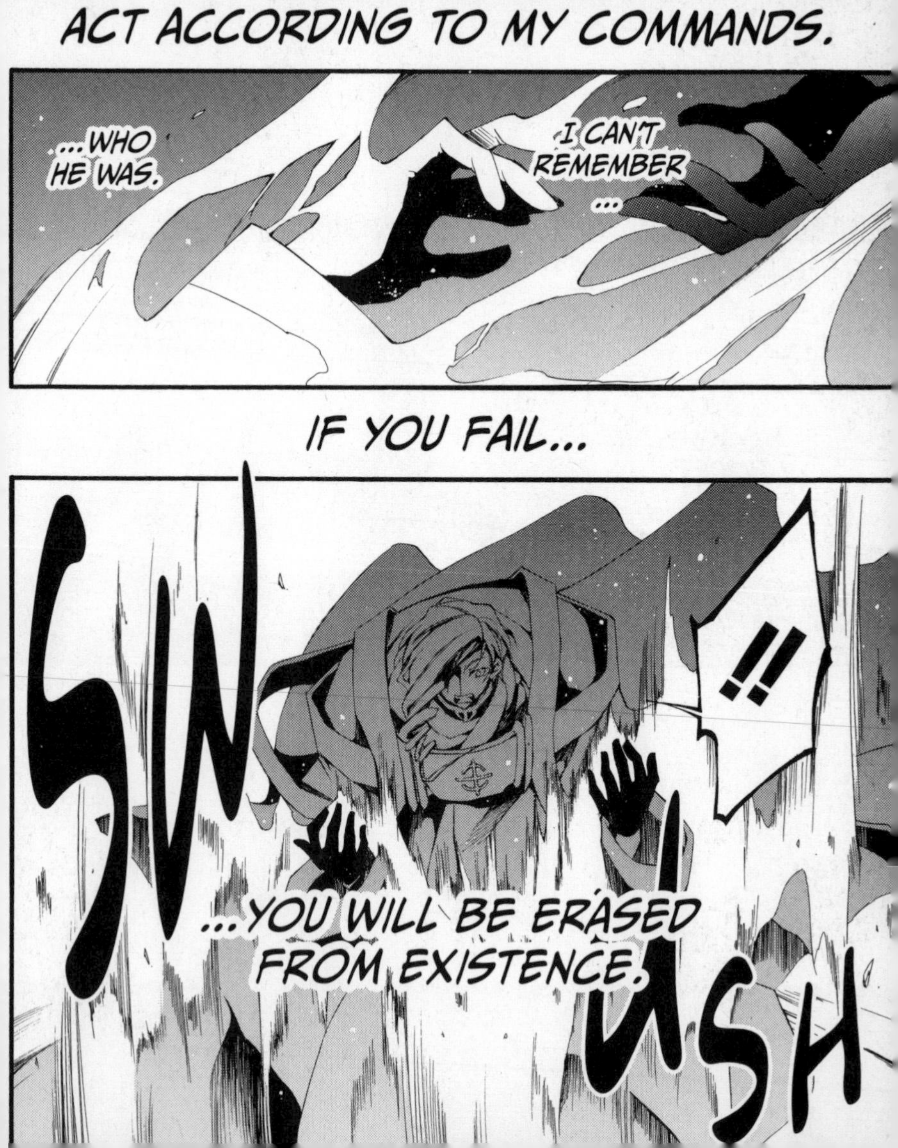
ACT ACCORDING TO MY COMMANDS.
I CAN'T REMEMBER...
...WHO HE WAS.
IF YOU FAIL...
!!
SWUSH
...YOU WILL BE ERASED FROM EXISTENCE.

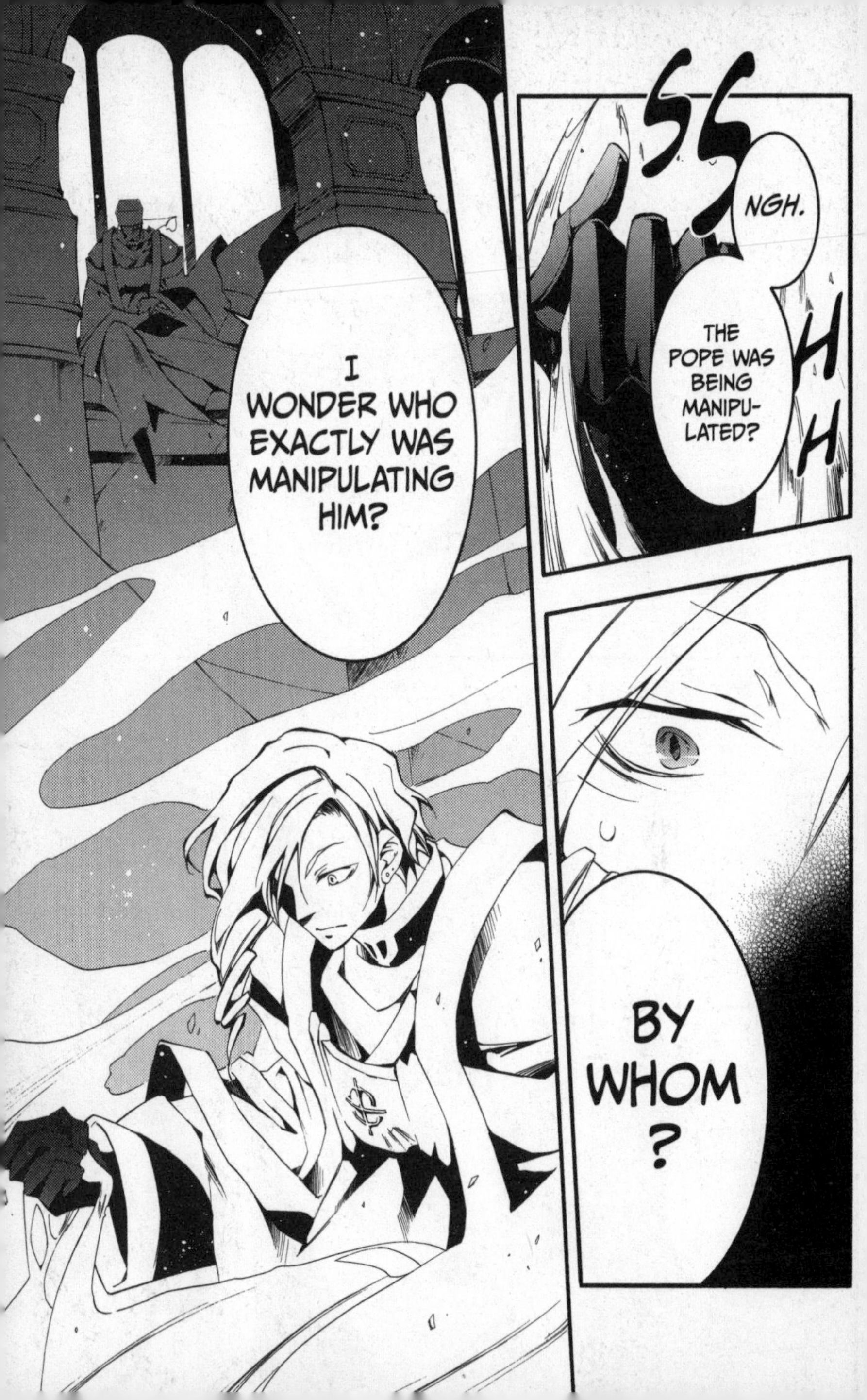
SS
NGH.
THE POPE WAS BEING MANIPU-LATED?
HH
BY WHOM?
I WONDER WHO EXACTLY WAS MANIPULATING HIM?

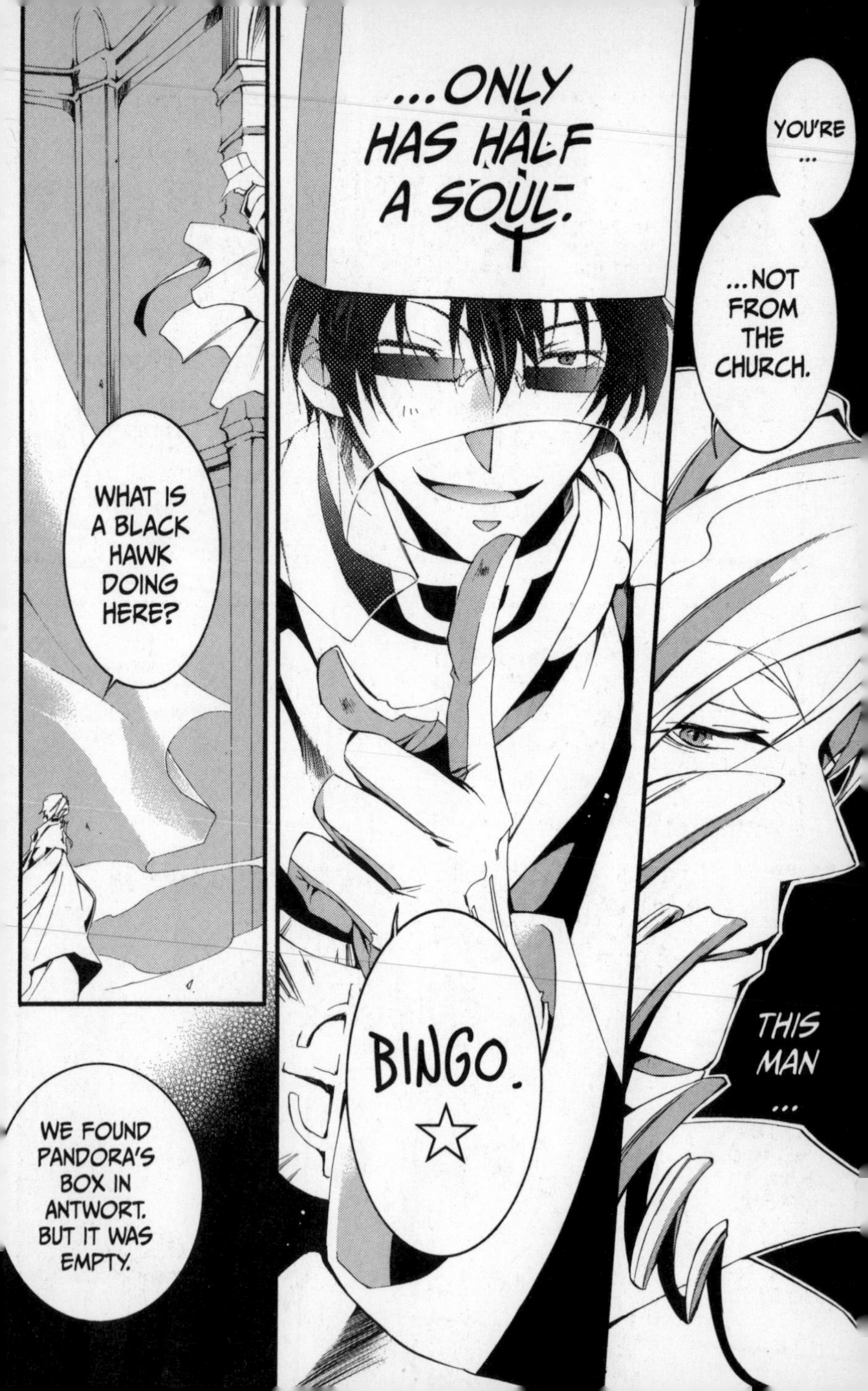
YOU'RE ...
...NOT FROM THE CHURCH.
THIS MAN ...
...ONLY HAS HALF A SOUL.
BINGO. ☆
WHAT IS A BLACK HAWK DOING HERE?
WE FOUND PANDORA'S BOX IN ANTWORT. BUT IT WAS EMPTY.

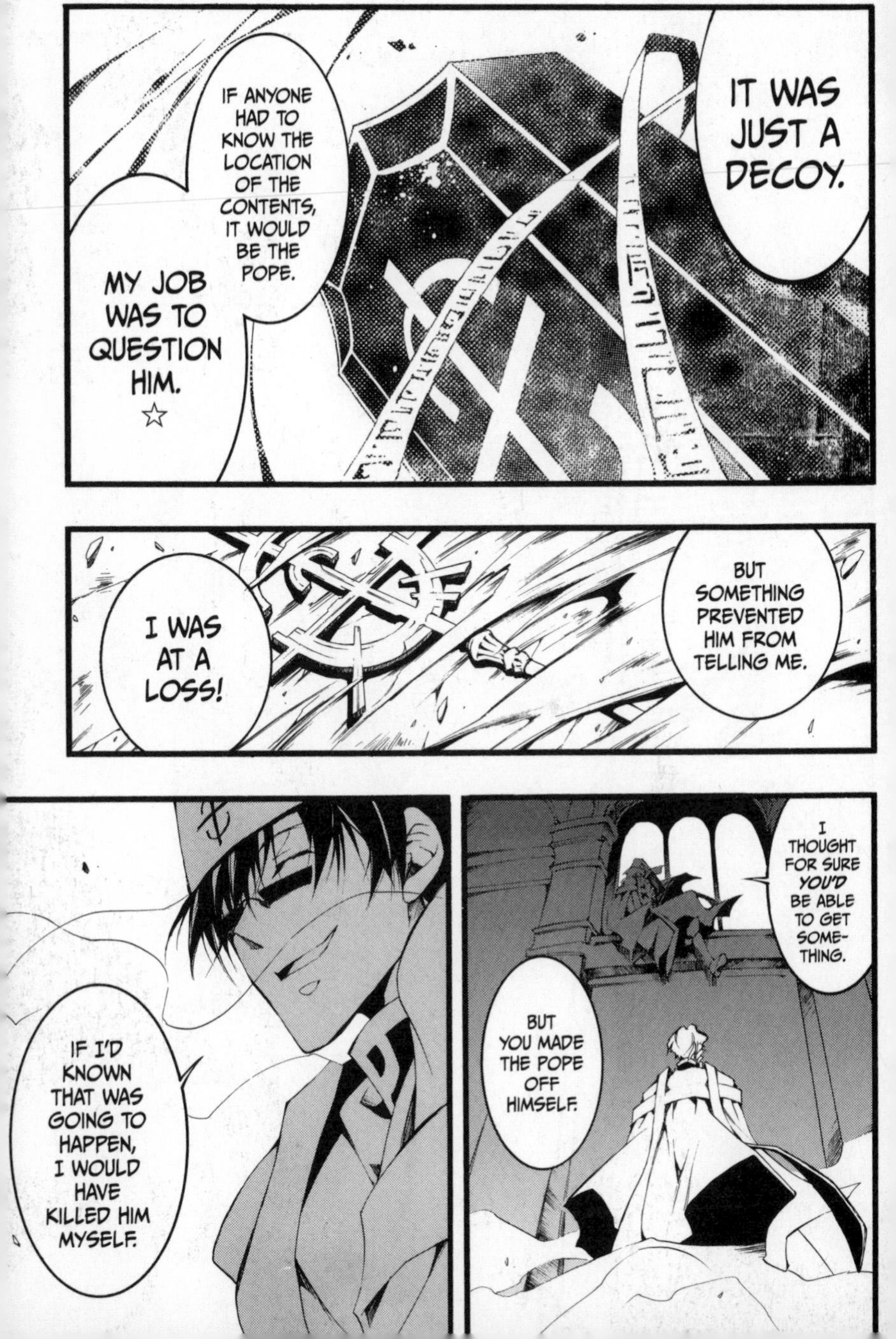
IT WAS JUST A DECOY.
IF ANYONE HAD TO KNOW THE LOCATION OF THE CONTENTS, IT WOULD BE THE POPE.
MY JOB WAS TO QUESTION HIM. ☆
BUT SOMETHING PREVENTED HIM FROM TELLING ME.
I WAS AT A LOSS!
I THOUGHT FOR SURE *YOU'D* BE ABLE TO GET SOME-THING.
BUT YOU MADE THE POPE OFF HIMSELF.
IF I'D KNOWN THAT WAS GOING TO HAPPEN, I WOULD HAVE KILLED HIM MYSELF.

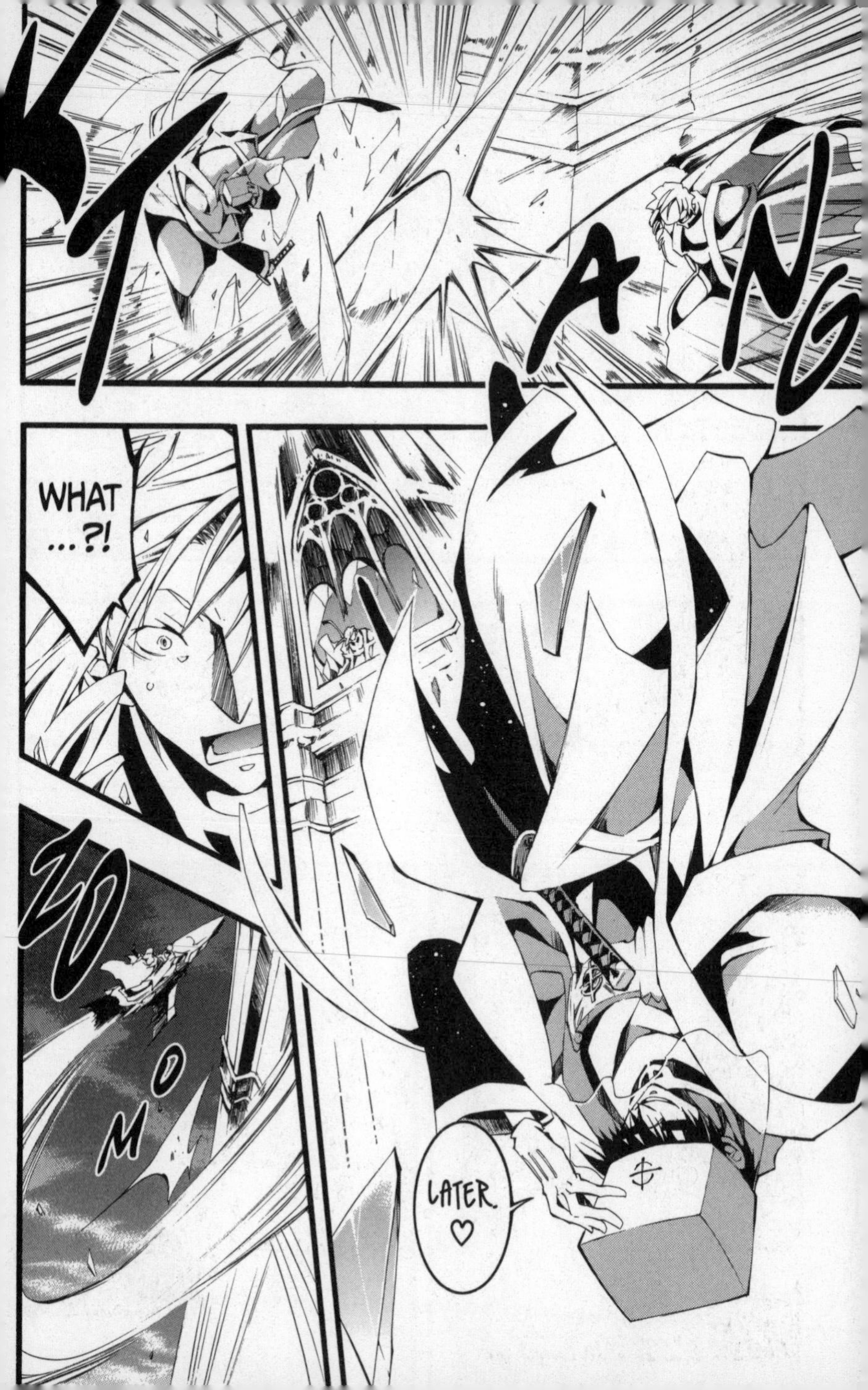
KYANG
WHAT...?!
LATER. ♡
ZOOM

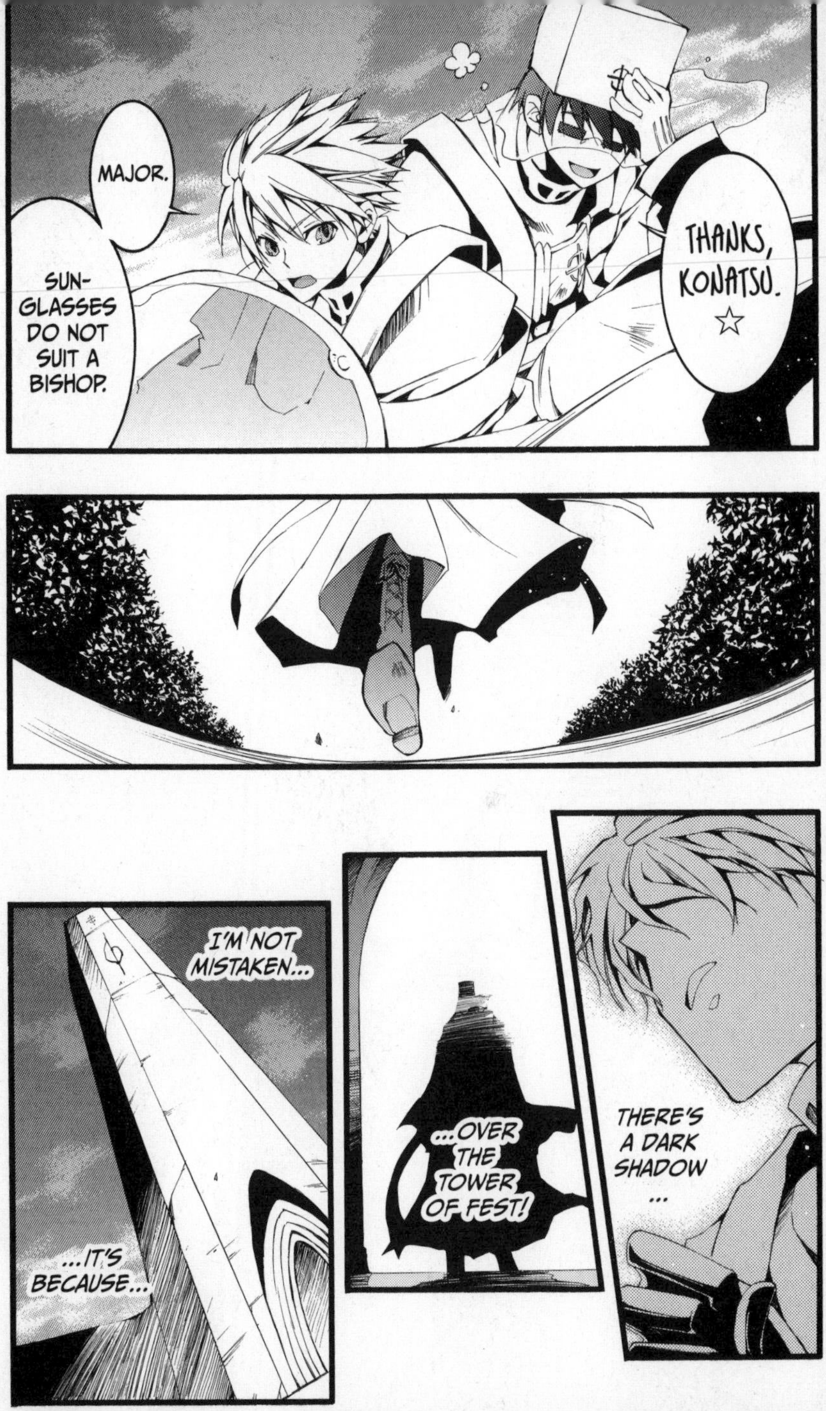
THANKS, KONATSU. ☆
MAJOR.
SUN-GLASSES DO NOT SUIT A BISHOP.
THERE'S A DARK SHADOW ...
...OVER THE TOWER OF FEST!
I'M NOT MISTAKEN...
...IT'S BECAUSE...

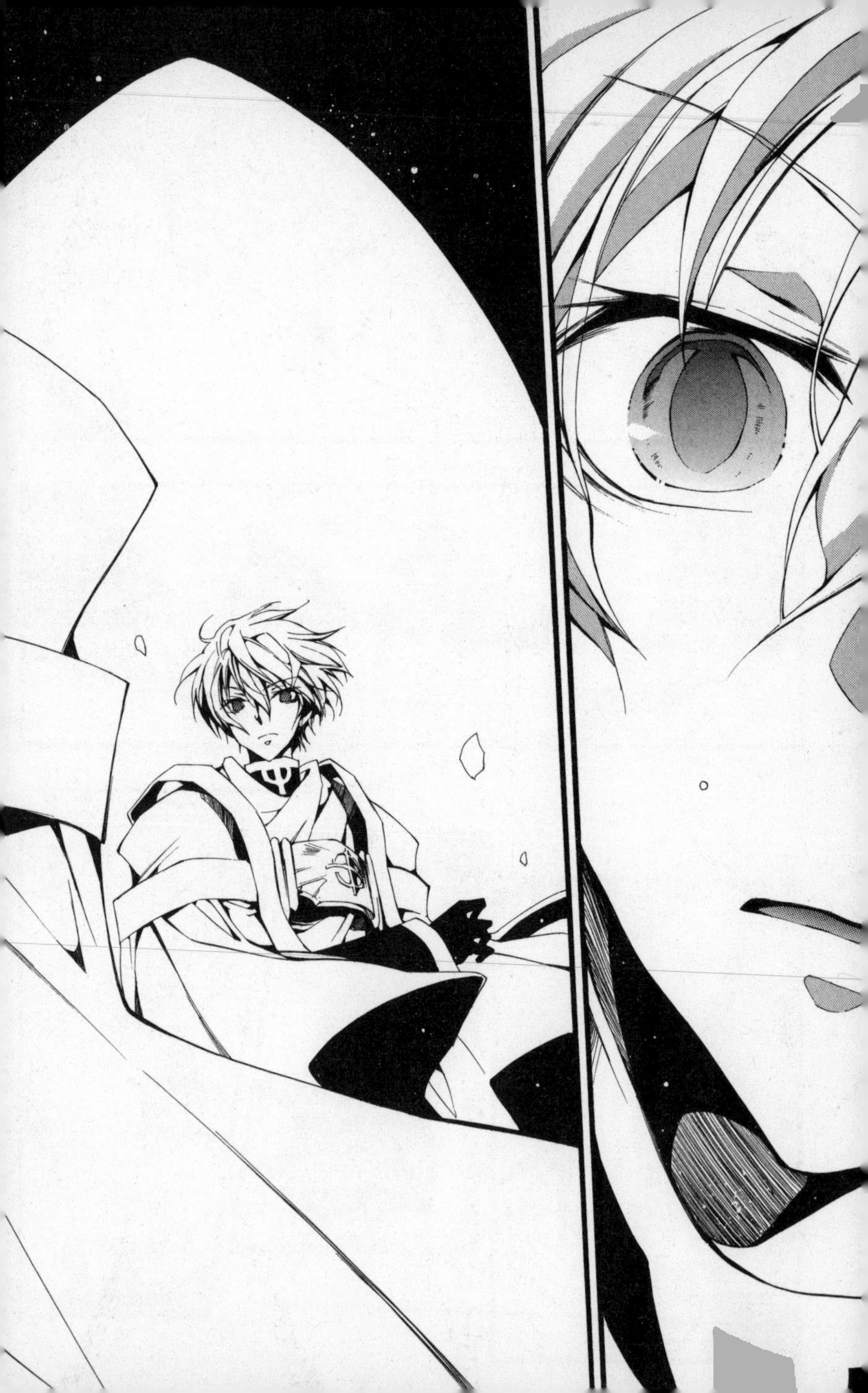

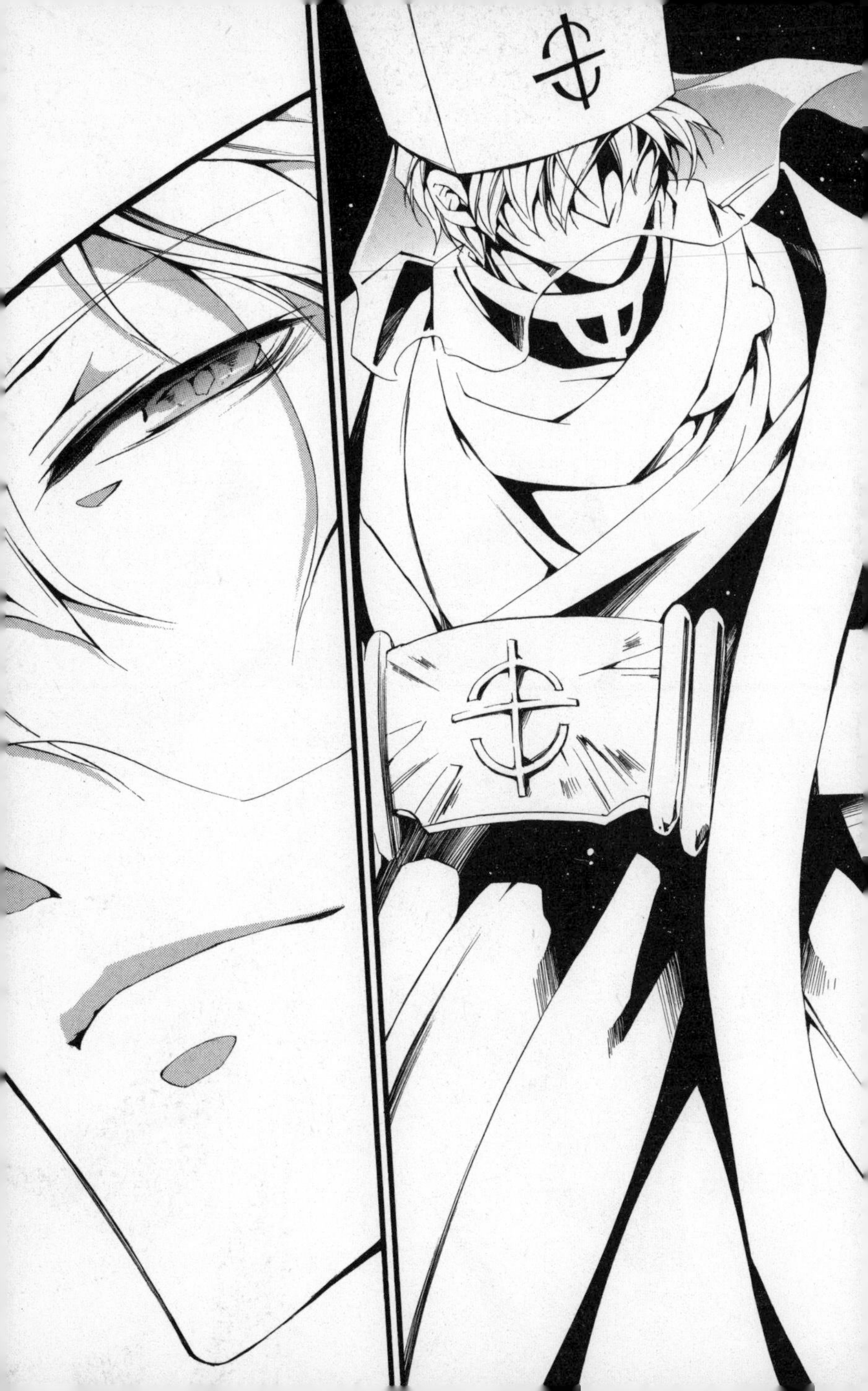

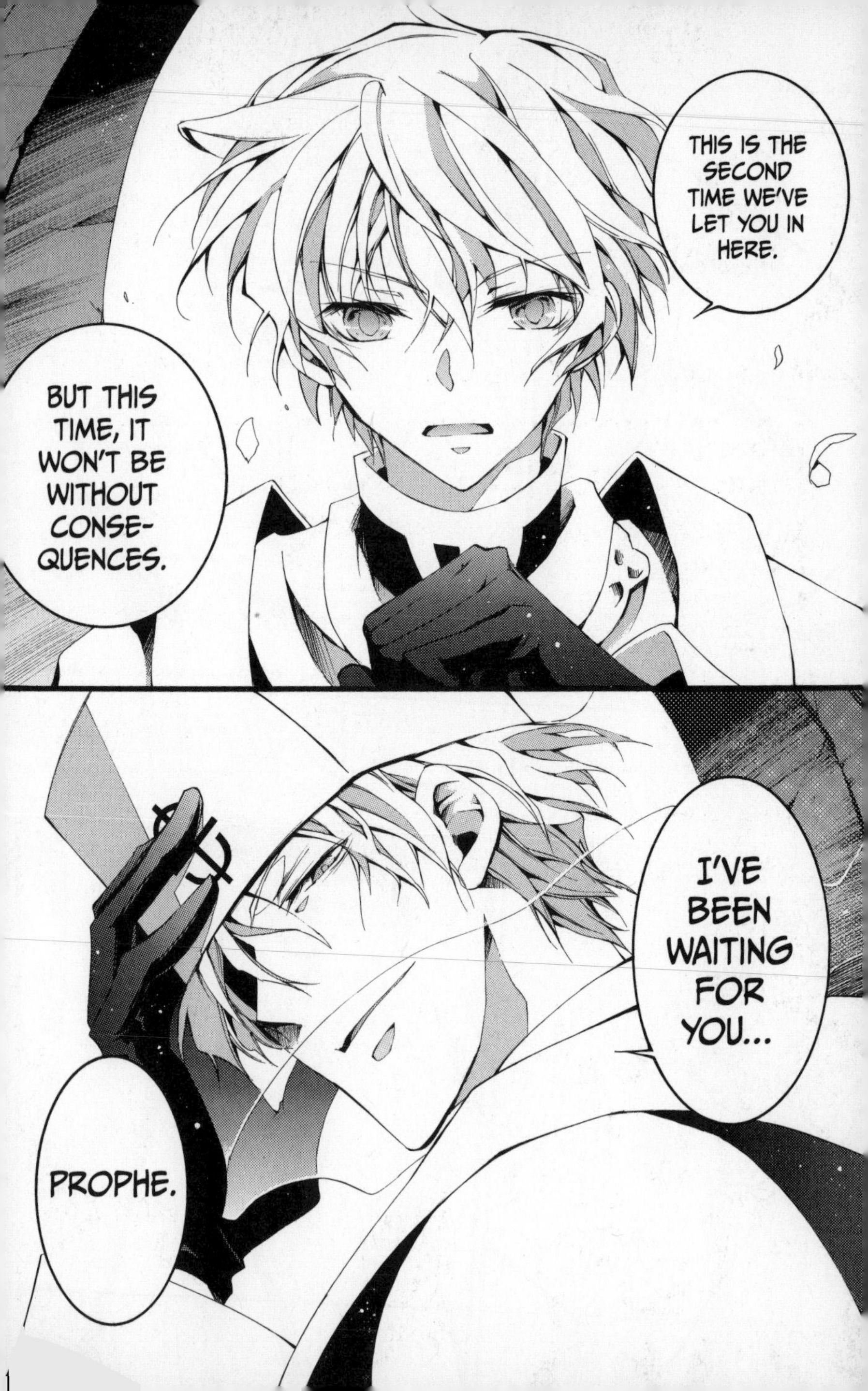
THIS IS THE SECOND TIME WE'VE LET YOU IN HERE.
BUT THIS TIME, IT WON'T BE WITHOUT CONSE-QUENCES.
I'VE BEEN WAITING FOR YOU...
PROPHE.

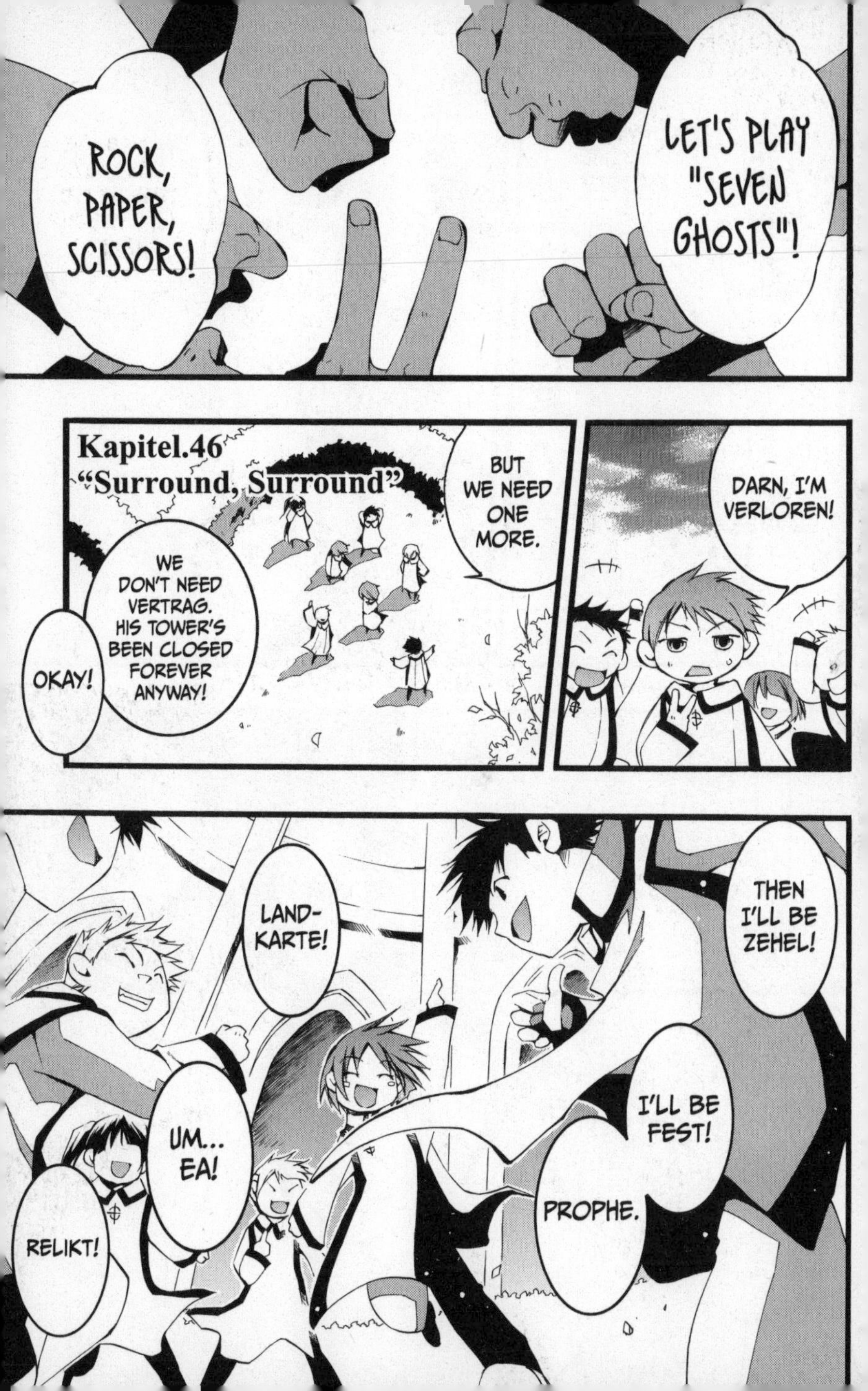
LET'S PLAY "SEVEN GHOSTS"!
ROCK, PAPER, SCISSORS!
DARN, I'M VERLOREN!
BUT WE NEED ONE MORE.
Kapitel.46 "Surround, Surround"
WE DON'T NEED VERTRAG. HIS TOWER'S BEEN CLOSED FOREVER ANYWAY!
OKAY!
THEN I'LL BE ZEHEL!
LAND-KARTE!
I'LL BE FEST!
PROPHE.
UM... EA!
RELIKT!

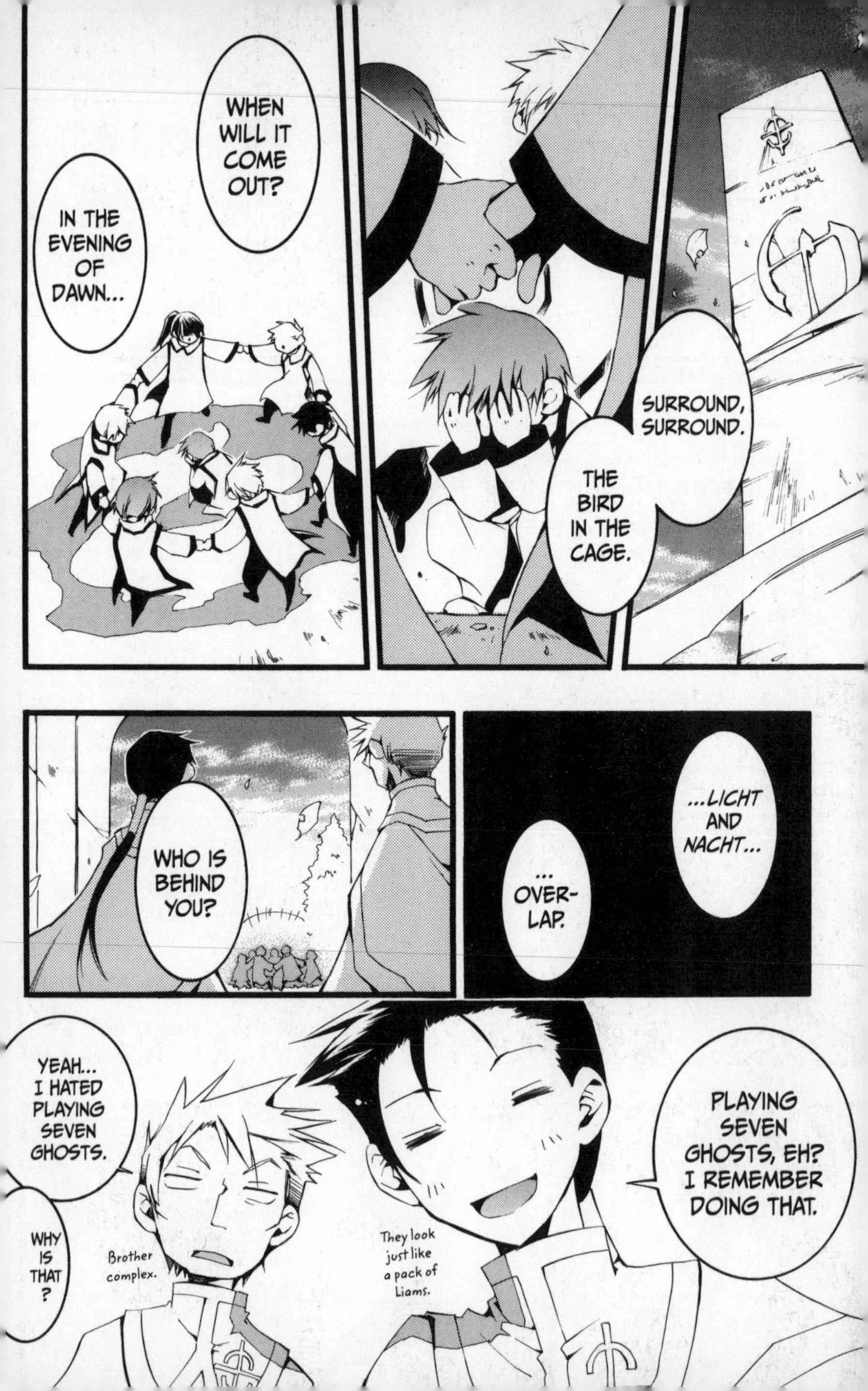
SURROUND, SURROUND.
THE BIRD IN THE CAGE.
WHEN WILL IT COME OUT?
IN THE EVENING OF DAWN...
...LICHT AND NACHT...
... OVER-LAP.
WHO IS BEHIND YOU?
PLAYING SEVEN GHOSTS, EH? I REMEMBER DOING THAT.
They look just like a pack of Liams.
YEAH... I HATED PLAYING SEVEN GHOSTS.
Brother complex.
WHY IS THAT?

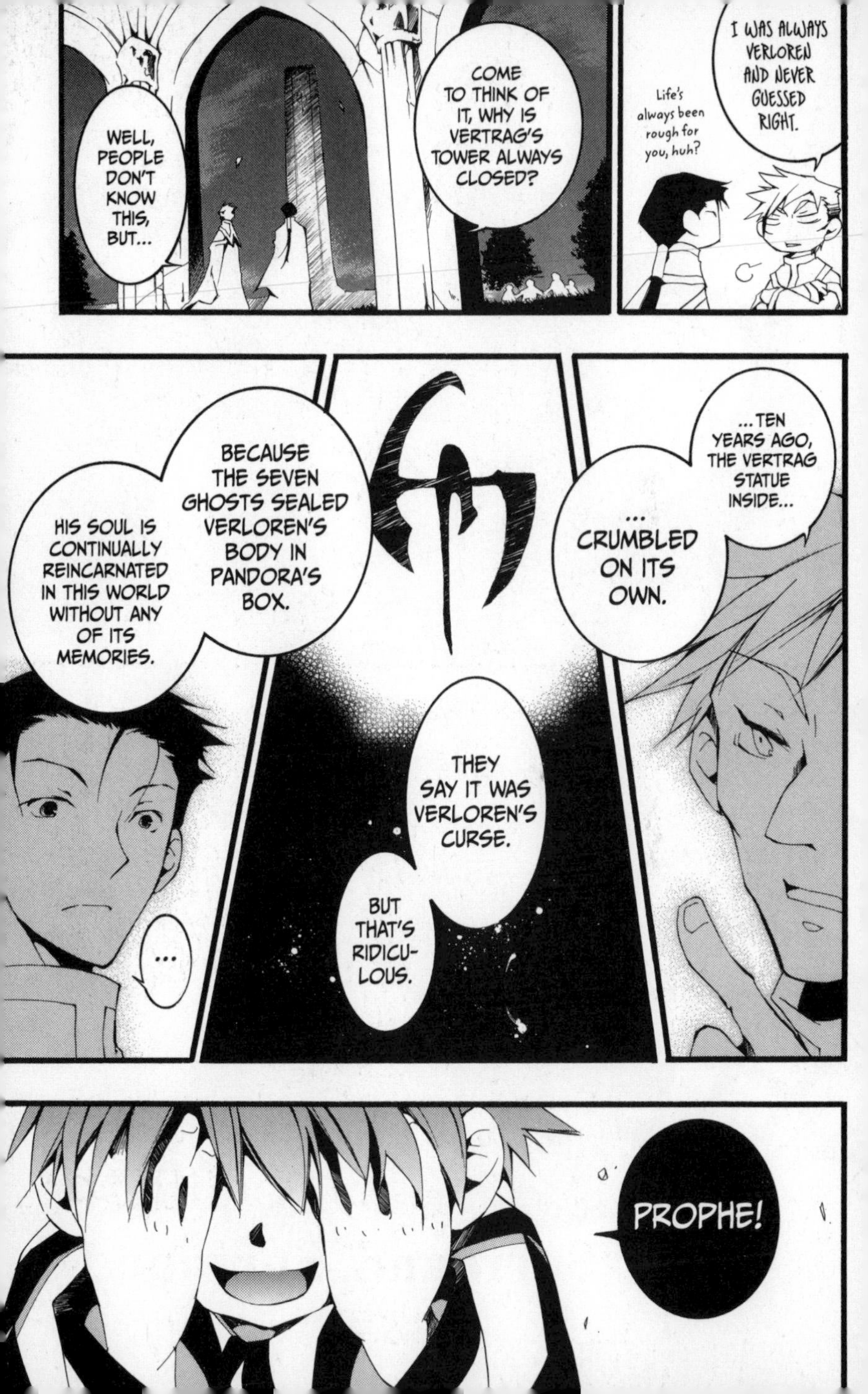
I WAS ALWAYS VERLOREN AND NEVER GUESSED RIGHT.
Life's always been rough for you, huh?
COME TO THINK OF IT, WHY IS VERTRAG'S TOWER ALWAYS CLOSED?
WELL, PEOPLE DON'T KNOW THIS, BUT...
...TEN YEARS AGO, THE VERTRAG STATUE INSIDE...
... CRUMBLED ON ITS OWN.
THEY SAY IT WAS VERLOREN'S CURSE.
BUT THAT'S RIDICU-LOUS.
BECAUSE THE SEVEN GHOSTS SEALED VERLOREN'S BODY IN PANDORA'S BOX.
HIS SOUL IS CONTINUALLY REINCARNATED IN THIS WORLD WITHOUT ANY OF ITS MEMORIES.
...
PROPHE!

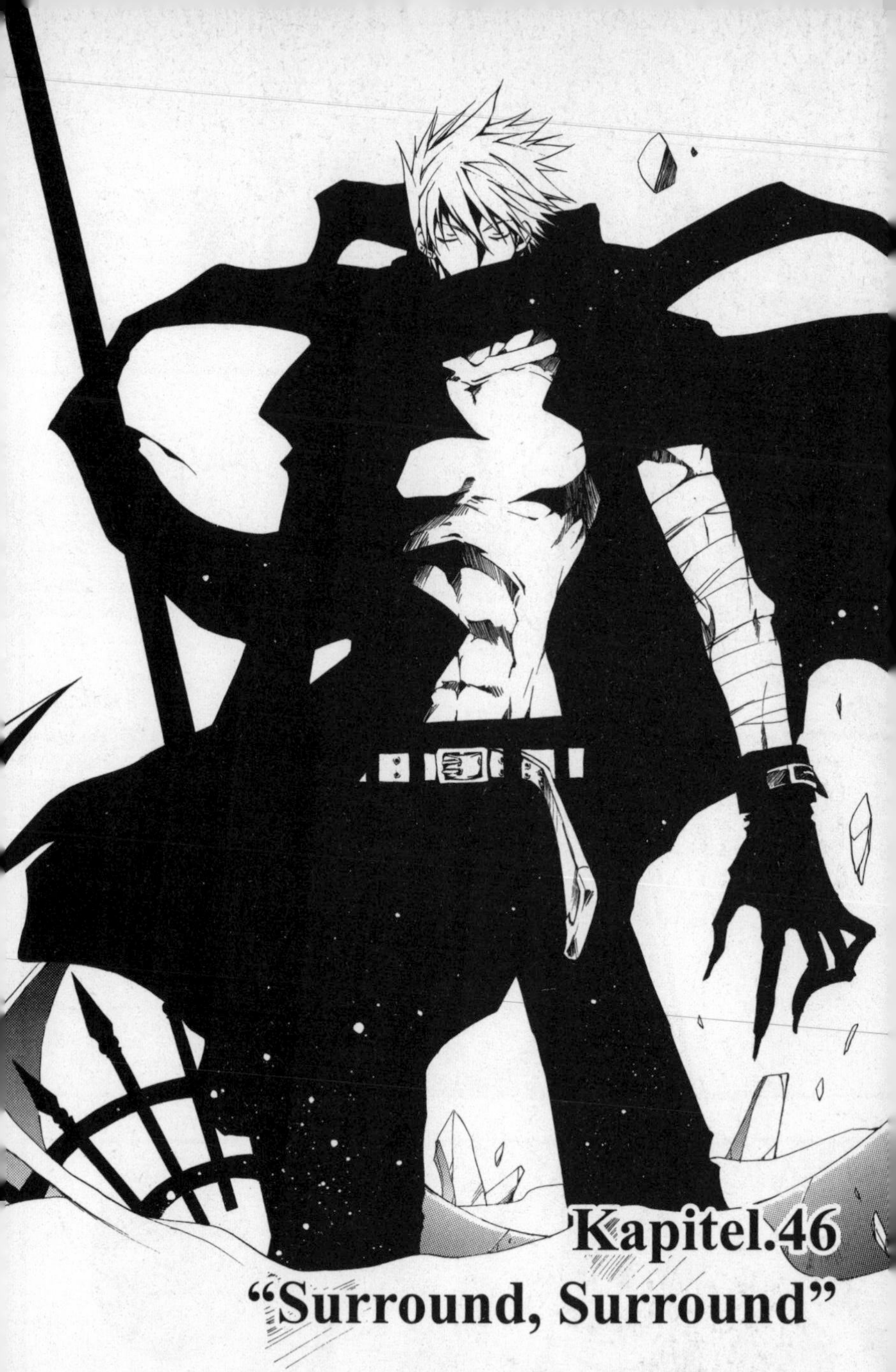
Kapitel.46
“Surround, Surround”

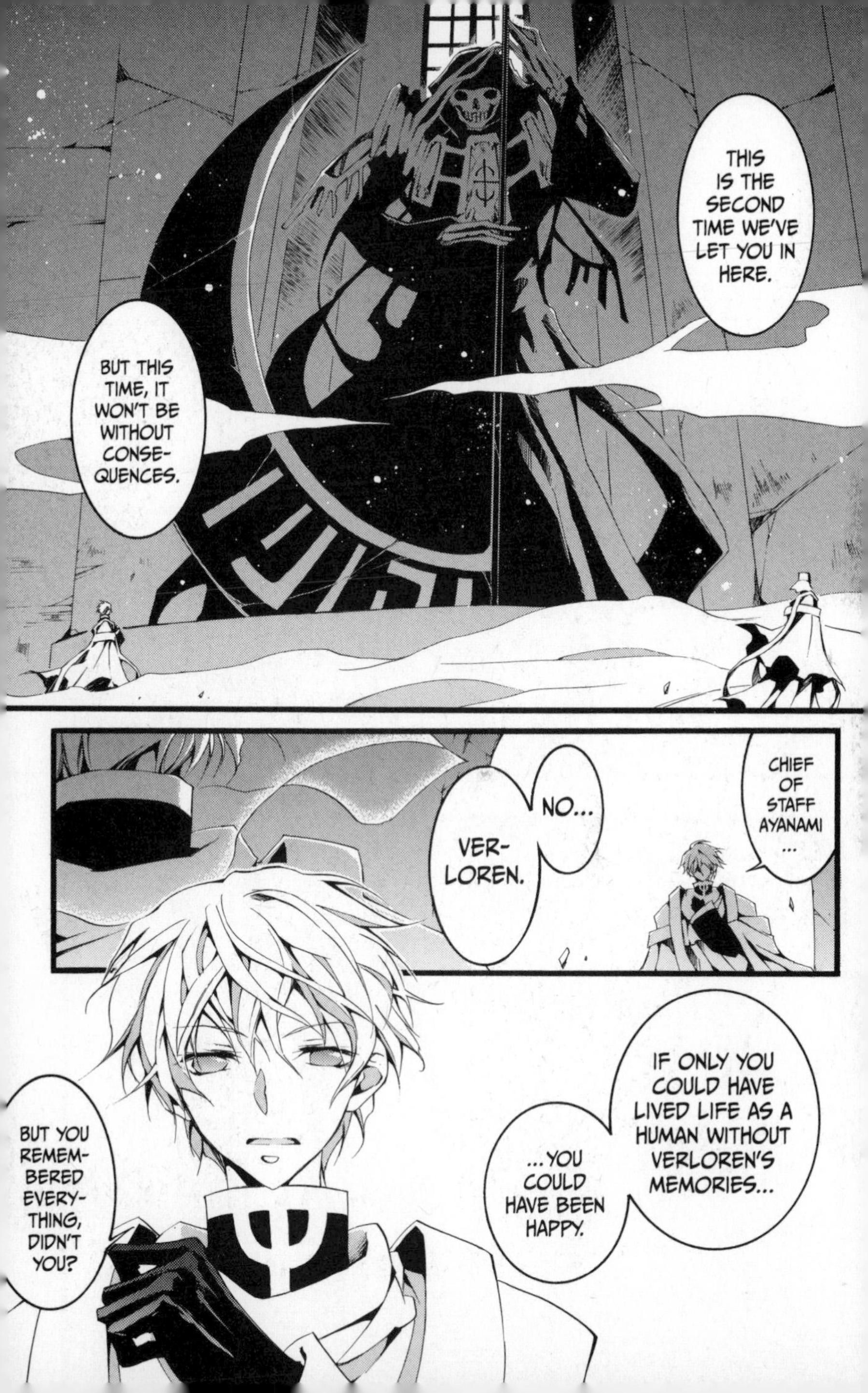
THIS IS THE SECOND TIME WE'VE LET YOU IN HERE.
BUT THIS TIME, IT WON'T BE WITHOUT CONSE-QUENCES.
CHIEF OF STAFF AYANAMI ...
NO...
VER-LOREN.
IF ONLY YOU COULD HAVE LIVED LIFE AS A HUMAN WITHOUT VERLOREN'S MEMORIES...
...YOU COULD HAVE BEEN HAPPY.
BUT YOU REMEM-BERED EVERY-THING, DIDN'T YOU?

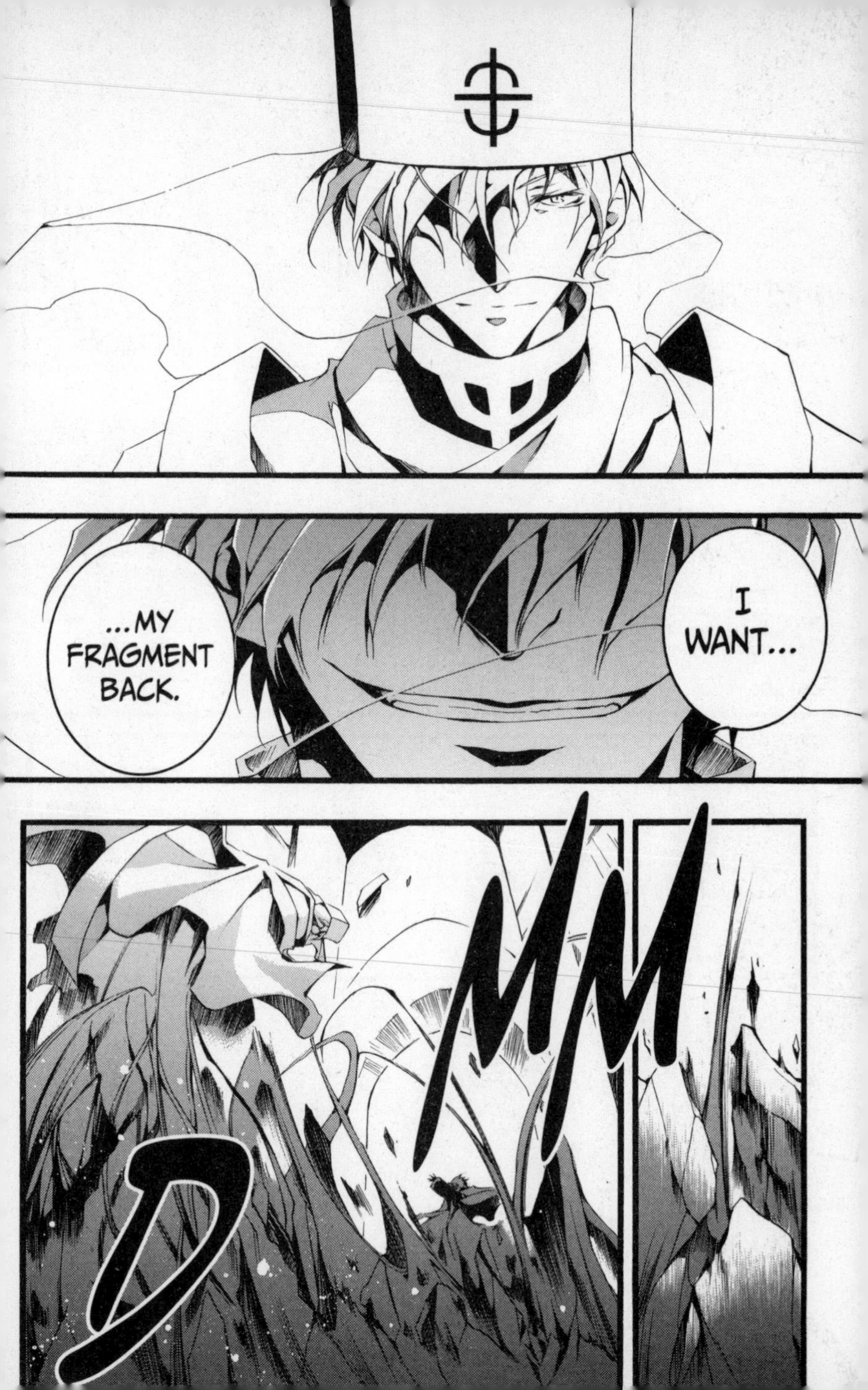
I WANT...
...MY FRAGMENT BACK.
DMM

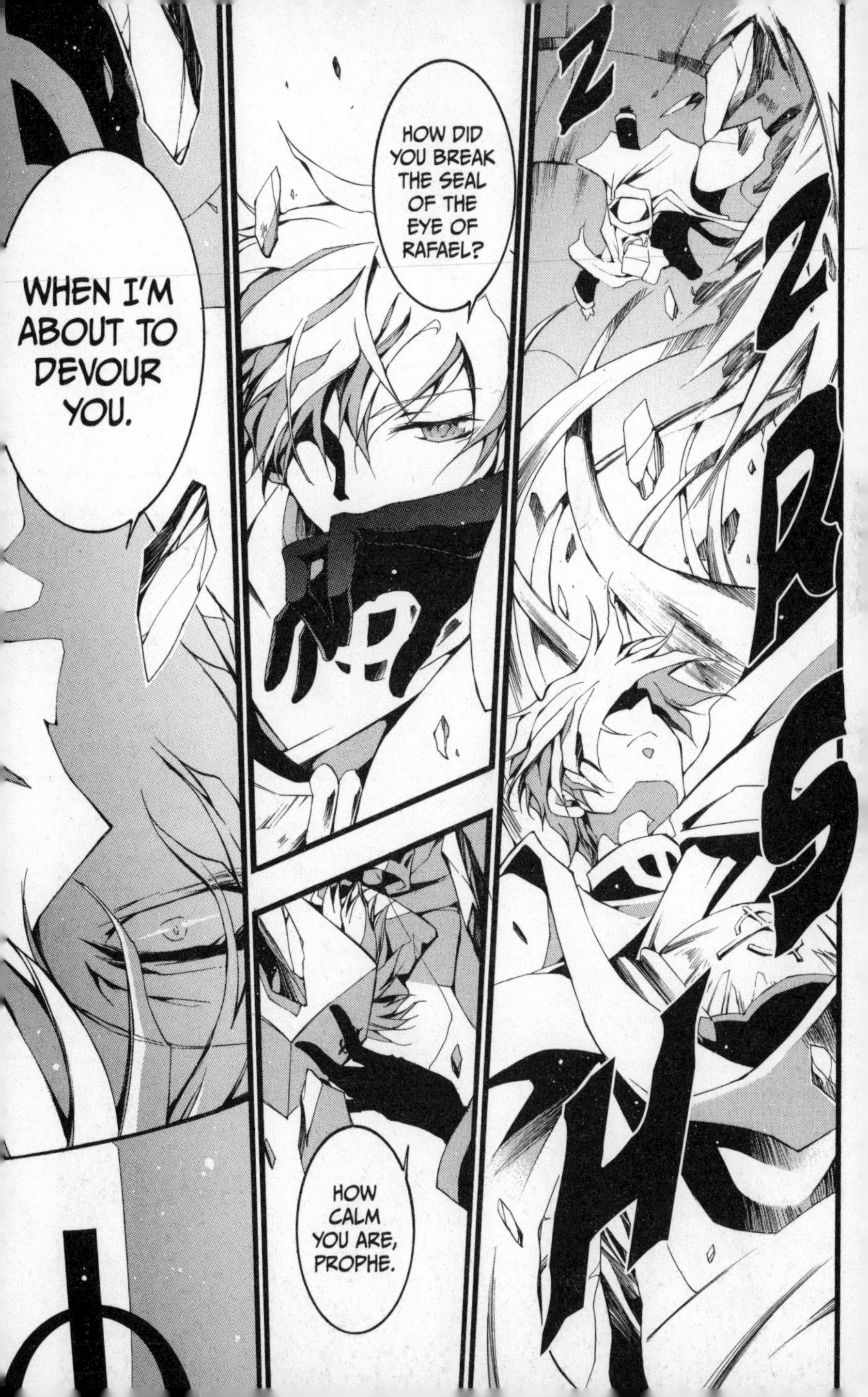
HOW DID YOU BREAK THE SEAL OF THE EYE OF RAFAEL?
HOW CALM YOU ARE, PROPHE.
WHEN I'M ABOUT TO DEVOUR YOU.

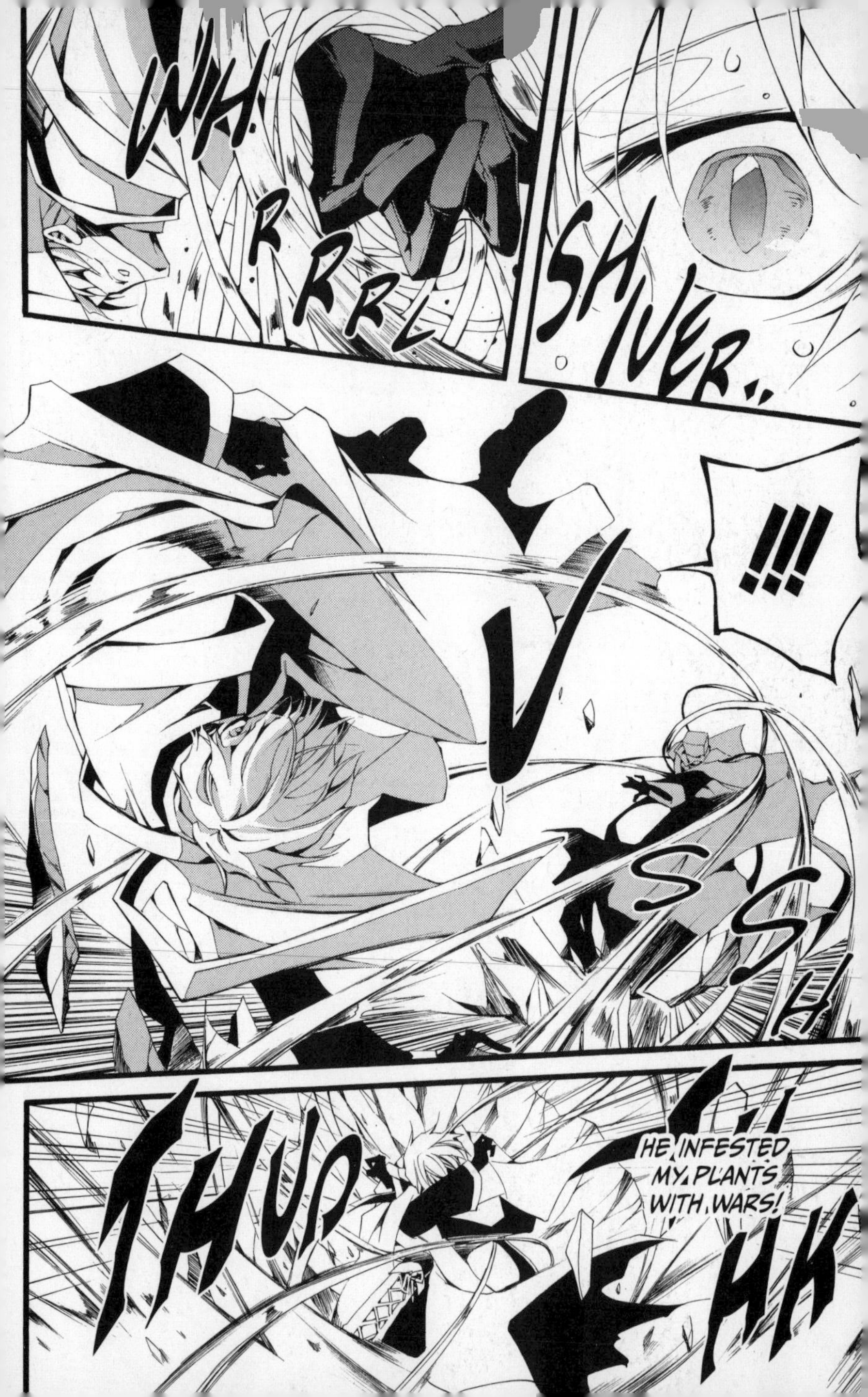
SHIVER...
WHRRRRL
!!!
VSSSH
HE INFESTED MY PLANTS WITH WARS!
...!
HK
THUD

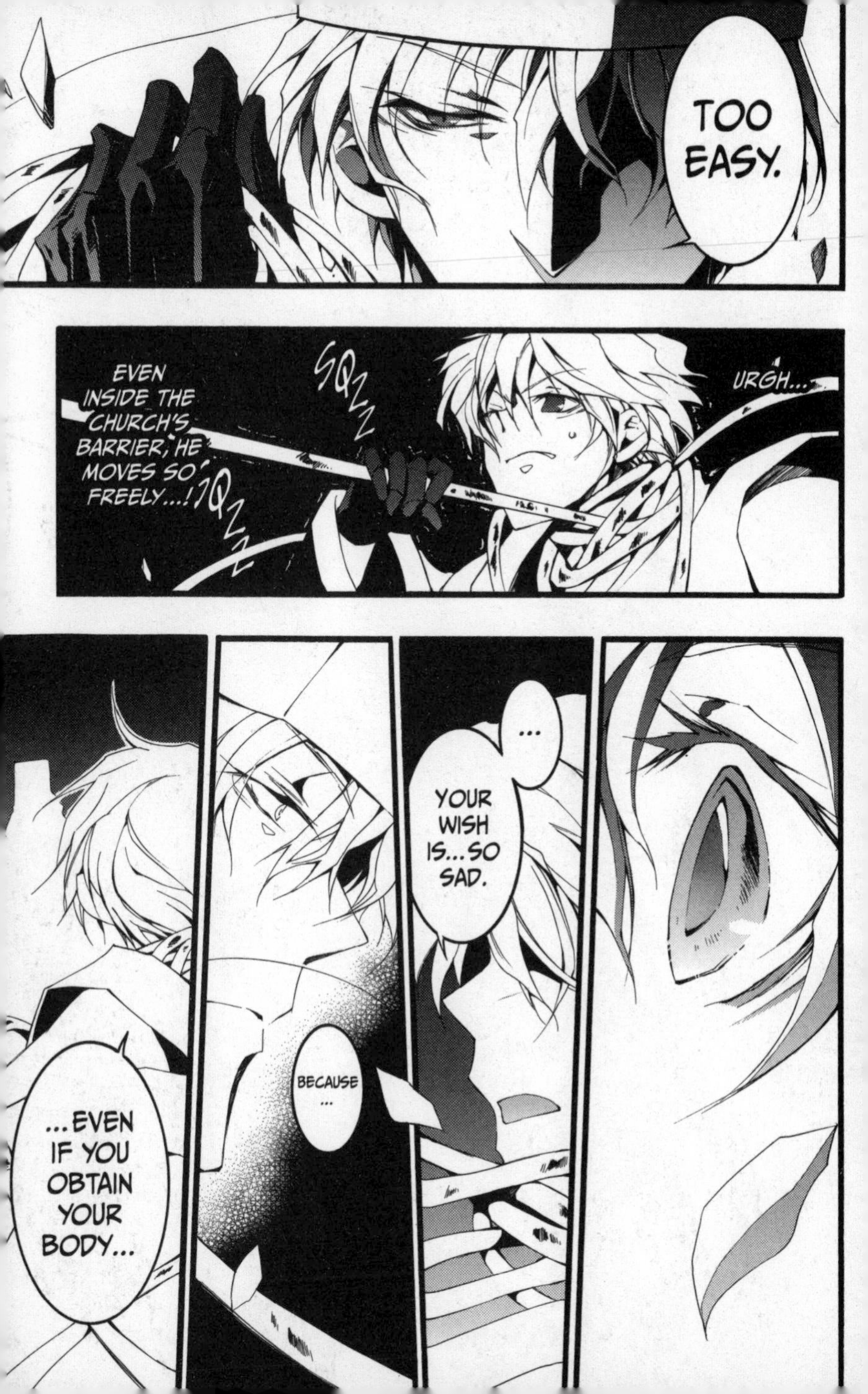
TOO EASY.
URGH...
SQZZZ
EVEN INSIDE THE CHURCH'S BARRIER, HE MOVES SO FREELY...!
SQZZZ
...
YOUR WISH IS...SO SAD.
BECAUSE ...
...EVEN IF YOU OBTAIN YOUR BODY...

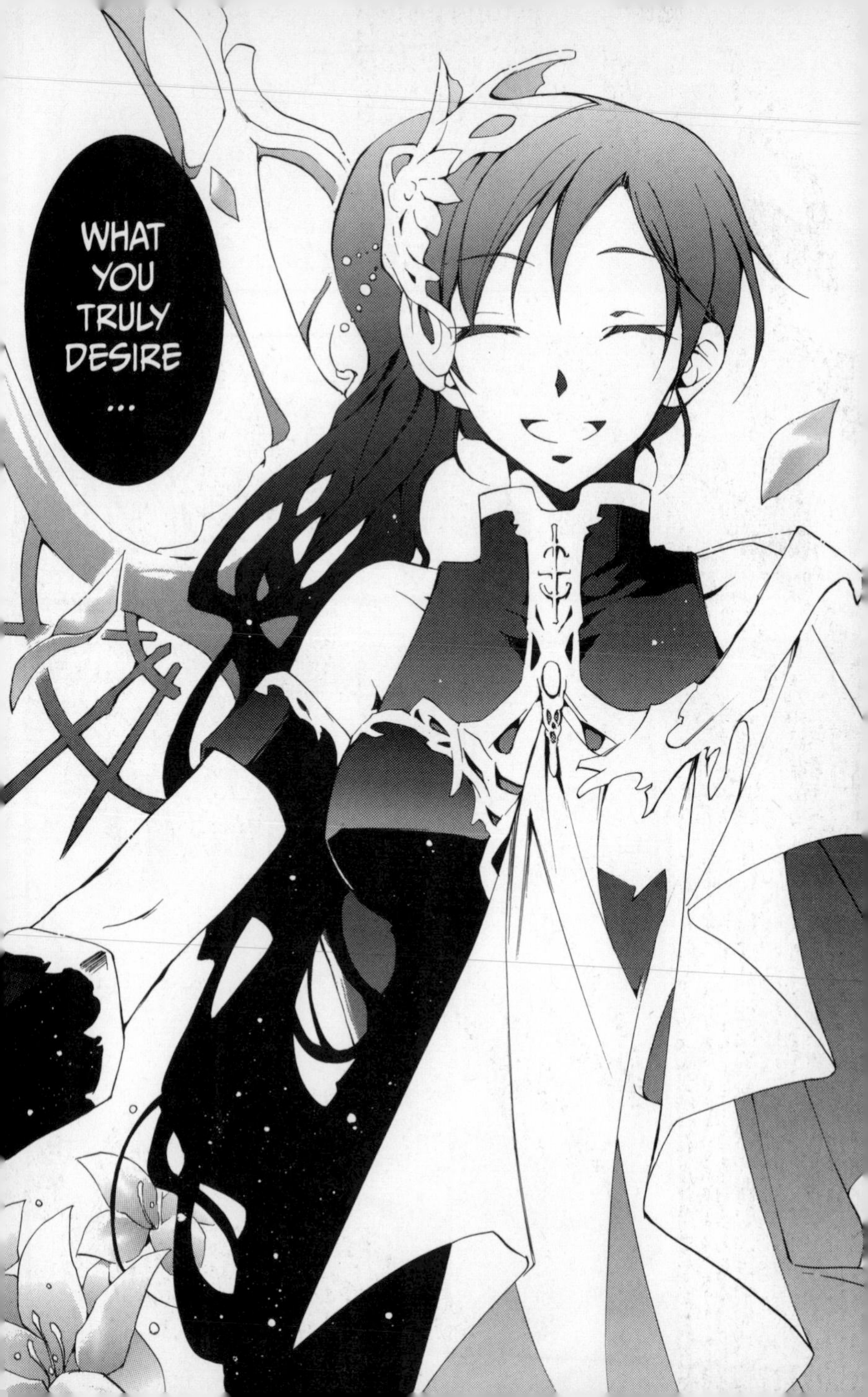
WHAT YOU TRULY DESIRE ...

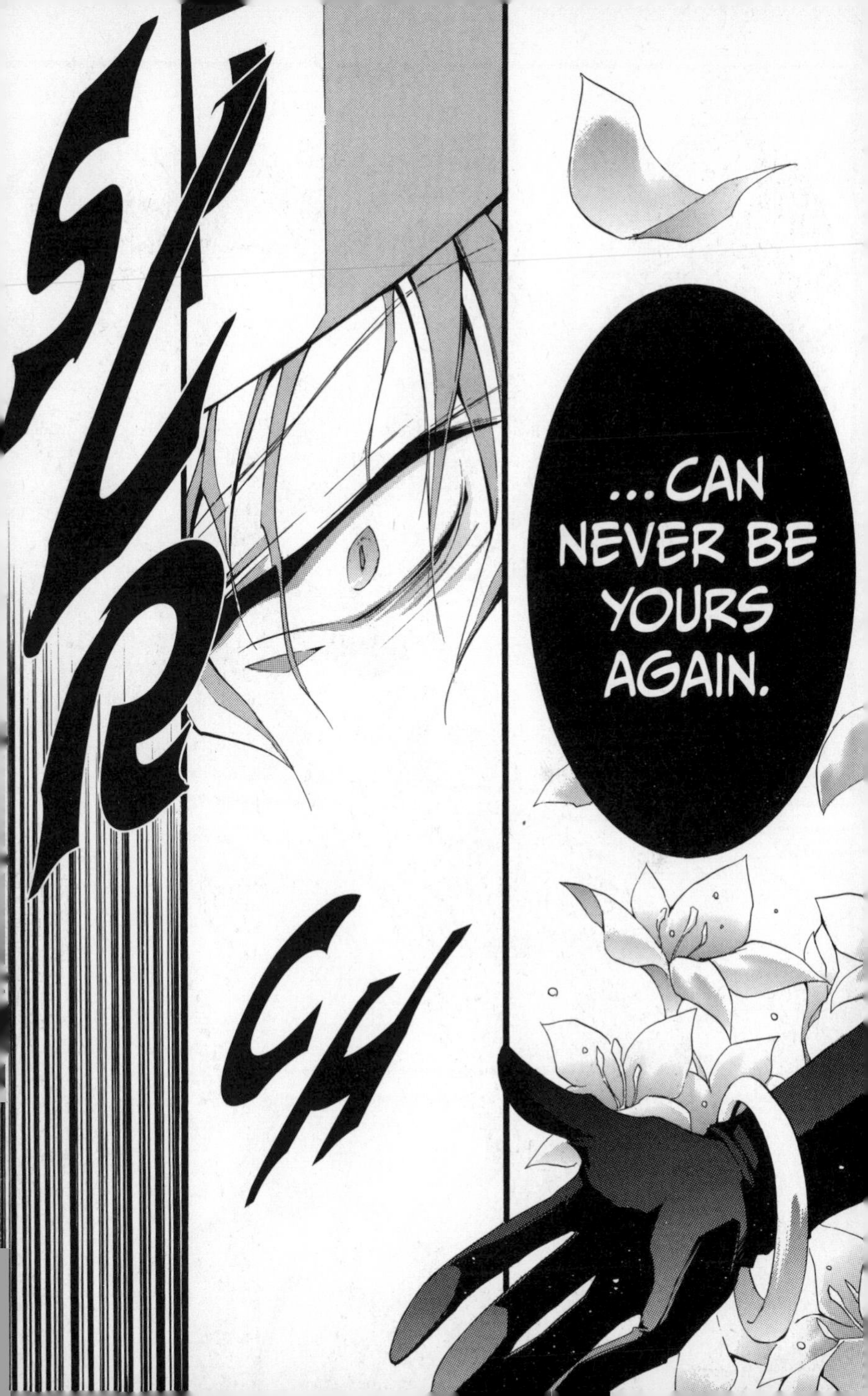
...CAN NEVER BE YOURS AGAIN.

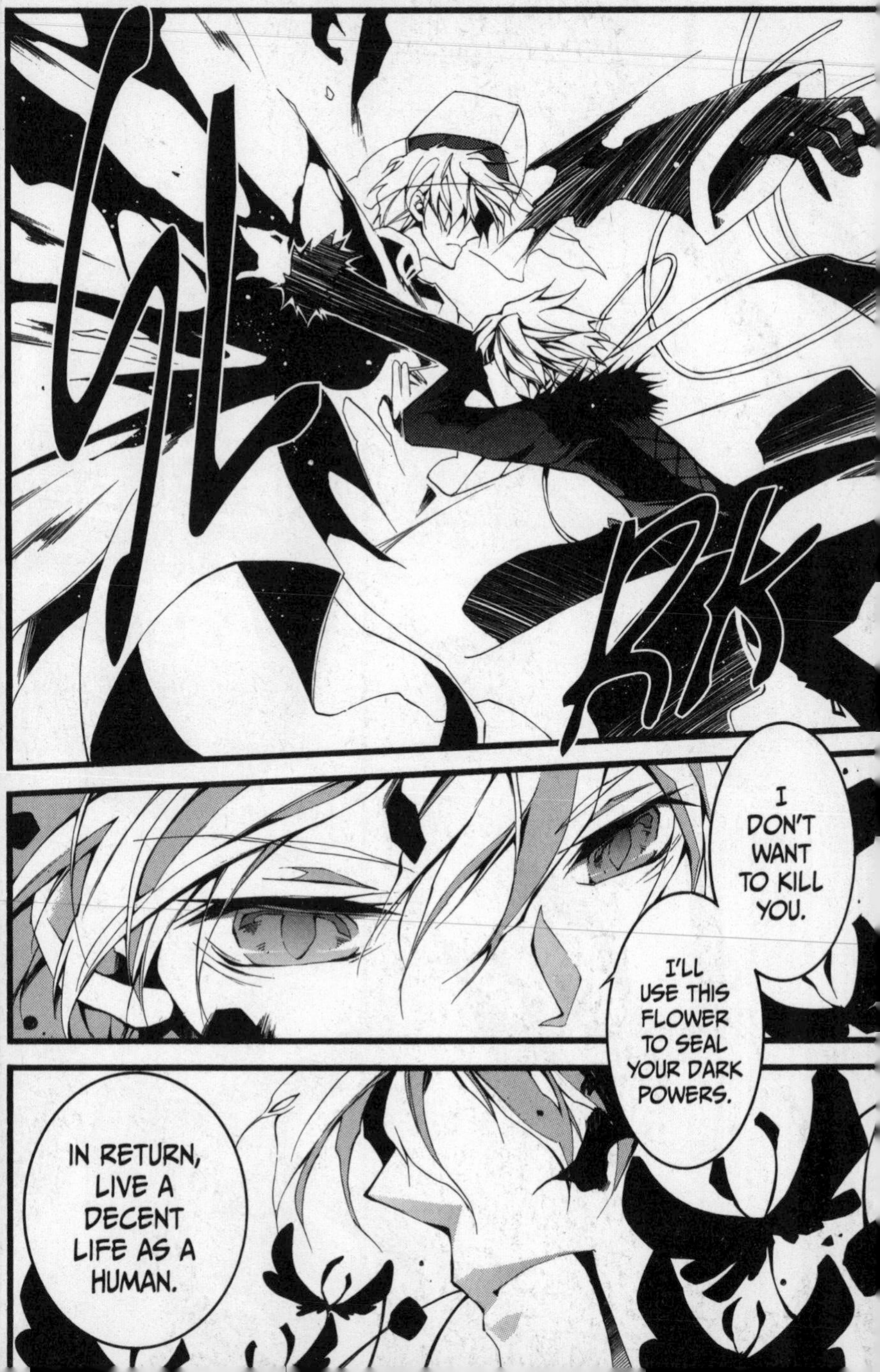
I DON'T WANT TO KILL YOU.
I'LL USE THIS FLOWER TO SEAL YOUR DARK POWERS.
IN RETURN, LIVE A DECENT LIFE AS A HUMAN.

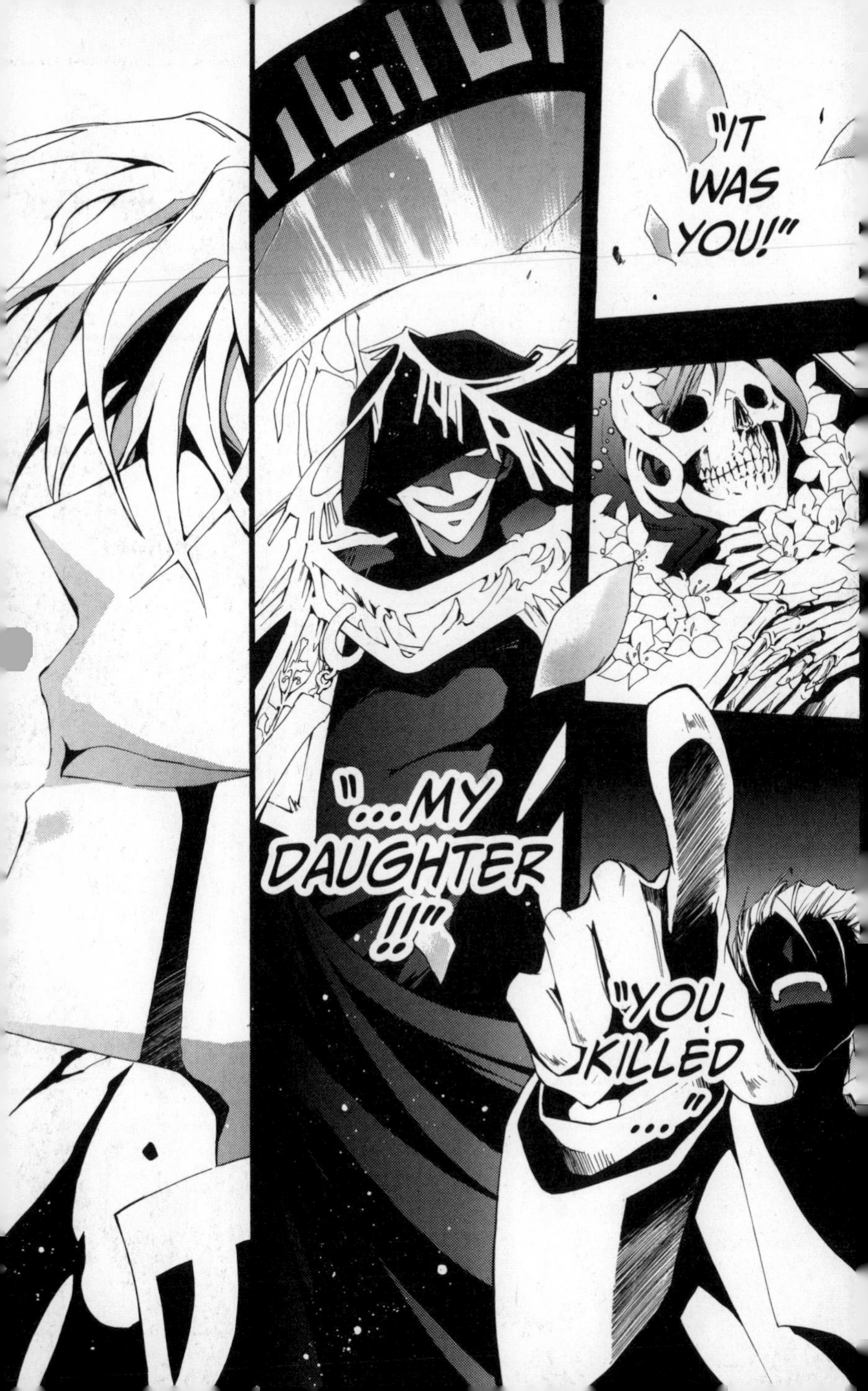
"IT WAS YOU!"
"YOU KILLED ..."
"...MY DAUGHTER!!"

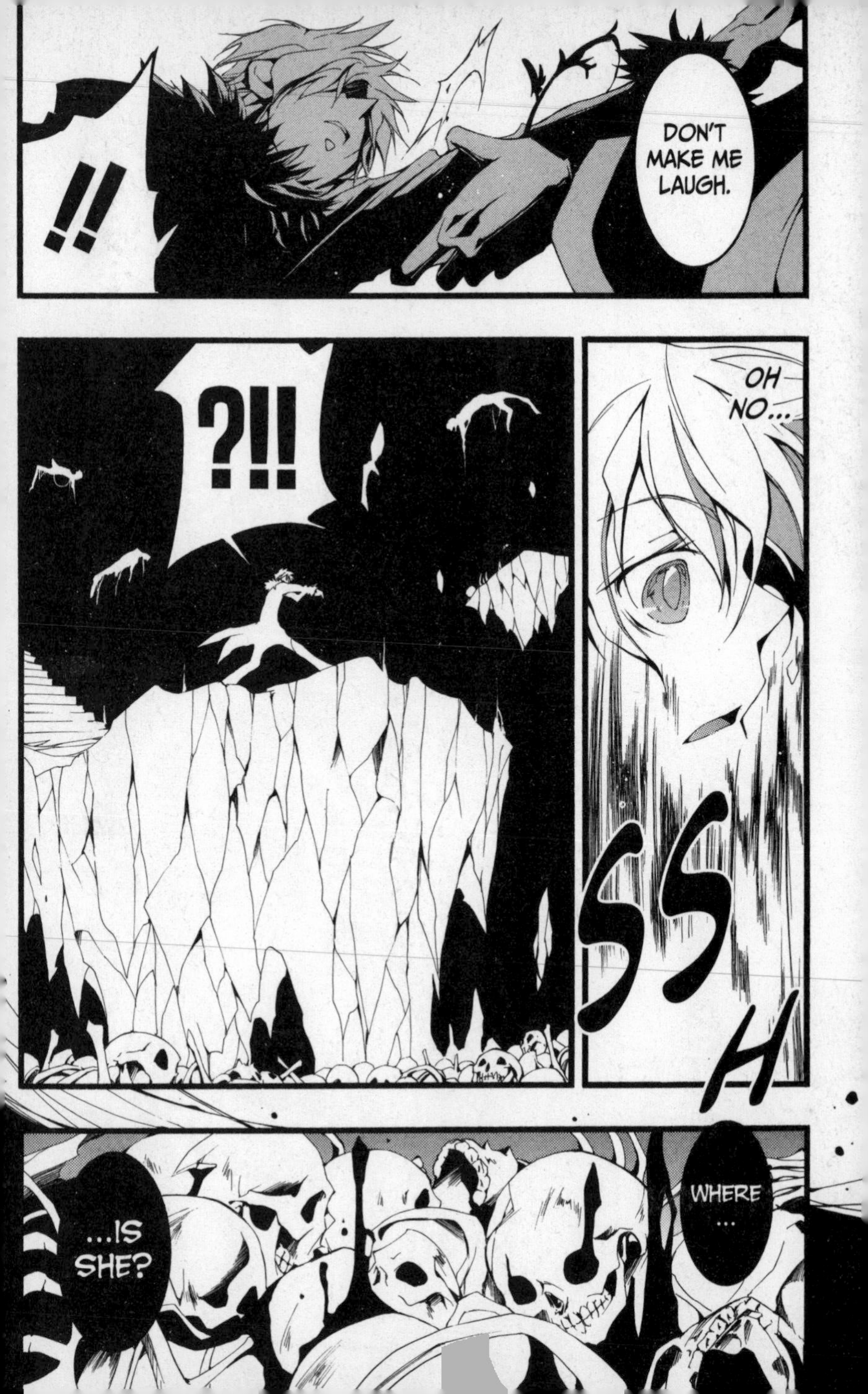
DON'T MAKE ME LAUGH.
!!
OH NO...
SSH
?!!
WHERE ...
...IS SHE?

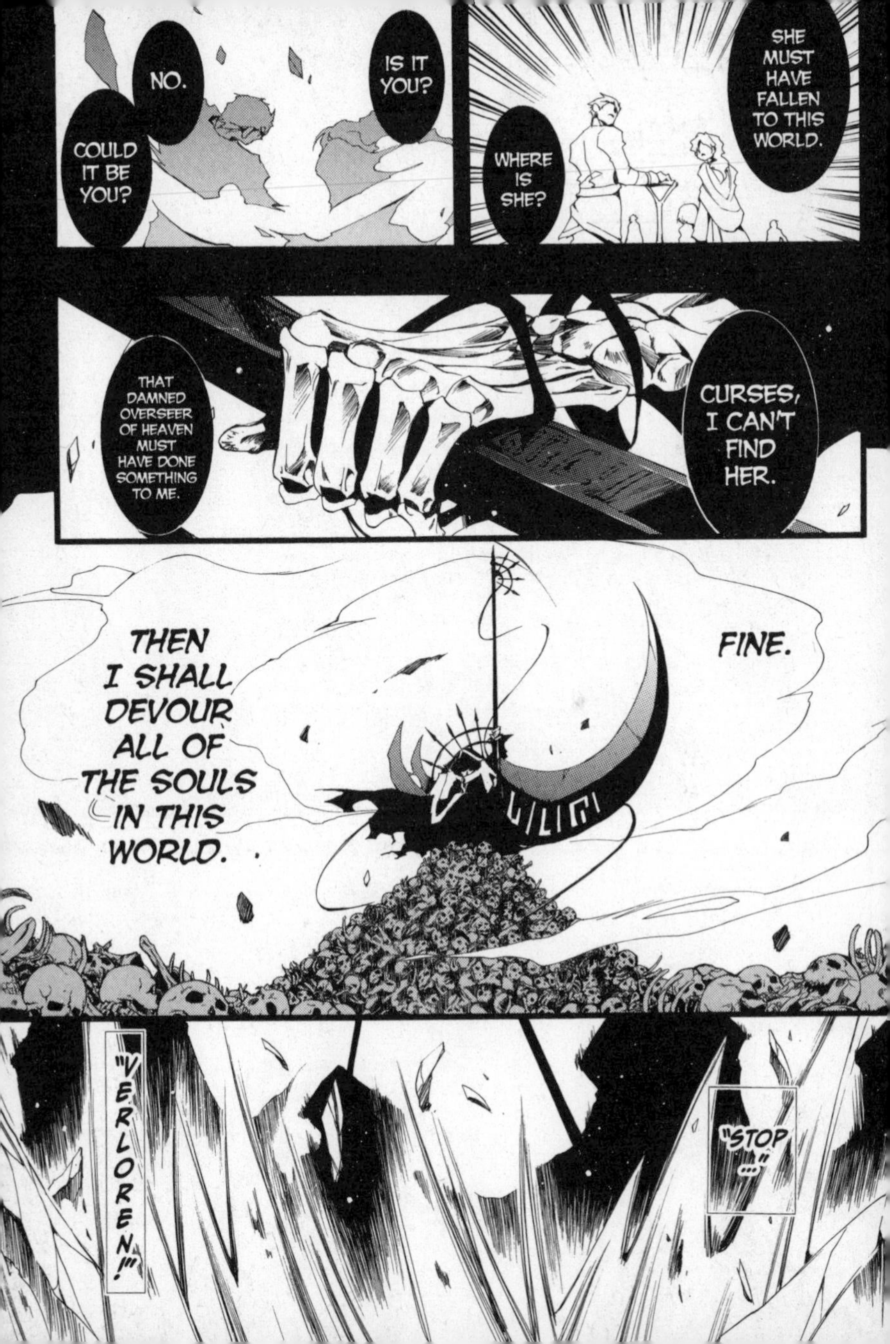
SHE MUST HAVE FALLEN TO THIS WORLD.
WHERE IS SHE?
IS IT YOU?
NO.
COULD IT BE YOU?
CURSES, I CAN'T FIND HER.
THAT DAMNED OVERSEER OF HEAVEN MUST HAVE DONE SOMETHING TO ME.
FINE.
THEN I SHALL DEVOUR ALL OF THE SOULS IN THIS WORLD.
"STOP..."
"VERLOREN!"

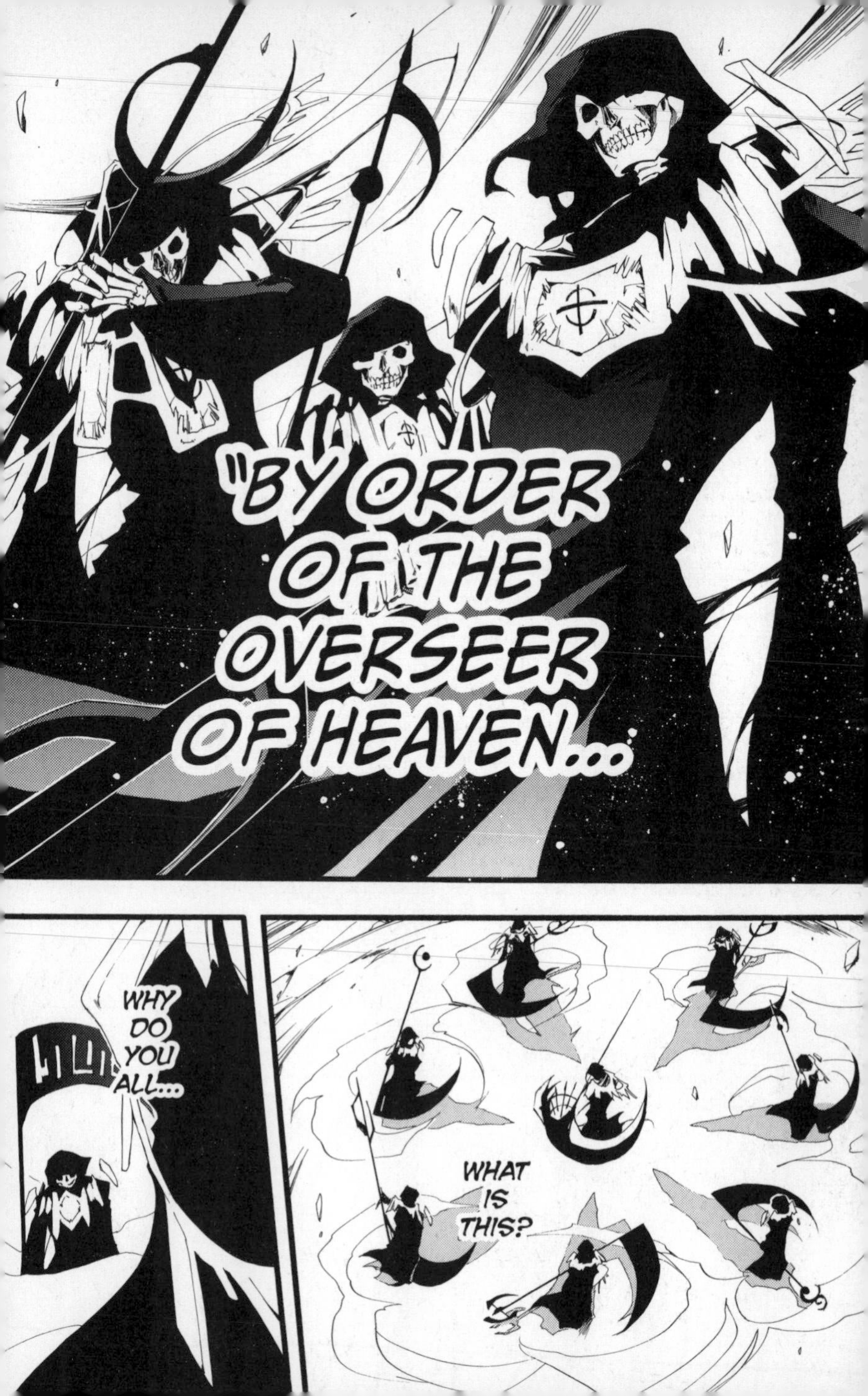
"BY ORDER OF THE OVERSEER OF HEAVEN...
WHAT IS THIS?
WHY DO YOU ALL...

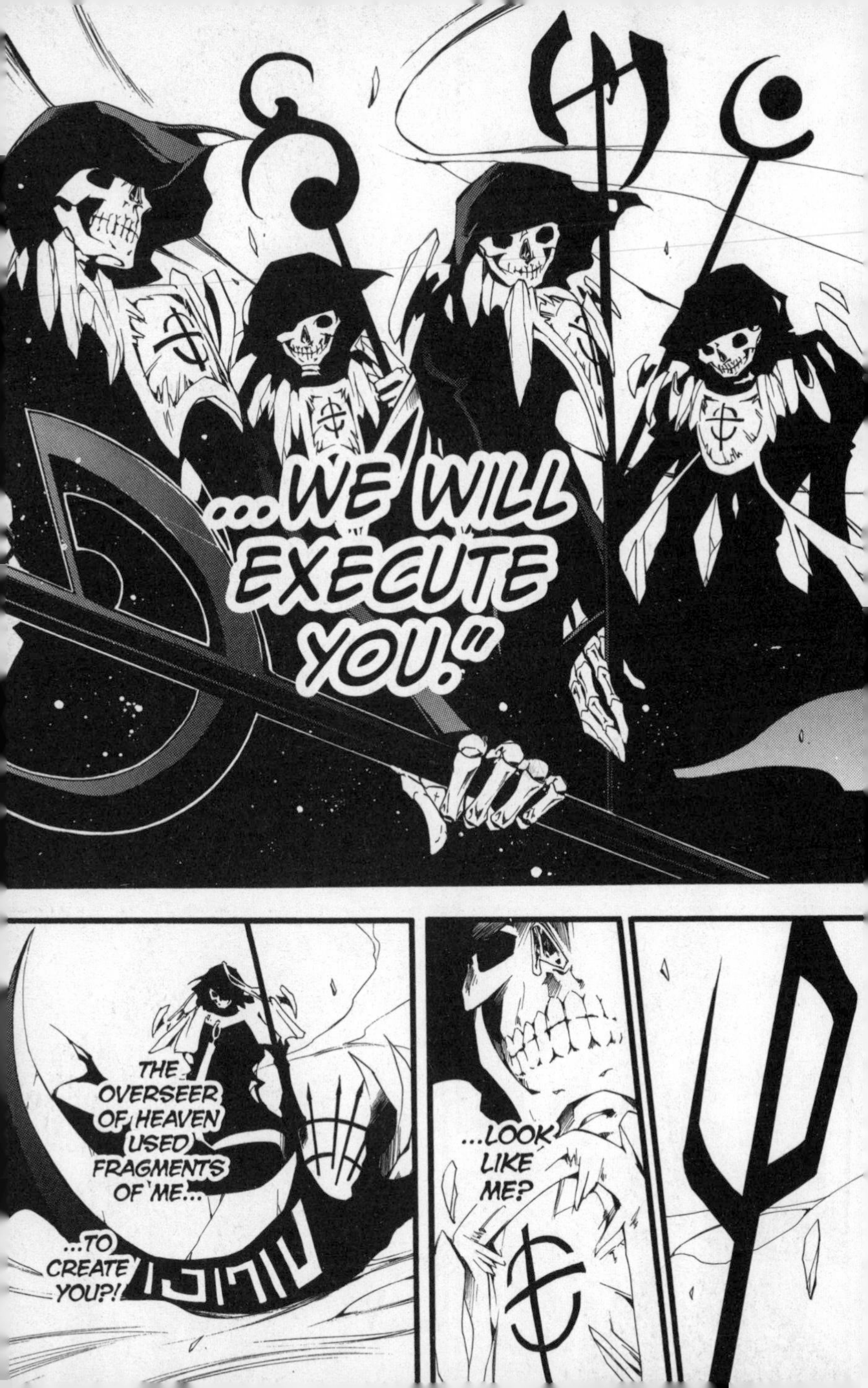
...WE WILL EXECUTE YOU."
...LOOK LIKE ME?
THE OVERSEER OF HEAVEN USED FRAGMENTS OF ME...
...TO CREATE YOU?!

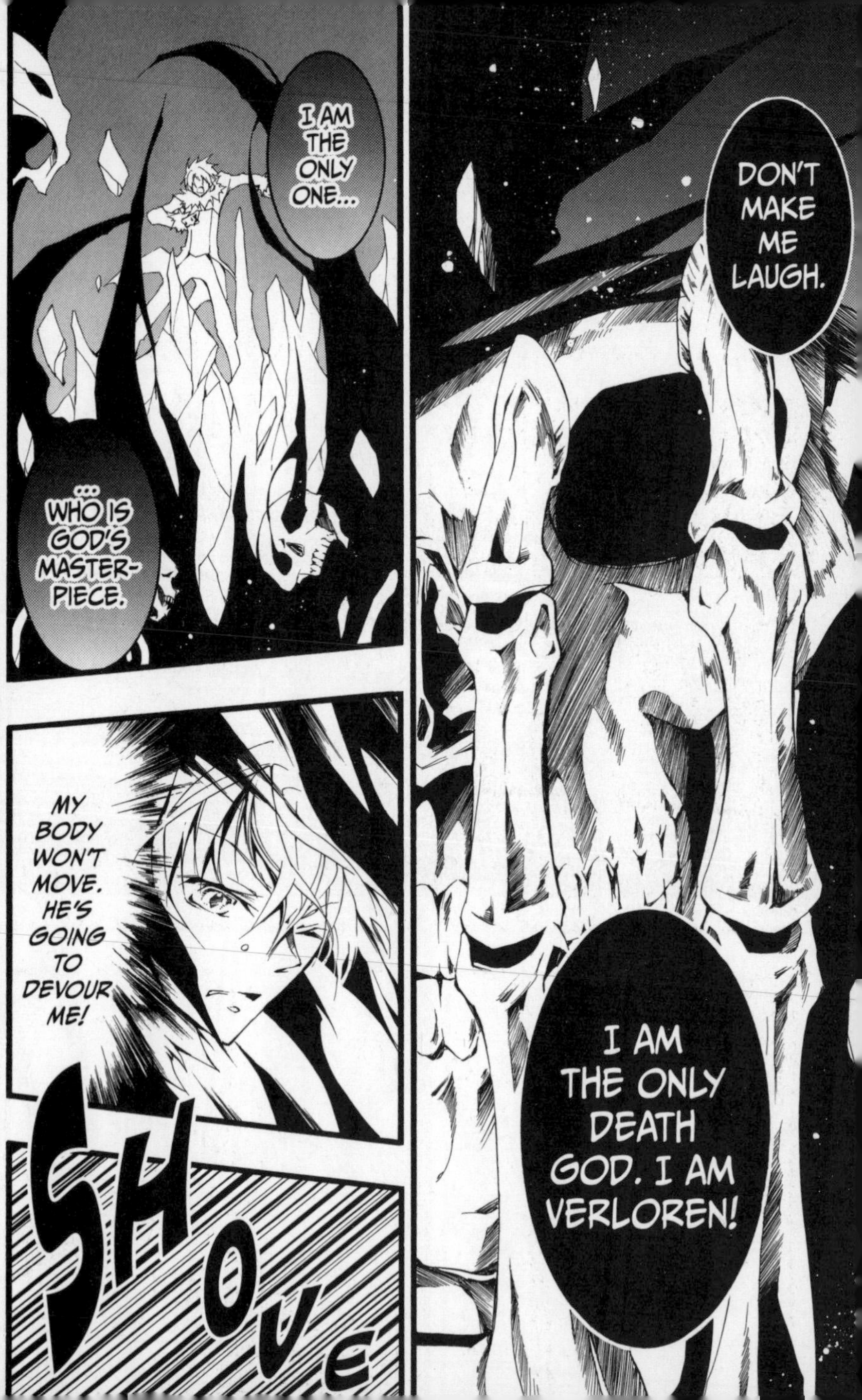
DON'T MAKE ME LAUGH.
I AM THE ONLY DEATH GOD. I AM VERLOREN!
I AM THE ONLY ONE...
...WHO IS GOD'S MASTER-PIECE.
MY BODY WON'T MOVE. HE'S GOING TO DEVOUR ME!
SHOVE

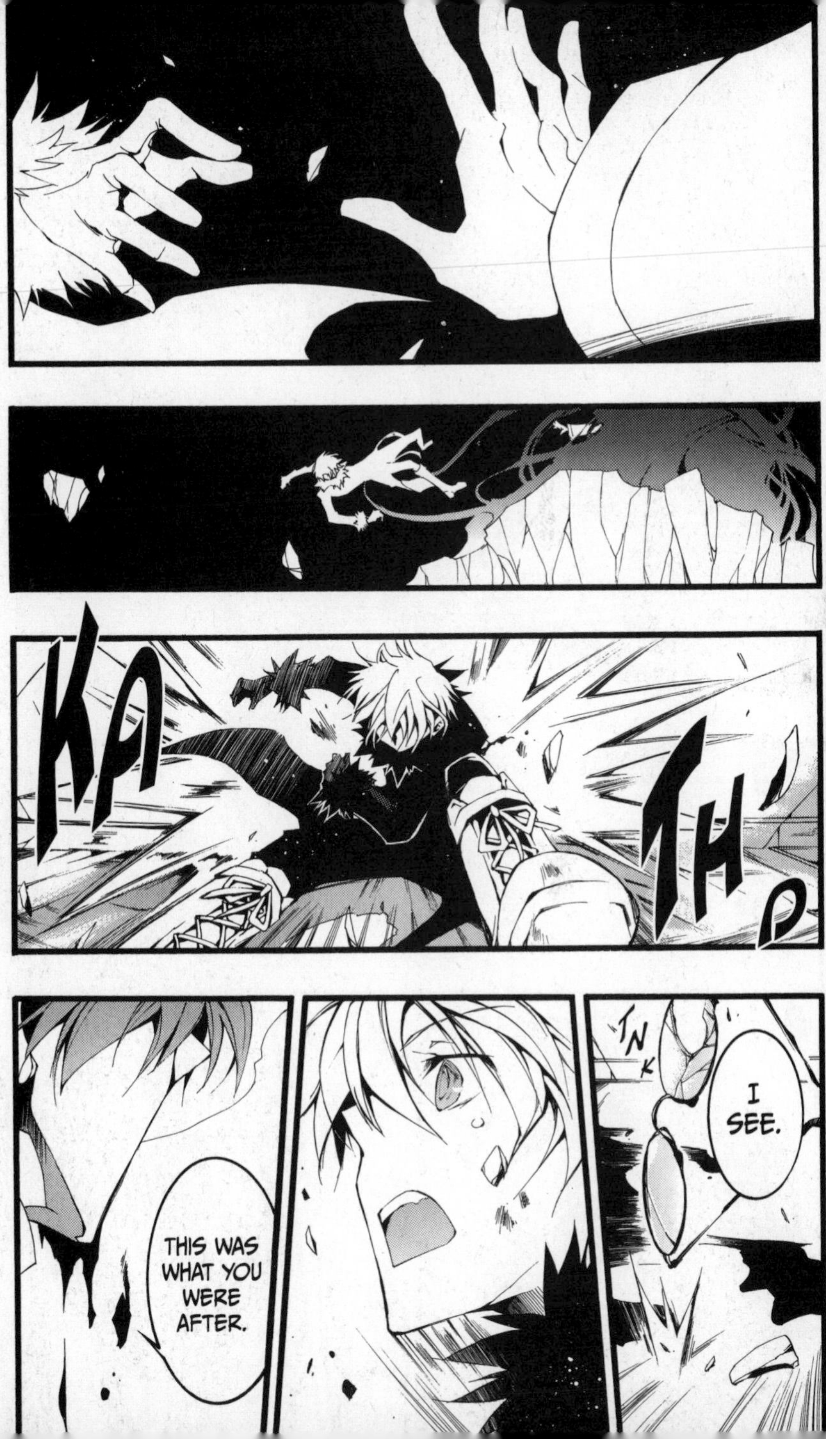
KA
THD
TNK
I SEE.
THIS WAS WHAT YOU WERE AFTER.

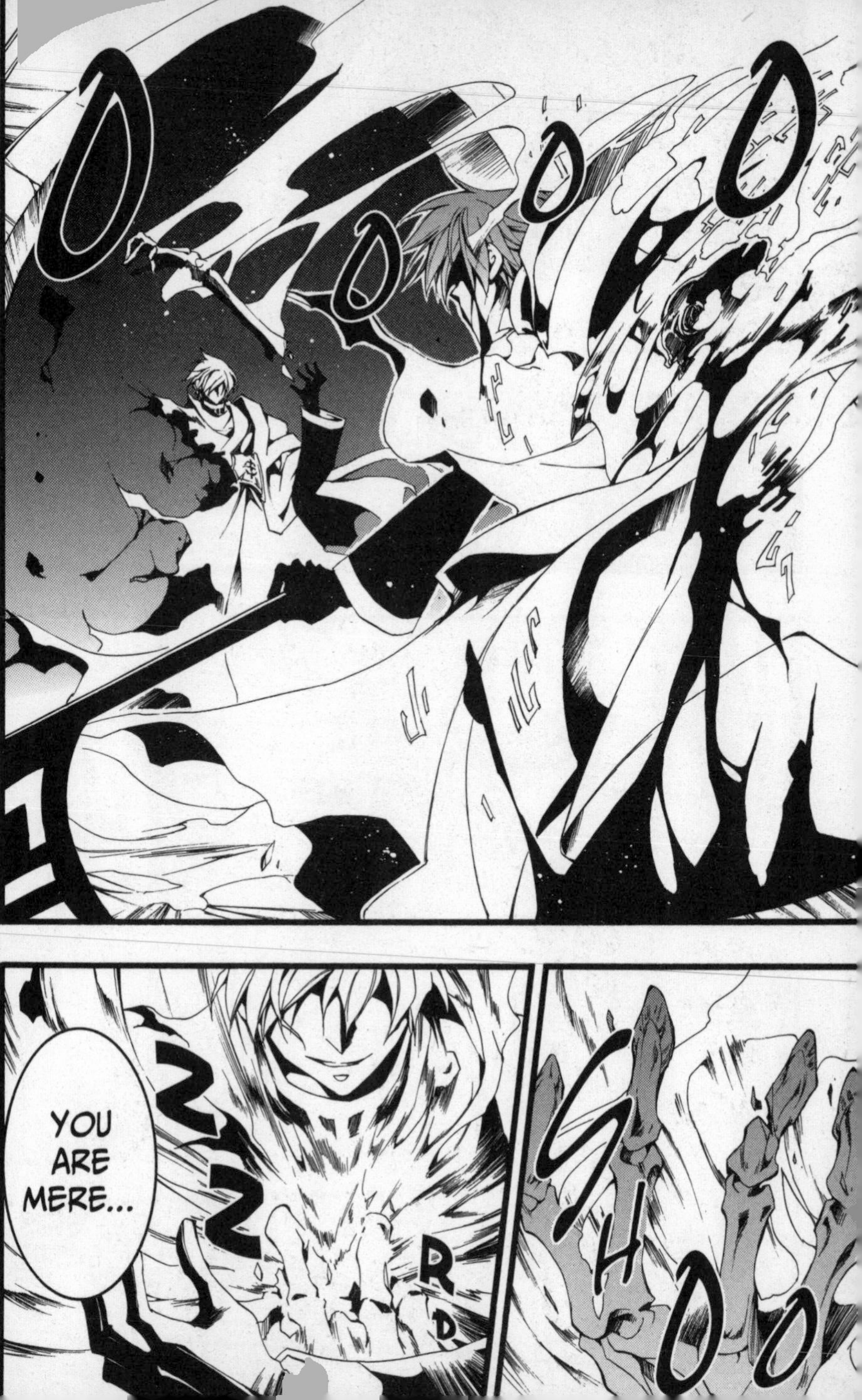
DODODDD
SHOOO
YOU ARE MERE...
ZZ
RD

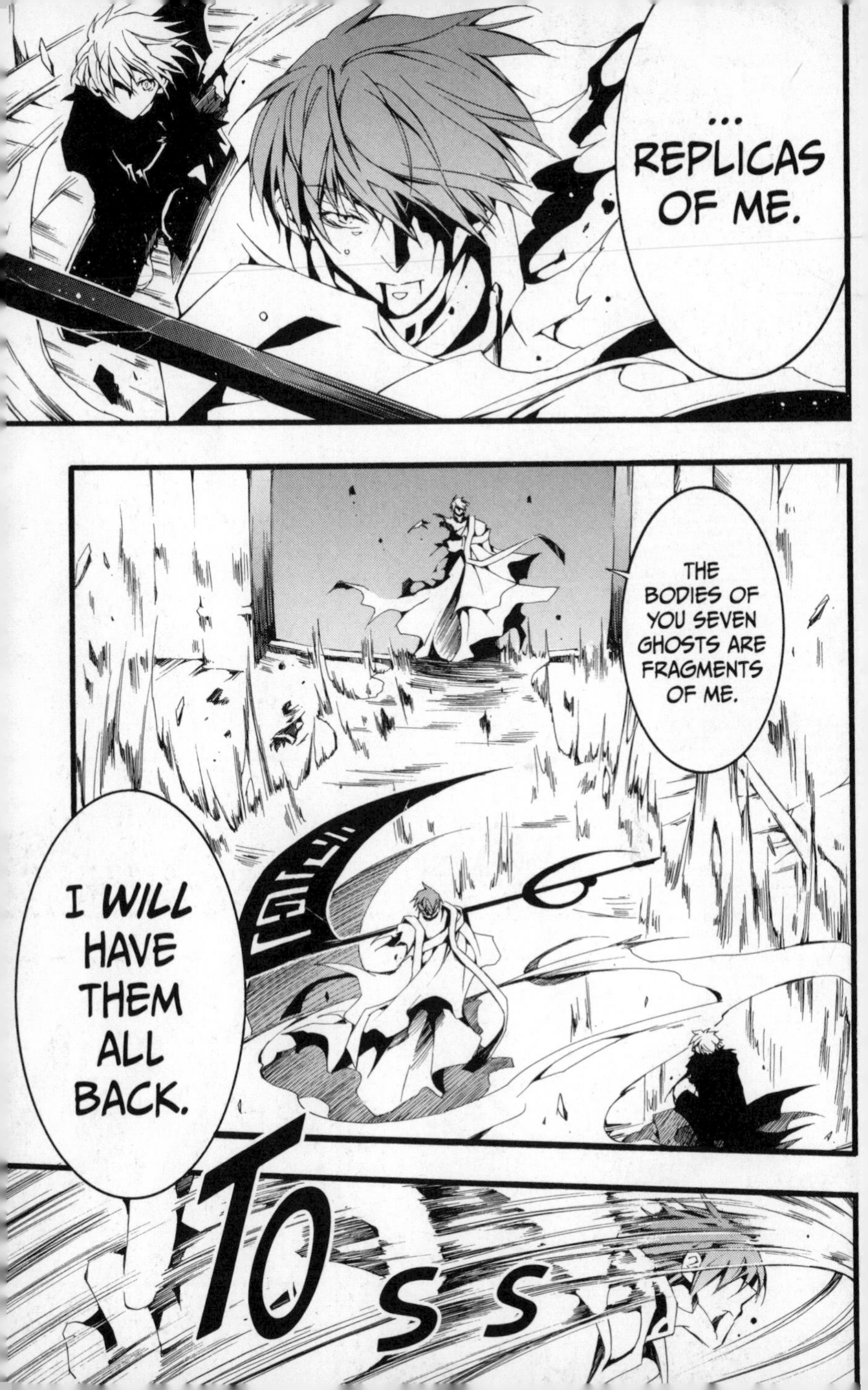
...REPLICAS OF ME.
THE BODIES OF YOU SEVEN GHOSTS ARE FRAGMENTS OF ME.
I *WILL* HAVE THEM ALL BACK.
TOSS

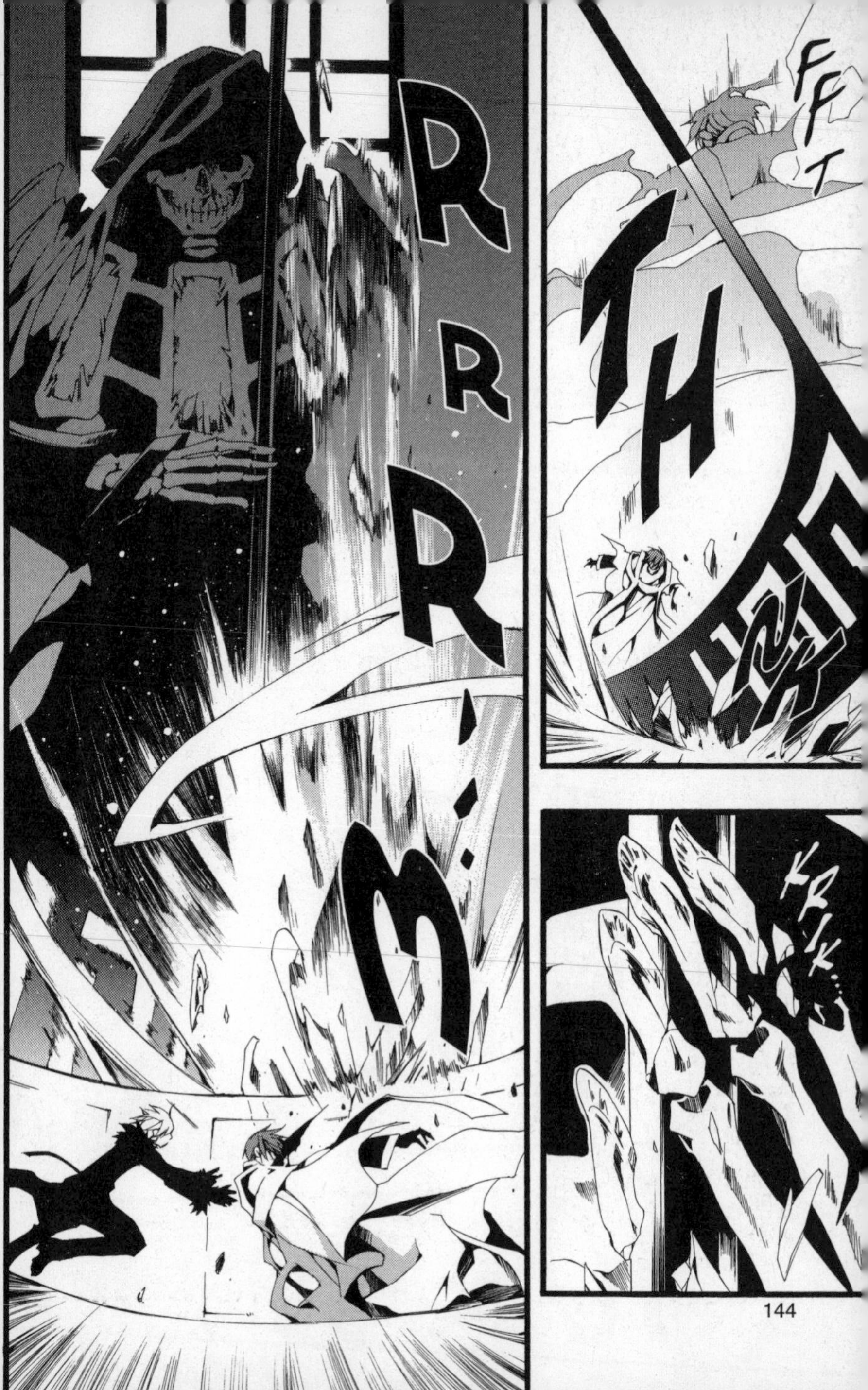
FFT
THUNK
KRIK...
RRRM

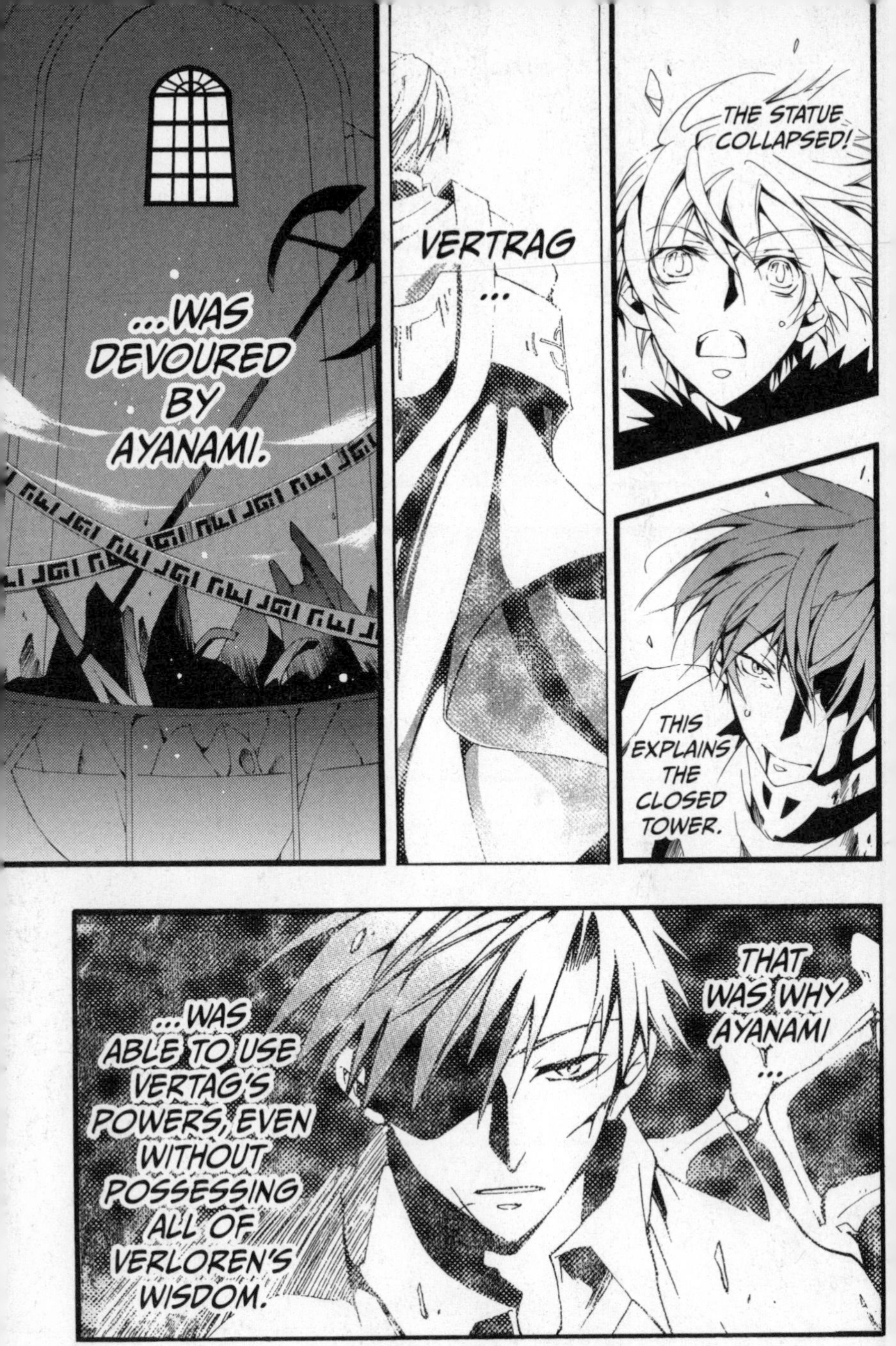
THE STATUE COLLAPSED!
THIS EXPLAINS THE CLOSED TOWER.
VERTRAG ...
...WAS DEVOURED BY AYANAMI.
THAT WAS WHY AYANAMI ...
...WAS ABLE TO USE VERTAG'S POWERS, EVEN WITHOUT POSSESSING ALL OF VERLOREN'S WISDOM.

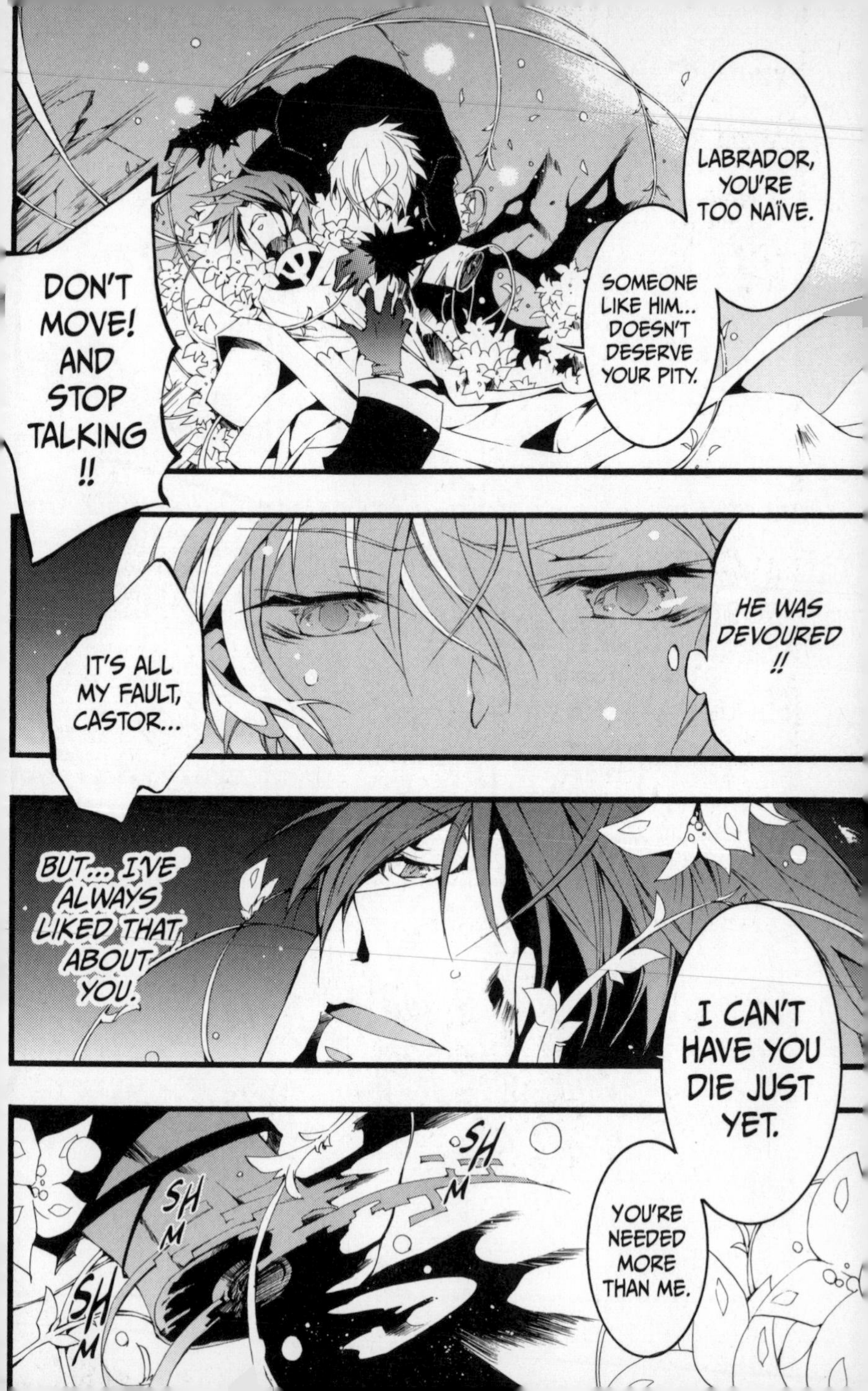
LABRADOR, YOU'RE TOO NAÏVE.
SOMEONE LIKE HIM... DOESN'T DESERVE YOUR PITY.
DON'T MOVE! AND STOP TALKING !!
HE WAS DEVOURED !!
IT'S ALL MY FAULT, CASTOR...
BUT... I'VE ALWAYS LIKED THAT ABOUT YOU.
I CAN'T HAVE YOU DIE JUST YET.
YOU'RE NEEDED MORE THAN ME.
SHM
SHM
SHM

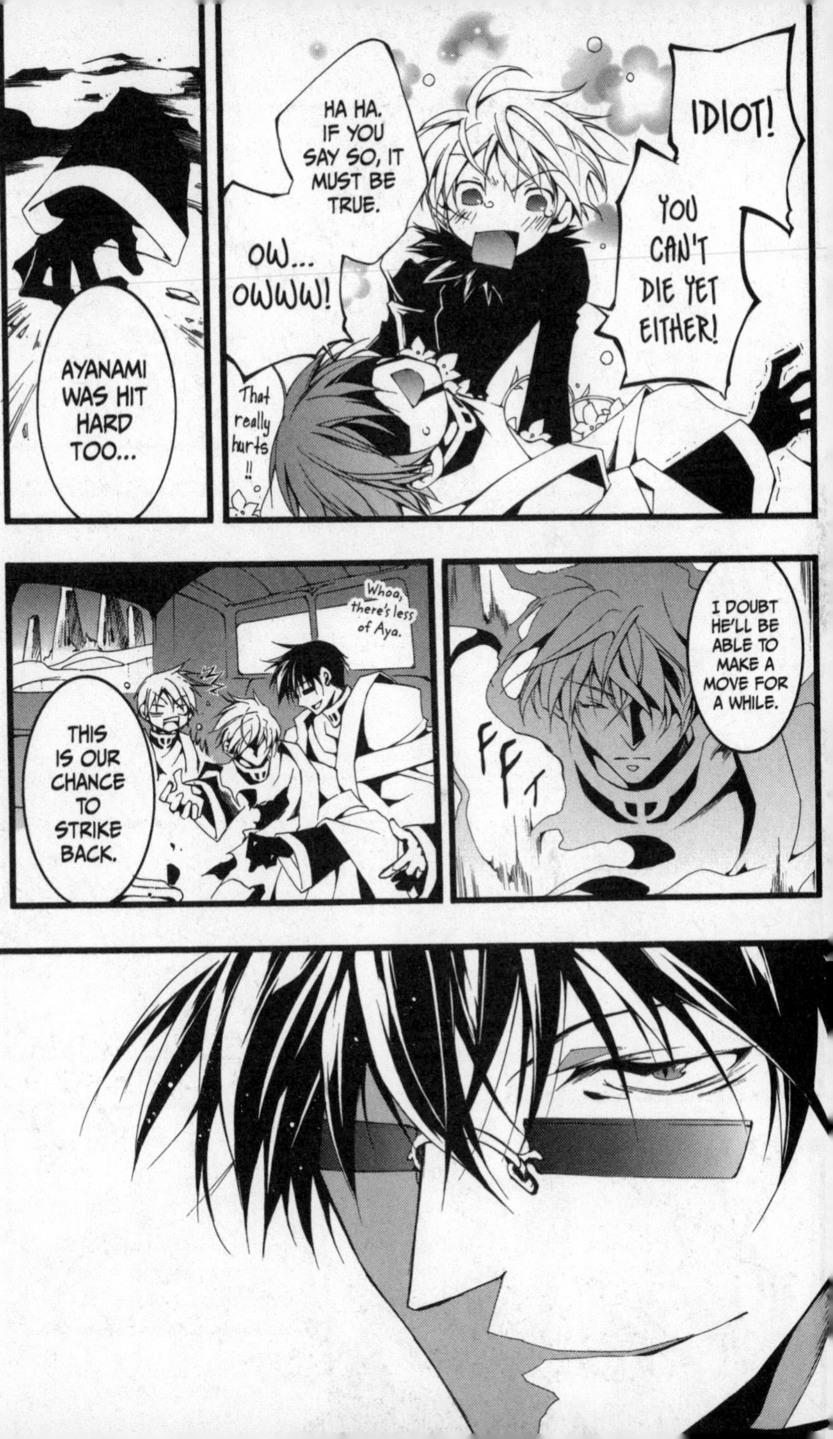
IDIOT!
YOU CAN'T DIE YET EITHER!
HA HA. IF YOU SAY SO, IT MUST BE TRUE.
OW... OWWW!
That really hurts!!
AYANAMI WAS HIT HARD TOO...
I DOUBT HE'LL BE ABLE TO MAKE A MOVE FOR A WHILE.
FFT
Whoa, there's less of Aya.
THIS IS OUR CHANCE TO STRIKE BACK.

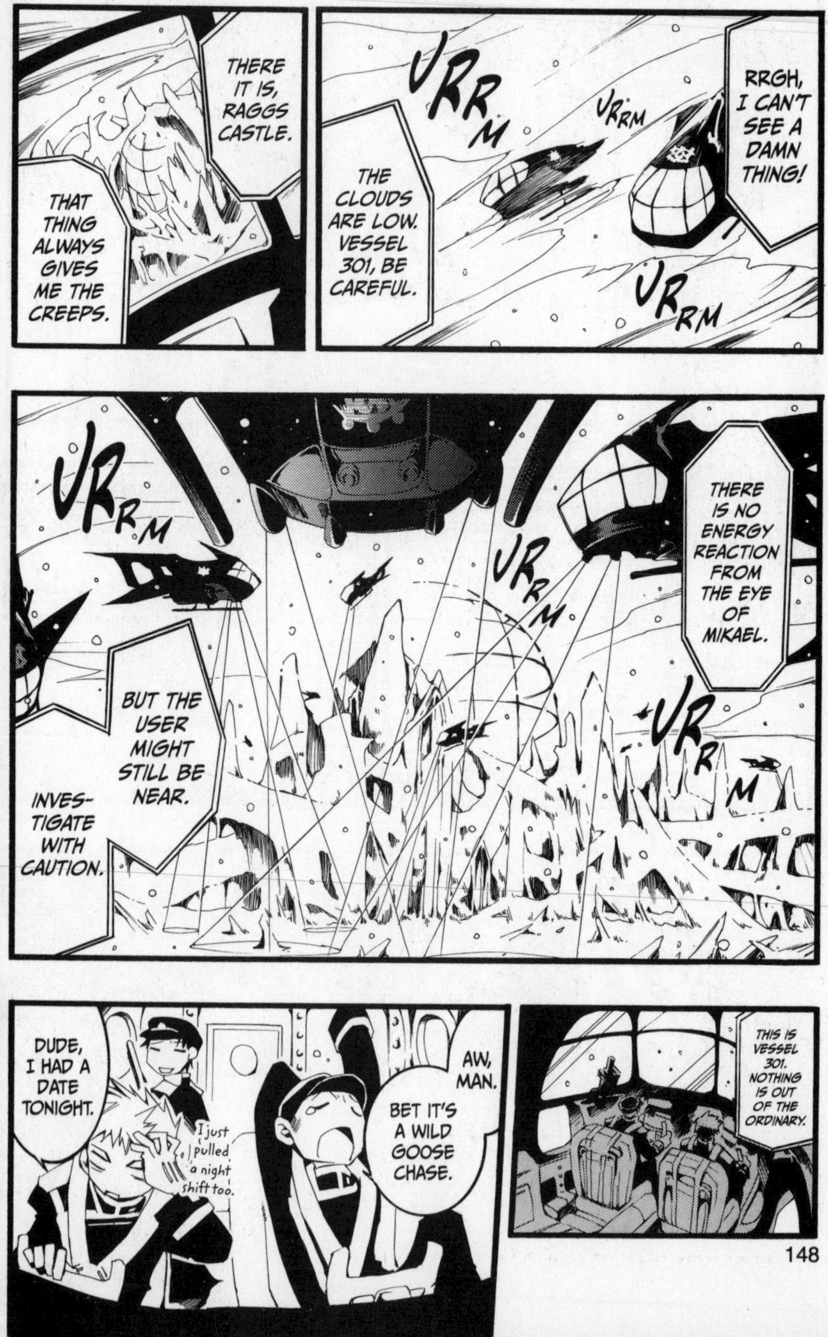
RRGH, I CAN'T SEE A DAMN THING!
VRRM
VRRM
VRRM
THE CLOUDS ARE LOW. VESSEL 301, BE CAREFUL.
THERE IT IS, RAGGS CASTLE.
THAT THING ALWAYS GIVES ME THE CREEPS.
THERE IS NO ENERGY REACTION FROM THE EYE OF MIKAEL.
VRRM
VRRM
VRRM
BUT THE USER MIGHT STILL BE NEAR.
INVES-TIGATE WITH CAUTION.
THIS IS VESSEL 301. NOTHING IS OUT OF THE ORDINARY.
AW, MAN.
BET IT'S A WILD GOOSE CHASE.
DUDE, I HAD A DATE TONIGHT.
I just pulled a night shift too.

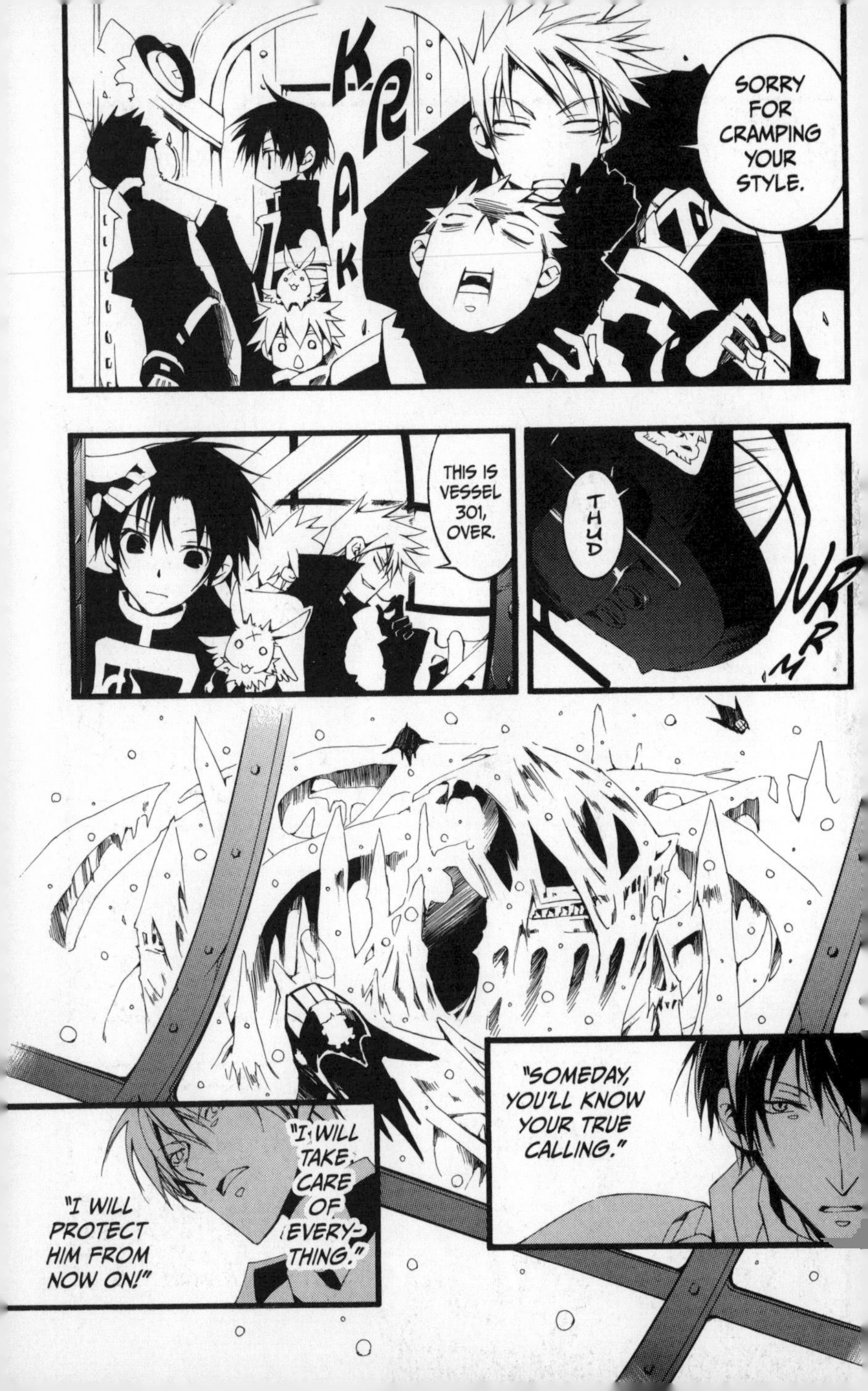
SORRY FOR CRAMPING YOUR STYLE.
KRAK
THUD
VRRM
THIS IS VESSEL 301, OVER.
"SOMEDAY, YOU'LL KNOW YOUR TRUE CALLING."
"I WILL TAKE CARE OF EVERYTHING."
"I WILL PROTECT HIM FROM NOW ON!"

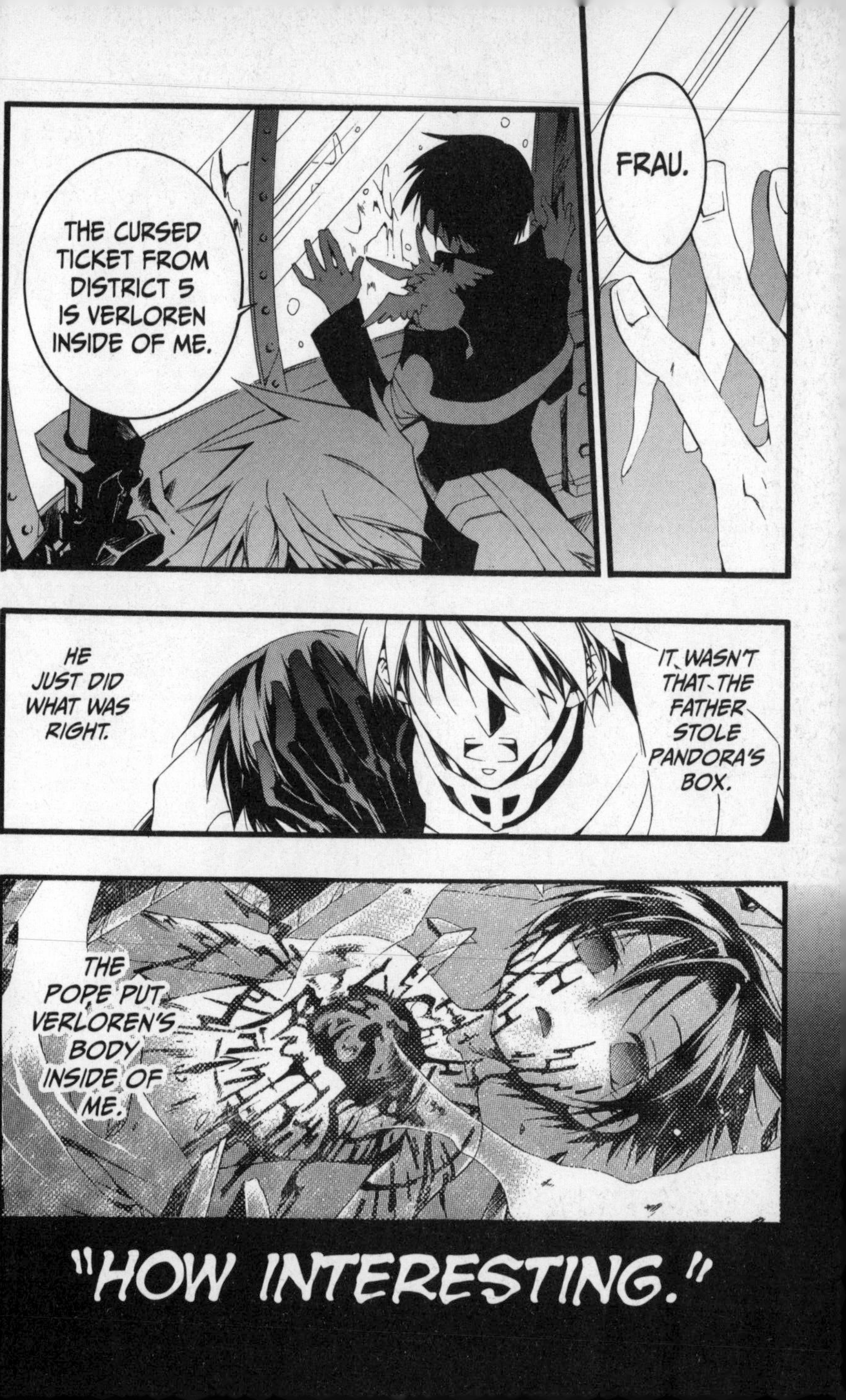
FRAU.
THE CURSED TICKET FROM DISTRICT 5 IS VERLOREN INSIDE OF ME.
IT WASN'T THAT THE FATHER STOLE PANDORA'S BOX.
HE JUST DID WHAT WAS RIGHT.
THE POPE PUT VERLOREN'S BODY INSIDE OF ME.
"HOW INTERESTING."

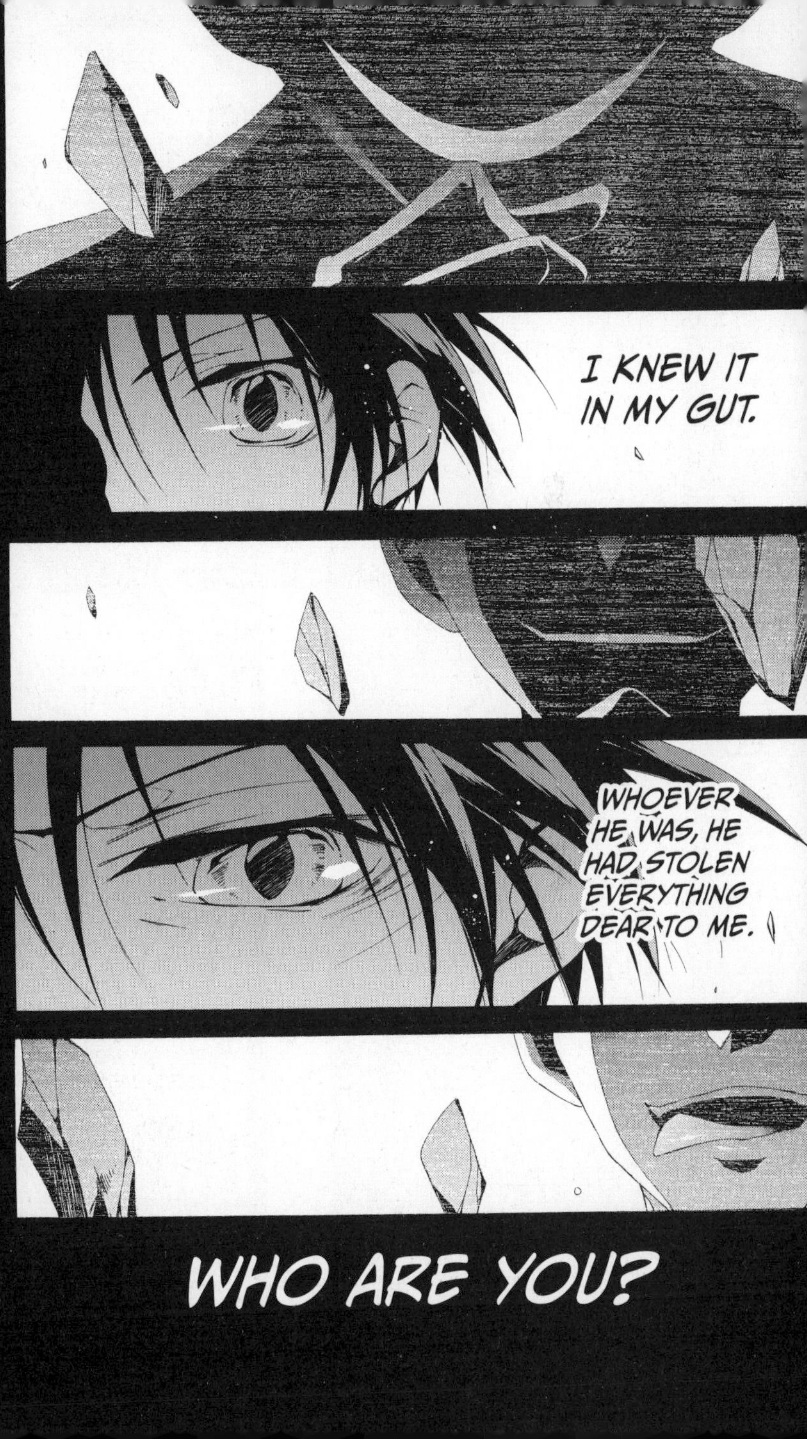
I KNEW IT IN MY GUT.
WHOEVER HE WAS, HE HAD STOLEN EVERYTHING DEAR TO ME.
WHO ARE YOU?

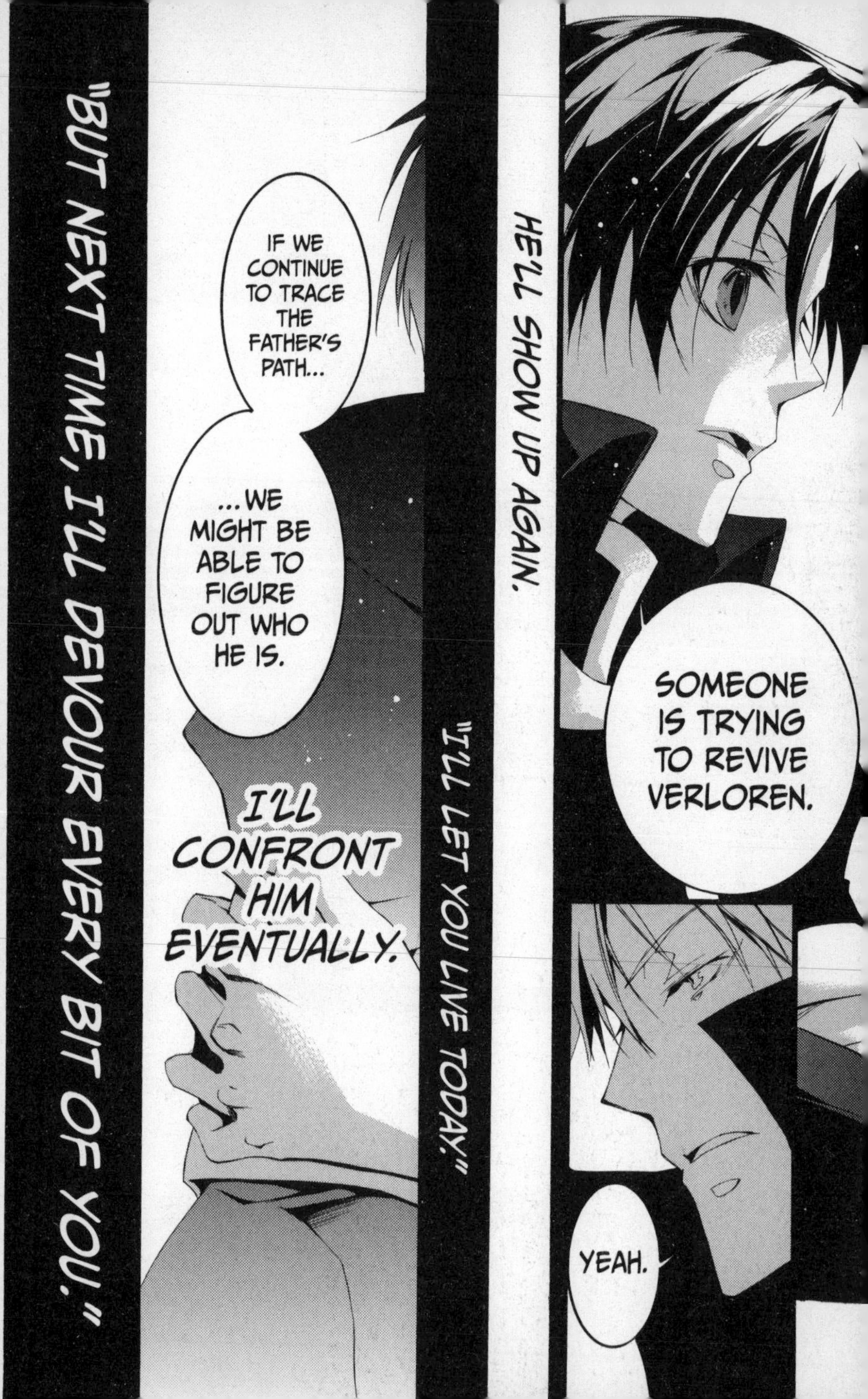
SOMEONE IS TRYING TO REVIVE VERLOREN.
YEAH.
HE'LL SHOW UP AGAIN.
"I'LL LET YOU LIVE TODAY."
IF WE CONTINUE TO TRACE THE FATHER'S PATH...
...WE MIGHT BE ABLE TO FIGURE OUT WHO HE IS.
I'LL CONFRONT HIM EVENTUALLY.
"BUT NEXT TIME, I'LL DEVOUR EVERY BIT OF YOU."

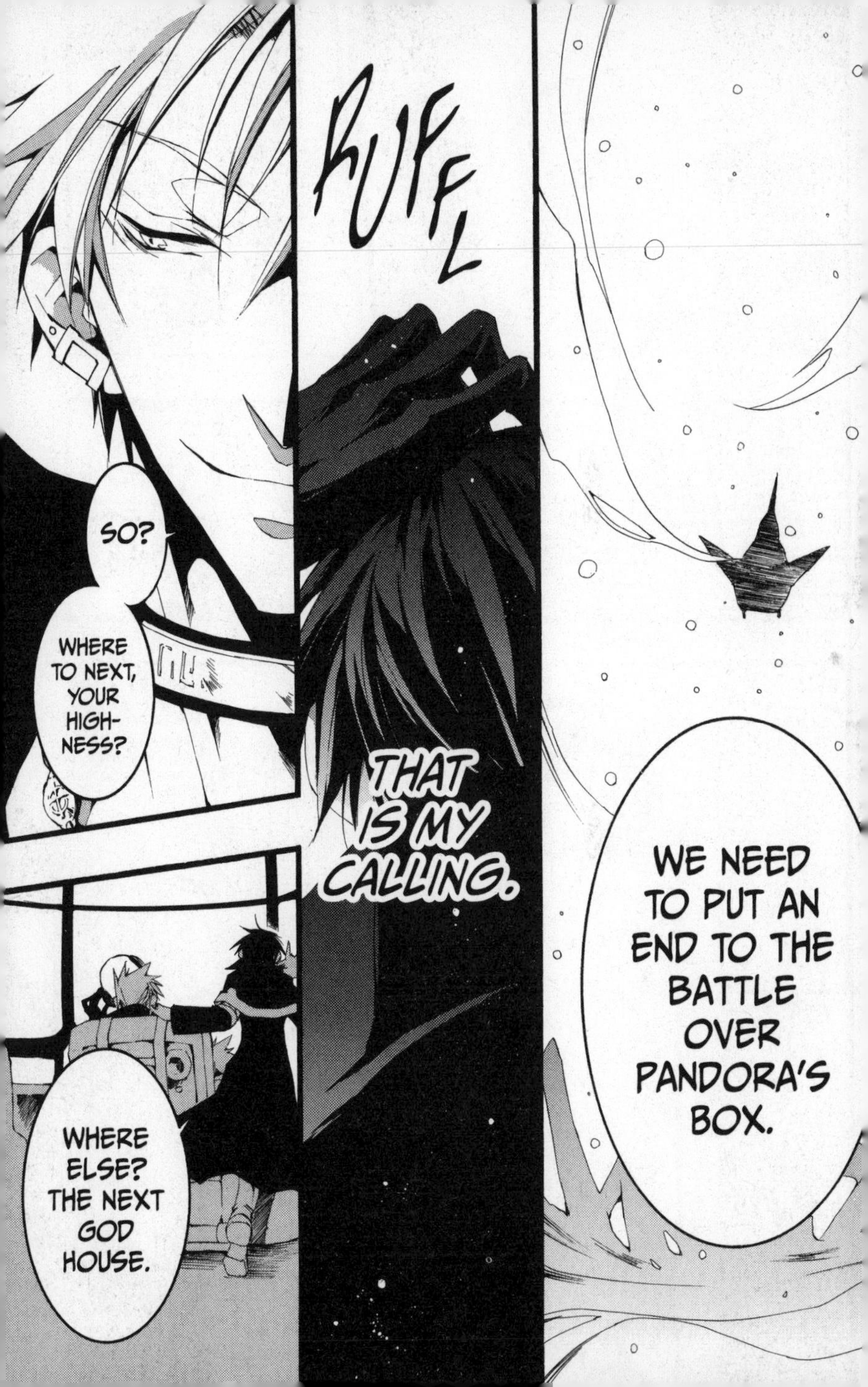
WE NEED TO PUT AN END TO THE BATTLE OVER PANDORA'S BOX.
RUFFL
THAT IS MY CALLING.
SO?
WHERE TO NEXT, YOUR HIGHNESS?
WHERE ELSE? THE NEXT GOD HOUSE.

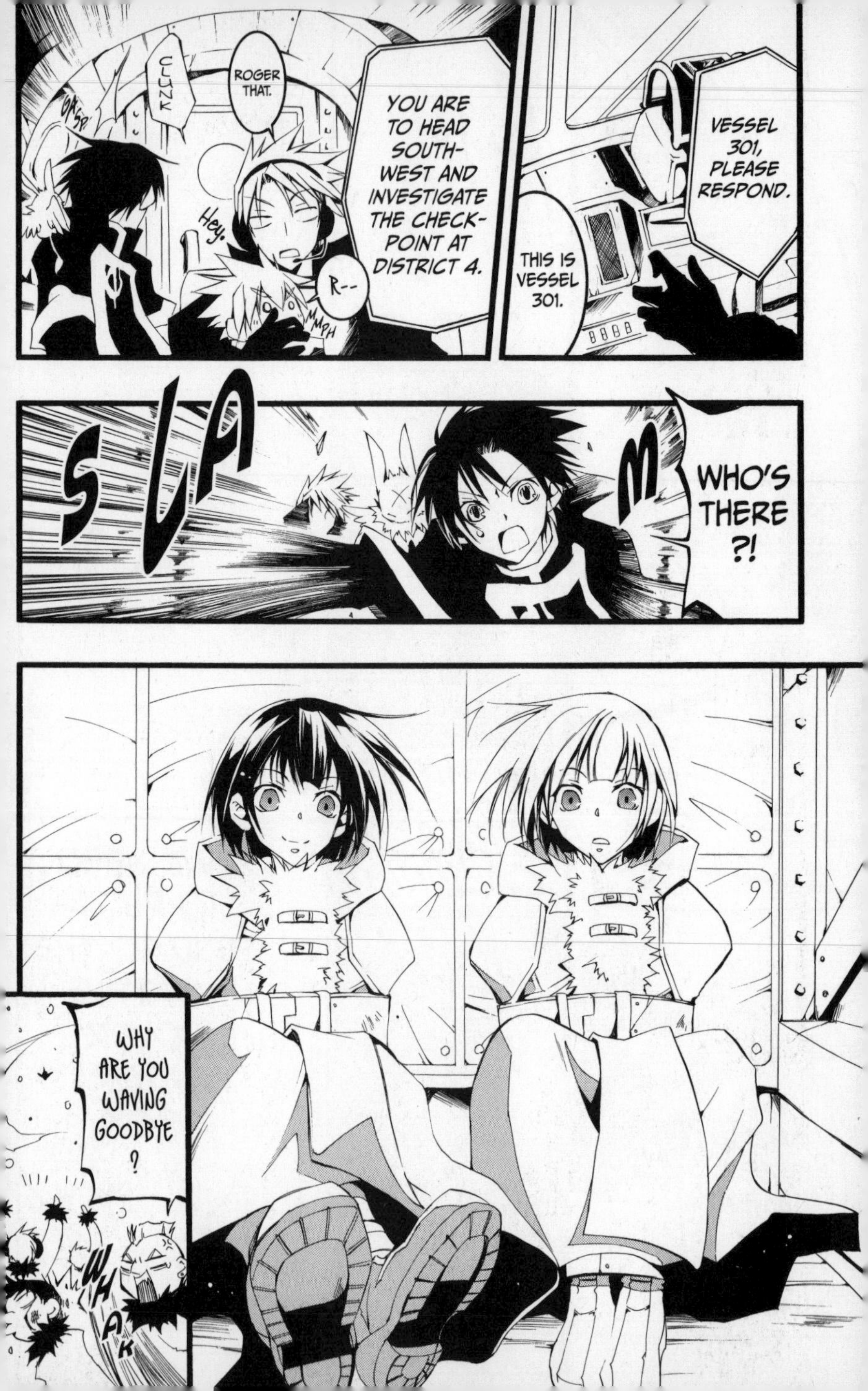
VESSEL 301, PLEASE RESPOND.
THIS IS VESSEL 301.
YOU ARE TO HEAD SOUTH-WEST AND INVESTIGATE THE CHECK-POINT AT DISTRICT 4.
ROGER THAT.
CLUNK
Hey.
R--
MMPH
WHO'S THERE ?!
WHY ARE YOU WAVING GOODBYE ?
WHAK

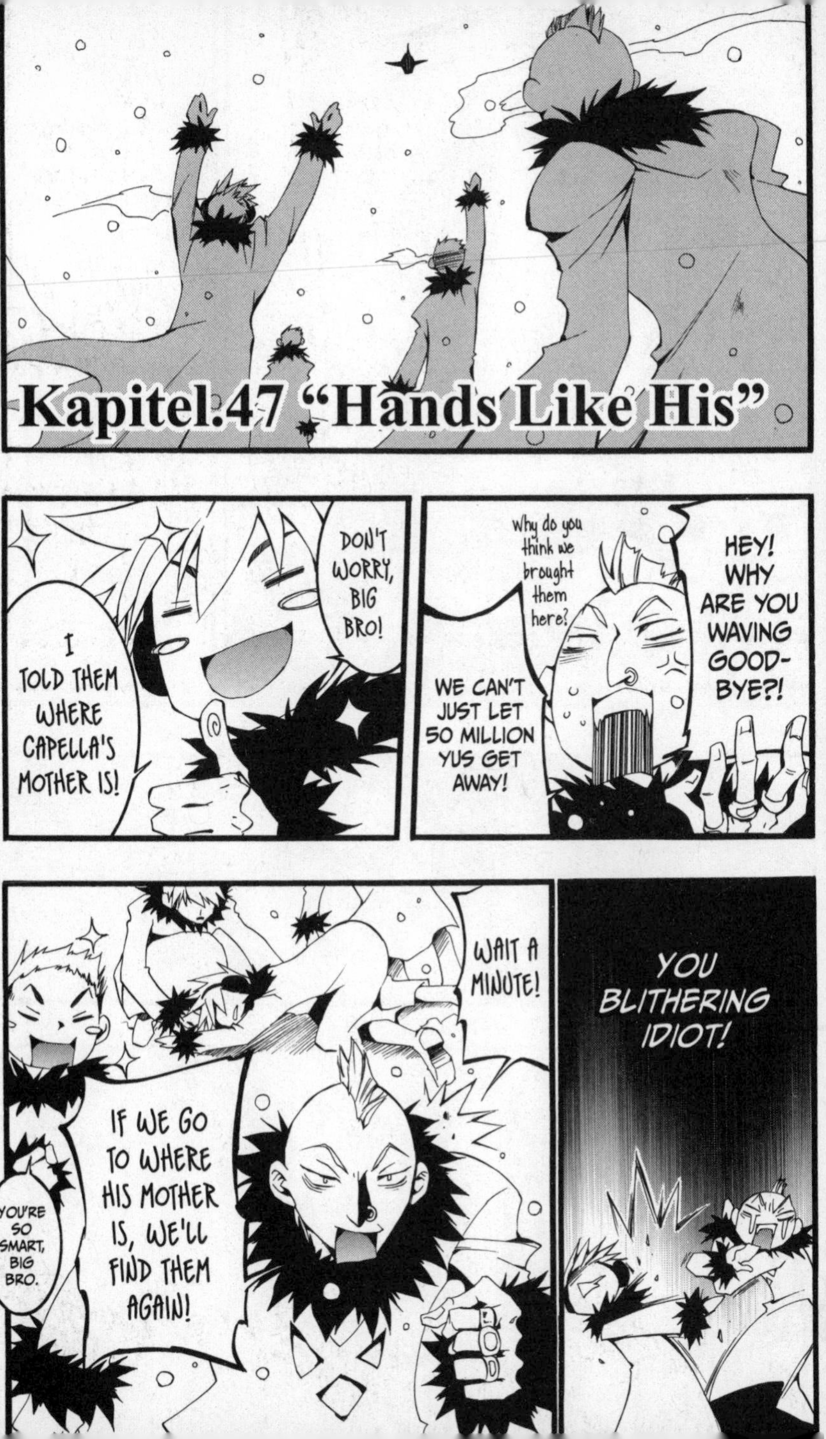
Kapitel.47 "Hands Like His"
DON'T WORRY, BIG BRO!
I TOLD THEM WHERE CAPELLA'S MOTHER IS!
HEY! WHY ARE YOU WAVING GOOD-BYE?!
Why do you think we brought them here?
WE CAN'T JUST LET 50 MILLION YUS GET AWAY!
WAIT A MINUTE!
IF WE GO TO WHERE HIS MOTHER IS, WE'LL FIND THEM AGAIN!
YOU'RE SO SMART, BIG BRO.
YOU BLITHERING IDIOT!

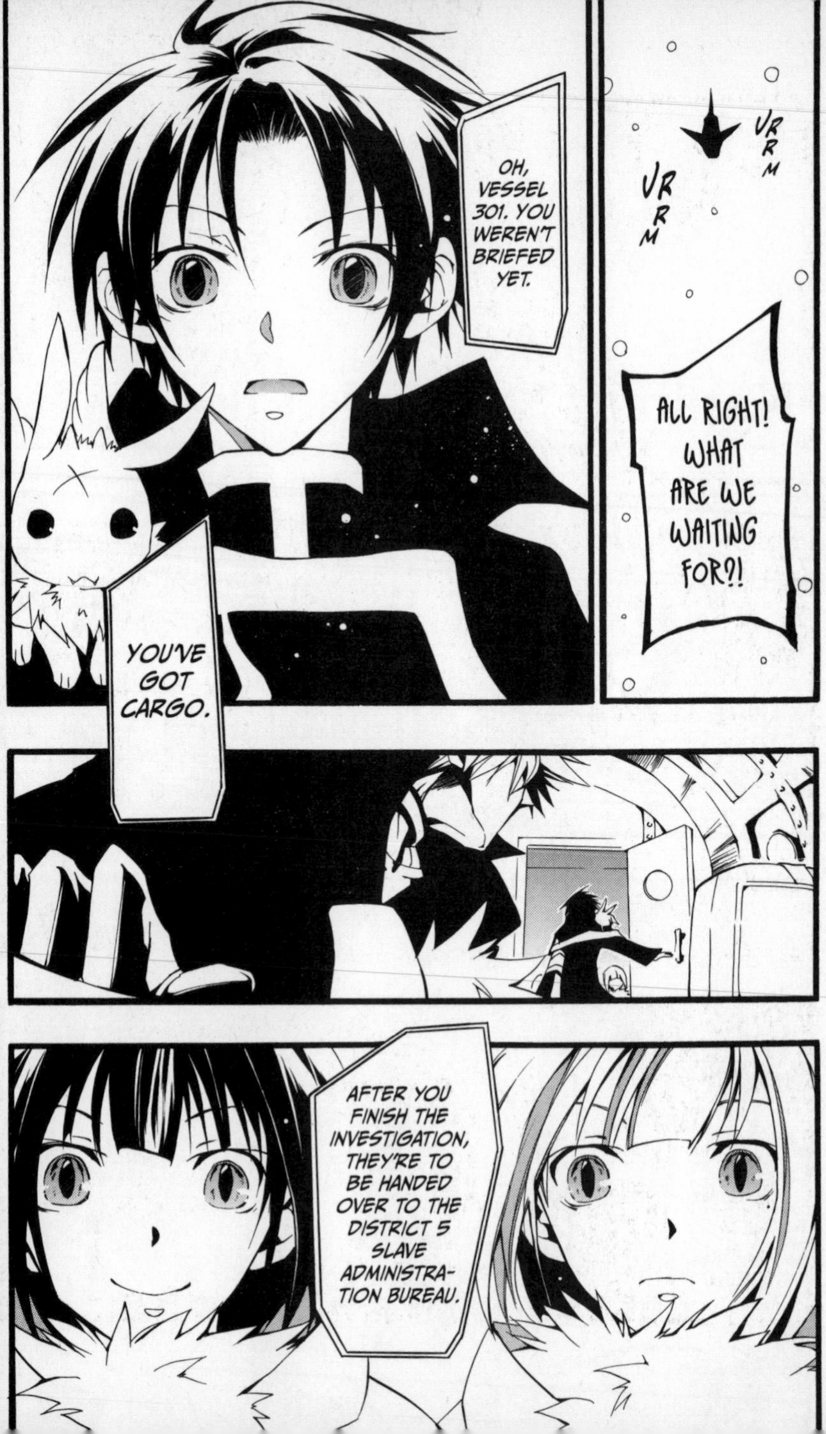
VRRM
VRRM
ALL RIGHT! WHAT ARE WE WAITING FOR?!
OH, VESSEL 301. YOU WEREN'T BRIEFED YET.
YOU'VE GOT CARGO.
AFTER YOU FINISH THE INVESTIGATION, THEY'RE TO BE HANDED OVER TO THE DISTRICT 5 SLAVE ADMINISTRA-TION BUREAU.

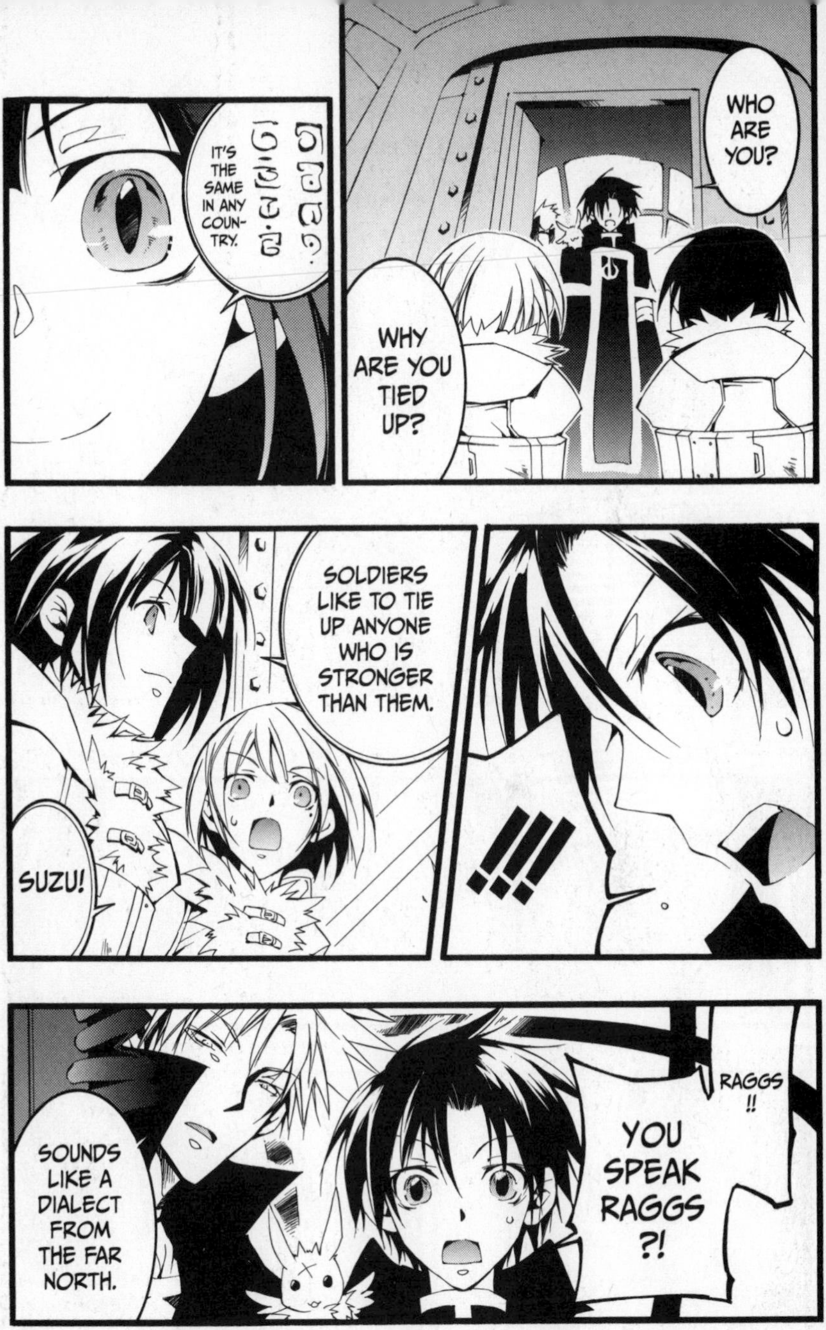
WHO ARE YOU?
WHY ARE YOU TIED UP?
IT'S THE SAME IN ANY COUN-TRY.
!!!
SOLDIERS LIKE TO TIE UP ANYONE WHO IS STRONGER THAN THEM.
SUZU!
RAGGS!!
YOU SPEAK RAGGS?!
SOUNDS LIKE A DIALECT FROM THE FAR NORTH.

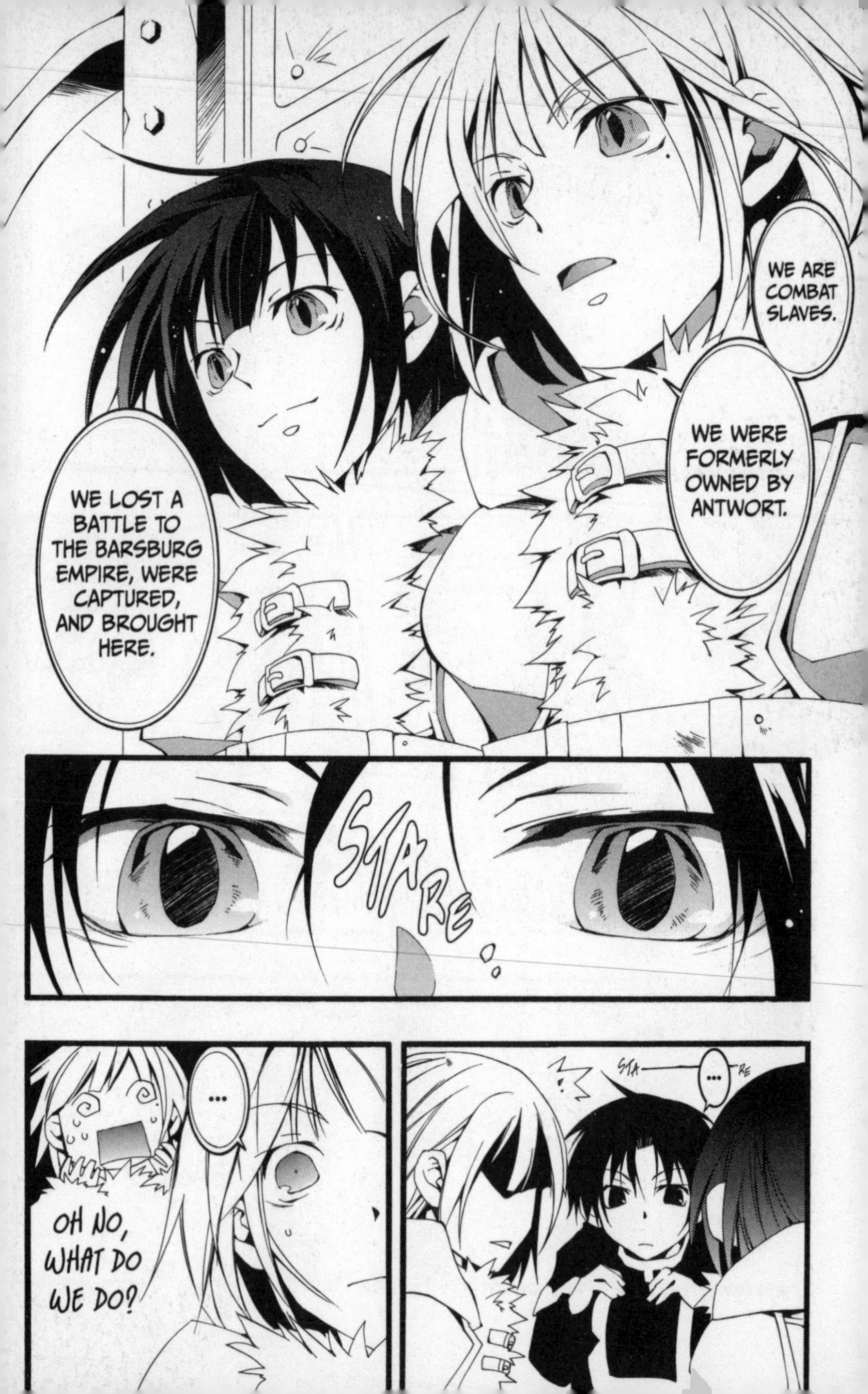
WE ARE COMBAT SLAVES.
WE WERE FORMERLY OWNED BY ANTWORT.
WE LOST A BATTLE TO THE BARSBURG EMPIRE, WERE CAPTURED, AND BROUGHT HERE.
STARE
STA— —RE
...
...
OH NO, WHAT DO WE DO?

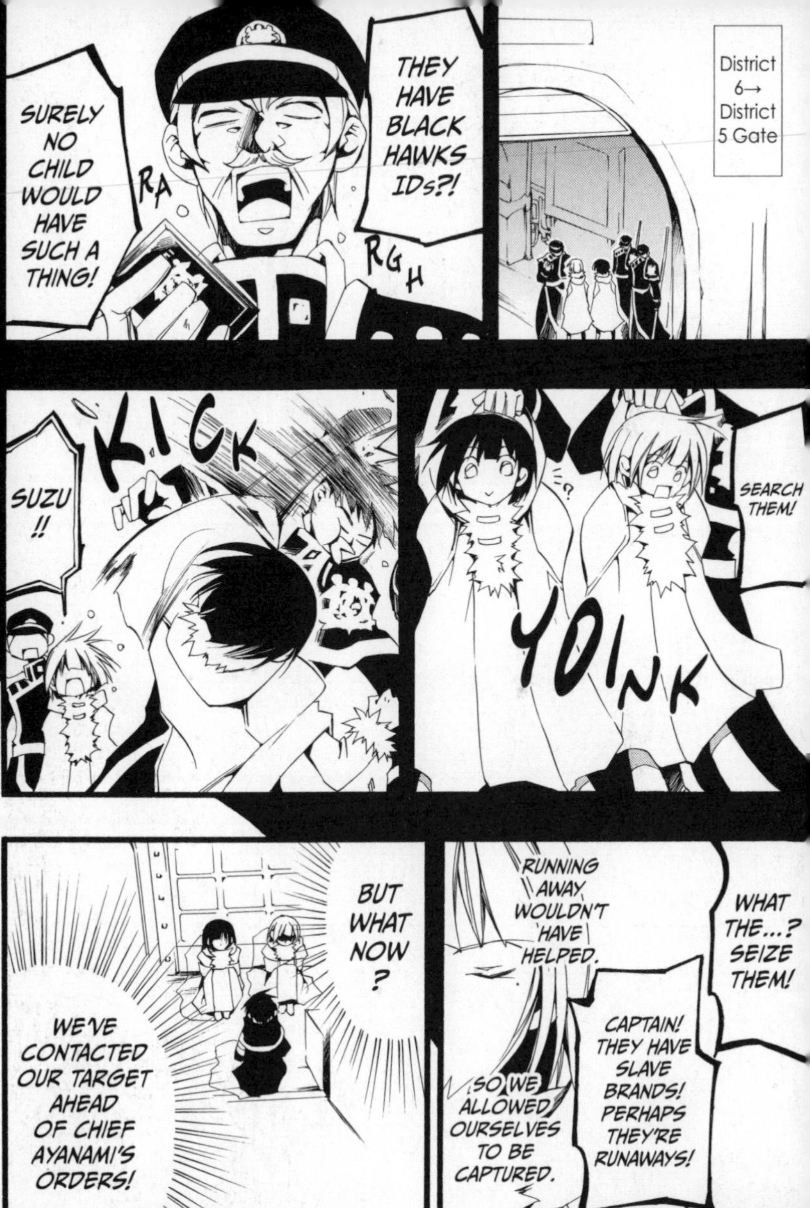
District 6→ District 5 Gate
THEY HAVE BLACK HAWKS IDs?!
SURELY NO CHILD WOULD HAVE SUCH A THING!
RARGH
SEARCH THEM!
YOINK
KICK
SUZU !!
WHAT THE...? SEIZE THEM!
RUNNING AWAY WOULDN'T HAVE HELPED.
CAPTAIN! THEY HAVE SLAVE BRANDS! PERHAPS THEY'RE RUNAWAYS!
SO WE ALLOWED OURSELVES TO BE CAPTURED.
BUT WHAT NOW ?
WE'VE CONTACTED OUR TARGET AHEAD OF CHIEF AYANAMI'S ORDERS!

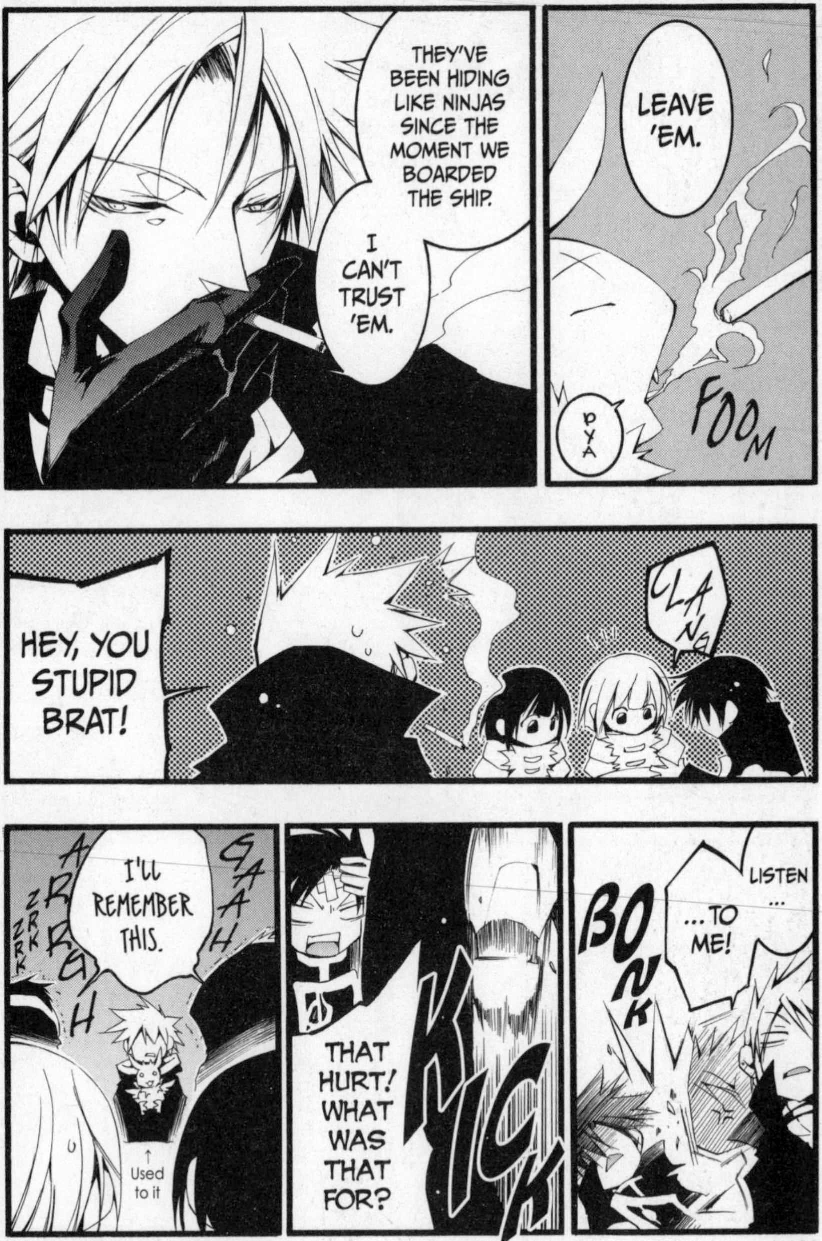
LEAVE 'EM.
PYA
FOOM
THEY'VE BEEN HIDING LIKE NINJAS SINCE THE MOMENT WE BOARDED THE SHIP.
I CAN'T TRUST 'EM.
CLANG
HEY, YOU STUPID BRAT!
LISTEN ...
... TO ME!
BONK
KICK
THAT HURT! WHAT WAS THAT FOR?
GAAH
I'LL REMEMBER THIS.
ARRGH
ZRK ZRK
Used to it

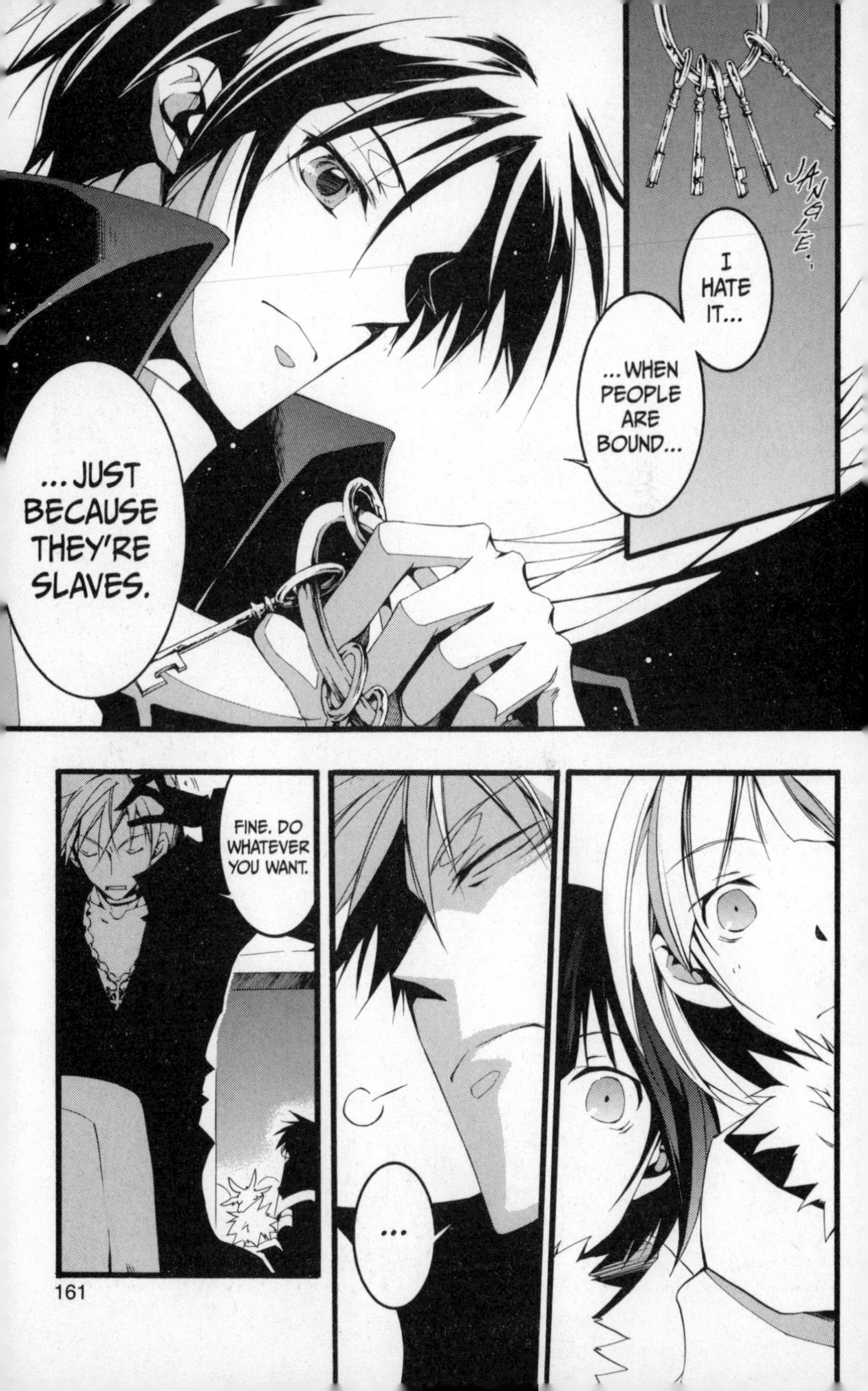
JANGLE...
I HATE IT...
...WHEN PEOPLE ARE BOUND...
...JUST BECAUSE THEY'RE SLAVES.
...
FINE. DO WHATEVER YOU WANT.

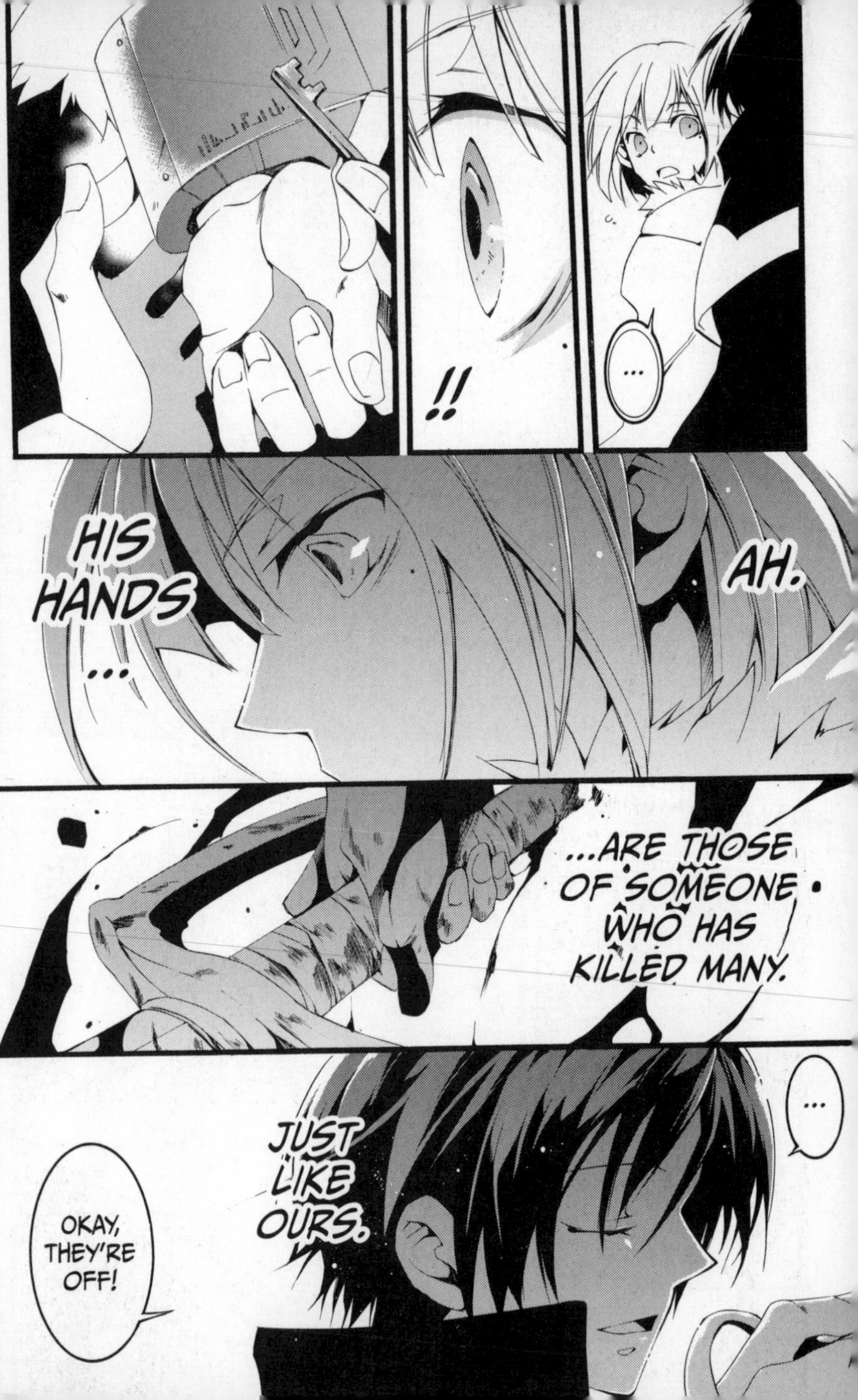
...
!!
AH.
HIS HANDS ...
...ARE THOSE OF SOMEONE WHO HAS KILLED MANY.
...
JUST LIKE OURS.
OKAY, THEY'RE OFF!

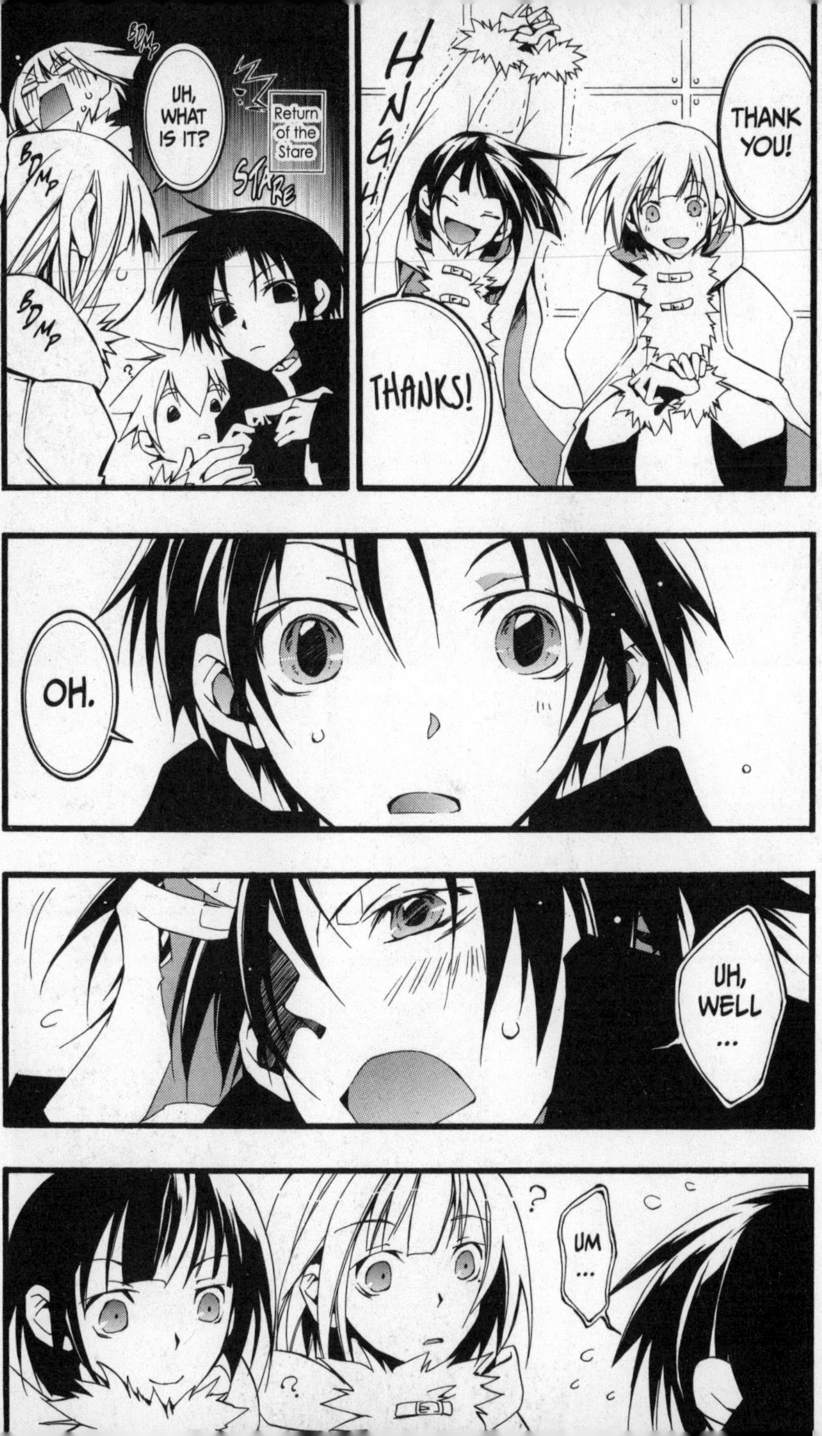
THANK YOU!
HNGH
THANKS!
Return of the Stare
STARE
UH, WHAT IS IT?
BDMP
YIKES!!
BDMP
BDMP
OH.
UH, WELL ...
UM ...

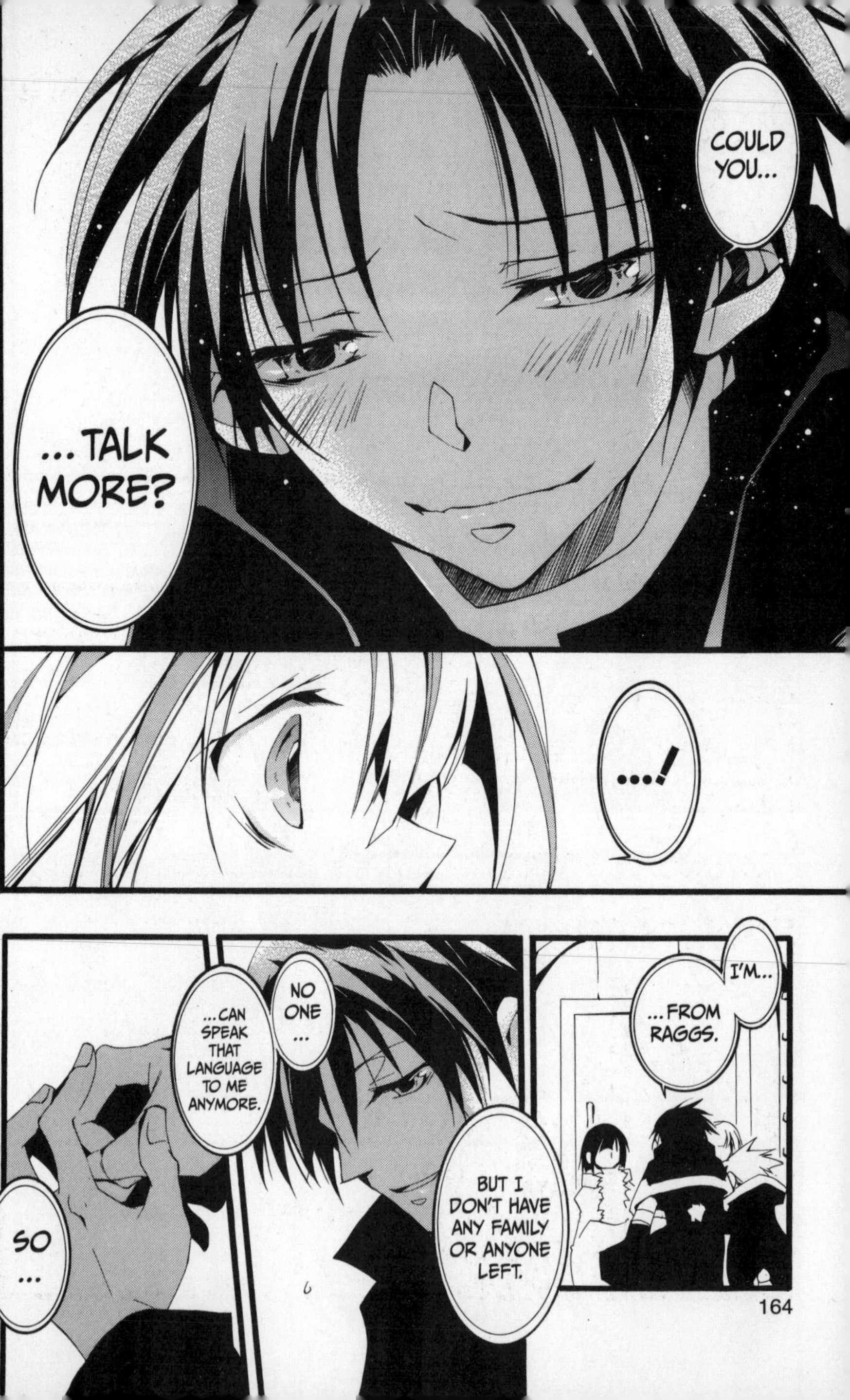
COULD YOU...
... TALK MORE?
...!
I'M...
...FROM RAGGS.
BUT I DON'T HAVE ANY FAMILY OR ANYONE LEFT.
NO ONE ...
...CAN SPEAK THAT LANGUAGE TO ME ANYMORE.
SO ...

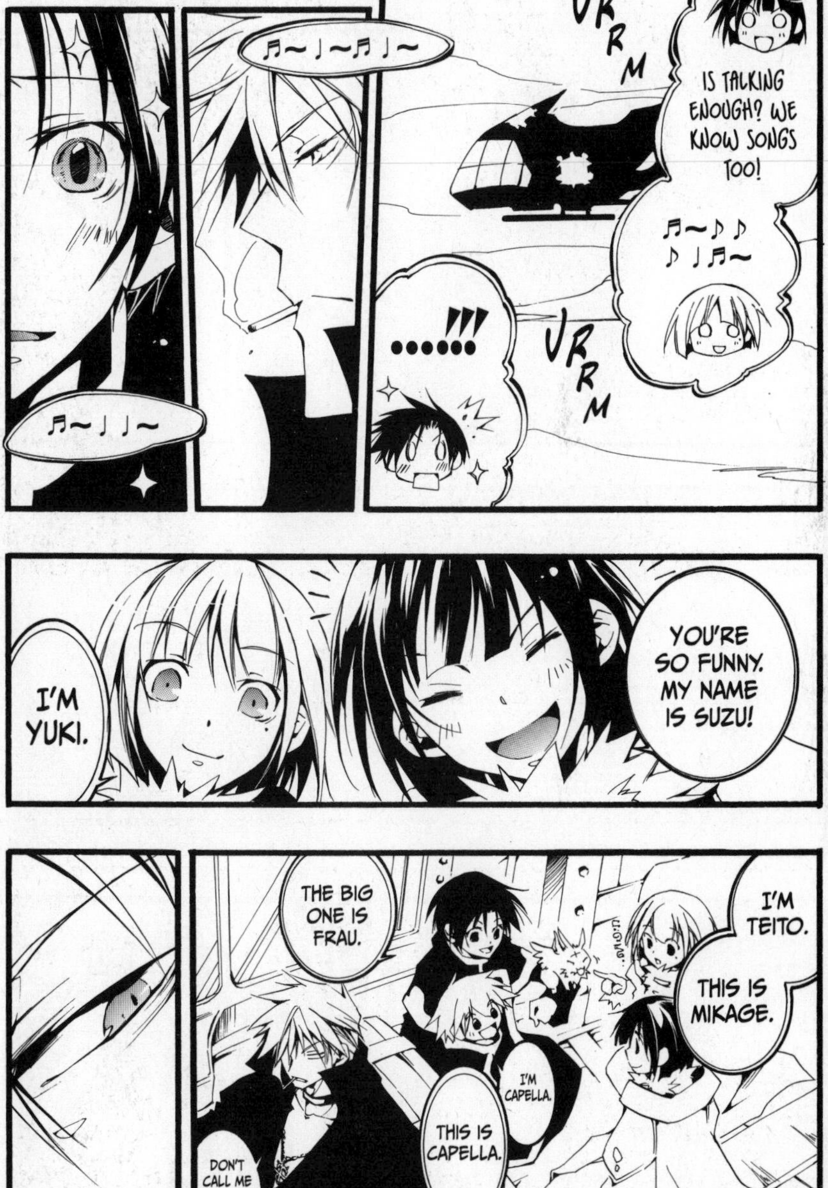
VRRM
IS TALKING ENOUGH? WE KNOW SONGS TOO!
♬~♪♪ ♪♩♬~
......!!!
VRRM
♬~♩~♬♩~
♬~♩♩~
YOU'RE SO FUNNY. MY NAME IS SUZU!
I'M YUKI.
I'M TEITO.
THIS IS MIKAGE.
THE BIG ONE IS FRAU.
I'M CAPELLA.
THIS IS CAPELLA.
DON'T CALL ME "THE BIG ONE."

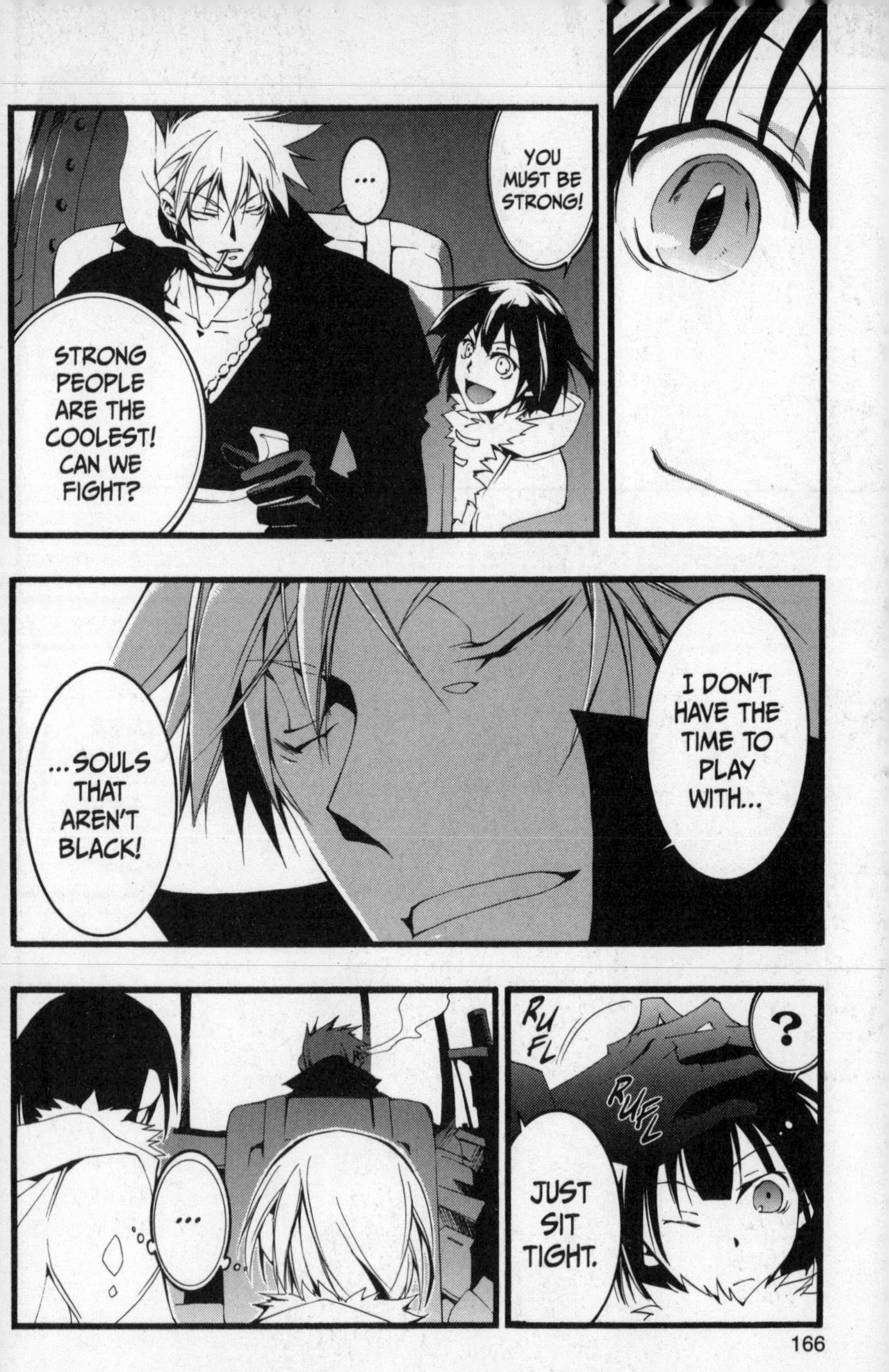
YOU MUST BE STRONG!
...
STRONG PEOPLE ARE THE COOLEST! CAN WE FIGHT?
I DON'T HAVE THE TIME TO PLAY WITH...
...SOULS THAT AREN'T BLACK!
RUFL
?
RUFL
JUST SIT TIGHT.
...

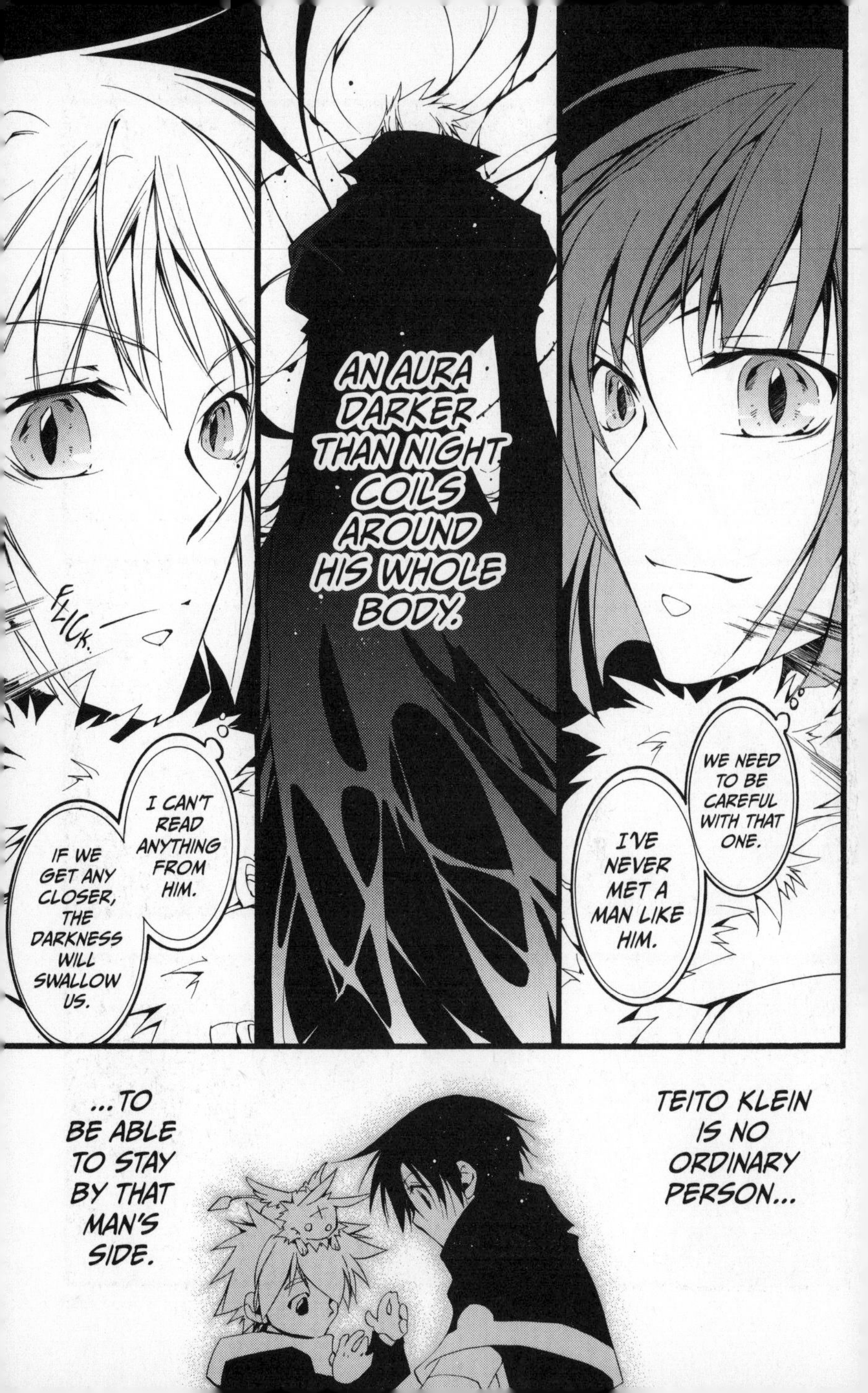
WE NEED TO BE CAREFUL WITH THAT ONE.
I'VE NEVER MET A MAN LIKE HIM.
AN AURA DARKER THAN NIGHT COILS AROUND HIS WHOLE BODY.
FLICK.
I CAN'T READ ANYTHING FROM HIM.
IF WE GET ANY CLOSER, THE DARKNESS WILL SWALLOW US.
TEITO KLEIN IS NO ORDINARY PERSON...
...TO BE ABLE TO STAY BY THAT MAN'S SIDE.

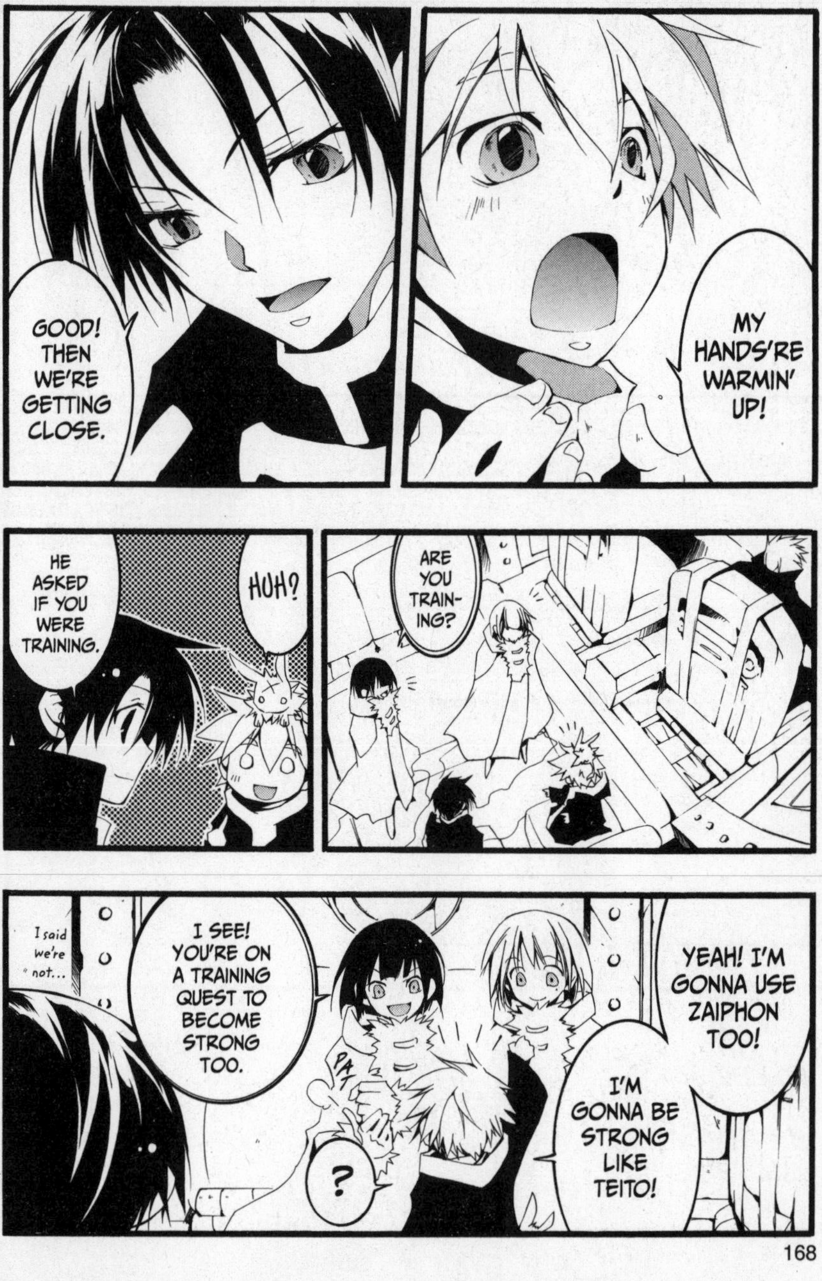
MY HANDS'RE WARMIN' UP!
GOOD! THEN WE'RE GETTING CLOSE.
ARE YOU TRAIN-ING?
HUH?
HE ASKED IF YOU WERE TRAINING.
YEAH! I'M GONNA USE ZAIPHON TOO!
I'M GONNA BE STRONG LIKE TEITO!
I SEE! YOU'RE ON A TRAINING QUEST TO BECOME STRONG TOO.
PAT
?
I said we're not...

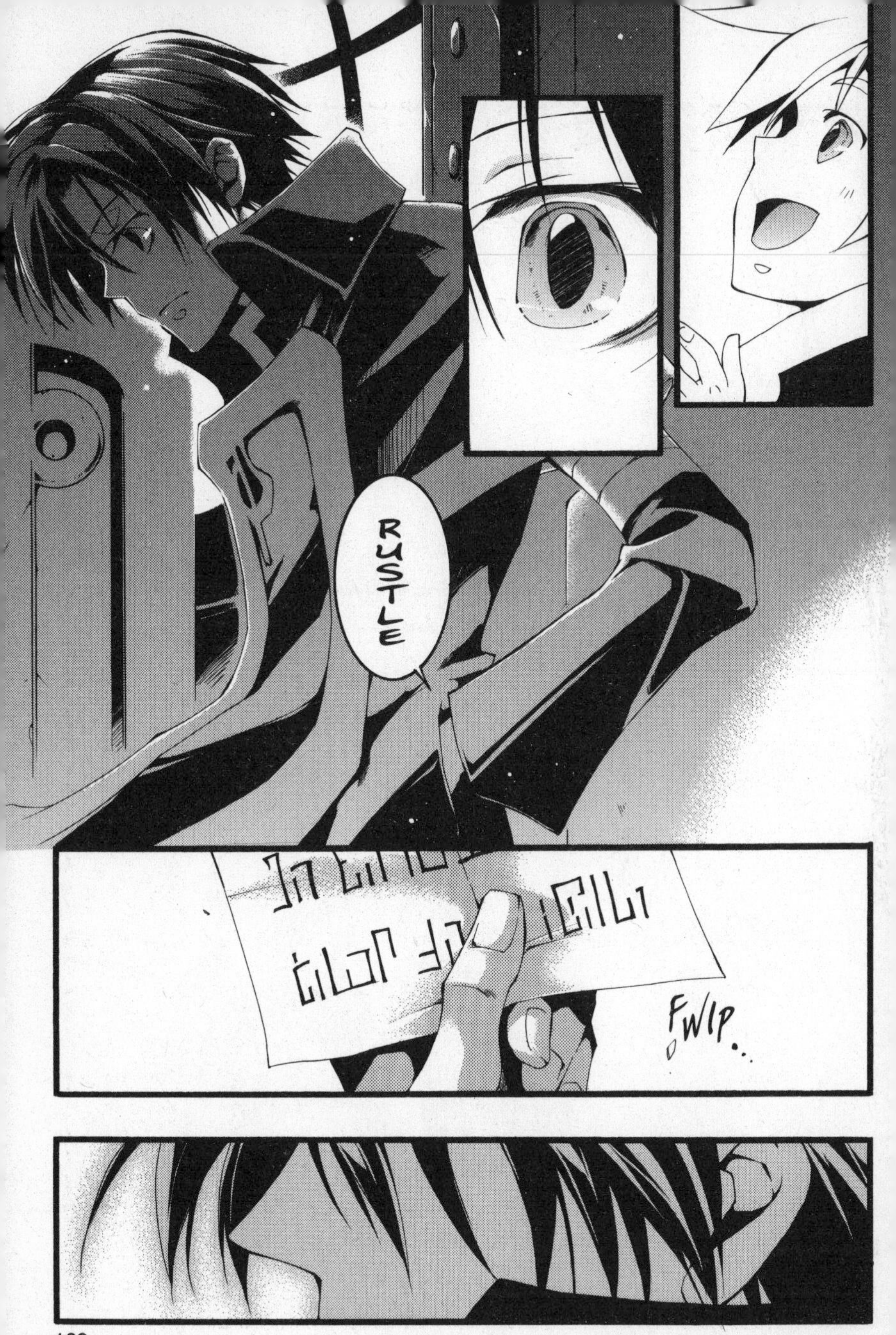
RUSTLE
FWIP...

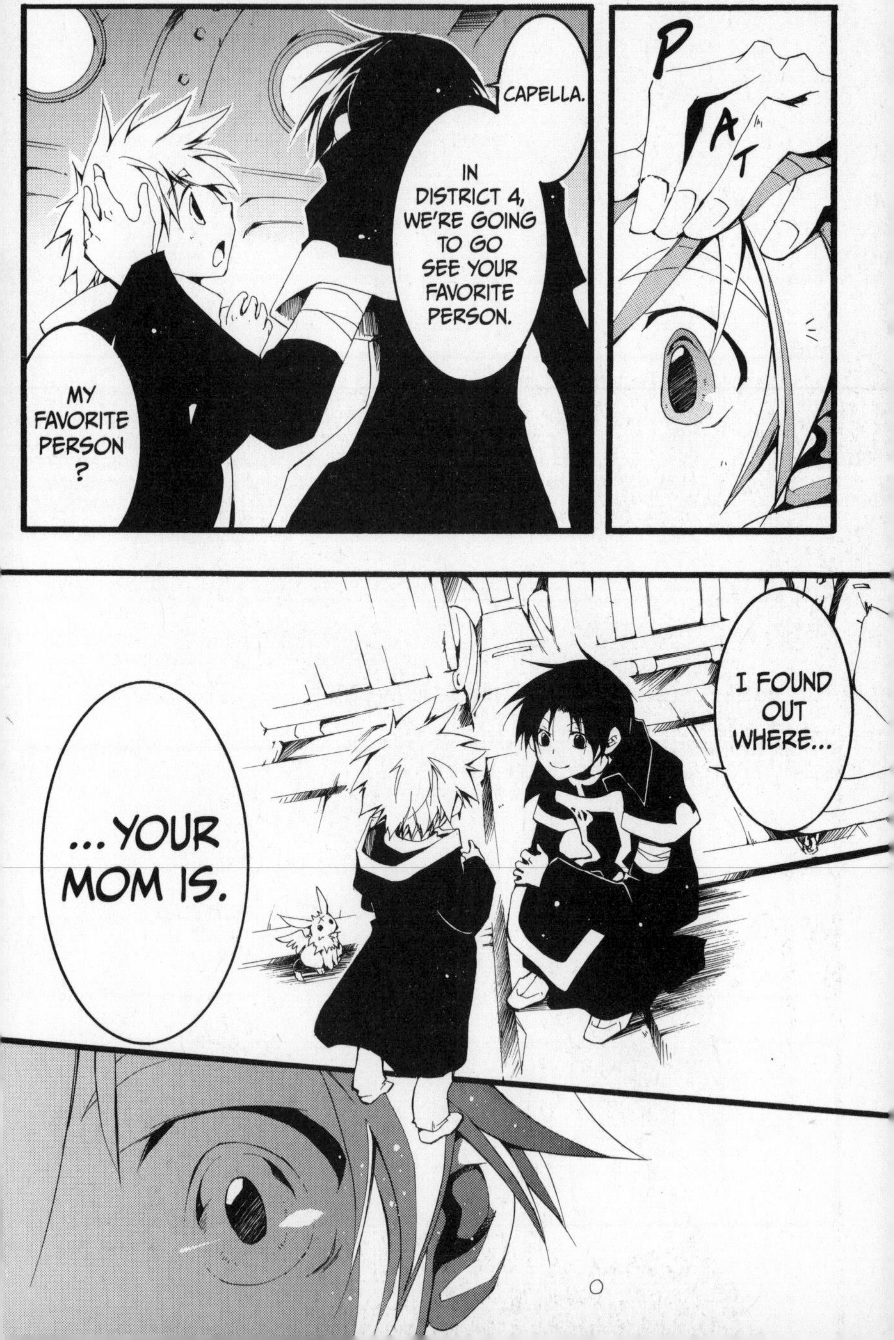
PAT
CAPELLA.
IN DISTRICT 4, WE'RE GOING TO GO SEE YOUR FAVORITE PERSON.
MY FAVORITE PERSON?
I FOUND OUT WHERE...
...YOUR MOM IS.

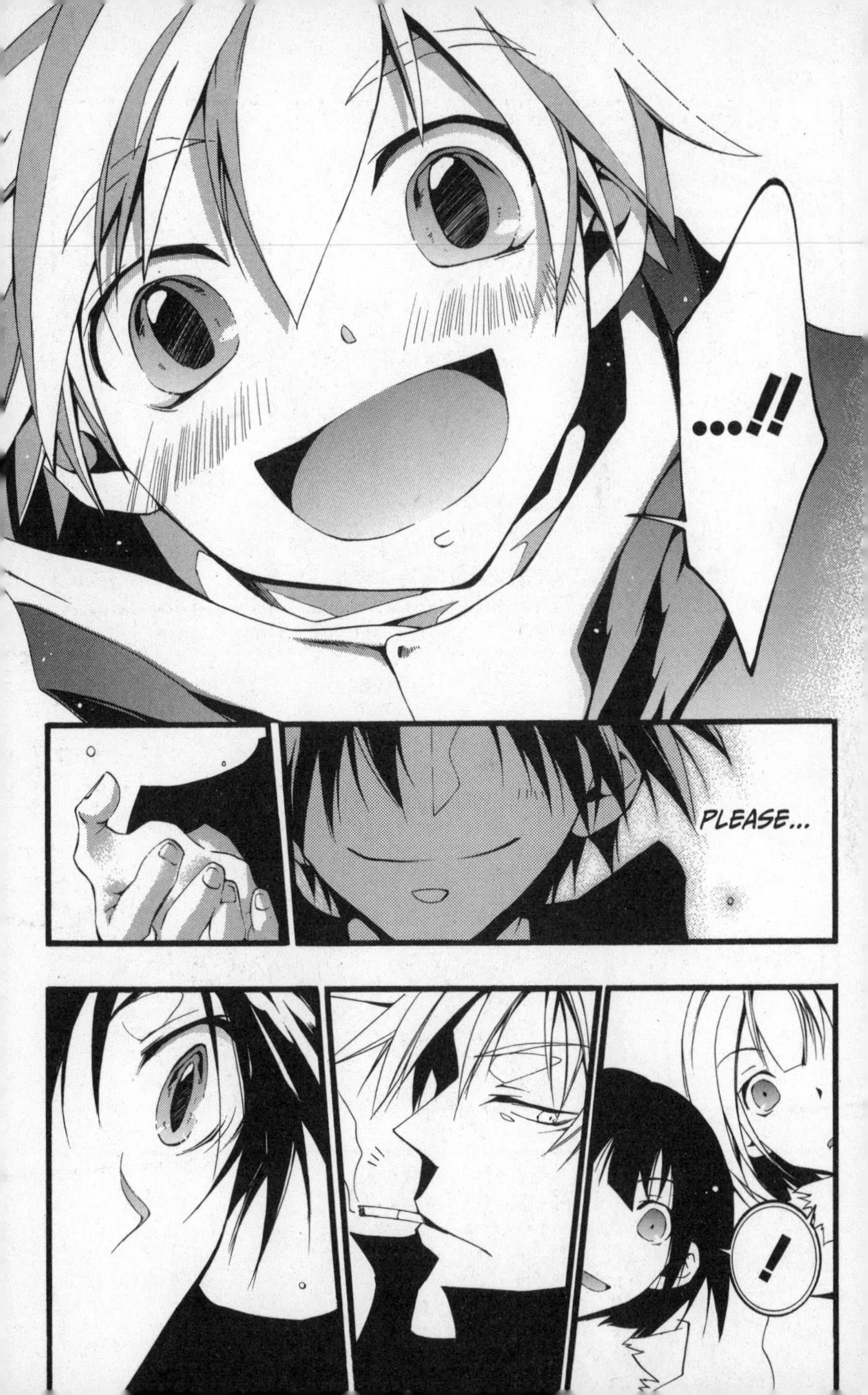
...!!
PLEASE...
!

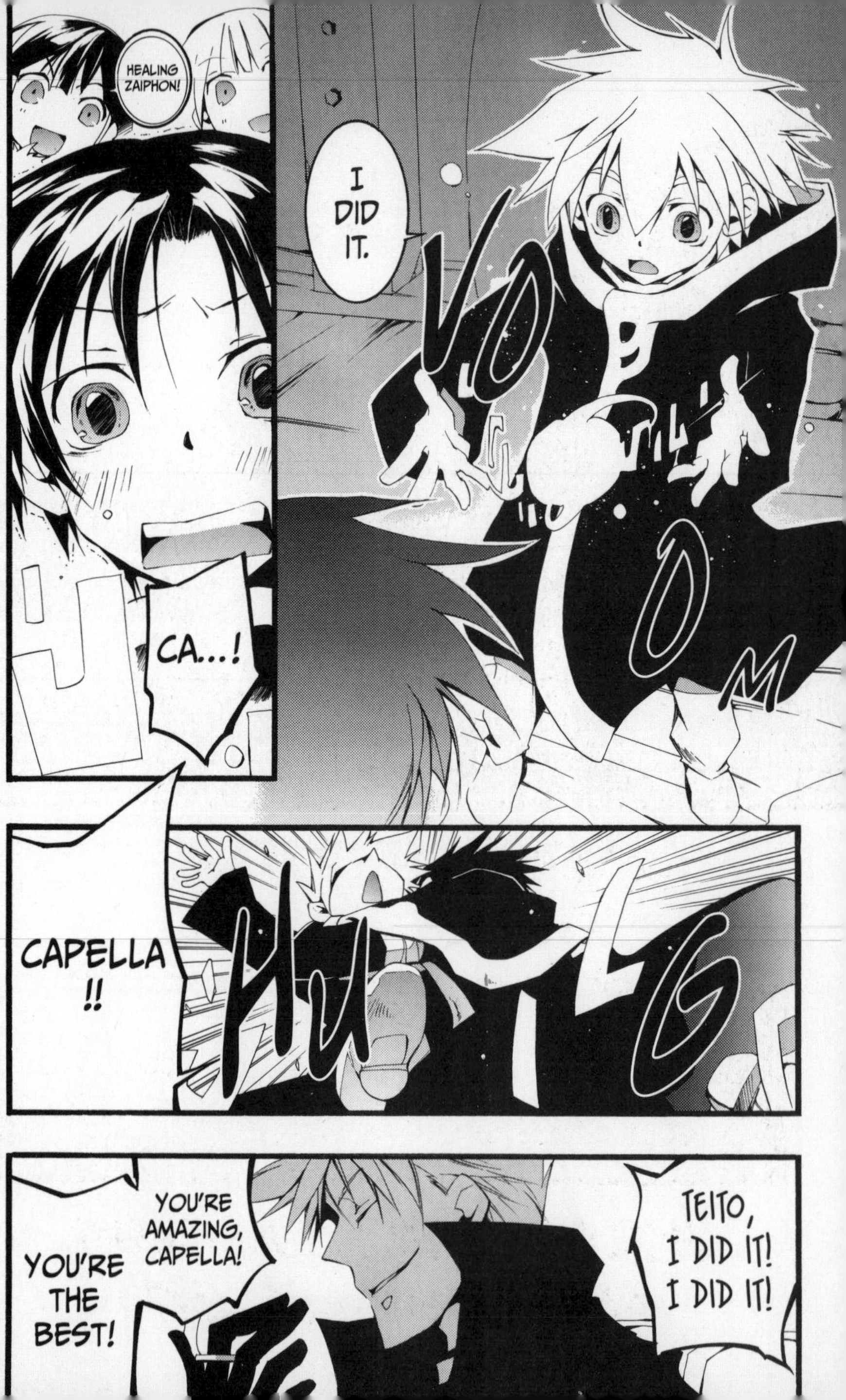
I DID IT.
HEALING ZAIPHON!
CA...!
CAPELLA !!
HUG
TEITO, I DID IT! I DID IT!
YOU'RE AMAZING, CAPELLA!
YOU'RE THE BEST!

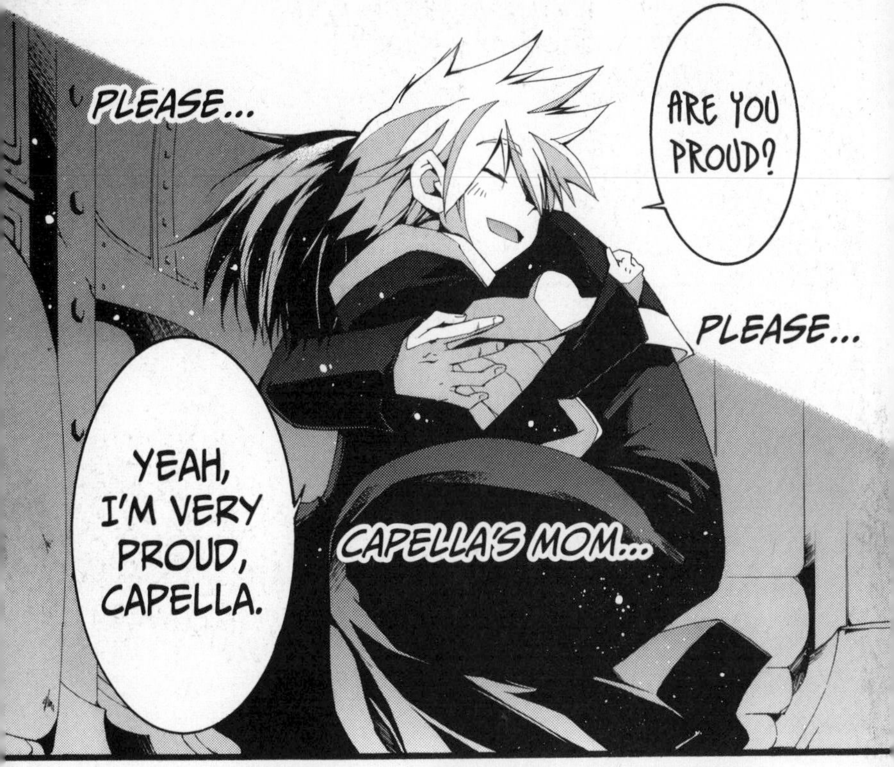
ARE YOU PROUD?
PLEASE...
PLEASE...
YEAH, I'M VERY PROUD, CAPELLA.
CAPELLA'S MOM...

...LOVE CAPELLA WITH ALL YOUR HEART.

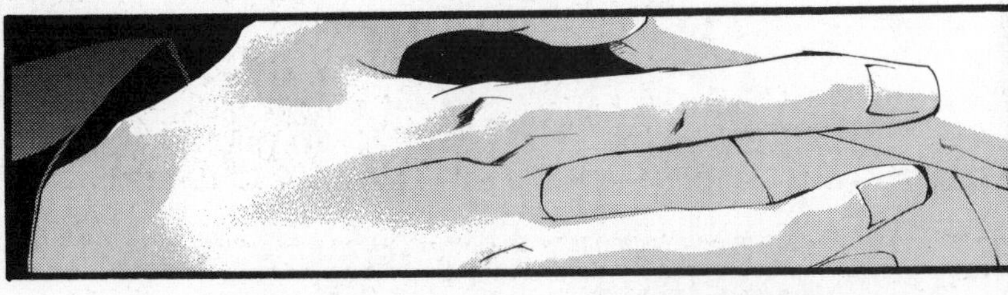

HOLD HIM IN YOUR ARMS AND NEVER LET GO.

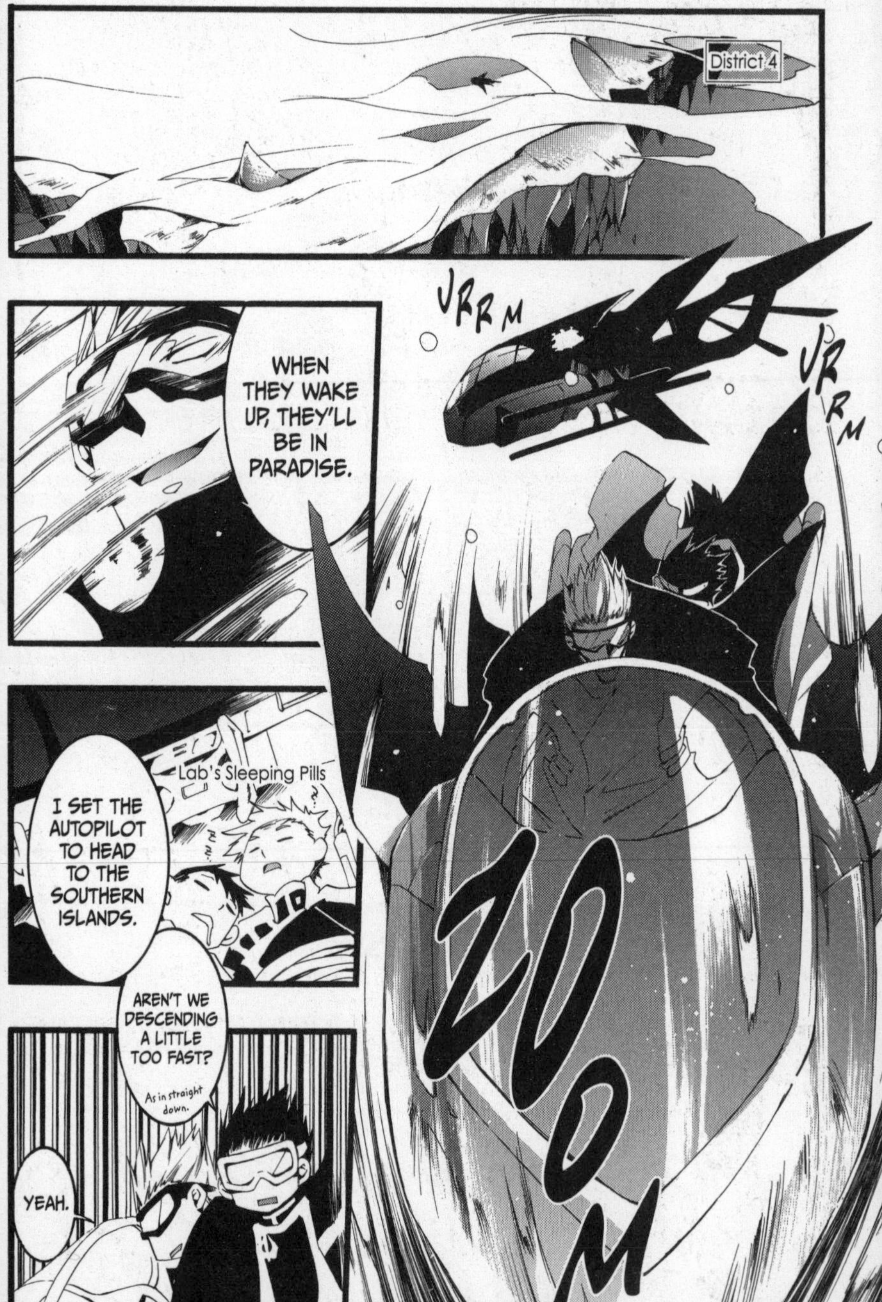
District 4
JRRM
JRRM
ZOOM
WHEN THEY WAKE UP, THEY'LL BE IN PARADISE.
Lab's Sleeping Pills
I SET THE AUTOPILOT TO HEAD TO THE SOUTHERN ISLANDS.
AREN'T WE DESCENDING A LITTLE TOO FAST?
As in straight down.
YEAH.

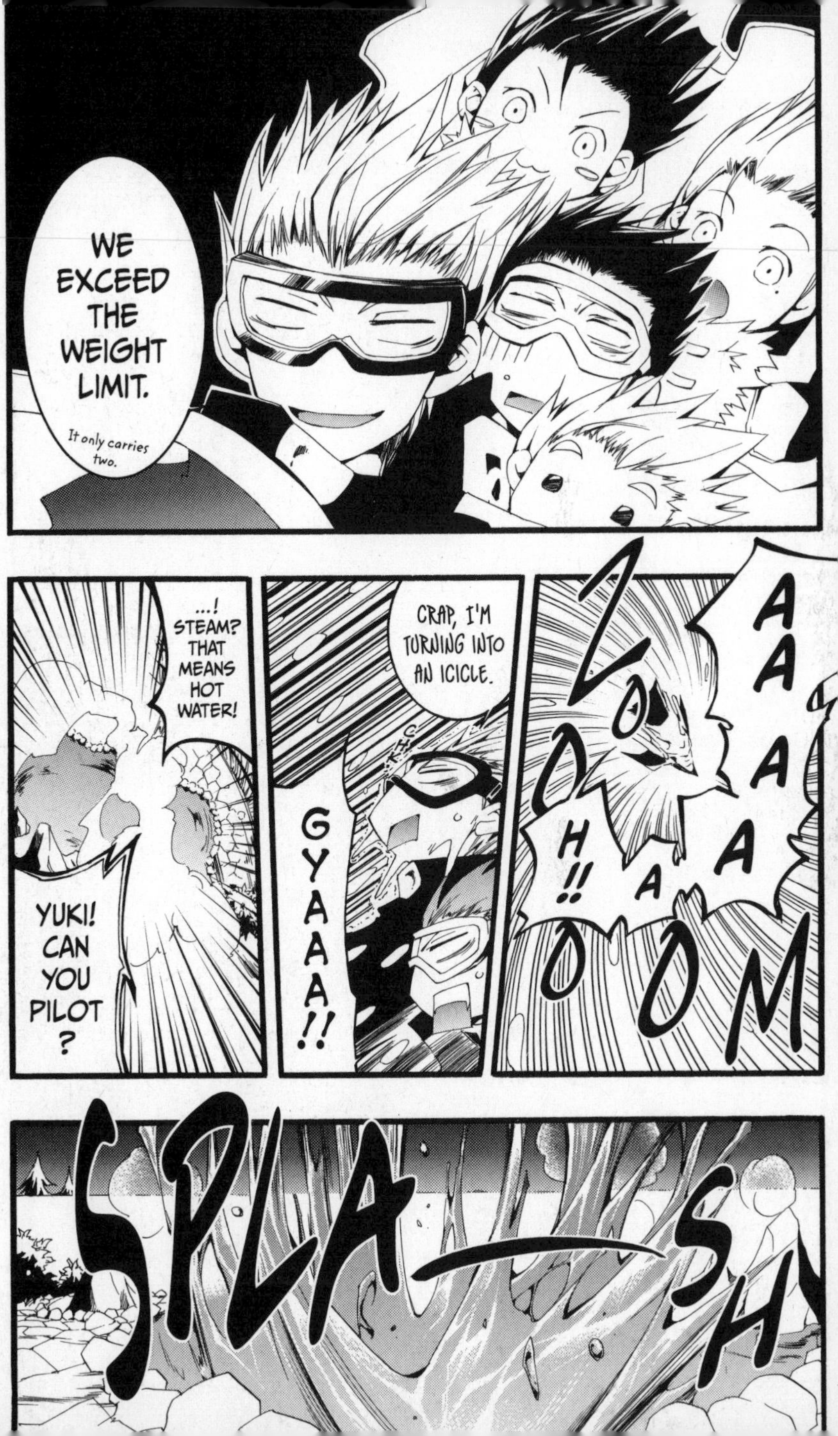
WE EXCEED THE WEIGHT LIMIT.
It only carries two.
AAAAAA
ZOOOH!!
CRAP, I'M TURNING INTO AN ICICLE.
GYAAAA!!
...! STEAM? THAT MEANS HOT WATER!
YUKI! CAN YOU PILOT?
SPLASH

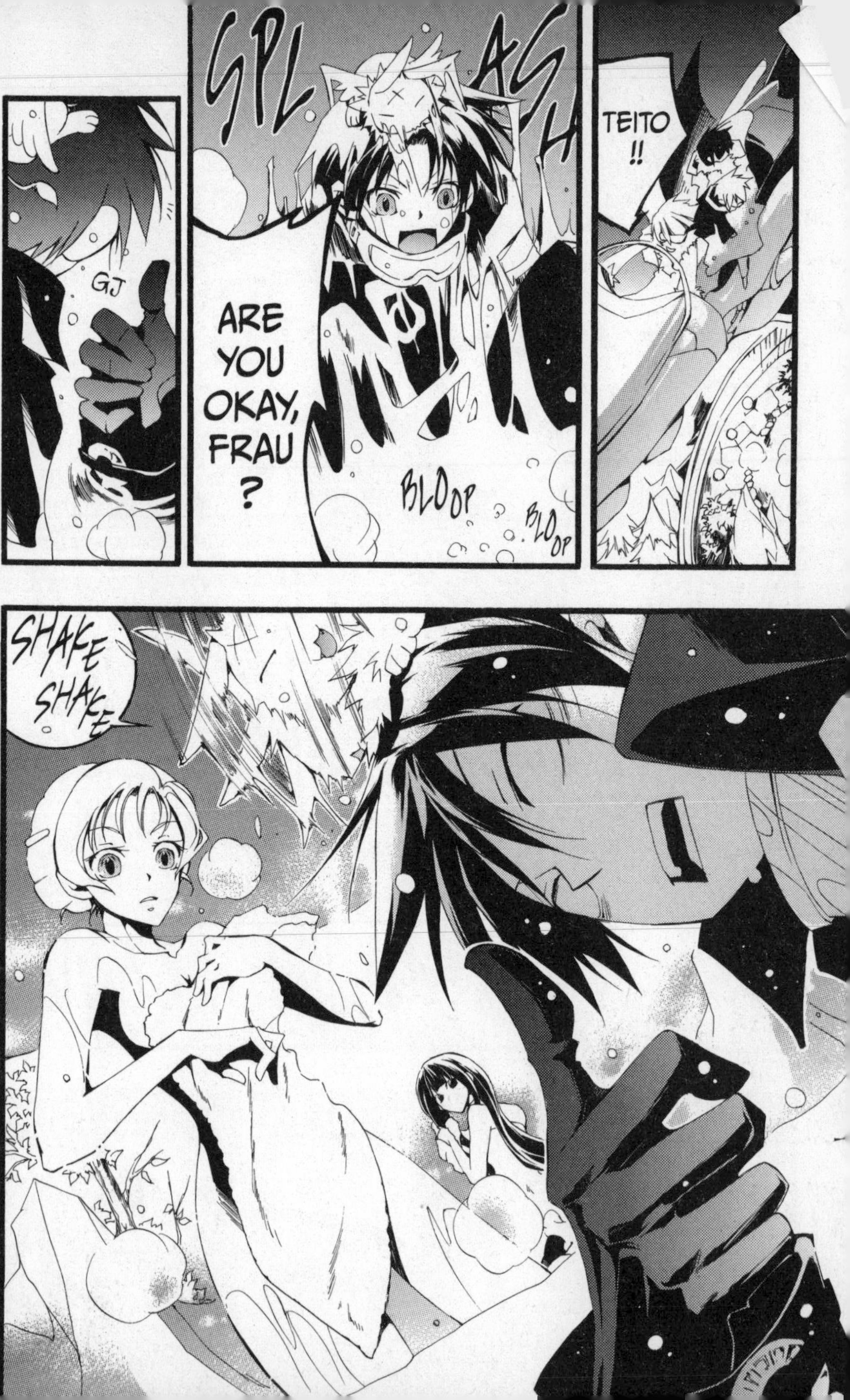
TEITO !!
SPLASH
ARE YOU OKAY, FRAU ?
BLOOP
BLOOP
GJ
SHAKE SHAKE

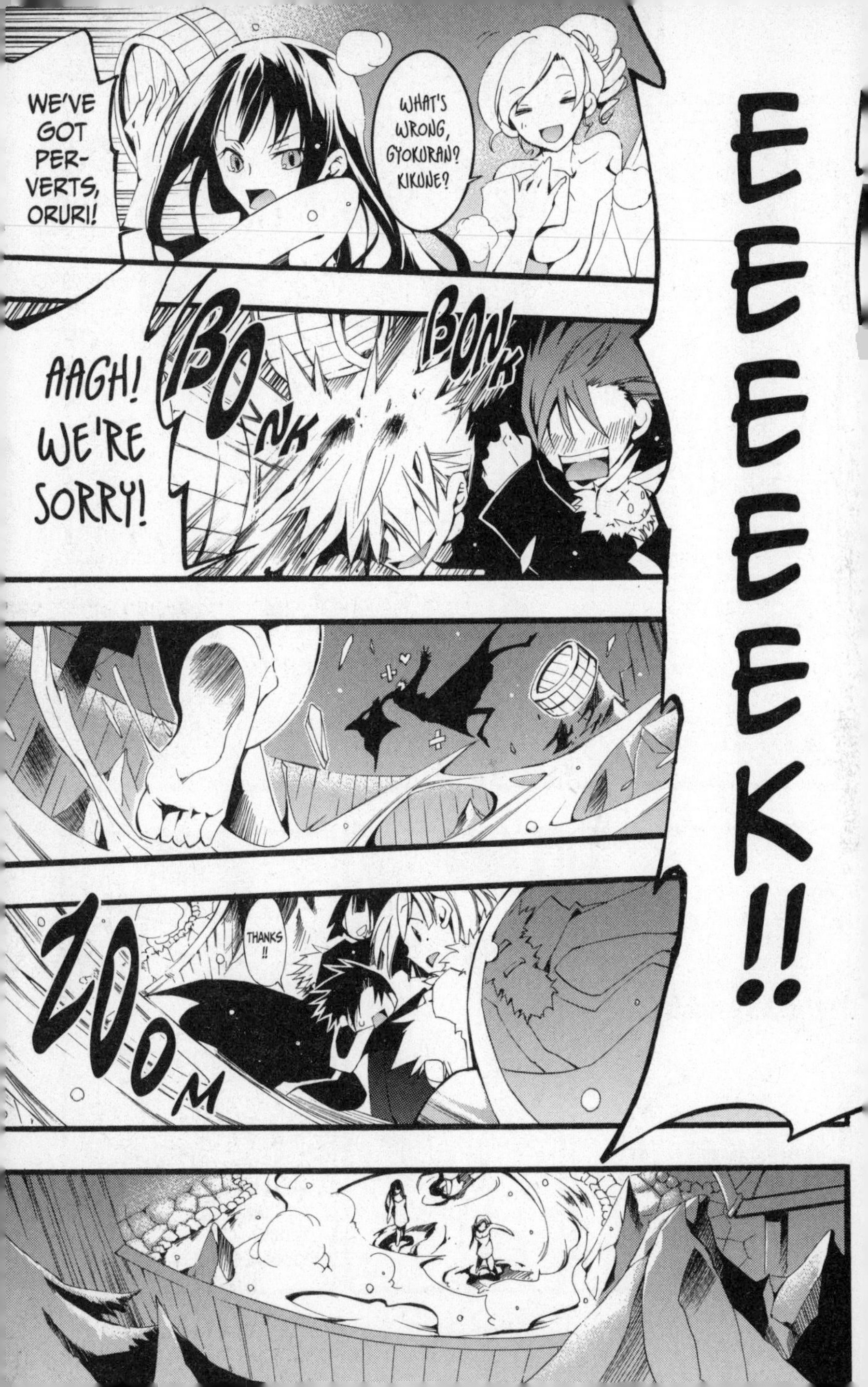
EEEEEEK!!
WHAT'S WRONG, GYOKURAN? KIKUNE?
WE'VE GOT PER-VERTS, ORURI!
BONK
BONK
AAGH! WE'RE SORRY!
THANKS!!
ZOOM

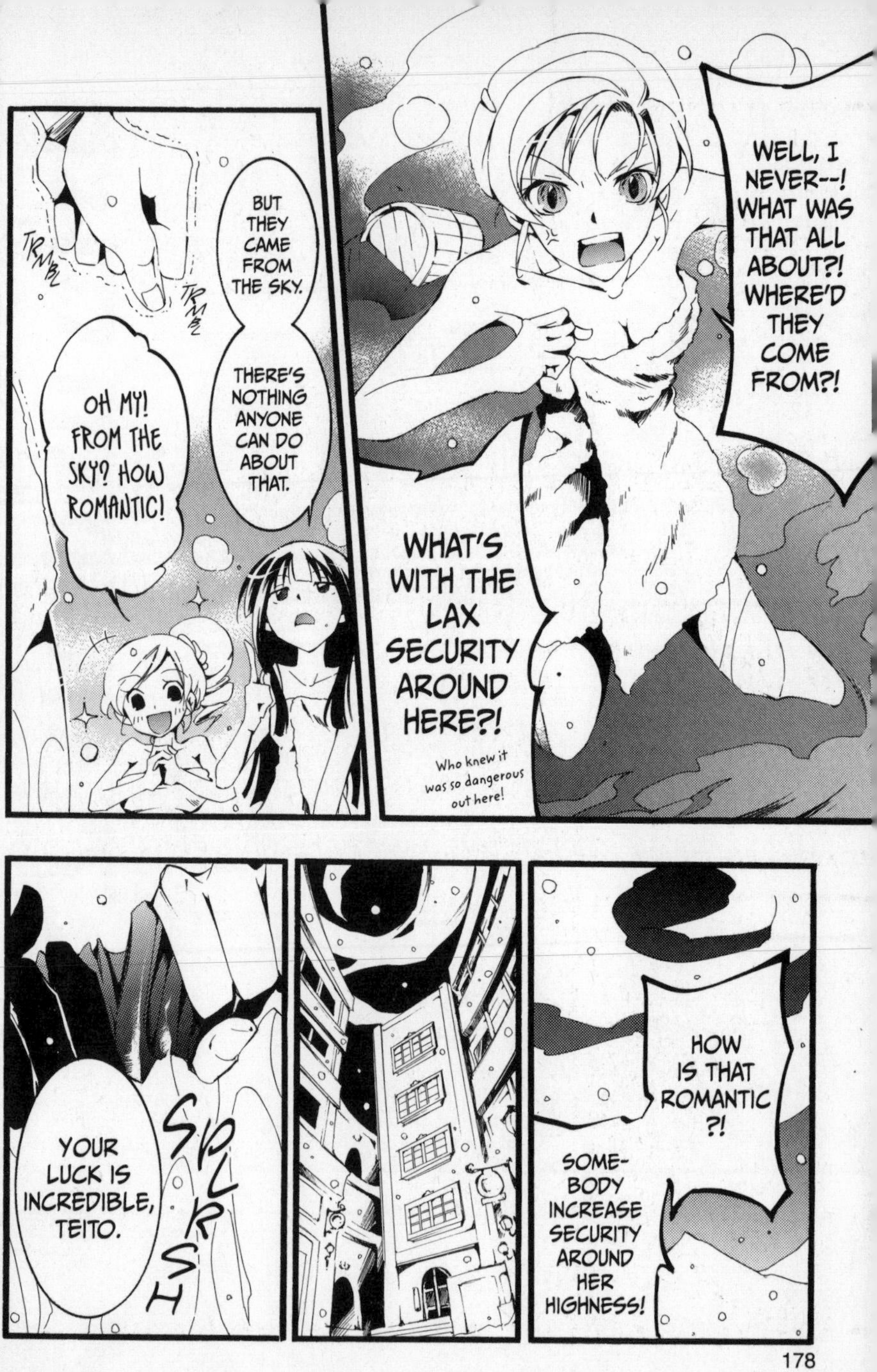
WELL, I NEVER--! WHAT WAS THAT ALL ABOUT?! WHERE'D THEY COME FROM?!
WHAT'S WITH THE LAX SECURITY AROUND HERE?!
Who knew it was so dangerous out here!
BUT THEY CAME FROM THE SKY.
THERE'S NOTHING ANYONE CAN DO ABOUT THAT.
TRMBL
TRMBL
OH MY! FROM THE SKY? HOW ROMANTIC!
HOW IS THAT ROMANTIC?!
SOMEBODY INCREASE SECURITY AROUND HER HIGHNESS!
SPLURSH
YOUR LUCK IS INCREDIBLE, TEITO.

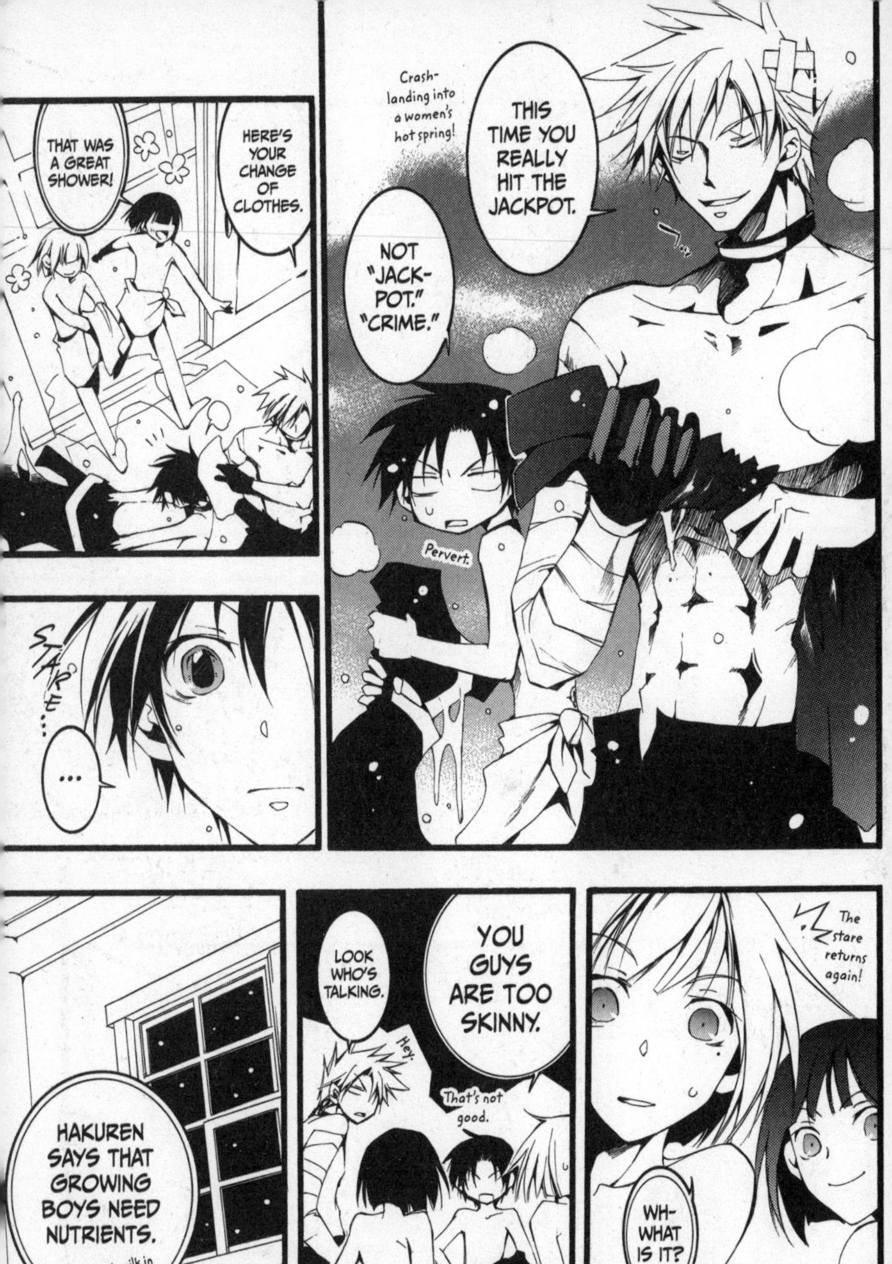
THIS TIME YOU REALLY HIT THE JACKPOT.
Crash-landing into a women's hot spring!
NOT "JACKPOT." "CRIME."
Pervert.
HERE'S YOUR CHANGE OF CLOTHES.
THAT WAS A GREAT SHOWER!
STARE...
...
The stare returns again!
WH-WHAT IS IT?
YOU GUYS ARE TOO SKINNY.
LOOK WHO'S TALKING.
Hey.
That's not good.
HAKUREN SAYS THAT GROWING BOYS NEED NUTRIENTS.
Let's drink milk in the morning.

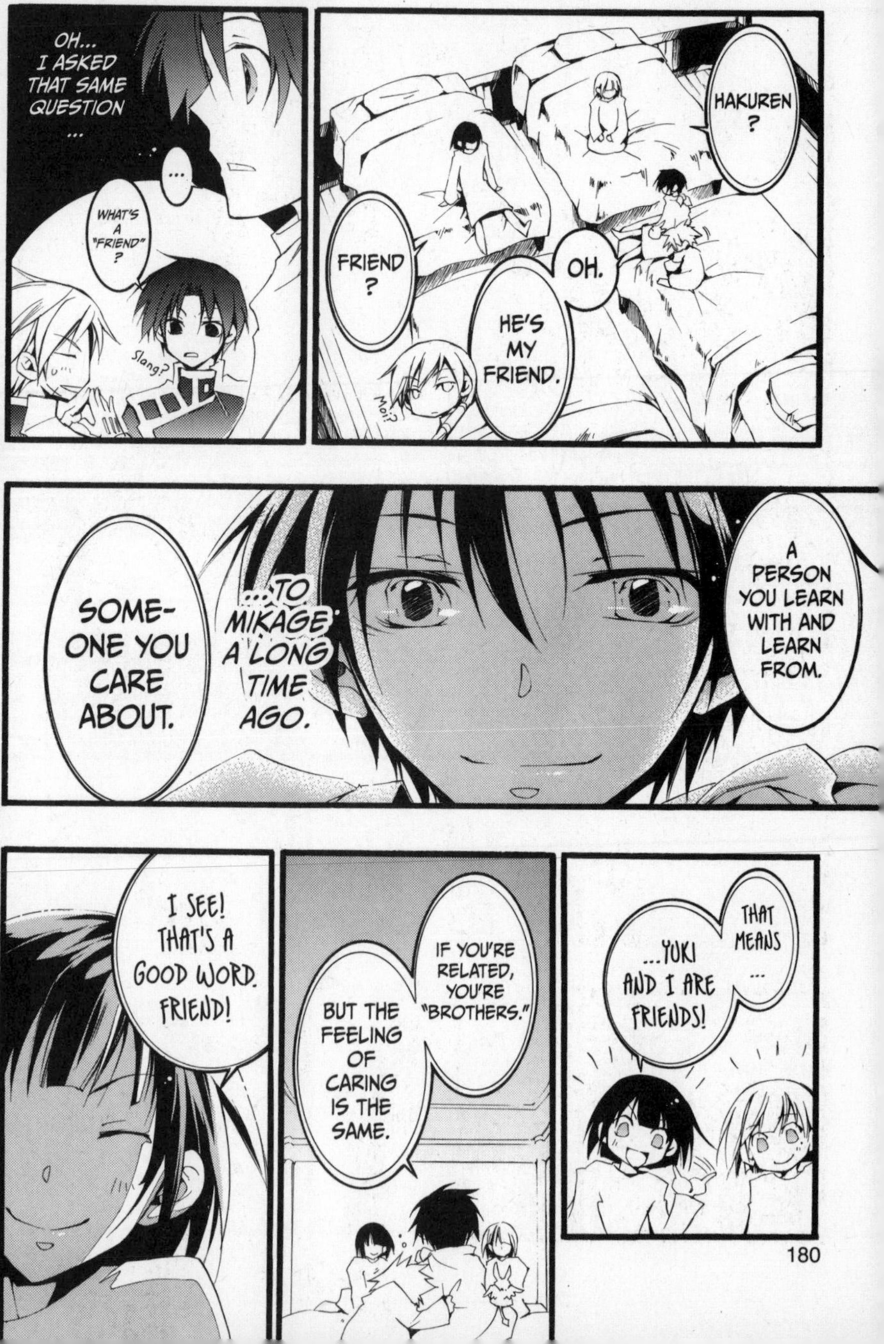
HAKUREN?
FRIEND?
OH.
HE'S MY FRIEND.
Moi?
OH... I ASKED THAT SAME QUESTION ...
...
WHAT'S A "FRIEND"?
Slang?
A PERSON YOU LEARN WITH AND LEARN FROM.
...TO MIKAGE A LONG TIME AGO.
SOME-ONE YOU CARE ABOUT.
THAT MEANS ...
...YUKI AND I ARE FRIENDS!
IF YOU'RE RELATED, YOU'RE "BROTHERS."
BUT THE FEELING OF CARING IS THE SAME.
I SEE! THAT'S A GOOD WORD. FRIEND!

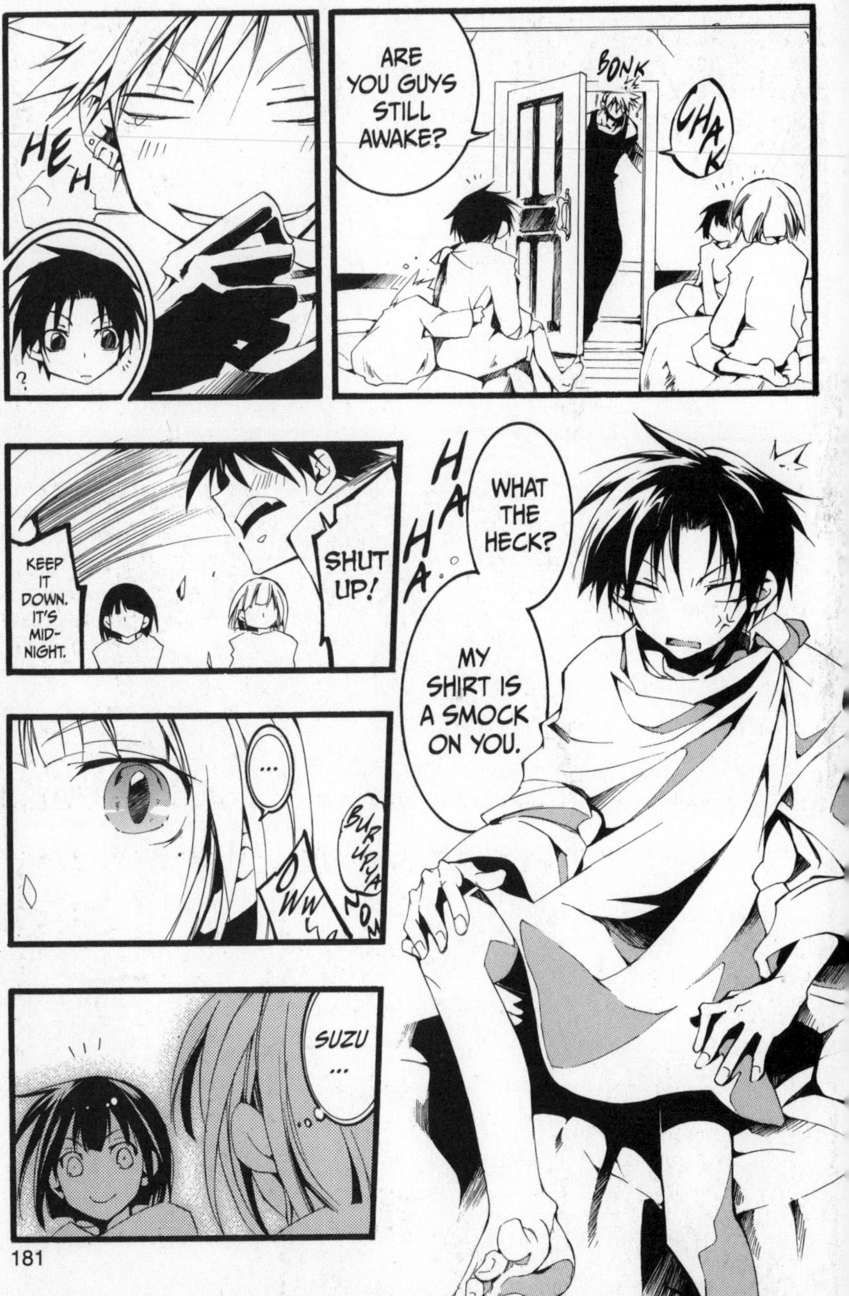
ARE YOU GUYS STILL AWAKE?
BONK
CHAK
HEH
?
WHAT THE HECK?
MY SHIRT IS A SMOCK ON YOU.
HAHAHA
SHUT UP!
KEEP IT DOWN. IT'S MID-NIGHT.
...
SUZU ...

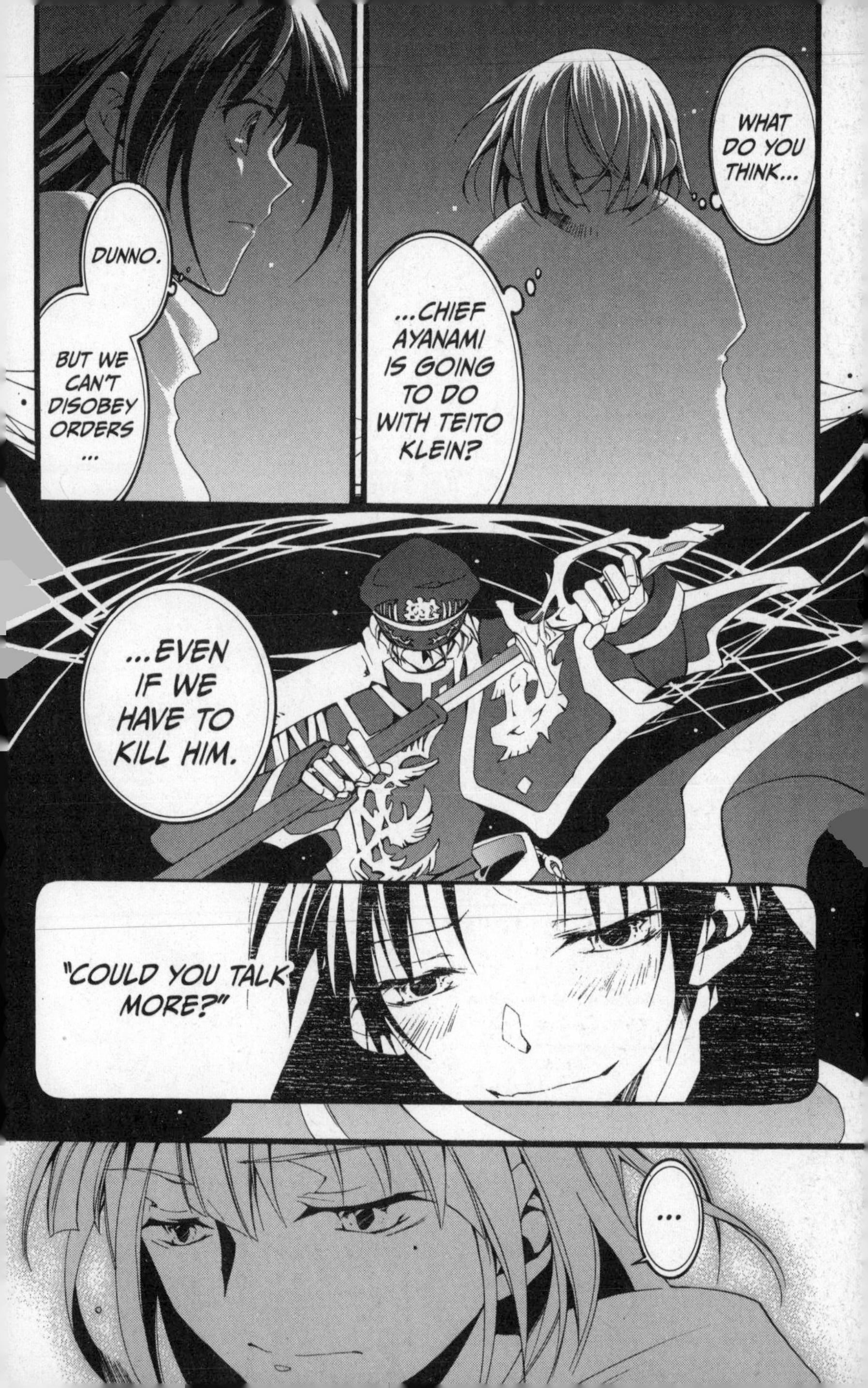
WHAT DO YOU THINK...
...CHIEF AYANAMI IS GOING TO DO WITH TEITO KLEIN?
DUNNO.
BUT WE CAN'T DISOBEY ORDERS ...
...EVEN IF WE HAVE TO KILL HIM.
"COULD YOU TALK MORE?"
...

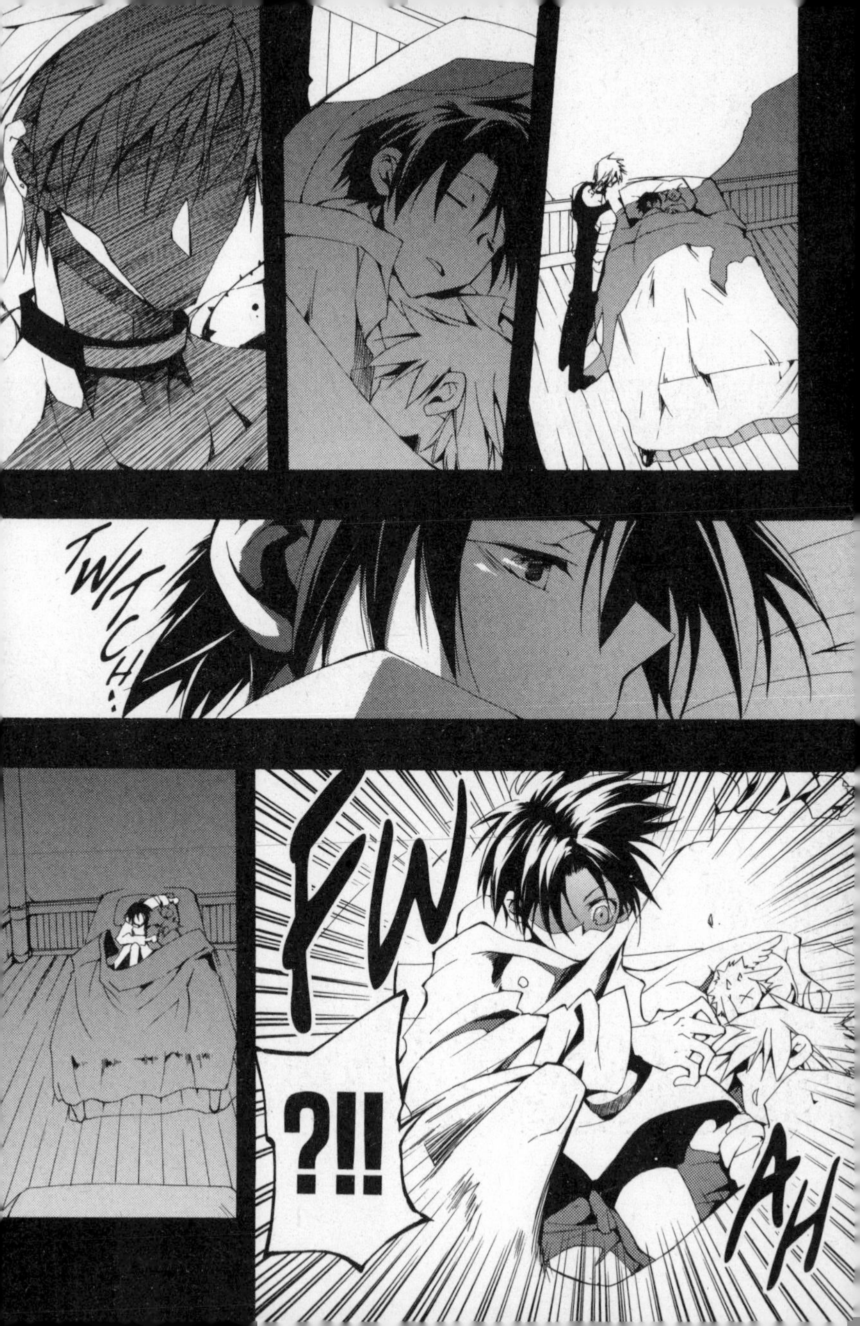

TWITCH..
FW
?!!
AH

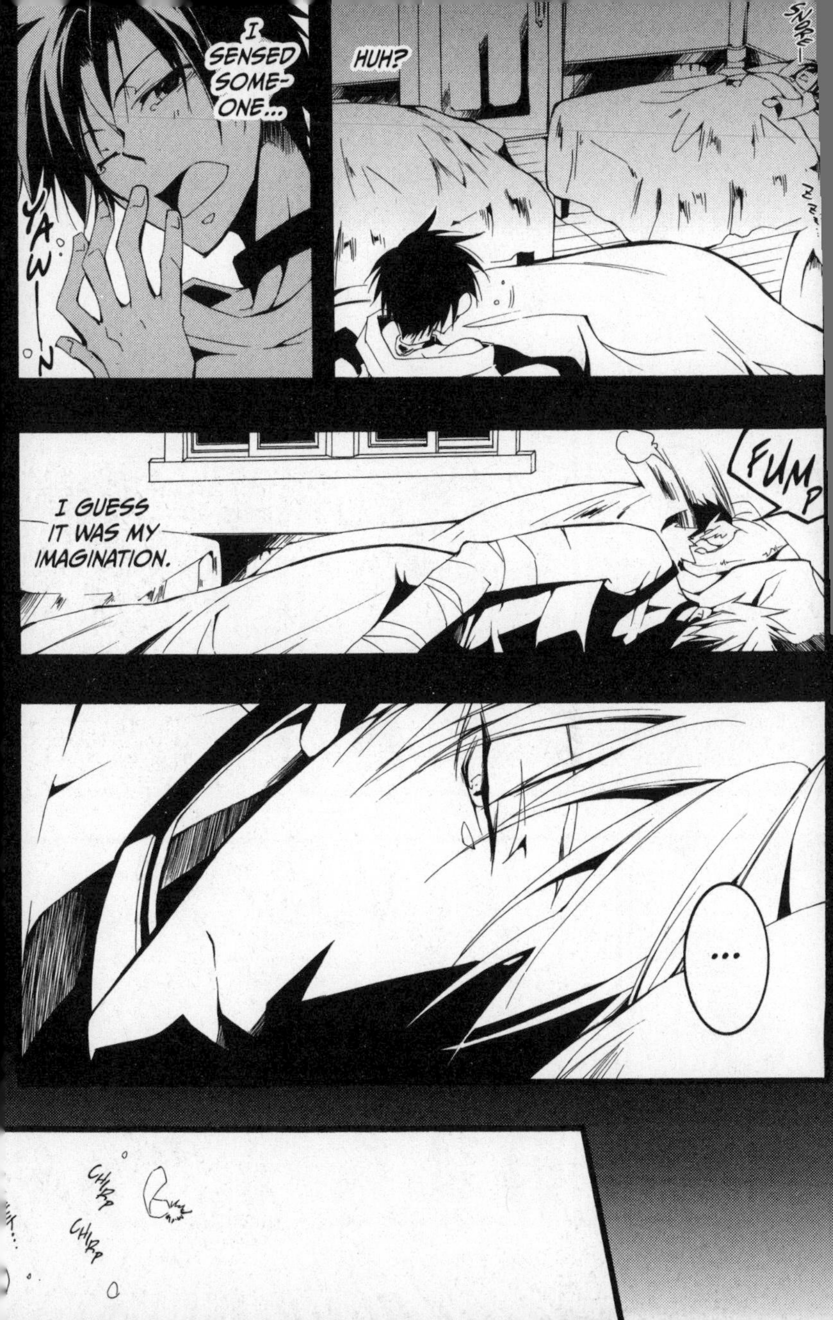
SNORE—
HUH?
I SENSED SOME-ONE...
YAWN
FUMP
I GUESS IT WAS MY IMAGINATION.
...
CHIRP
CHIRP

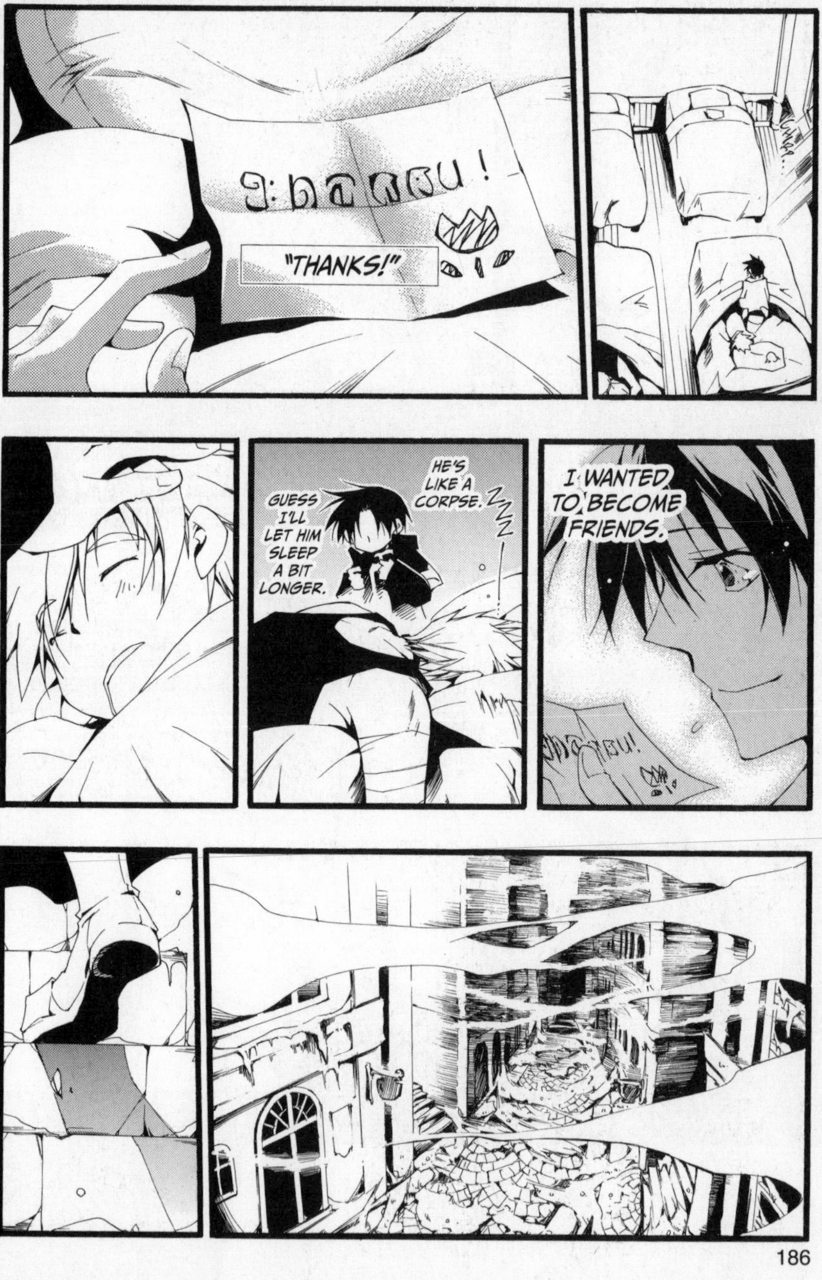
"THANKS!"
I WANTED TO BECOME FRIENDS.
HE'S LIKE A CORPSE.
ZZZ
GUESS I'LL LET HIM SLEEP A BIT LONGER.

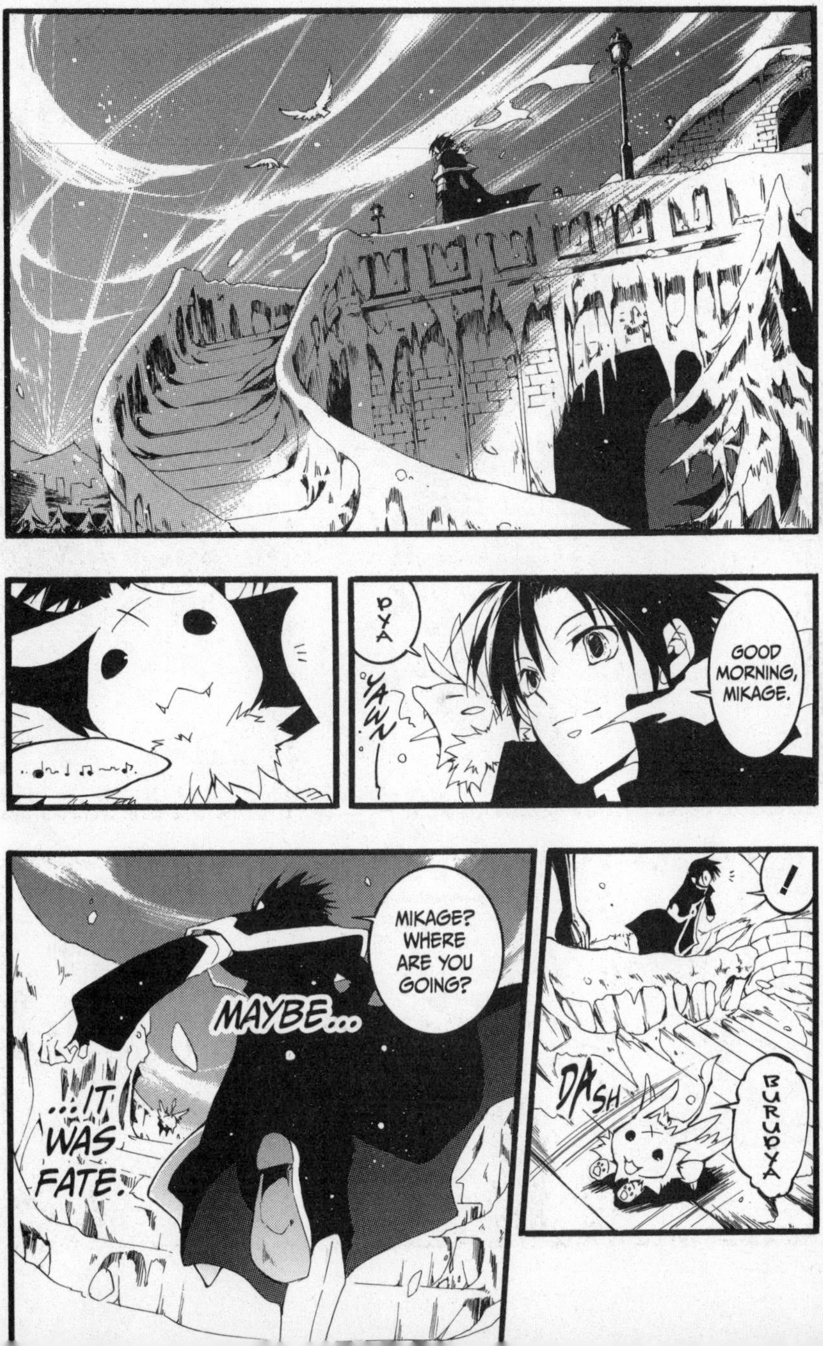
GOOD MORNING, MIKAGE.
PYA
YAWN
!
DASH
BURUPYA
MIKAGE? WHERE ARE YOU GOING?
MAYBE...
...IT WAS FATE.

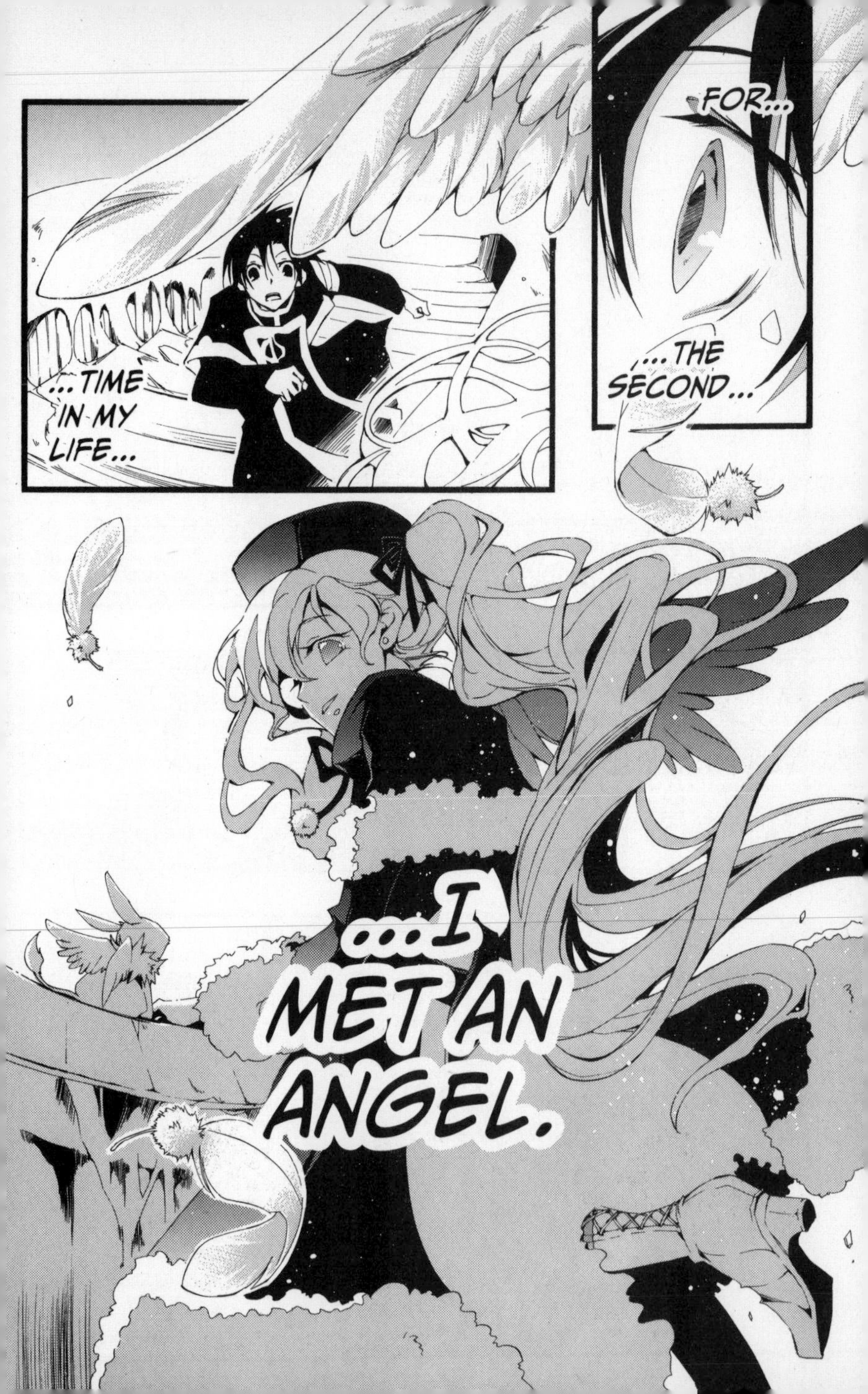
FOR...
...THE SECOND...
...TIME IN MY LIFE...
...I MET AN ANGEL.

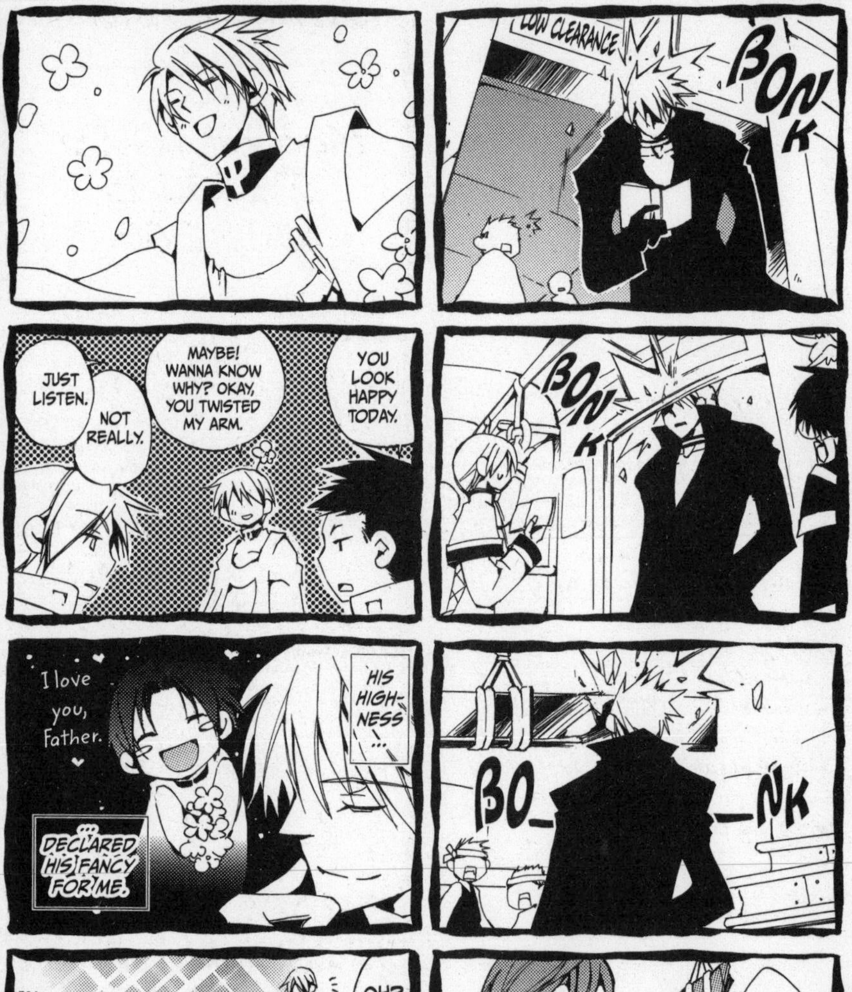
LOW CLEARANCE
BONK
BONK
BO—NK
GAH...
NO WONDER HE'S STUPID...
YOU LOOK HAPPY TODAY.
MAYBE! WANNA KNOW WHY? OKAY, YOU TWISTED MY ARM.
NOT REALLY.
JUST LISTEN.
HIS HIGHNESS...
I love you, Father.
...DECLARED HIS FANCY FOR ME.
OH?
"Fancy"?
So archaic...

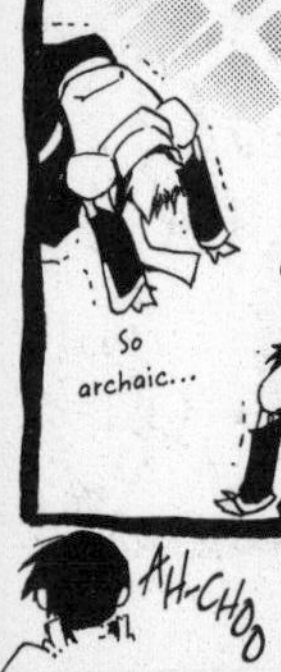
AH-CHOO

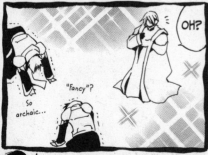

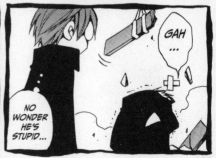

*Don't use this unless you're over 50

MY MASTER LOVES THE RAGGS LANGUAGE.
MASTER! THERE ISN'T A LANGUAGE I CANNOT SPEAK!
SO I SHALL SPEAK TO HIM IN IT AS MUCH AS HE WANTS.
BUT TEITO IS SLEEPING WHEN YOU'RE AWAKE, SO THERE'S NO POINT.
Shut up.
THOOM

Thank you for picking up volume 8.

The girl at the end was originally supposed to appear in volume 3. We finally managed to work her into the story in this volume. What an accomplishment! (It took so long...)

Thank you very much to all the readers who have stuck with us. Thank you very, very much!

In life, every day is a new adventure. We hope you stick around to watch all of Teito's new adventures.

Thank you very much. ♥ Amemiya & Ichihara
April 2009

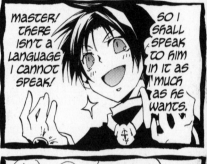

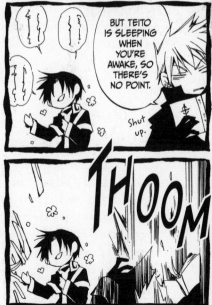

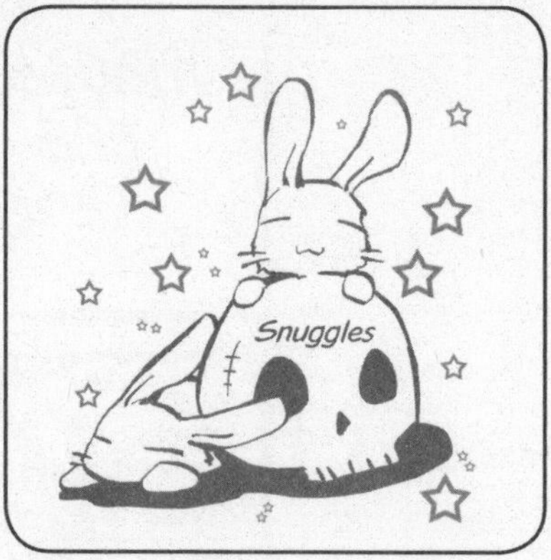
Snuggles

One morning, we opened the curtains to find a bunch of reporters loaded up with cameras outside our window! What was going on? Turns out a rare wild bird had been spotted outside our house. For the past few months, the wild bird association has been aflutter.

—Yuki Amemiya & Yukino Ichihara, 2009

Yuki Amemiya was born in Miyagi, Japan, on March 25. Yukino Ichihara was born in Fukushima, Japan, on November 24. Together they write and illustrate *07-Ghost*, the duo's first series. Since its debut in 2005, *07-Ghost* has been translated into a dozen languages, and in 2009 it was adapted into a TV anime series.

front

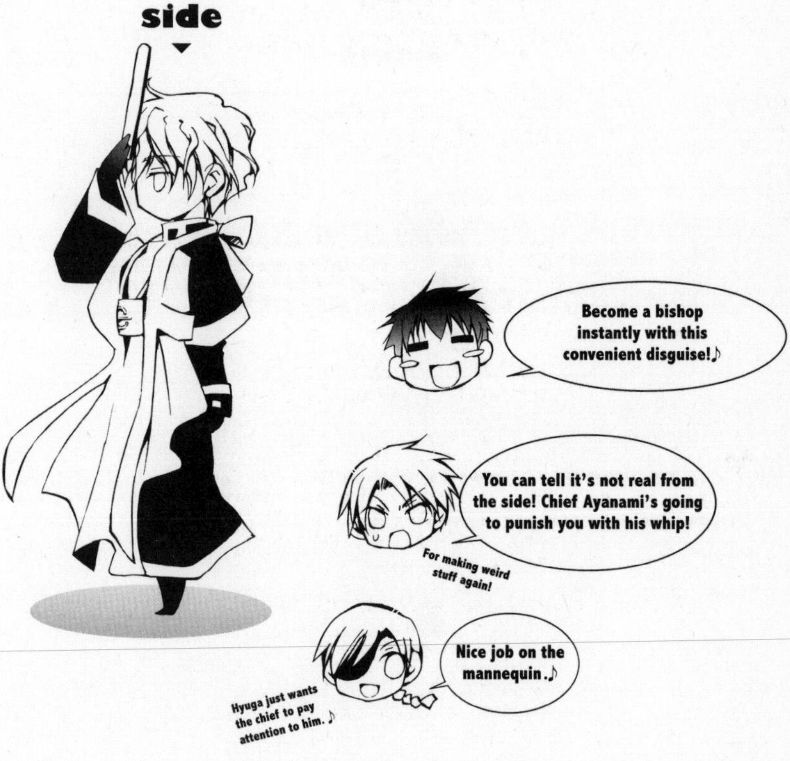

side
Become a bishop instantly with this convenient disguise!♪
You can tell it's not real from the side! Chief Ayanami's going to punish you with his whip!
For making weird stuff again!
Nice job on the mannequin.♪
Hyuga just wants the chief to pay attention to him.♪

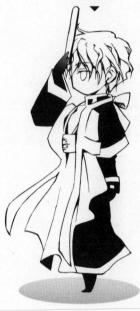

07-GHOST

Volume 8

STORY AND ART BY
YUKI AMEMIYA and YUKINO ICHIHARA

Translation/Satsuki Yamashita
Touch-up Art & Lettering/Vanessa Satone
Design/Yukiko Whitley
Editor/Hope Donovan

Printed in Canada

Published by VIZ Media, LLC
P.O. Box 77010
San Francisco, CA 94107

10 9 8 7 6 5 4 3 2 1
First printing, January 2014

PARENTAL ADVISORY
07-GHOST is rated T for Teen and is
recommended for ages 13 and up. This
volume contains realistic and fantasy violence.
ratings.viz.com

www.viz.com

VIZMANGA

Read manga anytime, anywhere!

From our newest hit series to the classics you know and love, the best manga in the world is now available digitally. Buy a volume* of digital manga for your:

- iOS device (**iPad®, iPhone®, iPod® touch**) through the **VIZ Manga app**

- Android-powered device (**phone or tablet**) with a browser by visiting **VIZManga.com**

- **Mac or PC computer** by visiting **VIZManga.com**

VIZ Digital has loads to offer:

- 500+ ready-to-read volumes
- New volumes each week
- FREE previews
- Access on multiple devices! Create a log-in through the app so you buy a book once, and read it on your device of choice!*

To learn more, visit www.viz.com/apps

* Some series may not be available for multiple devices.
  Check the app on your device to find out what's available.

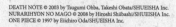

 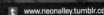

Hey! You're Reading in the Wrong Direction!

This is the end of this graphic novel!

To properly enjoy this VIZ graphic novel, please turn it around and begin reading from right to left. Unlike English, Japanese is read right to left, so Japanese comics are read in reverse order from the way English comics are typically read.

This book has been printed in the original Japanese format in order to preserve the orientation of the original artwork. Have fun with it!

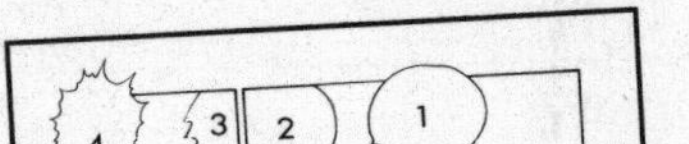
1
2
3
4
1
2
5
6
7
8
3
4
9
5
142

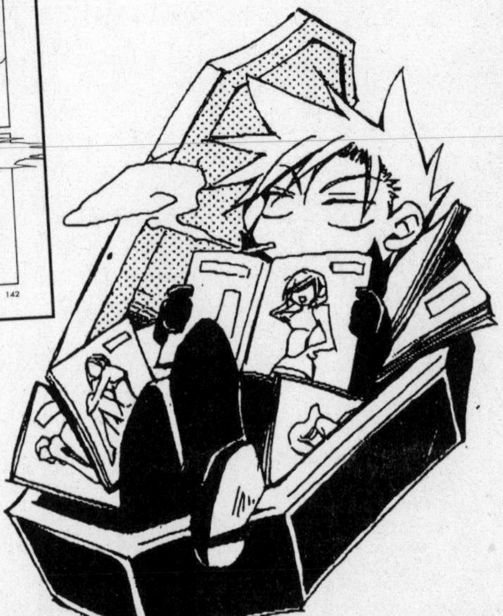